NOT WITH MY CHILD, YOU DON'T

NOT WITH MY CHILD, YOU DON'T

A Citizens' Guide to Eradicating OBE and Restoring Education

BY ROBERT HOLLAND

With testimonials from parent-activists who have made a difference in communities across America

NOT WITH MY CHILD,
YOU DON'T

Published by Wayne L. Sullivan
Executive Editor/Publisher
Chesapeake Capital Services
Citizen Projects Publishing Division
500 Forest Avenue
Richmond, Virginia 23229, U.S.A.

Printed in the United States of America

Publisher's Cataloging in Publication
(Prepared by Quality Books, Inc.)

Holland, Robert G.
Not with my child you don't : a citizens' guide to eradicating OBE and restoring education / by Robert Holland
p. cm.
Includes bibliographical references and index.
ISBN 0-9647408-0-X

1. Competency based education—United States. 2. Educational change—United States. 3. Education and state—United States.
I. Title

LC1032.H65 1995 379.1'54
QBI95-20287

To my wife, Allyne, a fine writer and editor herself, who has dealt with many of the intricacies of publishing that completely eluded my non-business-like mind.

To my daughter, Kristina, a computer whiz, who has bailed me out many times when I felt forsaken by the New Technology.

To my son, Bobby, a great baseball player, who urged me to write the book, and then, just as importantly, reminded me not to get so wrapped up in writing as to neglect my daily workout at the gym.

Acknowledgements

Many persons have helped, encouraged, and supported me, and I am grateful for all they have done:

• Wayne Sullivan advanced the idea of inviting citizen-activists to write mini-chapters about what they have experienced in their communities across America. It was a brilliant idea, because it is the citizens' contributions that make this book special. Wayne also devoted hundreds of hours to help get this book in publishable form.

• Jerry and Deana Parker provided crucial support to sustain this project.

• From opposite sides of the political arena, Patrick McSweeney and the Honorable L. Douglas Wilder have my gratitude—GOP leader McSweeney for his wise counsel and steadfastness, and Democratic Governor Wilder for his willingness to listen to the people and to grace my book with a Foreword.

• The good folks up in Alexandria, Virginia, at The Foundation Endowment have generously supported my research on OBE and multiculturalism and my attempts to clarify the issues at forums (some friendly, some not) around the country and in Canada. M. Stanton Evans and Sylvia Crutchfield, president and executive vice president, respectively, along with Joyce Dimitriou, special consultant Kathy Tucker, and other staff members have always had information and advice when I needed it.

• The Family Research Council, Gary Bauer's fine organization in Washington, D.C., and in particular education specialist, Bob Morrison, also have provided invaluable assistance in spreading the word about OBE.

• The entire Editorial Department at the *Richmond Times-Dispatch* earns the Medal of Patience for putting up with my long fascination (I thank them for not calling it an obsession) with this subject. One person in particular, Kathy Barnes, has handled the bulk of calls for OBE information and reprints that have flowed in from practically every state. She has done that with good humor and efficiency. Jean Vonderlehr also has been great. I deeply appreciate the work that production editors Patsy Arthur and Cindy Paris, and artists Gary Brookins and Bob Gorrell, did in putting together a booklet of my OBE columns that we have a hard time keeping in stock. And, of course, I am deeply grateful for the tolerance and guidance that Editorial Page

Editor Ross Mackenzie, and Editorial Board Chairman Ed Grimsley, have given my work over the years, and for the constructive suggestions offered by Commentary Editor Ann Merriman, Chief Editorial Writer Todd Culbertson, and Associate Editors Bart Hinkle and Melanie Scarborough.

• At the *Times-Dispatch,* I am also thankful for the leadership of chairman and publisher, J. Stewart Bryan, and for the backing of his father, D. Tennant Bryan, publisher emeritus, who deepened my interest in the curious education reform agenda when he sent me to a multiculturalists' national strategy session in Los Angeles in 1993.

• Through the miracle of computer networking, I have cultivated many new sources of information, a number of whom also have become good friends. On Prodigy, Cindy Duckett of Kansas has been a virtual one-person research library on education reform; and she has cheered me on in cyberspace. And folks like Karen Iacovelli of New York, Karl Bunday of Minnesota, and Rich Shalvoy of Connecticut have helped this Southern boy shed his provincialism.

• Finally, there are the countless persons—hundreds of them, really—who have called to urge me to continue writing about OBE and school reform. They tell me that there is no more important issue before us as Americans and that they are appalled at the general lack of coverage in the media. It is for them, and for the children, that I muster my energies.

Contents

To the Reader: Because this book examines many pieces of a complicated OBE puzzle and features citizens' write-ups of experiences in their communities at the end of each chapter, I am providing a Table of Contents in greater than usual detail. My hope is that it will be helpful in making the book a guide for those who wish to use it as such.

—Robert Holland

Eight
Breaking the Media Silence

FOREWORD

BY L. DOUGLAS WILDER
Former Governor
Commonwealth of Virginia

The technological advances and the improvement in the delivery of services in the post-war (World War II) era have caused Americans to reevaluate and/or discard tried and proven methodology. We have seen this in transportation, health services, electronics, energy, and any number of areas of human involvement. One subject that has loomed large on the scene, for revision, is education. Scholar after scholar, consultant after consultant, commission after commission, President after President have advanced theories, compacts, hypotheses, reports, exposes too numerous to cite here, which were to be the *raison d'être,* that last word, the cure. Among those things advanced was the proposal known as Outcome-Based Education.

Bob Holland has afforded this nettlesome subject an analysis worthy in its rendition of how the affected parties, the parents of the children, reacted as well as to how this affected his editorializing in his weekly columns on the subject in the newspaper. He has admitted to starting from ground-zero in his comprehension of the matter. Suffice it to say that he was light years ahead of most of us in appreciating the concerns of a public, already cynically disinclined toward public officials, which was most concerned with practicality and reality opposed to simple idealism.

As Governor of the Commonwealth of Virginia during this time, I was directly involved with having to decide the worthiness of the implementation of such a results-oriented program. I feel that Bob Holland has touched the nerve of the uneasiness of the public and captured it as well as the general mood and approach to its enactment.

The opposing view, as expressed by James P. Jones, then president of the State Board of Education, presents as poignantly as could be expressed, the observations as to the distastefulness of watching sausage or laws being made. Jones' Jacobean wrestling with Joe Spagnolo, then State Superintendent of Public Instruction, for ten days, illustrates that either whatever time that Jones had spent before in understanding the soundness of the measure was not enough, or that he had signed on prematurely and/or needed further justification. His assertion that he had sent me copies of a press release which he intended to release some time later that week shows that he felt that as the Chief Executive Officer of the state charged with the responsibility of effectuating and implementing the policy of the Commonwealth of Virginia, consistent with appropriate legislative guidelines, I was entitled to no more discussion than that. Incidentally, though I never saw any such copy, it obviously did not include his guesstimate that he felt reasonably sure that he could get five, of the nine members of the Board, to vote to recommend to Spagnolo withdrawal of the proposal. I had already concluded, with the hundreds of calls and letters and communications as I traveled across the state, that the best and most effective way of dealing with this ill-presented proposal was to cut the "Gordian knot" of confusion.

Jones, in whom I had confidence enough to appoint to the Board, a man with whom I served in the Virginia Senate and who has been a good friend and supporter, may not be intimately aware of how regulations become law in Virginia. Later in this book you will read his account where he quibbles with the authority of the Governor to invalidate decisions of the Board of Education as it relates to state policy. Nevertheless, he makes no case for its continuance.

When I pulled the plug on this half-baked measure, I directed the State Superintendent, via the office of the Secretary of Education, to withdraw the proposal, with appropriate notice by the Secretary to those affected entities. This was done with the clearest understanding, by me, that any actions to the contrary by the Superintendent or the Board would have resulted in new persons serving in those capacities, being that they served at the pleasure of the Governor. In my submission of the budget to the legislature, I removed any and all residue of funding for the measures. This was also made known in my press release, prior thereto, which gave the substantive reasons for the withdrawal of the proposal.

This work is not confined to Virginia. All across this country, there is general agreement that the delivery of services in education, which hasn't changed in this country in the past 100 years, must be changed. How to do that, with the involvement of the people most affected, the students and the parents thereof, is the ultimate problem. The problems of elitism, separatism, charter schools, vouchers, etc., will be discussed across this nation. But the question of what people can do, and how they did it, relative to stopping the juggernaut of *fait accompli,* is addressed in this book with a candor and clarity that enables those opposed or in agreement with the concept or the proposal itself, to be more enlightened.

Bob Holland has exposed, for all to see, the way government has heretofore operated both nationally and locally—with an attitude of indifference to what the people's thoughts on the matter were, other than the bureaucrats involved. On a personal note, I found his incisive probing and prodding to be helpful by raising questions and concerns which obviously had not been maturely considered.

It reaffirms my strong belief that government should be of the people, by the people, and for the people.

—L. Douglas Wilder
Richmond, Virginia

A Special Statement:

J. Stewart Bryan, III

Chairman and Publisher
Richmond *Times-Dispatch*

By one definition, a newspaper is a regular publication that contains news, opinions, features, and advertisements. Certainly each edition of the Richmond *Times-Dispatch* fills that definition; but, in so doing, it also attempts to fill a larger role in our community.

Part of that role—its most basic, perhaps—is to provide information for our readers of current events: what happened today or yesterday, and what will, or is scheduled to, happen tomorrow, in the world, the nation, our state, and our community.

An additional part of that role is to perform the traditional watchdog function that the press has long filled in this country—sometimes well, and sometimes not so well. That aspect goes beyond telling who, what, when, where, and why. It includes pointing out *how* our elected and appointed officials are performing their tasks.

Another part of our mission might be called community service. A newspaper should help its community see itself as it really is—with virtues and faults, accomplishments and failures, and with hopes and aspirations for the future.

To fulfill this role at the *Times-Dispatch,* we subscribe to definite principles and strive to be certain things: responsible, free, independent, truthful, accurate, and impartial. We believe in fair play and a sense of decency. We are committed to the concept of separate and distinct direction of news and editorial policies. Our opinions are confined to the editorial and op-ed pages. They play no part in our presentation of the news.

With this book, *Not With My Child, You Don't,* Bob Holland has clearly exemplified all of these notions so necessary to the effective functioning of the American press, but seemingly so out of favor today with many of our colleagues as they rush headlong onto the information superhighway.

In his writings about Virginia's encounter with Outcome-Based Education, in the *Times-Dispatch* and in this book, he has performed investigative reporting of current events that others found insignificant; he has provided the facts and analyzed them; and he has furnished a sort of report card on the principal players involved.

He has helped our community and our state see themselves as they really are: with virtues and faults, accomplishments and failures, and has helped them define their hopes and aspirations. By assisting our community and our state in this undertaking, I believe, he has also helped our nation understand a very complex issue.

1

The Awakening, or Brother, Can You Paradigm?

I remember clearly the telephone call in December, 1992, that turned my life upside down.

It was Mary Douglas Enghauser, a parent and home schooler who keeps herself up to date on governmental education policies, as home-schoolers must do in order to preserve their rights. I frequently devote my weekly newspaper column to issues in education. I had consulted with her on other issues, and found her to be well-informed.

"Bob," said Mary Douglas, "you have seen the news stories about Virginia's World-Class Education Initiative; but have you ever heard of transformational Outcome-Based Education? Do you know that it is the underlying philosophy driving education reform in Virginia?"

I had been writing about education off and on for three decades, but I had to admit that I had never heard of the precise term OBE. It sounded harmless enough, even praiseworthy. Wouldn't it be great to get some clearcut "outcomes" from the $450 billion we spend nationally on education every year?

But I decided on Mary Douglas' advice to look into this OBE thing. If I have learned anything over the years, it is that my readers are frequently ahead of me in spotting grandiose schemes in the social bureaucracies. It had been a tip in May, 1990, that enabled me to expose how the U.S. Department of Labor and state employment agencies secretly race-normed scores on job aptitude tests so that African-Americans and Hispanics were held to substantially lower standards than whites and Asian-Americans. That led to bipartisan support in Congress for a provision in the 1991 Civil Rights Act specifically banning that discriminatory practice (although other forms of deception have arisen in its place).

Little did I know when I first sought information about OBE that over the next two years I would write four dozen columns on OBE and its close cousins; or that my columns, which are syndicated mainly to small community papers in Virginia, would circulate underground by the tens of thousands all over the country, often via copying machine and fax; or that routinely I would receive calls out of the blue from Maine to Washington State to Florida to Wyoming and just about everywhere in between (47 states in all at last count) from citizens distressed by OBE in their communities; or that I would be asked to talk to such varied groups as the Eagle Forum in Birmingham and the National School Boards Association's communicators in Toronto.

Nor did I dream that I would be writing this book, in collaboration with some of the wonderful people I have met across Virginia and across the USA who give the lie to the notion that Americans have become apathetic. They—not Ed-Central's facilitators and change agents—are the real heroes of the school reform movement.

That has been the "up" side of OBE—the coming together of so many everyday Americans dedicated to preserving schools as places of learning as opposed to centers of psychological manipulation. The "down" side is that a powerful Juggernaut that doesn't look kindly on opponents—that considers them "resisters"—has forced these citizens to go to extraordinary lengths to present their cases, sometimes at the risk of becoming social outcasts. And with the passage by fall 1994 of key federal legislation (Goals 2000, School to Work, and the massive Elementary and Secondary Education Act reauthorization, all of which nurture elements of OBE), the hardest battles lie ahead. The conservative trend in the November, 1994, mid-term elections did not repeal automatically the rights-usurping federal enactments, nor did it alter the course of the powerful education/industrial complex that is pushing for nationally systematized education. But there is new cause for hope, and opportunities for those who want to secure the future of education freedom.

Believe me, not a day goes by that I don't think about how strange it is that people in faraway communities are contacting me in Richmond with worries that are so similar in every respect: "They are eliminating grades." "They are asking my child some very personal questions." "They have wiped out the honors course in Western Civilization." "They don't correct the students' misspellings." "They are promoting the idea that the school is our children's family."

I interpret the outpouring of concern cascading upon my cluttered editorial office as a sign, first, just how pervasive and single-minded the OBE movement is, and, second (and sadly), just how deficient the major media have become in reporting news about education and the general American culture in an even-handed way. The concerted effort by Big Government, Big Education, and even some corporate giants to force a radical transformation of American education (and, indeed, society) merited at least as much coverage as the proposal of First Lady Hillary Clinton and White House aide Ira Magaziner to nationalize the health care system. (These same two figures, as will be noted later in this book, were prime movers behind a plan to push OBE-style reform on schools through the Labor and Education departments, but there's been scarcely a peep about that in the Big Media.)

This book is intended to give concerned citizens hope, and, beyond that, practical guidance enabling them to become constructive activists in their own communities. The book will follow two tracks: I will tell what I learned as a journalist about OBE and systemic restructuring in roughly the order I learned it; then a citizen contributor will tell about what was happening down in the trenches. This is a many-faceted subject, because OBE is very much like the many-headed Hydra of classical mythology; therefore, the chapters have been written to focus on distinct elements of the problem. You may wish to read the book straight through, or you may prefer to flip back and forth and use it as a manual by referring to those sections most pertinent to what your own community is experiencing. In any event, I try in Chapter 12 to put together some Do's and Don'ts that would be useful to any citizen's group trying to make an impact on public policy.

So about my own rude awakening:

My first step after getting off the phone with Mary Douglas Enghauser was to ask the State Department of Education for copies of the draft of a "Common Core of Learning" (see Appendix) that had been touted as the centerpiece of World-Class Education reform. I had to rub my eyes and grab a third cup of coffee. There were obviously agendas embedded in the thick education jargon that went far beyond helping children learn the academic basics. Nor did this look much like the "grassroots" education reform that had been touted.

The 40-page draft, which liberally quoted Labor Department manifestoes, gave the impression that providing employers well-adjusted workers for a global economy was somehow the highest goal of education; however, industrial policy jargon merged weirdly with that of ed-school and campus leftists.[1] The draft flatly asserted that "relevancy" is the "most pressing issue facing education in America"—a clear echo of student radicals' demands of the Vietnam-era 1960s, when education standards went into a nosedive. Perhaps, I mused, that is more than coincidence—given that the student radicals of the '60s occupy many positions of power today, including, most certainly, in the Clinton Administration.

This early draft was quite candid about the intentions behind school restructuring. "The Common Core of Learning," it declared, "is based on a new paradigm, that of transformational outcome-based education. It begins with significant outcomes related directly to the requirements of important life roles, and asserts that everything done in and by a school should depend upon what attitudes, knowledge, and skills it takes for each student to accomplish those outcomes.''

Then and there I developed an acute allergy to proposals promising new paradigms or paradigm shifts. Paradigm is, of course, nothing but a prissy word for model. Intellectuals often conceal their real intentions behind such rhetorical fog. I also have developed a real suspicion about any program that has 2000 in its title,—i.e., America 2000, Goals 2000, Workforce 2000. Of course, my suspicion is not justified in every case, but many fuzzy theorists are implying that all of the accumulated wisdom of the ages, and all of our societal mores and traditional values, will disappear down a memory hole when we usher out the year 1999. That's bunk. Children will still need to learn to read, to write, to compute, to comprehend our common heritage as Americans, and to function as independent individuals—not be 24-hour-a-day slaves to a computer or calculator. They will need to learn to meet deadlines and to function in competitive environments. They will have to learn how to deal with and overcome failure. Schools that eliminate grades and failure do children an enormous disservice.

And, yes, children will need the wholesome values that only families, not nanny-state therapists, can transmit to them.

The architects of school restructuring, however, seemed to suggest that all of the basic structure would have to go: ''Artificial constraints such as time, resources, and organizational structures must give way to achieving specific results. Seat time, Carnegie units, grade structures, and 'bell-shaped curves' are not consistent with the philosophy of the 'Common Core of Learning.' ''

In place of structure would be the state-prescribed Outcomes—38 of them, arranged within seven Dimensions of Living. These outcomes would be the new graduation requirements for Virginia's students. The following were the Dimensions of Living:

- **Personal Well-Being and Accomplishment**
- **Interpersonal Relationships.**
- **Life-Long Learning.**
- **Cultural and Creative Endeavors.**
- **Work and Economic Well-Being.**
- **Local and Global Civic Participation.**
- **Environmental Stewardship.**

Let's look at some examples.

Under Local and Global Civic Participation, the Life Context included: ''a growing disparity in the distribution of wealth and resources worldwide . . . A world characterized by increasing interaction of racial, ethnic, and cultural groups . . . Increasing globalization of industry, coupled with a lack of understanding among consumers as to how foreign markets and economies affect personal economic decisions and circumstances." Those observations clearly reflected someone's worldview. Whose?

So that was the framework within which students would have to satisfy such "outcomes" as these:

- **Identify community problems and negotiate solutions contributing to the public good.**
- **Cooperate with individuals and groups in seeking social, political, and economic stability and improvement.**
- **Support and defend civil and human rights worldwide.**
- **Participate in and support community service activities.**

The subjectivity of many such outcomes was immediately apparent. Who would define "public good" or decide when a student had contributed to it? Who would decide what qualified as worthy community service? What about conflicting perspectives on civil rights? Would a student who wrote a paper criticizing the evolution of civil rights laws from equality of opportunity for individuals to equality of outcomes for groups be adjudged insufficiently supportive of civil rights? Would he or she have to take remedial work?

The same sort of vagueness and potential for attitudinal indoctrination infected many of the outcomes. To be an "Environmental Steward," a student was supposed to, "Use the environment responsibly, and encourage others to do so to improve the human condition." But, who would rule what's responsible? The state's education braintrust? Under "Work," a student was to "collaborate effectively in planning, producing, and delivering products and/or services." That seemed an oddly utilitarian outcome—one that suggested a student is less a seeker of wisdom than a cog in an industrial system. I didn't understand until months later the genesis of such outcomes, or how similar they were from one OBE state to another.

These were not, mind you, independent-study projects for high school seniors. They were the kind of immersion in "real-life" woes that the state's school officialdom would expect beginning in the very early childhood years. Part of the OBE plan contemplated mandatory schooling of all 4-year-olds in the state—or, at least, said the authorities, all "at-risk" pupils (however, they might be defined).

In one suggested unit, 8-year-olds would center their studies around the theme of homelessness: (1) researching homelessness in the United States, Canada, and Mexico; (2) conducting a survey to "examine individual perceptions" and to "develop solutions;" (3) debating the problem in the local community; and (4) presenting a solution to homelessness through a graphic display, a story in the student newspaper, or a letter to a local official. The first three activities would be done in a group, cooperatively—an approach much encouraged by OBE advocates. The last activity would be done individually, and the student would be assessed on his outcome. A student who concluded that homelessness is exaggerated and not amenable to a government solution apparently would be a candidate for remedial instruction and a retest. Supposedly the 8-year-olds—**eight-**year-olds!—would hone a number of fundamental skills through this thematic exercise, but the great potential would appear to be an enhanced level of political correctness. (I would later find that an elementary school in the vanguard OBE school system of Rochester, New York, would base its entire curriculum around the Genesee River that runs nearby.[2] Children were asked to put their critical thinking skills to work on such questions as, "Was there a beginning of the world?" "Who is in charge of the city?" "Why is the river water brown?" and "How will the river valley look in a hundred years?")

On first inspection, the "Common Core" looked more like a "rotten core." Certainly it could not be called a core curriculum demanding rigorous intellectual standards. A computer check found that the words reading, writing, and mathematics were not mentioned once in the entire document. How could this be? How did our supposed best and brightest state leaders develop this "new paradigm" of education reform?

I would recommend that any citizens who are concerned about proposals before their school officials start at the beginning by getting a copy of the original documents. Don't depend on the brief summaries carried by newspapers. And, even longer stories may not have the detail that you need.

Shocked and appalled, I made up my mind to learn everything I possibly could about OBE. I could not have imagined then how tangled the web would be.

A Middle-American Mom's Disillusionment

By Cindy Duckett
Kansas

It began in the fall of 1986, an eventful time for me. It was a year, I thought, that was supposed to be the beginning of "the good life." We had purchased a beautiful bi-level home in a nice, quiet middle-class neighborhood. My oldest child started kindergarten at the neighborhood school just two weeks after we moved in. This was Wichita, Kansas—the heart of America. I had lived here all of my life and had been educated in the city's public school system. I had some terrific teachers and had received a good education here myself, so I had no qualms at all about sending my children to these schools.

Oh sure, I had hear news stories about the crumbling educational system in this country, but that was happening someplace else—surely not here, and surely not at the school in this nice new neighborhood of ours. After all, I reasoned, the schools in this city were the same ones I grew up knowing. For the most part, the buildings all still looked the same and even some of the teachers I once knew were still around.

From the very beginning, I was involved in my son's school and that involvement had increased by the time my daughter started kindergarten two years later. I did all of the typical things that parents are "supposed" to do. I was room mother in at least two classes each year. I drove for nearly every field trip. I helped put up bulletin boards and volunteered to work in the classroom or the office whenever I was needed. . . . I monitored my children's homework and attended every parent-teacher conference. I knew every employee in the building from the janitors to the teachers to the principal.

The first thing I saw that I didn't like started during my son's second year at school. A new program called "Writing to Read" was introduced. The foundational belief of that program was that if a child could say a word, he could write it and if he could write it, he could read it.

At first, I thought this sounded great because it seemed to be using a phonics base combined with computer technology. What I saw in actual use, however, were words like "kite" spelled as "kit" and "key" spelled as "ke." At the time, I didn't know that this approach actually had a name, but I've learned since then that this is invented spelling—whereby any way a child wants to spell a word is okay. Parents were instructed **not** to correct their child's spelling when they saw words written in this manner. The thought was that children should "feel good" about their writing and that the technicalities of correct spelling would naturally come later.

I remember my mother saying that she was told something similar to this 20 years earlier when my sister was taught to read and spell in a similar way, yet she never did learn to read or spell very well. I was concerned but when I expressed those concerns, they fell on deaf ears. My own children started school already knowing how to read and how to spell many words. I continued to work with them at home to counter what they were learning in school, in spite of what I had been told to do; and today both of my children are excellent readers and spellers but not every child who went through that program was as fortunate. One of the things I volunteered to do was help teachers grade papers. This program started when my son was in first grade, and by the time he and his classmates were in fifth grade and ready to move into middle school, I saw that many of them could not read at grade level and could not spell even some of the most basic words correctly.

(Cindy then describes a new superintendent who came to town describing himself as a "change agent," and the turmoil that ensued.)

Meanwhile, back at the school building, I was seeing more and more "progressive" education philosophies being implemented. My daughter spent her third grade year working in group situations most of the year. Parties and "fun" activities were frequently taking place and seemed to get about as much time as academic work. I had grown almost to detest the month of May because I spent more of my time driving for field trips, many of them picnics and other non-educational activities, than working in the school.

My son spent a fair amount of his time tutoring students in lower grades rather than learning something new himself. Spelling books were taken out of the schools. Penmanship books were removed. Arithmetic books were replaced with "math manipulatives." Grades were inflated—a fifth-grade student working at second-grade level but doing very well at the second grade level received the same "A" as the fifth-grade student working well at the fifth-grade level—all in the name of promoting "self-esteem." Parents were pulling their hair out over a new middle school program called advisement whereby their students were spending time in Pseudo-counseling situations rather than in academics. Standardized test scores were on the decline districtwide and per-pupil expenditures (along with property taxes) were soaring to record levels. Discipline in schools had become almost meaningless and violence in the schools had reached near-epidemic proportions.

By this time, I was going through a major "attitude adjustment." I was almost completely disillusioned by the very same public school system that I had once thought so wonderful. For the first time, I began to consider placing my children in a private school, but I had always thought that option to be too expensive to even think of, so I didn't act on pursuing that idea just yet. . . .

Surely Some Pages Were Missing In the State's Plan

By Lil Tuttle
Virginia

Our little group of parents and former teachers was formed in April, 1993, before we knew anything about "OBE." We were all displeased with the reduced emphasis on the academic subjects in our schools; and we were tired of hearing our children say, "But I don't have to know that!" or the school say, "Mrs. Smith, you're the only one ever to raise that question." We knew better. Collectively, we hoped to stem the tide of declining academic standards in our local schools. Ours would be a local advocacy group, providing parents with the kind of support needed to hold our schools accountable. We called ourselves, "Academics First" because we believed teaching academic knowledge and skills is the primary—if not the sole—mission of the public schools.

The "Virginia Common Core of Learning (CCL)" was one of the earliest documents we obtained. Robert Holland's columns about it had caught our attention, and we wanted to know what was in it. The first reading left us totally bewildered. It was the most bizarre education plan we'd ever read—it didn't even mention the academic subjects! Surely some pages were missing? Several readings later, the realization dawned that the state intended to radically alter both the mission and the structure of public education. By becoming something akin to Big Mother, the restructured school's mission was to develop the whole child socially, emotionally, personally, and intellectually. This Outcome-Based plan would judge student achievement (outcome) in seven developmental categories: Personal Well-Being and Accomplishment; Interpersonal Relationships; Lifelong Learning; Cultural and Creative Endeavors; Work and Economic Well-Being; Local and Global Civic Participation; and Environmental Stewardship. These categories would replace English, math, history, science, etc.

After the shock wore off, the anger set in. By whose authority? With whose consent? Certainly the governed hadn't been consulted. If the State went unchallenged, Virginia's public schools would become places of indoctrination, not education. The reaction was a resounding, "Not with my schools and certainly not with my children!"

We began showing the state's plan to neighbors, friends, and local groups. Telephone calls to friends and family-friendly organizations revealed how widespread this sort of restructuring was. Contacts in Pennsylvania provided books, articles, and research to bring us up to speed. Before the 1993 school year ended, the Virginia Family Foundation arranged for an all-day meeting of about 50 people from around the state to exchange information and documents. It was decided there should be no single statewide organization—that would be too easy a target for the state. Instead, there would be many local groups networking together. By the end of that day, we suffered no illusion about the task ahead, but we were no longer isolated.

This "Reform" Was Bought Right Off A Consultant's Shelf

Dr. Jeffrey Satinover, Ken Von Kohorn, and Kay Wall
Connecticut

In 1992 Governor Weicker established the Commission on Educational Excellence (CEEC), which included some of the top Connecticut business leaders. Its purported purpose was to study Connecticut's public schools and to design a plan to improve them. They never did study the public schools, but instead brought in outside consultants who advocated an Outcome-Based Education (OBE) system with "high academic standards."

If the CEEC had in fact set up high academic standards and had recommended them to the General Assembly to beef up Connecticut's public schools, our efforts would not have been needed. But the CEEC didn't do that. Instead, it followed a blueprint used by similar commissions in other states. Research into those other states turned up several items of interest. In all the other cases in which similar commissions had recommended OBE— or a comparable system under a revised name—those states had turned over tremendous power and authority to their state departments of education for implementation, allowing the education bureaucracy to set the "outcomes" and assessments, moving away from local control of school curricula. What we further discovered was that the state goals were a combination of watered-down academics and attitudinal-type outcomes. **And they were virtually identical from state to state.** For example, in Pennsylvania: "All students will understand their worth as unique and capable individuals and exhibit self-esteem." In Connecticut (From the "Common Core of Learning" or CCL): "Each student should be able to appreciate his or her worth as a unique and capable individual and exhibit self-esteem."

We did a count of the Connecticut CCL, and found that of its 110 goals, 51 are "affective," or behavioral-type, non-academic outcomes.

Observing this process being duplicated in Connecticut induced us to form the Committee to Save Our Schools (CT: SOS). We quickly learned that a small number of dedicated people can accomplish a tremendous amount in a political unit as manageable as a state if their methods are effective, and if the issue is the right one—and this one is. Nothing is more important to people than the well-being and future of their children.

What Did Any of This Have To Do With Education?

By Joe Gwynn
Virginia

My first introduction to Outcome-Based Education (OBE) was when a friend gave me a copy of the proposed draft of Virginia's Common Core of Learning (CCL) , dated February 15, 1993. I was unaware of the first draft, written in late 1992, or the second, dated February 1, 1993. She told me that it was to be voted on by Virginia's General Assembly in the near future. To say I was shocked as I read the CCL would be an understatement. What does being an Environmental Steward mean—population control? What has being a Lifelong Learner to do with the time a child spends in public school? In yet another Outcome, each child was to become a Fulfilled Individual by the time he or she leaves public school. I'd certainly like to see that curriculum! The other Outcomes were equally vague. Students were to become Supportive Persons, Expressive Contributors, Quality Workers, etc. Give me a break! How could intelligent legislators not see through that nonsense?

What has any of that got to do with education? What compelling state interest had suddenly granted them the right to usurp our God-given rights? Had not the Supreme Court always upheld the rights of parents to educate their children as they saw fit? Then, as I began to see that Outcome-Based Education had cropped up all over the country, I called parents in other states. I discovered that the same Outcomes had mysteriously surfaced everywhere. That seemed strange to me, since we had been told that Virginia's Outcomes were developed right here in Virginia.

After a while one learns to weigh carefully each word written by the "educrats." As with the Newspeak of George Orwell, it is nearly impossible for the uninitiated to decipher their codes. Family Life Education now means teaching children that the values of traditional families are obsolete. And "accelerated learning," usually implemented in poorer school districts, means dumbing-down schools to their lowest common denominator. In the Preface to Virginia's CCL, we read: "The weight of authoritative opinion is that schooling must concentrate not only on what students are able to demonstrate but also on what we expect them to be as adults." Where does one begin to unravel the meaning of those words? Whose "authoritative opinion" . . . what "weight?" . . . and when, pray tell, did it become the role of the schools to decide what our children are to "be"? We send them off to school not to be taught "what" to think, and certainly not what to "be," but to be given the tools to think for themselves. And therein lies the main problem with Outcome-Based Education.

2

Affective Ed

As I began discovering how extensively OBE was being seeded in my own backyard, I also learned that this was far more than just a Virginia creeper. Offshoots were cropping up in state after state. If you turn to the Appendix of this book, you will find an illuminating comparison of "Outcomes" across the nation. The similarities are striking, particularly given that OBE advocates invariably claim to be promoting "grassroots" reform.

In Michigan, a group of parents even produced a guide entitled, "How to Know If Your School Has OBE." (See Appendix.)[1] That was a clever way of relating Outcome-Based Education to a social disease or to an infestation of gypsy moths. But to the Michigan folks and many other citizens in communities with full-blown OBE, this is neither a joke nor an exaggeration. They have ample reason to fear an insidious effect on their children's academic preparation and their values.

One of the first symptoms many parents encounter—sometimes before they are even aware of the existence of an OBE plan—are strange test or survey questions that their children tell them they have been asked in school. From a Kansas Outcomes-Based Health Education survey in 1991 came such attitudinal queries as, **"Are there people in your life you trust to give you advice? Are there people in your life with whom you share your deepest thoughts and feelings?"**[2] (If the answers are "no," is the school free to presume a dysfunctioning family?)

From a middle-school survey in Kentucky, a key OBE state, children are invited to "get in touch" with their feelings by completing such sentences as these: **"I'll never forget the first time I . . . . I remember how angry I was when my father. . . . I'll never tell anyone about the time. . . ."**[3]

And from Ohio came a "values questionnaire" (discussed by Chris Helm later in this chapter) in which children are supposed to say "okay" or "not okay" to . . . **"sex before marriage . . . having sex so I will be popular . . . having sex so I won't be lonely . . . having sex for fun . . . having sex to repay a favor . . . using birth control."**[4]

These are assessments of what educationists antiseptically call the children's "affective domain." A more humane term might be their zone of privacy, which schools ought to respect but in many cases are violating.

One of the first questions parents usually have when they learn of the inquiries Affective Education makes of student attitudes is: "How on Earth are the schools going to test the children for **that?**"

The answer is that they aren't going to test at all, because testing as we knew it when schools were places to train the intellect is going out the window along with objective standards. No longer will there be right and wrong answers. Schools steeped in the OBE philosophy are going to be conducting "pupil assessments." That ties back in to the Affective realm: It means that schools will be assessing how students feel about themselves, and the nitty-gritty issues of "real life." What are their attitudes toward homelessness, clear-cutting of forests, premarital sex, racial diversity, or homosexuality? Affective Ed and Assessment go together like, well, love and marriage once did.

Affective, let me confess, was not a word in my daily vocabulary—at least not until shortly after I began my investigation of OBE. "Affection," "affectionately?" Sure, those are words we use for a particular kind of feeling—a sweet, Valentine's Day kind of feeling—we have toward others. But "affective" looks like a misspelling of "effective" (and by no means should the two words be confused!). So it took me aback to read that "student completion of affective inventories" was part of a new system of pupil assessment under consideration by my state's department of education. The affective inventories would be conducted in an assessment of "personal well-being and accomplishment."[5] My research began with my Webster's (which admittedly is not always a reliable guide to the strange language of educationese) where I found that "affective" was a term from psychology meaning, "pertaining to or resulting from emotions or feelings rather than from thought."

Very well, then. Students were going to be asked to inventory how they **felt** about various matters; but what did that have to do with what they **knew,** or what they ought to know—reading, writing, literature, mathematics, history, science, geography, economics?

This same state assessment would have a section on "Interpersonal Relationships," calling for "teacher observations of student interactions." Teachers also would take note of the "group process during a collaborative project." Later, I would discover to what inordinate lengths OBE went in stressing working in a group as opposed to individual initiative. And it made me wonder: What happens to the child who is gifted but a loner? He doesn't work well in a group, but he must learn to mix in a group before moving on to the next level. Encouraged in his individualism, the bright kid might grow up to be a Nobel Prize-winning scientist or a Pulitzer Prize-winning author, enriching the lives of us all. But the OBE philosophy discourages the idea of individual brilliance in favor of homogenized groupthink. The highest and best use of this bright child in an OBE school would be as a peer tutor, helping the slow pupils.

The proposed state assessment also contemplated such activities as:

• Student response to a vignette requiring the analysis of conflict and a discovery of cooperative resolution. (Your basic old conflict resolution—the idea that any dispute can be compromised. How America would have defeated Fascism and Communism were such a mindset dominant beats me.)

• Student journal of leisure activities. (Perhaps, "How I Got in Touch With My Inner Self While Hanging Out at the Mall"?)

• Student self-reporting of participation in community service activities. (Some school systems, including Maryland's, are requiring school-approved community service for graduation, which drains the spirit of voluntarism right out of such labors. Sounds rather more like involuntary servitude.)[6]

• Develop and implement a plan that encourages others to use some aspect of the environment responsibly. (Again: Who defines *responsible* ?)

In contemplating students toting their journals everywhere to complete their affective inventories, I decided to dive into the pedagogical murk to seek the origin of the psychobabble. And it turns out that in teacher training institutions (ed-schools) across the land, the 1956 work, "Taxonomy of Educational Objectives," by psychologist Benjamin Bloom of the University of Chicago, is presented—yea verily—as holy writ on Affective Ed.[7] Bloom, who was influenced by the earlier research on behavior modification by Harvard University psychologist, B.F. Skinner, neatly divided thinking skills into "higher order" and "lower order." Somehow, knowledge and comprehension get shoved into the lower order, while the higher realm has to do with applying, synthesizing, and evaluating. In 1994, HR6, the House version of the reauthorized Elementary and Secondary Education Act, would have asserted the primacy of "higher order" thinking, slamming the so-called "disproven theory that children must first learn basic skills before engaging in more complex tasks. . . ."[8] Protests by advocates of phonics in reading instruction, led by the National Right to Read Foundation, succeeded in convincing a conference committee to expunge that absurd language. But such edubabble frequently slips into the law of the land unnoticed.

Bloom theorized that thinking was either "cognitive" (which usually connotes rational thinking, but in educationese also has an affective element) or "affective" (feelings, beliefs, emotions, attitudes, values).[9] He asserted that by focusing on the affective domain, teachers could instill higher order thinking skills in their pupils. Evaluation, the highest of his "higher order" skills, Bloom described as "formulating subjective judgment as the product resulting in personal values/opinions with no real right or wrong answer." This morally relativistic and manipulative theory owed much to the B.F. Skinner's laboratory research on behavior modification which culminated in programmed learning /teaching machines, and hideous "Skinner boxes" for rearing children in a controlled environment. However much today's OBE advocates might deny it, the taproots of OBE are Skinnerian.

Beyond the realm of theory, the National Education Association has aggressively promoted Affective Ed for many years—no doubt in part because it dovetails nicely with the NEA's radical political agenda. Dr. Dennis L. Cuddy, a former Senior Associate with the U.S. Department of Education, has traced the NEA's affection for the affective back to the 1960s and a former NEA division, the Association of Supervision and Curriculum Development (which remains today, through its journal "Educational Leadership," a pre-eminent cheerleader for OBE).[10] In 1969, the ASCD/NEA published "Improving Educational Assessment & An Inventory of Measures of Affective Behavior." (Another inventory!) In it, Dr. Cuddy notes, another guru among the behavioral psychologists, Ralph Tyler, pontificated on the need for "diagnosis," or "an assessment of the student's environment in order to evaluate his potential success in moving ahead—home environment, language used in the home, types of behavior values by the student's peer group, and interests and previous experience." Harking to his work with education progressivists (the OBE of yore), Tyler wrote of setting educational objectives that "represented desirable and attainable human outcomes. Now as the people from (Skinnerian) conditioning have moved into an interest in learning in the schools, the notions of behavioral objectives have become much more specific."

At a 1993 meeting in Washington on revamping the Elementary and Secondary Education Act according to OBE principles, NEA senior lobbyist Dale L. Lestina made this statement on higher-order versus basic skills: "The National Education Association believes that all students should be challenged to meet higher academic standards, and that there should be a greater emphasis on higher-order thinking skills that will help them to be critical thinkers, *i.e.*, better learners and innovators, and better workers." (Suppose the critical-thinking pupils rejected the idea of compulsory unionism for America's schoolteachers as pursued by the NEA, fittingly labeled the National Extortion Association by Forbes magazine? Naw, the NEA surely doesn't favor **that** kind of thinking in the schools.)

Reality, not lofty theory, is what confronts parents when they find that their children's deepest feelings, emotions, and attitudes have been probed by affective surveys and exercises in their schools—typically, without the parents' knowledge. When Congress was considering Goals 2000 early in 1994, Senator Charles Grassley of Iowa collected samples of intrusive surveys from across the nation, and had printed in the February 4, 1994, edition of the Congressional Record almost 20 pages of the rankest examples.[11] One of the most blatant was from his own state: the infamous Bettendorf Survey. It listed a large assortment of hyphenated-American nationalities (Irish, Hispanic, African, Anglo, French, Polish, German, Japanese, etc., as well as Jews, Catholics, and Protestants, and then asked such outrageous questions as these:

- **Which of the above do you think is responsible for the decline of the U.S.'s economy?**
- **Which of the above do you think is the most likely to raise a large family (8 or more children)?**
- **Which of the above do you think is most subject to suspicion of criminal activity?**
- **Which of the above do you think would be most likely to eliminate an entire race?**
- **If you could eliminate an entire race, would you?**
- **If yes, which one? (Responses will not be published).**

What possible justification can there be for schools asking such hateful questions? To ferret out and expose bigotry? It seems at least as likely that such questions will plant ugly thoughts in young minds—that perhaps it is okay to scapegoat distinct ethnic or religious groups, and even to commit violence against members of such groups.

Author and syndicated columnist, Thomas Sowell, uses a blunter term for Affective Ed—brainwashing. He argues that affective exercises such as taking children to a funeral home to touch corpses ("death education"), X-rated sex-ed, and lifeboat dilemmas in which students must decide whom to toss overboard to keep an overloaded boat from sinking actually are ventures in de-sensitizing students.[12] The object is to rid them of the attitudes and values they bring from home so they will be receptive to a new, socially prescribed way of thinking. Sowell's thesis gained credence with me when I attended a four-day conference of the National Association for Multicultural Education in Los Angeles in February, 1993, and heard one educator after another emphasize the necessity of changing the attitudes that children bring with them from home. Lily Wong Filmore, a graduate education professor at Berkeley and the keynote speaker (and a participant in the U.S. Department of Education study that in 1994 produced HR6, the legislation to "reinvent" the Elementary and Secondary Education Act in an OBE mold), delivered the following charge to an enthusiastic audience of multiculturalists:

"When you consider the kinds of things I am proposing as necessary additions to the school curriculum for a multicultural society, there will be some definite clash with the practices, beliefs, and attitudes that are taught in many homes. In fact, that is precisely why such curricular changes are needed and why the changes have to be for all children, not just those we serve . . . No matter what their parents and families think about others or the environment . . . we are going to have to inculcate in our children the rules that form a credo that will work for a multicultural 21st Century."

Parents do not have to sit back and let such arrogance rule the day. They have the force of considerable constitutional interpretation on their side. In some landmark cases, the United States Supreme Court has upheld the primacy of parents in child-rearing. In Pierce vs. Society of Sisters, 268 U.S. 510 (1925), still a landmark case, the High Court held that an Oregon law requiring all children between the ages of 8 and 16 to attend public schools until the completion of the eighth grade unreasonably interfered with the liberty of parents to direct the education of their children. In ensuing cases, it is true that the courts have not been models of consistency, but there also are statutory enactments intended to protect parental rights.

Parents have to be alert to what's going on with their child's education. They need to go over the lessons of the day, and listen intently to what their child has to say. This does not mean the parent ought to go ballistic over every dubious sounding comment that comes home. But, if Affective Ed surveys and exercises are intruding heavily into personal zones of privacy, parents have a right to have access to the materials and to see to it that their children are not exposed to it.

Senator Grassley, you see, did more than talk about the outrageous ventures in attitude adjustment. He successfully sponsored an amendment to Goals 2000 (one of the few freedom-expanding features of that law) that builds on the Hatch Amendment of 1978 in protecting pupil rights. Senator Orrin Hatch's provision applied only to school materials directed funded by the federal government, but the Grassley Amendment contains no such limitation.[13] The Protection of Pupil Rights section of Goals 2000 states, in part:

• Sec. 439. (a) All instructional materials, including teacher's manuals, films, tapes, or other supplementary material which will

be used in connection with any survey, analysis, or evaluation as part of any applicable program shall be available for inspection by the parents or guardians of the children.

(b) No student shall be required, as part of any applicable program, to submit to a survey, analysis, or evaluation that reveals information concerning . . .

(1) political affiliations;

(2) mental and psychological problems potentially embarrassing to the student or his family;

(3) sex behavior and attitudes;

(4) illegal, anti-social, self-incriminating, and demeaning behavior;

(5) critical appraisals of other individuals with whom respondents have close family relationships.

(6) legally recognized privileged or analogous relationships, such as those of lawyers, physicians, or ministers; or

(7) income (other than that required by law to determine eligibility for participation in a program or for receiving financial assistance under such program),

without the prior consent of the student (if the student is an adult or emancipated minor), or in the case of an unemancipated minor, without the prior written consent of the parent.

School systems are supposed to notify parents and students of their rights under this new law. Granted, it may not be realistic to expect the federal bureaucracy to act expeditiously in enforcement of this protection of parental rights. The Secretary of Education is supposed to set up an Office and Review Board to "investigate, process, review, and adjudicate" violations of parents' rights. But not for six years after the Hatch Amendment's passage were implementing regulations written, and in the 10 years since then the feds have investigated only 17 cases.

The best bet may be for parents and other citizens to use the law as a weapon in local fights—publicly exposing violations of federal law. And they can lobby their legislators for passage of state versions of pupil and parental rights laws, with clearcut enforcement mechanisms. Utah has already passed its own version of a parental rights statute.

Thwarting a few affective questionnaires, however, will not solve the problem. OBE is part of a wide-ranging agenda backed by a powerful assortment of vested interests that joined forces behind one model of education for all as we shall see in Chapter Three.

Out in the Cold at "Warm and Cheerful" School

By Chris Helm
Ohio

March 4, 1988, ice covered the streets. It would not dampen my spirits. This was moving day. We had purchased a home in one of the best school districts in the state. My daughter would be attending the local elementary school and the twins would follow in two short years. I was a 33-year-old housewife with a loving husband, three healthy kids, Labrador retriever, mini-van in the garage, and a new tri-level. I couldn't wait to become the ultimate "burb" mom and grinned to myself as we passed the sign, "Welcome to Warm and Cheerful Centerville." I was living the American dream.

It was soon to become a nightmare.

The first three years found me busy with Girl Scouts, PTO, homeroom volunteer, and little league. I had convinced my husband and myself that to be "involved" meant a better education for my children. I was on a first-name basis with the principal, never missed an Open House or teacher's conference. I was willing to volunteer for anything I could fit in between lunches with the ladies and decorating my spotless house. As I was leaving for lunch one day, I whispered a quiet prayer of thanks for how good life was and also asked if there was anything more that I could be doing. . . .

Not long after that, I was reading the paper when my 13-year-old daughter sat down beside me. "Mom," she said, "we had to fill out a really funny survey in health class this week and I feel uncomfortable about it. The questions ask if certain things are okay or not okay. Things like masturbation, having sex to repay a favor, and birth control." When she was done with her story, I asked her to repeat it for her father. "What do they think they are doing asking questions like that of a 13-year-old girl? What business is that of theirs?" I exploded. We decided that Dave would pay a visit to the school. This was one of the top school districts. Surely officials would admit their mistake and apologize. Instead, my husband was asked not to "tell anyone about this because it would blacken the eye of the school." Further phone calls to board members and the superintendent brought cold responses, if any. I began to call other parents to see if they were aware of this survey. Then the local news station called to ask if I would make this public. I knew it was the quickest way to reach all the parents, so I agreed. Phone calls to my home numbered over 200—from parents with more stories. Some parents feared telling me their names.

One phone call that I received during that time came from Brenda Miller. She convinced me to do a local radio show. After the show, Brenda came to my home with a book titled, *Child Abuse in the Classroom*. I was hooked.

I will never forget the first time I met Brenda's sister, Debbie Stevens. She was a tiny, long-haired brunette whose mind was the closest thing to a computer that I had ever seen. We were complete opposites. I was the party girl in high school; she was the bookworm. While I was entertaining neighbors, Debbie had been reading documents. She started to discuss President Bush's plan called America 2000 and something called Outcome-Based Education. She began explaining all the "affective" areas in Ohio's curriculum. She zeroed in on a new guidance curriculum that was being implemented in my district. She pulled document after document out of the boxes she had brought with her to my home.

"Look at these words, Chris. Why do they have words like experiment in this program? What kind of psychological files are they referring to?" she asked. I was convinced that I could never allow my children to sit in on this "guidance" class.

The following month at the school board meeting, I requested to opt out my children from the guidance program. Permission was granted based on certain conditions. I was expected to come to school and personally remove my twins from the classroom, or they would be sitting in the office. No area would be provided for us to work during that time. It was not uncommon to find us sitting outside on the front porch steps of the school. Somehow the school district had forgotten the city's slogan. It was no longer "warm and cheerful."

Why "We Three Moms" Headed for Sacramento

By Carolyn Steinke
California

To become an activist is not a choice but a call. Mine came more than five years ago, in September, 1989.

I was very content with my niche in life—a mother of seven wonderful children, with a loving husband, a great Bible-believing church, involvement in the church's Teenage Youth Ministry . . . my plate was full.

Little did I imagine that coming to the aid of a disgruntled mother from church—regarding a story her daughter was reading in public school—would be the vehicle to turn my whole world around.

The story was about a white witch, "Strega Nona," portrayed with a white dove on her shoulder and a staff in her hand (like Moses). The priests and nuns would come to *her* for potions when God didn't answer their prayers.

"Strega Nona" was not just an isolated inappropriate story for the public classroom. She represented an introductory role model character for Reading and Math Skills, thus making this part of state-approved curriculum for second and third grades.

Part of the program included a study of *past* knowledge of witches, a one-week study of *new* knowledge of witches, an essay on how the students' perceptions of witches had changed—all culminating with a celebration of cooking spaghetti in a cauldron and each child casting his own spell over it!

The principal's response to our respectful protest was, "I'm sorry, there is nothing we can do other than to opt your child out of this segment of the class." The only problem was that it was too late; little Marrisa had already been exposed.

From that moment on, my eyes were opened, and the power of word of mouth began.

A short time later, a mom from another school called me to express concerns with her third-grader's radical personality change since school began. The children in her class were twice-weekly involved in a "magic" circle—a teacher-directed, self-esteem program written by Jack Canfield ("1,000 Ways to Improve Self-Esteem in the Classroom").

The program instructed little children how to chant mantras, and it encouraged them to share very personal feelings with the group with such questions as "Which parent does the child care for most? Did the child ever wish one of his or her parents were dead? If so, which one and why?"

The child was not sharing as the group passed the stuffed teddy bear around. Unbeknownst to the mother, a male school counselor was called on the scene. The child's lunch was taken away until she gave the counselor a hug—a **forced** hug! Her lunch was given back to her. Recalled a parent aide, "she walked to the trash barrel and threw her lunch away."

I remember well attending my first California Eagle Forum convention, hosted by Dr. Jo Ellen Allen. One of the speakers had a tremendous impact on me: Dr. William Coulsen, one of the founding fathers of Circle-Based, Non-Directive, Self-Esteem Therapy—yes, therapy!—in the classroom. He shared with us from his heart, tearfully, the damage such programs cause. It was very apparent to me the regret he suffered over his part in their creation, along with Dr. Carl Rogers and Dr. Abraham Maslow. Further evidence of the failure of self-esteem programs came from research of the QUEST program showing among participating students (1) elevated drug use, (2) earlier sexual involvement, and (3) a reduced perception of risk.

Armed with our new information, we three moms took off our aprons and flew to Sacramento to meet with the head of curriculum for California schools. We were sure that, presented factual research, the gentleman would advocate halting this state-mandated program, a graduation requirement. His response? "I'm sorry, there is nothing I can do, once a program is already in place. You see, federal funds are involved here."

I guess I am a Pollyanna by nature. I was so sure that once the truth was presented no one would continue to promote any program that would be detrimental to our children.

I was wrong.

Honor Roll

(Honoring grassroots organizations that have made a difference for the better in their communities.)

Parents Involved in Education, Inc. (P.I.E.)

P.O. Box 3004
Palm Desert, California 92261
(619) 564-1717

Carolyn Steinke, Executive Director

P.I.E. (Parents Involved in Education, Inc.) and P.I.E. P.A.C. (Parents Involved in Education Political Action Committee, Inc.) grew out of the need for parent representation in our State Capitol—a voice that speaks for the folks back home, most of whom have precious little time to look over the shoulders of their elected officials to be certain that their best interests are being served.

P.I.E.'s mission is to restore academics in education, eliminate dangerous psychological practices in the classroom, and to ensure parents that their natural right to, and expectation of, laudable moral standards in curriculum shall be affirmed.

P.I.E. is endorsed by the California Republican Assembly and Senate, Traditional Values Coalition, Citizens for Excellence in Education, Capitol Resource Institute, Concerned Citizens in Education, Concerned Women for America, The Claremont Institute, United States Justice Foundation, and Moms in Touch.

P.I.E. currently boasts over 50 chapters in California and several other states.

3

The Bandwagon

The deeper I looked into OBE, the more amazed I became at two parallel findings:

(1) How extensive was the agenda of "systemic change," or restructuring of American education, of which OBE was only the most visible part, and

(2) How monolithic was the aggregation of power elites—in government, big business, and the education establishment—pushing OBE, and its ugly sister philosophies.

As for the agenda, concerned citizens may waste too much time trying to label specific school programs as, definitively, OBE. Some practices may spring from the same strain of thought as OBE, yet not literally be OBE because of the absence of learner or exit outcomes. One can fall into a semantic trap and let promoters of the systemic agenda off the hook by insisting too adamantly that "this is OBE."

To be sure, there is a distinctive jargon that usually accompanies OBE: "what children should know and be able to do," and "authenic assessment," to cite just two examples. And where OBE goes, you normally will find advocates slamming memorization and structured drill, any form of ability-grouping, competition, and standardized testing. At the same time, you'll hear high praise for group or cooperative learning, portfolio assessment, thematic (or interdisciplinary) learning, whole language (as opposed to phonics) to teach reading, "real-life" or socially relevant projects, the overriding importance of self-esteem, mandatory community service, and a lot of the trendy "isms," such as globalism, multiculturalism, and environmentalism. Still, just because your neighborhood educrat spouts nonsense about "global citizenship," don't automatically assume that your school system has full-blown OBE.

Think more broadly of an OBE Philosophy, as opposed to literal OBE. (Its advocates keep changing the name anyway to try to throw opponents off the trail.) I am indebted to Lil Tuttle, an academics-advocate *par excellence,* for helping to clarify thinking about the competing strains of education philosophy. (See her excellent analysis at the end of Chapter 7.) All of the controversy over American education, now and way back to the eras of Deweyism and Progressive Education, really comes down to a competition between two approaches to educating children.[1] These might be called . . .

Objective Education
versus
Affective Education

Objective: For you, um, "mature" readers of this book, education according to objective standards may remind you of the schools of your childhood—before the decline of SAT verbal and math scores, and the rise of disruptive behavior. Instruction is teacher-led, the assumption being that there is a body of objective knowledge and skills that the teacher is paid to pass along to the children. The knowledge is taught in well-defined courses, along the lines of the classical disciplines: history, English, geography, civics, mathematics, and the sciences. Values? Yes, values are taught; but they are hardy civic virtues like the work ethic, responsibility, integrity, and honesty—not sociopolitical attitudes or personal feelings. Competition is not a dirty word: Children are graded on the A–F scale, and those who make the Honor Roll are recognized. In specific subjects, children often are grouped according to their achievement levels (advanced to slow) so that teachers are better able to tend to individual needs. Standardized tests, permitting comparisons with national norms, are used.

This is basic, teacher-directed education—the Three R's, plus a lot more.

Affective: In an earlier era, this was called Progressive Education, or Life Adjustment. Now the label is Outcome-Based Education, or Mastery Learning, Benjamin Bloom's progenitor of OBE. Developmentally Appropriate Practice (DAP) is another label, particularly for the primary grades.

The teacher is no longer a teacher but rather a "facilitator." Much of the learning is child-directed or -initiated, or at least child-centered. Tremendous emphasis is put on the child's feeling good about himself (self-esteem) and about learning in general. Because social development is paramount, teachers routinely evaluate the pupils' attitudes, feelings, and emotions. Grouping by ability is a big no-no. Instead, pupils of varied achievement levels and ages are mixed together and older or faster students are asked to be peer tutors to younger or slower ones. Grades typically are either A/B or "Not Yet" (or some euphemism like "Emergent") to avoid wounding self-esteem. Failure is banished in favor of universal "success." Rather than earning credits in traditional academic disciplines (derogated as "seat time"), students graduate—or earn Certificates of Mastery—by completing "outcome performances," i.e. projects showing themselves to be Environmental Stewards or Quality Workers.

Does this have to be entirely an either/or choice? Probably not. Even if most children learn best from a structured, teacher-directed, academically demanding approach, a few elements from the School of Relevance could enliven instruction. There is nothing intrinsically wrong with having pupils amass portfolios of their essays or experiments—so long as they proceed from a sound knowledge base, and are tested on that objective knowledge. And the best teachers make pupils aware of the relevance of their classwork to the competitive world that awaits them. Surely, however, no child is done a favor by being shielded from all possibility of failure. Sink or swim is part of what awaits them beyond the school walls. It is unrealistic to think of some grand compromise between OBE/affective and basic/objective education that will satisfy both sides. One or the other must prevail as the foundation of schooling, although of course true schools of choice would permit a wide range of approaches.

The Affective or Progressive approach long has been favored by many in the education establishment, especially education-school pedagogues and state departments of education. But not until OBE came along has the collective might of the federal government and multinational corporations been gathered in support of one model of education for all of American schooling. This is the ultimate outrage of OBE: that so many political and industrial elitists, whatever their individual motives, have hopped on a Bandwagon they call Systemic Reform and that they wish to force all the rest of we lesser beings on board—no matter what approach we may prefer for our own children, or what local school boards or independent-minded teachers may think about the new progressivism.

They want to settle the age-old debate over education approaches by fiat—and that is simply wrong.

But, this is no deep, dark, one-world conspiracy. By combing government reports and (mostly obscure) academic and business journals, I found that the leading OBE advocates were on record with regard to their objectives.[2] Because of the paucity of media coverage, however, it was an immense help to have the services of a private, *pro bono* researcher who pulled scads of documents out of the ERIC data system for me. This person has chosen to remain nameless because of the possibility of economic retribution; but I hope he/she knows how sincerely grateful I am for the invaluable assistance.

So who are the movers and shakers behind the monolithic effort to remake American education on a nationally prescribed method? Well, an interesting tipoff to the extent of the collaboration came in the summer of 1994 when the executive director of the National Association of State Boards of Education was assembling a coalition of heavy-hitters to strike back against the opposition to "systemic reform."[3] Membership in the coalition promised such benefits as "message tool kits including sample speeches, model presentations, issue briefs, materials on opponents, and an advocacy video." **Materials on opponents?** So now you can go in some bigwigs' dossier simply for speaking up for a sound basic education for your child?

Anyway, these organizations had joined the systemic-change coalition by summer's end:[4]

- The Association for Supervision and Curriculum Development.
- The Business Roundtable.
- The Council for Basic Education.
- Council of Chief State School Officers.
- National Alliance of Business.
- National Association of Secondary School Principals.
- National Association of State Boards of Education.
- National Association of State Directors of Special Education.
- National Education Association.
- National Middle Schools Association.
- National School Public Relations Association.
- New American Schools Development Corporation (a non-profit group formed under President Bush's America 2000, precursor of Goals 2000).

The only invitees that had turned down the invitation were the National Association of Independent Schools, National Conference of State Legislators, and National Governors Association.

The Business Roundtable, the "facilitator" of the coalition, was to pick up much of the $125,000 tab. The Roundtable also has bankrolled the "Keep the Promise" media campaign that seeks to drum up support for Goals 2000. Chapter 9 will discuss the role of Big Biz.

The OBE movement—until then largely confined to educationist circles—began coalescing after the federal government's 1983 report, "A Nation at Risk." That report complained of "a rising tide of mediocrity" and the fact that 23 million adult Americans were illiterate. Ironically, however, the message the elitist reformers took away was that America needed less concentration, not more, on the academic basics. In 1989, President Bush convened the nation's Governors in an education summit at the University of Virginia, where the august assembled leaders propounded the idea of legislating National Education Goals. One of the leading education intellectuals in the Reagan-Bush years, **Chester E. Finn, Jr.,** actually was a proponent of a national curriculum and national testing. Bush's America 2000 would provide a vehicle for OBE riders, but the major move would come after Bush's defeat for re-election in 1992 by the lead Governor at the Education Summit, Arkansas' William Jefferson Clinton.

Here are some of the major riders on the OBE bandwagon:

The National Center on Education and The Economy, Marc Tucker, president. Originally located in Rochester, New York, where Tucker was a professor of education, the center opened a second office in Washington when Bill Clinton was elected President. And small wonder. Shortly after the 1992 election, an ebullient Tucker released a report in which he declared that, "The advent of the Clinton administration creates a unique opportunity for the country to develop a truly national system for the development of human resources, second to none on the globe."[5] Tucker said the center, and the organization from which it sprang in the mid-'80s, the Carnegie Forum on Education and the Economy, had been "elaborating" a national agenda for eight years. Among Tucker's collaborators (whom he called "a small group with close ties to the Center") were **Michael Cohen,** who would become a full-time consultant to Education Secretary Richard Riley and write the Goals 2000 legislation; and **David Hornbeck,** the Business Roundtable's star OBE consultant to several states.

The center really got the OBE bandwagon rolling in 1989 when it set up and paid for under the Labor Department's wing the **Commission on the Skills of the American Workforce,** with **Ira Magaziner,** then an industrial consultant, as chairman. Although **Hillary Rodham Clinton,** a trustee of the center and then a lawyer at Arkansas' Rose Law Firm, was not on the commission at the start, she was made co-chair for implementation when in June, 1990, the commission released a report, **"America's Choice: High Skills or Low Wages!"**[6] This duo would achieve much notoriety a few years later with the First Lady as chair of the secretive—and ultimately rejected—health care reform committee, and Magaziner as her Svengali. Magaziner's convoluted scheme for nationalized health care (the bill ran to more than 1,300 pages) would attract extensive media coverage, and rightly so. Yet, the major media failed to note that this pair's plan to nationalize education has achieved a high degree of success.

In an education journal article they co-authored in 1992, Mrs. Clinton and Magaziner argued that it was critical to have a new national system of performance-based standards that virtually all students would meet by age 16. Without the **Certificate of Initial Mastery (CIM),** they argued, students would not be allowed to go on to work, preparation for college, or technical training. And those who dropped out would be rounded up and sent to Youth Centers, which they called "an essential component of the whole strategy for national human resource development."[7] The element of forced early choice between work and college is basically on the German model.

The Magaziner Commission also argued that sociability was more important for the new American worker than basic literacy and math skills; that a new student assessment system should let students take and retake and retake tests as often as they needed until they could succeed; and that in place of objective testing schools should go to the three P's—performances, portfolios, and products—collections of student work evaluated subjectively. Traditional knowledge-based tests won't do because they "sort out" people too much (the dumb from the smart?).

That was vintage OBE.

It is instructive that parents were mentioned in the commission's thick document not a single time. Basically, the report was all about the need for government schools to instill the attitudes in children favored by the power elitists.

The Ira Magaziner/Hillary Clinton report had a powerful impact at the state and national levels. It spurred state **Workforce 2000** task forces that led to numerous state departments of education bringing in OBE consultants like sociologist **William Spady** (a development discussed in more detail in Chapter 5). And it led to the Labor Department's stepped-up involvement in elementary and secondary education through its SCANS system. SCANS is an acronym for **Secretary's Commission on Achieving Necessary Skills.** SCANS has supplied the work specs for the New American Child and indeed for every workplace in the nation.

The 1993 release of a **SCANS Blueprint for High Performance** had a revealing prototype of the student resume the SCANSers wish to substitute for academic report cards. Be on the alert for these.[8] The resume would contain a student's name, address, home phone, date of birth, and, of course, Social Security number. It would carry ratings for "workplace competencies," such as "interpersonal skills" and "systems thinking." And students also would be rated for their self-esteem (measured by attitudinal surveys), sociability, self-management, and integrity/honesty. Furthermore, the SCANS Blueprint reported that the Educational Testing Service, the nation's largest test-maker, was developing a **"Worklink"** program to enable businesses to call up students' resumes electronically. Subsequently, the National Center for Education Statistics released a **Student Data Handbook for Early Childhood, Elementary, and Secondary Education** detailing a system for collecting detailed data on every American child and sharing it through the SPEED/ExPress electronic data system.[9]

The implications for personal rights and privacy of all this tracking are chilling. This is intrusion on a scale beyond Orwellian imagining. Consider how much of a chance you would have to land a job if somewhere along the line a school had given you a low mark (for whatever reason) for integrity/honesty. Perhaps you would have to go to a government re-education center to have your attitudes properly retooled.

The SCANS Blueprint goes so far as to state that "all school systems should make the SCANS skills and workplace competencies explicit objectives of instruction at all levels." It says the federal government should take the lead in bringing this about, and with the passage of the Clintons' Goals 2000, that can happen, because that law puts the Department of Labor in the thick of certifying the skills of all American workers. The companion School to Work law calls for the total integration of work-based learning into the curriculum and the tracking of students into specific occupations from an early age. This is vocationalism writ large. Whatever happened to the ideal of liberal learning to enable students to become free-thinking, well-rounded individuals?

With the National Education Standards and Improvement Council set up under Goals 2000 to certify acceptable standards for states wishing to receive federal aid, the **New Standards Project** has become an ever more important member of the bandwagon. Again, this is a Marc Tucker production, having been started by his center in January, 1991, in collaboration with the Learning Research and Development Center at the University of Pittsburgh. Again, the linkages are suggestive of an interlocking directorate. **Lauren Resnick,** the testing expert at Pitt and co-NSP director with Tucker, serves on SCANS. And Hillary Clinton is a major presence, having served on NSP's founding board.

The NSP has as its stated purpose "a radically new approach in the assessment of student progress that would drive fundamental changes in what is taught and learned."[10] It is preparing the **Certificate of Initial Mastery** as a replacement for the traditional high school diploma. The underlying philosophy is egalitarian to the point of being utopian. Resnick and Tucker have condemned current tests as being "designed to sort out those who would enter the elite from those who would not." Therefore, in designing a new system, the NSP intends to destroy "the primary mechanisms of the sorting system in American education that have lowered expectations and limited opportunity for countless people over the years." Having one standard for everyone—and allowing unlimited time for slower students to meet it—will dictate the abolition of all ability-grouping.

Picture one big group—its collective self-esteem off the top of the charts—earning at a common dumbed-down level, which shall be called "world class." All Children Can Learn. Lower the basketball hoop to three feet and All Children Can Slam-Dunk, too.

One additional key player deserves mention—**Labor Secretary Robert Reich.** The NSP's objectives were anticipated by Reich, then a Harvard political economist, in a presentation to the National Education Association's leadership in April, 1988. His paper was entitled, "Education and the Next Economy," and the NEA leaders gave it their hearty endorsement.[11] Wrote Reich:

"Young people must be taught how to work constructively together. Instead of emphasizing individual achievement and competition, the emphasis in the classroom should be on group performance. Students need to learn how to seek and accept criticism from their peers, to solicit help, and to give credit to others, where appropriate. They must also learn to negotiate—to articulate their own needs, to discern what others need, and see things from others' perspectives, and to discover mutually beneficial outcomes."

Classroom ability-grouping, said Reich:

". . . is another vestige of high-volume, standardized production—the deluxe models moving along a different conveyor belt from the economy cars. This may be an efficient way to cram information into young minds with differing capacities to absorb it; but tracking or grouping can also reduce young peoples' capacities to learn from and collaborate with one another. Rather than separate fast learners from slow learners in the classroom, all children (with only the most obvious exceptions) should remain together, so that class unity and cooperation are the norm. Faster learners would thus learn how to help the slower ones, while the slower ones would be pushed harder to make their best effort."

Thus are the flower children and university radicals of the 1960s—Reich, Ira Magaziner, Bill Clinton, Hillary Rodham Clinton—in a position to translate their woolly theories into public policy. And, joining with them on OBE, incredibly enough, have been crusty outcomes-oriented capitalists who imagine they will get Quality Workers from schools turned into temples of Political Correctness. Republicans helped get the bandwagon rolling with America 2000 (though some of them, like former Secretary of Education Lamar Alexander, now oppose Goals 2000). And, virtually the whole education establishment—seeing a chance to enshrine their progressivist doctrines—is on board.

What chance does the average citizen have against such a powerful Juggernaut? Well, for encouragement, one might look to membership of the Board of Trustees of the National Center on Education and the

Economy. The honorary chairman is Mario Cuomo, who as Governor of New York channeled heavy funding in the floundering OBE experiment in Rochester's schools; but Cuomo is governor no longer, having been defeated for re-election in the wave of revulsion against Big Government scheming that swept the nation in the 1994 mid-term elections. And now the Clintons' face the first Republican-controlled legislature in 40 years, with its leaders vowing to "revisit" Goals 2000 and perhaps remove provisions that threaten local and parental authority over education of the young.

Bandwagons may look unstoppable, and the one carrying OBE is still running strong; however, there are ways for citizens to exert their will and have an influence, even as David did against Goliath. For examples of how, please read on. . . .

The Politics of Pork and School Restructuring

By Donna Shedd
Kentucky

We had been fighting Outcome-Based Education in Kentucky for a full two years before we discovered that it had a name.

It was in early 1992 that the various tentacles of our education restructuring, known as KERA, all came together to form one obfuscating OBE octopus. The revelation came at the Constitutional Coalition's annual Education Policy Conference in St. Louis, Missouri, where a presentation was given on OBE. The discourse hit us right between the eyes. KERA was OBE!

Education restructuring in Kentucky went into full swing in the late 1980s. Back in 1985, 66 property-poor school districts had joined together to file a complaint regarding the inequity in funding from one district to another. By 1989, their case was being heard in the Kentucky Supreme Court. In June, the Court declared Kentucky's entire school system unconstitutional and ordered the General Assembly to fix it "part and parcel," post haste. The court presumed to tell the legislators what a "fixed" system would encompass.

In January, 1990, a conference was held on what the legislature was concocting for the schools. The reformers were already on their second and third drafts by then—all written by David Hornbeck, the lawyer/consultant. It had been 15 years since I taught school, but I recognized the fads from the 1960s. The inane drive to have everything "fair": nobody fails, everyone succeeds, nobody competes, everyone cooperates, everyone equal, everyone well and everyone happy.

A handful of citizens joined together to lobby against the bill. It was a brand new experience for most of us. We were moms and grandmoms. We learned a lot—it was the proverbial school of hard knocks. We learned about pork barrel projects and their weight in voting versus the weight of just-plain-moms. It doesn't turn out as in the movies. In the real world of politics, it always comes down to power, which translates into money and re-election. The KERA bill contained 75 pork projects—from swimming pools to golf courses to parking garages. And then there were the threats. Six of eight legislators from northern Kentucky stood firm and voted no. So the leadership stood firm on its threat and funds for the University of Northern Kentucky's convocation center were crossed off the budget on the morning of the vote in the House. Thus was the legislative deed done.

Speaking Out as an Independent Voice on Education

By Linda Murphy
Oklahoma

In October of 1992 I was appointed to the steering team of our local school to implement a pilot program that would fulfill the mandates of our state's education reform legislation, HB 1017, which passed in 1990. I asked for information about the program and was given a file that had some education journal articles and handouts from education seminars. As I read this information, and later the pilot application form, I found that our school system, and, in fact, our entire state was positioned to be totally restructured in a process called Outcomes-Based Education, OBE, and Outcomes Accreditation System, OAS.

Our new state law requires schools to meet or exceed the outcomes accreditation system established by North Central Accreditation Association. I found that a sociologist, William Spady, received a federal grant in 1984 to implement OBE in schools around the nation. He has been in our state on several occasions and was scheduled to be in Fort Gibson to train our teachers. I read Spady's writing in *Educational Leadership* (October 1991), and found his statement that the results of OBE are not yet certain. In other writings he said we should write exit outcomes based on assumptions regarding the future and prepare students to be oriented with certain attitudes. He said they should be prepared to deal with religious and political orthodoxy, intolerance, fundamentalism—and conservatism.

Since the fall of 1992 when I discovered the political world view that OBE is based on, I have been speaking out about the very serious concerns I have regarding the paradigm shift that is being politically forced in our lives. Since part of the OBE and Outcomes Accreditation system is to set and meet goals or outcomes for all students in the affective (emotions and feelings) domain I knew this philosophy would be especially dangerous.

I first shared my findings with my husband, Dan, who fully agreed with the concern I had. We talked to Tom and Debbie Gann who are our friends and neighbors. Tom is also on the school board and served on the district steering team with me. They, too, agreed that this new program was one they did not want. From this point on the research and underlying information about the education restructuring plan for our state has just traveled like wildfire.

My initial feelings and thoughts of alarm about this radical philosophy were always calmed by a strong belief that most of the people in our state would not want or agree to implement this philosophy if they only knew what it was. I felt a strong sense of responsibility to speak out to the public. Because my career had involved a great deal of public speaking, I readily agreed when asked to share the information I had gathered. It did not take long to have boxes and boxes of files with information from our state department of education, the federal Labor Department, schools, and numerous contacts around the country. My speaking requests grew and grew. Our local school board did ultimately reject the OBE pilot project after much debate and deliberation, but it wasn't easy. The superintendent and other administrators were pushing hard to put it in place. There were many divisive statements made and public meetings held to discourage resistance to this "change" in educational philosophy.

From November, 1992, through January, 1994, I had given approximately 150 presentations on education restructuring. I had testified before the House Education Committee to delay implementation of the 7,000 learner outcomes that had been written and were to be required in all schools. I had also testified at a public hearing before the board of regents of higher education about the undermining of academics by education restructuring.

At each step of the way at the local, state, and federal levels there have been those who eagerly want to hear the truth about the underlying philosophy of OBE and OAS and those who have rejected or even fought against exposing this information. I've learned through past experience to do what I think is right and go on without being discouraged by those who get angry or try to stop me.

The very deceptive nature of the wording in our state legislation, the words of those selling this philosophy and the fact that the plans were not presented publicly to start with has been a big red flag. Obviously the resistance to this philosophy was expected and those planning the implementation had deliberately made it difficult to make closure on the big picture. Initially finding a piece of information here and then there was like discovering an automobile that had been brought in a piece at a time, first the hood, then the bumper, etc.

I have networked information to and from people across the state and nation for the past two years but have not joined nor did I previously belong to any organization. I held statewide networking meetings for 10 months until November, 1993, when I decided I would run for the position of State Superintendent of Public Instruction. It has been important not to be tied to anyone else. I have remained independent and not controlled. As you will quickly learn if you have concerns about the restructuring process, one of the first political attacks is to be labeled by the opposition as some kind of radical nut. Those belonging to a group are often more vulnerable to this. I am not talking about what is fair or accurate, just what is actually happening t everyday citizens in communities around the country.

I learned in presenting this information that if you do your homework first, speak clearly and honestly, many people will listen. You have to be calm and confident, but not pushy. Don't force your concerns on others, but be available and willing to discuss your findings. The words of the "experts" are the most revealing whether they are local or nationally known. Let their own words speak for themselves. Quote Bill Spady and others. I most often just presented facts without my own opinion until I became a candidate and my opinion was of importance to the listeners.

If I had been concerned about being accepted, I would have never gotten off of first base in sharing this information. It seems that many in the political bureaucracy including the education arena have high stakes vested in the success of education restructuring. Look at the money trail, and you will understand what is really happening.

(Editor's Note: As this book was going to press, Linda Murphy had been nominated by the new Governor of Oklahoma to be the state's Secretary of Education.)

Concerned Parents Were An Early-Warning System

By Dr. Karie E. Dawkins
Virginia

In 1990, concerned parents in Virginia realized that a major change was coming to Virginia schools when they were told that the Standards of Learning were no longer available because they were being replaced by "something"—but no one knew what. Little did the parents know how massive and in what philosophical direction those changes would be.

Parents soon learned that the Common Core of Learning (CCL), one of the many semantic covers for Outcome-Based Education (OBE), was being implemented in Virginia on the recommendation of sociologists acting as consultants—not just to Virginia, but to many other states. (Note the term **sociologists**—not teachers or academicians.)

Using behavior modification, all students were to be trained to become so-called "team players" easily manipulated by their "teachers" to follow a particular philosophical viewpoint. Although told that the desire was to allow local schools to control their curriculum, the parents quickly discovered that this would be impossible because **National** tests would in fact drive the curricula. And, predictably, those controlling **national** (not local) standards were being reformulated at the federal level by the sociologists and "progressive educators" who had experimented with parents and their children for the past 40 years, and had failed miserably. The bottom line and thinly veiled intent became all too obvious: societal control and power by a self-appointed few, to the personal loss, deprivation and bondage of many.

In addition, the parents learned that, under OBE, graduation requirements would no longer be based on completion of academic course work and credits earned. Instead, students could only "graduate" with a Certificate of Initial mastery (CIM) based on "demonstrated achievement" of "learner outcomes." To obtain a CIM, a student would have to demonstrate the achievement of predetermined "values, attitudes, and behavior." The CIM would be necessary for that student to receive a permit to work or drive a car. According to Ira Magaziner and Hillary Clinton in the March, 1992, issue of Educational Leadership magazine, "A new educational performance . . . established nationally . . . should be set for all students, to be met at or around age 16 . . . (A) Certificate of Initial Mastery . . . would qualify the student to choose among those going to work, entering a college preparatory program, or studying for a Technological or Professional Certificate. . . ." This subjective assessment and life/career manipulation of students by a controlling few—based on **their** predetermined attitudes, values, and behaviors—obviously was intended to lead our country down the dead-end road of socialist government.

Confusing references to changes coming to Virginia's school system prompted several parents to independently research the implementation of OBE in other states. The individual conclusions were the same: OBE was being implemented in Virginia in the same manner that it had been foisted on the unsuspecting public of other states, including Pennsylvania, Arkansas, and California. Upon review of copies of the draft CCL and of objective, in-depth critiques of the CCL by various analysts, parents quickly realized that the educational system in Virginia was being moved in a direction that would be harmful to students, by requiring less academics and more emphasis on controversial attitudes and values, and that would be harmful to taxpayers and the general society as well. Although the Department of Education denied that it had anything to do with OBE, many of the same terms, goals, and authors present in other states' education reform packages were in Virginia's CCL, too.

The frightening aspect of OBE was the emphasis on behaviors and attitudes instead of academics. Examples of questions from assessment tests in Pennsylvania and across the country proved that much of the "testing" was not of academic material, but behavioral and philosophical. These assessments included questioning children about private family matters and their own sexual activities. Even in Virginia where OBE-type standards had not been **formally** adopted, emotional and intrusive questioning of young children in routine classroom situations was evident. Example: For Mother's Day, a second-grade class was given a questionnaire asking the children about their mothers. Included among various "cutesy" queries such as "How tall is Mom in feet and inches," "How much does she weigh (Guess—be nice)," and "How much would she like to weigh", were more intrusive questions such as "Name her first boyfriend," "My mom handles stress by: running, cooking, eating, yelling, sleeping (circle one)", and "What is the one thing your mother does that your father can't stand". Excuse me, but teachers have no business asking such inappropriate questions of their students, much less second graders. What was the academic purpose of such a questionnaire? It is a far cry from taking a few minutes to make a nice card of appreciation for Mom on Mother's day! Children should be focusing on positive attributes of their family; not looking for problems that may not exist. Even if problems are there, emotional games should not be used in the school system. Most parents will agree that academics should be the main focus of school. What was most alarming in this second grade classroom example was that the parents of the students were afraid to complain about the intrusive questioning of their children because they were **afraid** of placing a stigma on their child—or on themselves! Parental intimidation by a publicly unaccountable system is always a serious problem. But parental **immobilization** when the family is threatened in **any** way is disastrous.

Evidence of inappropriate psychological and emotional questions are abundant and documented in *Child Abuse in the Classroom* by Phyllis Schlafly and *Educating for the New World Order* by Bev Eakman. Educrats still claim that Goals 2000 does not demand politically correct attitudes and behaviors, but emerging National Standards (as in U.S. and world history) are direct evidence that such is not the truth. The Pennsylvania state developed assessments were actually personality tests disguised as an "achievement" test. Evidence of grading students on politically correct attitudes (not grammar and literacy) was demonstrated in several counties in Virginia on the state's "Literacy Passport Assessment Test." Examples abounded (with media attention and public consternation expressed) of children's compositions that, when politically correct, were deemed "acceptable" and "passed" even when the writing was replete with atrocious errors in syntax, spelling, grammar, punctuation, and capitalization, while **honor students** who wrote beautifully and techncially superior compositions were **not** passed, being deemed insufficiently "creative" because of their politically **in**correct themes (such as expressing a positive, admiring attitude toward their family and parents). Parents began waking up to realize that the same mindset responsible for developing the "assessments" in Pennsylvania, Arkansas, California, and even Virginia, were obviously heavily involved in the development of our nation's new **national** standards and tests.

Honor Roll

(Honoring grassroots organizations that have made a difference for the better in their communities.)

(Oklahoma) Parents' Rights in Determining Education (PRIDE)

Formed in early 1992 by an initial group of approximately 40 parents, grandparents, and concerned patrons, this organization quickly became the largest of its kind in Oklahoma. At its peak, PRIDE was sending out 1,500 newsletters per month.

The fact that PRIDE is located in the state's largest population center contributed to its size and the fact that Oklahoma City is also the state capital contributed to the group's effectiveness. By May, 1992, as a result of a highly successful information exchange and effective contact with State Representatives and Senators, a reversal of sorts was announced. Our Department of Education backed down from its initial stance; OBE now would be optional at the district level. We are, however, still fighting the philosophy and practices of this wrongheaded reform.

PRIDE and other groups continuously monitor legislation and education policy, passing updated information on to an active core of concerned patrons. PRIDE is a non-profit organization, incorporated in Oklahoma. Current information and points of contact are available by sending a stamped, self-addressed envelope to: OK PRIDE, P.O. Box 7495, Oklahoma City, OK, 73153.

4

The Citizens' Mobilization

Clearly, the forces lined up behind the OBE style of school reform are powerful, well-financed, and determined. They control the budgets and regulations of federal, state, and local governments, they lobby for national associations with larders made fat with members' dues, and they are the captains of the world's wealthiest corporations.

Against this mighty Systemic Change Gang, which is so certain that outcome-based rather than freedom-based change is what all schools require, what chance do those who beg to differ—Moms and Dads and teachers and taxpayers—have of even starting a debate, much less winning it?

A good chance, actually. One of the inspirational lessons I have learned from observing OBE/culture wars across the nation is that in many communities citizens are halting the Juggernaut and forcing a re-evaluation of the kind of school restructuring that will truly benefit American children. The task is not easy. Some Big Education elitists—the National Education Association among them—have tried to demonize all opposition to statist school reform as right-wing radicals and religious zealots.[1] That's poppycook, of course. But perhaps if you are over as far to the political Left as the NEA is, Middle America does look to be far to the right.

So how does the citizen mobilization begin—with masses of disgruntled consumers of education marching on the State Capitol? No. That might be a culminating event, but not the start. It is a truism that there is strength in numbers, but I am increasingly convinced that in variety there is strength, too.

By variety I mean citizens who come from many different backgrounds all doing their own investigating and inquiring—maybe together with a few neighbors—after first becoming concerned about the new education dogma. In the age of the fax machine and the computer modem, a few citizens can quickly collect a mass of information and make connections nationwide with like-minded citizens. You don't have to be a part of a formal organization to get started.

The new sentinels for American freedom don't ride horses from town to village; they spread the word on the computer networks or via the fax machines.

I think of Kansan **Cindy Duckett,** keeper of an amazingly well-organized library on OBE, posting the latest news—and downloading vital documentation—at 1 a.m. almost every night. Cindy communicates to America from its Heartland at such a bracing hour because she doesn't want to take time from her family earlier in the evening (and also because she is a self-confessed "night owl" who likes to work when the phones aren't jangling. Me, too, Cindy!)

I think of Californian **Carolyn Steinke,** whose strike force against affective ed consisted in the beginning of "We Three Moms" traveling to Sacramento and learning first-hand what the bureaucrats and the special interests had in mind for the state's children.

I think of Ohio's **Chris Helm**, who spoke in dozens of church basements, schools, and libraries across the state—taking care to juggle her schedule so as to have time for her children. She and her compatriot, **Debbie Stevens,** would drive to the State House once a month to deliver thousands of letters denouncing the OBE and Goals 2000 scams.

I think of **Ken Von Kohorn, Kay Wall,** and their cohorts in upscale Westport, Connecticut—long home to some of the nation's finest schools—taking the time to do research so meticulous and to prepare an alternative reform plan so persuasive that no Big Education flack could credibly taint them as loopy aginners.

But when I think of a one-person "citizens' mobilization" I think inevitably of **Kerri Vailati**—a Hampton, Virginia, homemaker who is the wife of husband Rick, a shipyard worker. The cherubic faced, auburn-haired Mrs. Vailati—a political moderate—is living proof that one person (even if by her own admission not terribly well organized) still can make an impact on public policy by sheer energy and force of will.

By saving scraps of information, she was able to expose the State Superintendent of Public Instruction's disavowal of a direct association between the state's OBE plans and the work of OBE consultant William Spady. When the State Department of Education trotted out transparencies explaining its outcomes-laden Common Core of Learning, Kerri went back to her files and found identical transparencies from Spady's outfit. *Voila!* The state had simply scratched off "High Success Network" and presented the transparencies as its own.

In addition to persistence, it is a sense of humor that sets Kerri Vailati apart. (We should remember to keep our own; a smile wins more friends than a scowl.) When she nervously approached the podium to speak to the State Board of Education for the first time, she heard her name mispronounced. So she began by saying she was Kerri Vailati—"it rhymes with spaghetti"—and that bit of imagery has stuck in many minds and softened hard feelings.

At the meeting, the Board adopted the OBE plan (later to be withdrawn by Governor Doug Wilder) despite Mrs. Vailati and 20 other citizens speaking out strongly against it.

"We were frustrated," she remembers, "but at the same time thrilled to find other parents and teachers who were also questioning what was being railroaded through in Virginia's public school system. We met in the hallway and we compared notes for hours. We traded addresses and phone numbers. We networked in the hall for the remainder of the day. We were what is called the grassroots."

And hear how Kerri has kept up her one-woman mobilization:

"I wrote to friends in other states and asked them about education reform in their area and if they had heard of OBE. I read books, magazine articles, and newspaper articles. My children (Kristi and Ricky) wouldn't leave the house without their Nintendo Gameboys because they needed something to keep them busy in case their Mom would stop and talk to someone about education."

"You see, I would approach people about education while standing in line at the grocery store, while at church, while eating at restaurants, at the mall, at the bus stop, virtually everywhere I went. If they knew anything about school restructuring and were willing to talk, my children knew to sit down and keep themselves busy. The poor kids knew they were in for the long haul. They didn't especially like it, but they knew how important it was to Mom."

"A helpful hint: I found out that lines at the bank were the best for asking strangers about education. The lines were usually long and no one wanted to get out of line and go to the back. *You have a captive audience!* One time my family saw me 'accosting strangers' at a local restaurant's dessert bar. I had overheard a lady discussing schools and I asked her a few questions. My family was mortified watching the lady trying to get away from me as her ice cream melted away."

In order to keep current in the education cause, she and husband Rick refinanced their home and purchased a second computer, a fax modem, and a post office box. Friends held a yard sale to raise money to buy Kerri a tape recorder to use at public meetings. Rick, she says, "became a slight bit excitable when he realized I had put over 20,000 miles on our new car within only 11 months." But he calmed down when she kept the monthly phone bills under the goal of $150.

Here is Kerri's idea of a mobilization plan:

"It is important to have a good friend working with you who will be a runner. I did the running by myself for months and almost wore myself out. Once we had four or five runners, we could all take flyers out to groups and hand them out in neighborhoods when a big meeting was coming up, or when there was a crisis. You always need a thinker—someone around who can figure out what to do with ideas once you get them. You also need a phone caller. The last category of person who meant so much to me was the listener. I kept getting myself into hot water in one way or another and needed a listener not only to listen but to say a prayer for me from time to time when the alligators seemed to be snapping hard."

Since her baptism in the politics of OBE in 1993, Kerri Vailati has attended every State Board of Education meeting. Once that meant hitching a nine-hour ride across the state with a newspaper reporter when the Board went on the road. Often it has meant sleeping in friends' spare bedrooms.

"People were so hungry for information," she explained. "It didn't matter that I was not someone important. I may be 'just a mom,' but I am an informed mom!"

Another one-Mom mobilization with special powers of persuasion is **Sylvia Kraemer,** a member of the Federal Executive Service in Washington, D.C. Dr. Kraemer, the mother of two children in Alexandria, Virginia, public schools, defies the establishment's stereotypes of OBE foes: She is a "left-of-center Democrat and lapsed Episcopalian." She also is highly educated—and an educator herself: Possessor of a Ph.D. in history from The Johns Hopkins University, she taught the social and intellectual history of the United States, as well as Western Civilization, while serving as a member of the faculties of Vassar College, Southern Methodist University, and the University of Maine (Orono).

Dr. Kraemer penned blistering, but extensively documented, essays on the glaring deficiencies in Virginia's "Common Core of Learning." [2] These gained a wide underground circulation, like the *samizdat* in the former Soviet Union. Her learned dissection of OBE was merciless; the educrats at Ed-Central had no comeback:

"Translated into the political agenda that follows from these 38 (and highly arguable) soothsayers' cliches, Virginia's public schools would be charged with training our young people to become well-adapted servants of environmentalism, multiculturalism, Total Quality Management (TQM), technological determinism, and public entitlements. . . (This may be your political agenda, and it may be my political agenda; but it is not the business of taxpayer-funded schools to train followers for our political agendas). . . .

"We also find buried here the Virginia Department of Education's requirement for heterogeneously grouped classrooms, and its "Robin

Hood's approach to classroom learning: Pupils who have the misfortune to be high academic achievers (to the extent that academic achievement will be noticed at all under the 'new paradigm') will be required to 'function as a teacher or mentor' for the less able or slower learners. . . .

"Half of our trial attorneys can be kept busy litigating cases arising from the attempt of Virginia public schools to require high-achieving students to spend their precious in-school hours tutoring lower-achieving students. The other half will be busy litigating privacy statute violations arising from the Common Core's necessarily intrusive 'assessments' to determine whether students are acquiring the 'attitudes' and personality traits required for their 'life-roles'. . . .'

Wow! Sylvia, you would have made a great editorial writer.

Dr. Kraemer also exposed the fallacious assumption that OBE is an anti-elitist program that somehow will benefit racial and ethnic minorities:

"Some have argued that the kind of schooling proposed in the Virginia 'Common Core'—a fundamentally anti-intellectual and behaviorist strategy for personality modification and group socialization—is now necessary because of the changing population our public schools. This argument assumes that for the increasing proportion of (primarily) Asian-American, Latino, and African-American youngsters in our public schools, the traditional curriculum of academic subjects has no value. From this assumption follows the notion that these ethnic 'minorities' (which in some school systems are in fact majorities) should not aspire to a solid grounding in the liberal arts—which *remains the optimum foundation for professional or post-graduate training* for most of our 'white-collar' employment.

"Where is it written that young African-Americans should not aspire to become physicians, scientists, business executives, and government leaders? Are our educators so poorly educated themselves that they do not know that history itself provides the best training for a 'changing world'? That political science itself provides the best training for citizenship? That the thoughtful study of good literature provides the best preparation for the manifold experiences of the human condition? That a thorough grounding in the basic sciences and mathematics provides the best training for the many changes we are likely to see in technology and manufacturing—not only as workers and consumers, but as managers and policy-makers? Are our educators so lacking in genuine achievement themselves that they cannot recognize the importance to all kinds of 'success' of ordinary and sustained hard work, patience, and perseverance?"

Eileen Hunt, leader of a group of African-American, Christian women in Richmond, strongly supported Dr. Kraemer's observations at a standing-room only town meeting at a predominantly black school on August 31, 1993. That was the last of the jam-packed town meetings. Two weeks later, **Governor L. Douglas Wilder**—who had made history in 1989 by becoming the first elected black Governor in America—surprised many Virginians by asking the State Board of Education to take the "Common Core of Learning" off the table. The Governor heard the people. And he responded.

Some Virginians were cynical about the decision. The race for Governor was heating up and OBE was becoming a red-hot issue. In Virginia, a Governor cannot stand for re-election, but some thought Doug Wilder was trying to protect his fellow Democrats—or to cover himself in a future race. And some noted acerbically that OBE wasn't really dead; it was still out there in dozens of school experiments, just wounded, and the beast surely would be coming back. (And that was true enough).

Nevertheless, I have known governors—Republican as well as Democrat—who would never have had the good grace to take another look at a heavily backed administration program; governors who would let false pride or hubris get in the way of listening to citizen complaints and reassessing the plan. Governor Wilder deserves a great deal of credit for acting after concluding that the state's laudable reform efforts had gotten off the track of solid academics. It may well be, as State Board of Education President, James Jones, states later in this book, that the board was on the verge of taking the CCL off the table anyway; but the Governor's intervention gave the decision much more impact. Calls came in for months from all over the country. Governor Wilder had inspired many Americans to believe that everyday people can win some battles, after all.

The trio of activists mentioned above—Vailati, Kraemer, and Hunt—are among more than four dozen members of a commission the new Governor, Republican George Allen, has appointed to chart an education reform for Virginia that is not supposed to be laden with affective OBE. Allen was elected in a landslide in the fall of 1993 running on an anti-OBE platform against Democratic Attorney General Mary Sue Terry, whose stand was ambiguous. His appointee as State Superintendent of Public Instruction, Dr. William Bosher, Jr., was one of few school administrators in the country courageous enough to speak out against OBE as a local superintendent. A final report of Allen's Champion Schools Commission was due by December, 1995.

As Kerri Vailati has said of the many small citizens' groups that compared notes at State Board meetings, "Each of us had found a small piece of the puzzle." A real advantage of organizing groups ad hoc and spontaneously in local neighborhoods—and later networking with others across the state and nation—is that it becomes harder for the education establishment to pigeonhole the opposition as "Religious Right." As Cathy Reid of North Carolina suggests, it is a good idea to use multiple and verifiable sources.

In variety there is strength.

As a journalist I am an observer, not an organizer. But I had a rare opportunity to midwife the birth of a grassroots organization. When I started writing weekly op-ed columns about Virginia's OBE plan, I was swamped with dozens of daily calls. One day a quiet unassuming man, the husband of a schoolteacher, called. He had never been an activist, wasn't looking to be one now, and had to be discreet because of his wife's job; but he was concerned about what was happening and would be willing to help people get together if I would refer to him all of my callers who wanted to know what to do. So I did. Soon, Sharon Thompson (whose thoughts appear elsewhere in this book) had become co-coordinator of this group. And then, practically overnight, there was a brand-new organization, Concerned Virginians for Academic Excellence, affiliated with no other group nationally or locally, but having a membership of several hundred. And its members were speaking at school board meetings, doing research, and making contacts far and wide.

Now, please understand: I am not implying that there is any reason to be apologetic for approaching the OBE controversy from a religious perspective. Some of the contributors to this book come from that direction, others not. Nor am I suggesting that national organizations ought to be shunned. To the contrary, many such organizations have extensive storehouses of information about school reform and the culture war in general, and they can be excellent resources. You may want to join one or more such groups. But you may also want to keep your local focus, remembering that, yes, in variety there is strength.

The Alexandria, Virginia-headquartered Foundation Endowment has built itself into a fine clearinghouse of information on OBE and political correctness, and the Family Research Council in Washington, D.C., turns out well-documented studies on education as well as other family issues. Two groups with dynamic leadership are Concerned Women for America, and Phyllis Schlafly's Eagle Forum (publisher of *Education Reporter: The Newspaper of Education Rights*). Liberal mediacrats and educrats may sneer at such figures, but these are good people with strong ideas about strengthening parental rights. Perhaps the most dynamic presentation on that topic I have ever heard in person came from Janet Parshall of Concerned Women for America at a Virginia town meeting on OBE.

The lesson of mobilization is that you should not fear to start small—a committee of one, if necessary—and then to look for good and true friends wherever you can find them.

With the Advent of OBE, People Are Ready to Face the Truth

By Anne M. Barbera
Pennsylvania

Here in Pennsylvania, education has been moving away from academics for over 25 years. In the late 1960's our state chose to revise its regulations and base them on the 10 (later changed to 12) Goals of Quality Education, which were written by behavioral psychologists. Only four of these goals were academic.

The basic difference between the Goals of Quality Education (GQE) and Outcome-Based Education (OBE) is that our regulations based on GQE still required successful completion of so many credits in the major academic categories. In addition, schools were required to raise standards in the attitudinal testing while the OBE regulations require the child to pass social (attitudinal) development standards. Under our new OBE regulations, the children are merely required to take a few academic subjects which can be integrated in order to help the child complete social development.

In 1970, the Educational Quality Assessment test (EQA) was begun. This was the first statewide attitudinal test to be given and provided data at the school and district levels for curriculum and planning purposes. When I saw copies of this test in the 1980s, I was shocked to realize how low educators had stooped. As a former full-time teacher and at that time a substitute teacher, I could not believe anyone would rape a child's mind in that way.

As I mentioned previously, we were able to get pockets of parents to remove their children from the tests and to protest to the state, but it was not possible to awaken the entire state. Academic education continued to decline in Pennsylvania while educational costs continued to rise, causing a steep increase in many local taxes. Then Outcome-Based Education (OBE) hit the scene. People were now ready to face the truth and to go to battle in order to keep control of their children.

In late 1991, we were made aware of public hearings to be held for the revision of the Pennsylvania education regulations. When we obtained a copy of the proposed new regulations from the Department of Education, we exploded. The regulations had been totally rewritten, the academic basis was gone, the academic testing was gone, local control was stripped, and learning outcomes became the basis for our children's education. There were 45 pages of outcomes (more than 500 individual outcomes). They were vague and open to subjective interpretation. Only a small percentage of the outcomes were strictly academic, the others being attitudinal and social. The purpose and focus of our children's education was changed.

Established organizations throughout the state joined together under an umbrella group to gain strength in doing battle with the state. Leaders from various organizations took on different roles, according to their talents; some were researchers, others the strategists, and others statewide communicators. People throughout the state fed materials to these leaders. Contacts were made in the Department of Education and much in-house material was received. Our legislators also aided in getting documents the Department refused to give us. Local school superintendents shared material; they received from the Department by electronic mail. Materials came by mail from known and unknown sources.

Realizing I had to become more involved in this battle for our children's minds, I joined the Pennsylvania Parents Commission, an education activist group headquartered in the neighboring county. The chairman of this group, Peg Luksik, was to become one of the driving forces in the battle. I had worked closely with her on previous educational encounters.

Because the state supposedly had completed its regulations (which were now undergoing required public hearings), with the hope of implementing them in January, 1992, we knew we had to work quickly to stop the steamroller. Basically, we followed the four steps outlined above: we read, critiqued, and summarized the volumes of material we were receiving. We testified at hearings, lobbied our legislators for help, and slowed the pace at which the regulations were moving forward.

The Strange Odyssey of OBE Imported to Carolina

By Cathy Reid
North Carolina

On February 8. 1993, a friend I was having dinner with told me that she had just heard that our local school board was getting ready to select three school sites for an experimental program for which it had received a $20 million grant from The New American Schools Development Corporation. The things she had heard about it alarmed her, and as I listened to what she was telling me, I was convinced that she must be the victim of some terrible misunderstanding. After all, there was no way that our school system would try to eliminate our grading system, contract out our high school sports programs, do away with grade levels, and put our children in school starting at the age of three. Obviously, someone was confused and was spreading rumors that were likely to upset the entire community.

The next morning, I drove up to the local junior high school and asked to see a copy of the memos regarding something called "The Odyssey Project." After reading the materials, I realized that I was the one who had misunderstood. All that my friend had told me was not only true, but only the beginning of what ended up being a long, hard fight for our local education system—a fight that still has not ended.

After reading the memos, I requested a copy of the actual proposal that was submitted to the corporation issuing the 19 grants for the "break the mold" schools. I had never heard many of the terms mentioned in the proposal; however, I have heard them many times since from people all over the country. It turns out that the plan we were told by our school board and school administration was totally unique in every way, was actually an almost carbon copy of plans being implemented in school systems all over the country. The first thing I read that alarmed me was on Page One of the proposal: "The Odyssey Project will use an outcome-based education model that focuses on the knowledge, skills, and attitudes that students should possess when they graduate." Question number one was: "Where do they get off thinking they have the right to decide the attitudes my child should possess, and who would decide what those attitudes were?" The second part of that question was answered in the very next statement: "During Phase I, the Gaston County Design Team (GCDT) will determine essential outcomes for all students, the nature of the instructional program, and the time required for individual students to achieve these outcomes." This design team was made up of 20 persons in the education field and was split into three parts: Team Archimedes, Team Epsilon, and Team Diogenes. The team members were the people in charge of writing the proposal and then implementing the program once the grant was awarded.

Another disturbing feature was that they were replacing normal grade levels with "four formal levels of schooling and a developmental **prenatal** (emphasis mine) to age 3 component." "Alpha" would designate the pre-formal component of schooling children ages 0–3, "Beta" would be the center for learners ages 3–6, "Gamma" for learners ages 7–10, "Delta" for learners ages 11–14, and "Odyssey" for learners age 15–18. Our design team also had decided that it would contract out for our sports rather than have them run within the school. They also would require students to perform "at least 220 hours of quality community service time." Even course names were to change: language arts was to become "communications"; social studies was to be "global cultures"; mathematics was to become "numeracy"; and science was to be called "naturology." These and countless other concerns led citizens in the three communities involved in the site selection process to hold informal meetings to decide what steps to take.

Within two weeks of citizens having first found out about Odyssey, the Board of Education held a meeting to choose the sites for implementation. More than 600 parents showed up at that meeting. They filled the board room and the yard of the administration building. There were hundreds of signed petitions asking for nothing more than 30 days to study this project. All requests were ignored; the board voted on three Dallas, North Carolina, schools for the site and went full speed ahead with the project despite the outcry from the parents.

At that point, we realized that the school board and administration had no intentions of working with us. Therefore, several of us banded together and began having weekly meetings to decide what course to follow. There were about 32 of us comprising the core group, from six different towns in the county. We formed subcommittees and began to do as much research as we could in our spare time. I began to use my Prodigy service to hook up with people all over the country who were experiencing many of the same things we were. Many of us spent hours on end at the library and on the phone to find out what place some state and federal laws played in this. And, of course, we obtained everything we could from our school administration office.

Within a couple of weeks, we had enough information to hold a public meeting to let as many people as possible know what we had found. We had also obtained a copy of the Peg Luksik video, "Who Controls The Children?," which was a great tool, if only for its value of shocking some of these parents out of their complacency. After viewing the video, at least some people began to have a partial realization of what we were being faced with. This was no minor curriculum change; this was a full-scale assault on our parental rights.

Shortly after our first public meeting, the headlines in the local papers began to refer to "The Religious Right" and the "Christian Fundamentalists" who were against the Odyssey Project. Funny, I don't remember anyone ever asking me anything about my religious or political affiliations. After reading the articles, we realized our first mistake: Never, never quote from someone else's materials; always quote directly from the actual source. In our public meeting, one of our speakers read one line from a newsletter from Citizens for Excellence in Education (CEE), and from that point on, the newspaper consistently printed that we were getting much of our information from CEE. In actuality, our information was coming from dozens of sources and from intense research done by a few dozen dedicated individuals. Once you are branded as being affiliated with any other group, whether accurately or not, anything that group says, does, or participates in directly influences public perception of you. And of course you know you can't control what anyone else does. Luckily, we learn from our mistakes.

We soon realized that defeating Odyssey was not going to be any easy task. We had an arrogant Superintendent and Odyssey Design Team, who thought that they knew best for our children, and that we were a loud minority of uneducated, anti-progressive idiots. By the time we realized that the administrative staff was not going to listen to anything we were trying to tell them, the community was already beginning to split. The head of the Odyssey Design Team was found dead in his garage of carbon monoxide poisoning, and our Superintendent had taken over his position. Anonymous phone calls started coming to various members of our loosely formed group with accusations of a whole variety of things relating to Odyssey, such as, its funding, its funding source, and the Design Team. We were even told by someone that they personally saw a stack of several folders, each with personal information on each person in our small group. It was time to get serious. We realized that the most important thing we could do was keep the public informed. Without public outcry, there would be no defeat of Odyssey.

Unfortunately, keeping them informed would cost money, and we all had been digging pretty deeply into our own pockets. We decided that the best thing that we could do was to incorporate. There are pros and cons to becoming a corporation. By becoming a 501C3 non-profit corporation, we could accept donations to fund our ads, meetings, newsletters, etc. On the other hand, 501C3 organizations cannot in any way support or endorse candidates, even though we could as individuals. It is a fine line to walk. Also, if anyone in the organization, especially an officer or board member, says anything out of line, or gives incorrect information to the media, it definitely reflects upon the entire organization. You definitely have to watch what you say, and you can't be as outspoken as you'd sometimes like to be. Weighing all of those things, we realized that time was short and we had to incorporate in order to be most efficient. We found a good attorney sympathetic to our cause, and Concerned Citizens for Public Education was born.

We capitalized on each member's talents. One lady had a background in accounting, and she was able to run down how the grant money, as well as public funds, were being spent. Another member had good public relations skills. She was the one we had to go on the local radio shows and deal with the television media. We also chose designated spokesmen. If asked anything regarding CCPE by a reporter, any member was to refer them to one of the spokesmen. Others researched and compiled information by all means available. Prodigy, a computer online service, proved invaluable to me because I "met" people all over the country and learned what was happening in other places and how they were handling it.

CCPE began having monthly public meetings. We always tried to advertise the meeting in the local paper as well as by faxing public service announcements to all of the radio and television stations in the area. At these meetings, we always handed out copies of information that we found pertinent, as well as the phone numbers for all of our elected school board members, the superintendent, and the Odyssey Design Team. We also passed around a notepad to get the names, addresses, and phone numbers of those attending. Pretty soon we had a mailing list of more than 600 people. We were able to use this list to send out notification cards of our most important meetings, such as the one at which Peg Luksik spoke, and later a very well-done, informative newsletter. The format of our meetings was simple. A few of our people would get up and explain our latest findings, what we were doing, and what our audience could do to help. We would then open the floor for questions.

After repeated attempts, the Odyssey Design Team agreed to hold a public forum of sorts . . . on their terms, of course. There were to be three supporters of Odyssey, and three who were against. They would have the chance alternately to ask three questions each and make a closing statement. At that time, members of the audience were given the opportunity to ask the Design Team questions. In my opinion, the entire meeting was a farce. The opponents of Odyssey asked pointed questions and were given long, drawn-out explanations that did not answer the questions at all, and the supporters of Odyssey asked few questions, but rather took up the allotted time for questions with statements of support, with one girl even comparing the Odyssey opponents to those who crucified Christ.

Our school administration and the Odyssey Design Team had been holding their own public meetings around the county to explain Odyssey, which we also attended in force. They were blaming the entire controversy on the fact that they had used certain words in the proposal and other literature that the public surely couldn't understand—words such as "facilitators," "Paideia," "learning cadres," etc. On the contrary, we had become very well-informed on all of their terminology. This is important. You need to be able to understand what they are saying even better than they do.

CCPE, and many other dedicated individuals, continued tirelessly to research and educate others on the pitfalls of Outcome-Based Education and other elements of Odyssey. Call after call was made to NASDC to state in no uncertain terms that we didn't want their $20 million. No matter how many times we were pushed back, we kept pushing forward.

Summer eventually rolled around and it was time for NASDC to make decisions on continued funding of its 19 grants. NASDC chose to cancel funding of two—Odyssey being one of them. Local officials deny that the "vocal minority" had anything to do with the decision. We know better.

Unfortunately, the struggle continues. Even after funding ended, the school administration continued with elements of Odyssey. The battle will continue until we get some level-headed people in office, at all levels.

Starting Kindergarten: Not So Nice After All

By Sharon Thompson
Virginia

Excitement ran high in our house when my oldest child, a daughter, started kindergarten. I remember thinking, "At last, the real learning will begin." I was so happy that she would be undertaking the adventure of learning to read, something we had refrained from teaching her ourselves because of the advice of a preschool teacher. "She'll just be bored when she starts school," she said.

So we taught her colors, shapes, how to write her name, how to count, and beginning adding and subtraction, because we had thought these were things that preschoolers needed to know to be able to go to school ready to learn, a phrase I had picked up somewhere. I didn't know where I had heard it, but didn't it sound nice?

Taking my preconceived notion of school being just the way I remembered it from my own childhood, I started getting acquainted with my daughter's school. Right away, it seemed different, but warning bells did not go off immediately. It seemed . . . nice. There were nice pictures on the wall, nice teachers, nice books on the shelves. And what was this chart on the bulletin board by the principal's office? America 2000. Six national goals. Oh, yes, that's where I'd heard that phrase about coming to school ready to learn. Isn't that nice?

Then my daughter started coming home with school papers. You're learning circles, triangles, and squares? But you've known that since you were two. You are counting one through ten? Ditto. Obviously, the teacher had not had a chance to get very well acquainted with her yet. A discussion with the teacher should help her realize that Ariana needed more stimulating work.

Two discussions with the teacher and the principal later, we started realizing that stimulating work was not forthcoming. "It wouldn't be developmentally appropriate," she said. Professional jargon, I thought. They've certainly gotten to be more psychological in their approach than when I was in school. And I withdrew, confused and still very concerned. When I later learned that "developmentally appropriate practices" was a part of Outcome-Based Education, I realized just how much this had permeated my neighbordhood school.

Then my daughter started bringing home the papers with "inventive spelling." "It is called whole language," said a neighbor, who was submitting an application to a private school for her second grade daughter. "It is causing concern for lots of parents."

I began to think something was not right, but I could not afford private school. Homeschooling? Surely the teaching professionals could handle that better than I. A look at how teachers are trained would change my mind on that.

Then an article by Bob Holland changed my life forever, along with my children's future. I say that with deep gratitude. It was first in a series of articles about multiculturalism in the public school, and I was horrified. The next several weeks brought more articles, including articles about Virginia's own Common Core of Learning. Finally, I could no longer stand feeling all alone with this new-found knowledge. I called Mr. Holland. He put me in touch with a few of the many other parents who had contacted him and through one of them I acquired a copy of the October draft of the "Common Core of Learning." Reading it, I learned that multiculturalism was just one of my many growing concerns.

On March 28, 1993, thirteen of us sat down in my living room to discuss the Common Core of Learning. We came from Chesterfield, Henrico, and Middlesex Counties. We started an organization that came to be known as Concerned Virginians for Academic Excellence. We also developed a list of ten reasons why we were concerned about the Common Core. This list was printed on a flyer, which we dropped door-to-door in several neighborhoods, inviting people to come to a meeting at a high school in Chesterfield County. Ninety people came to that meeting where several people spoke about concerns. We also had available packets of information made up of various articles and documents that were coming to us through a network that would link us up with every state in the union before the year was out.

The way our network developed was a purely awesome experience for me. It was done with very little help from the media, and it was a first-hand look at what "grassroots" really means. It happened mostly by word of mouth, people talking to people sharing their concerns with each other. I would hear about someone who was working with the issue and would give them a call to share information. I myself got calls from total strangers who had heard about me from someone. I was always happy to talk and share information. The more concerned people we were in touch with, the more powerful we were. Mr. Holland helped once again by writing an article about our group including the name and address. That article eventually brought many letters even from other states. Several times we contacted folks who had written letters to the editor expressing their concern. They readily joined our cause.

Politics and Politicians: What Makes Policy?
or
America's System Works, But Not Why You Think!

By Michael I. Rothfeld
Political Consultant

Few of the lectures I give on political technology and campaigning make people as angry as this one.

None is more important.

Simply put, politics is not about the common good, appealing to men's better angels, nor serving our Lord. These may be your motivations. Occasionally, they will be a politician's motivation.

Politics is the adjudication of power. It is the process by which people everywhere determine who rules whom.

In America, through a brilliant system of rewards and punishments, checks and balances, and diffusion of authority, we have acquired a habit and history of politics mostly without violence and excessive corruption.

The good news for you and me is that the system works.

The bad news is it is hard, and sometimes dirty work, for us to succeed in enacting policy.

There is absolutely no reason for you to spend your time, talent, and money in politics except for this: If you do not, laws will be written and regulations enforced by folks with little or no interest in your well-being.

The following pages may challenge everything you thought you knew about politics, and everything you have been told about politics from your high school civics teacher to the lead editorial writer in your local paper.

But if you will read carefully and understand, you will become capable of leading a successful fight for your values.

Politicians, Not Education, Make Policy

The first mistake most folks make when they set out on a good-faith crusade to do good is to completely misunderstand their targets.

Sometimes, the local newspaper or media is the target. The thinking goes, "If we can just get them to understand the problem, things will change." It is fortunate that this is not correct, because the media in the U.S. is overwhelmingly committed to big government, abortion, and the supremacy of state-controlled education over parent-controlled education.

The fact is newspapers cast no votes. Dan Rather controls no elections. If this were not true, Ronald Reagan would never have been President.

An even more common mistake is to believe that the key to victory is education.

The "education is the key to political victory" theory goes that if we educate people as to the problem and the solution, then the elected officials will fall in line. **Wrong.**

Polls show huge majorities in favor of parental notification before a minor has an abortion. Yet the mere mention of the issue drives most politicians into fits of terror. Similarly, three-quarters of the American people oppose forced-unionism and favor Right to Work laws; however, such laws exist in only 22 states.

There is a kernel of truth to the "education is the key" mistake, but it is only a kernel.

Before explaining the kernel, it is important to understand two reasons why the education theory of politics is a mistake.

First, the theory assumes no opposing "education" effort. This is rarely the case.

Polls showed a majority in California in favor of education choice, yet the 1992 School Voucher Referendum lost 2–1 on election day. Why? Because the teachers' unions and pro-public-school-monopoly forces out-organized us, had a more focused message, and spent a lot more money.

The second, and more important, reason the "education is the key" theory fails lies in the nature of politics and politicians.

Policy in the Margins or Why Grass-Roots Politics Works

What follows is a generalized breakdown of voting in any given election:

People	Percent for Victory
100%, all people	50%, plus 1
70% eligible to vote (excludes aliens, felons, and minors)	35% plus 1

40% registered to vote (approximately 60% of eligible)	20% plus 1
20% vote on election day (50% of registered voters)	10% plus 1
7% almost always vote Republican 7% almost always vote Democrat 6% swing votes	3% plus 1

Three percent of the population plus one voter. Here is where politicians live and die.

In some local and state elections where turnout may be only 20 to 30 percent of registered voters, the margin may be far less than three percent plus one.

The average politician lives in constant fear of alienating any substantial portion of this three percent plus one voter he needs to win re-election, or to gain higher office.

What is the best way not to alienate these voters? Do nothing to make them mad, which almost always means . . . do nothing.

This is why even when new politicians are elected, little seems to change. Inertia—or the status quo—is the most potent force in politics.

However by mobilizing and directing (leading!) a relatively small group of voters rallying around a specific issue, you can change the political environment for a politician, or even a group of politicians. Your relatively small group can make it more costly for the politician not to act than it is for him or her to act as you want him to.

This is what I mean when I say that policy is made at the margins.

This is also why the homosexual lobby, labor unions, and organized liberal groups so often get legislation they want. They have groups of voters who can, and will, vote on their issue alone.

By becoming a grass-roots leader, you can, too.

That's where the fun, and the danger, begins.

How Politicians React to Pressure

In a perfect world, you would mobilize, the politician would immediately agree to do everything you want, the policy would be changed, and we would all live happily ever after.

Of course, it rarely happens that way.

When a provision harmful to home-schooling parents was located in the 1994 Education Bill (HR6), Mike Farris' Home School Legal Defense Association directed some one million calls and letters to Congress in a three-week period. The amendment to strip out the offending language passed the U.S. House of Representatives 424–1 and another amendment by Representative Richard Armey (R-TX) to positively protect home schoolers passed 374–53.

It was a rout.

The rout was not just because the home school community was so mobilized (though they were) but because they were mobilized for a very specific purpose, to which there was virtually no organized opposition.

It was an easy decision for members of the House of Representatives.

This is not the case for most controversial issues. It is certainly not true of the fight to end the public school monopoly of education.

So how will a politicians react to your organized pressure when he knows there is, or is certain to be organized pressure against your position?

The first thing the politician will do is try to make you go away without giving you anything of substance. If he gives you anything of substance, then those organized on the other side will be mad.

So most politicians will try to make you quit by intimidation, explanation, or buying you off.

Many politicians—especially those used to being treated like royalty rather than public servants—may try to threaten and intimidate you. This course seems especially common when the grassroots leader is female. Statements such as, "If you ever try something like this again, I'll vote against you for sure," or, "I'll tell the newspaper you're a trouble-maker" are not uncommon. A rudely spoken, "I don't know who you think you are, but that's not how we do things here" followed by a slammed-down phone receiver is another favorite.

Remember, you are not running for office. The politician is. Then remember the three percent plus one voter margin, and double your efforts to mobilize.

Before long, even this politician will go to a new tactic.

Most likely, a politician (whether or not intimidation is attempted) will seek to placate you by "explaining" what he or she calls "the political reality."

This usually takes the basic form of, "Believe me, I share your concerns but we just can't pass that bill right now," or "Even if we could pass what your people want, the Governor (or President or a judge) will kill it."

First of all, so what? Rome was not built in a day, nor is major policy passed overnight. Sometimes it may take years.

Policy is changed one vote—one politician—at a time.

Second of all, the reason this is often true is that politicians succeed in ducking difficult votes, thus preventing voters from ever knowing exactly where they stand.

Your job as a grassroots leader is to convey to the politician your supporters' insistence on the success of the policy you are fighting for. Of course, you do want to pass your legislation, but first and foremost, you want his or her complete public support. As an aside, a commitment in writing is better than a verbal commitment, and a vote on the full bill (not just some piece) is better than a written commitment.

When you have insisted on the politician's support for your position, they will then try to buy you off. Here is where most grassroots leaders fail.

Power and Influence and Selling Out

Politics can be seductive.

The chance to rub elbows with elected officials being looked up to by people in your community as someone in the know, invitations to and recognition at special events, or even an appointment to some committee or task force—all this could be yours if you become a grassroots leader. These are the trinkets for which leaders sell out their political agenda.

Of course, most everyone thinks he is strong enough, smart enough, and committed enough not to sell out. Few people are.

Before long, instead of delivering to the politician the grassroots' message to pass legislation, you become the politician's representative, telling the people what they must settle for.

Right now, today, decide whether you want influence or power.

Influence is calling a politician and having him take your call. He listens to what you want, and may or may not do it. It is what most grassroots leaders end up settling for.

Power is the ability to tell a politician what you want, and either get it or get a new politician at the next election.

Again I urge you to remember the three percent plus one voter. You and your grassroots group may be able to single-handedly bring the politician down. Or perhaps you will be one of a handful of groups organizing at the next election.

No matter what, you will make it harder for the politician to win re-election, costing him extra time and money.

If the politician loses, every other elected official will fear you and your group. If the politician wins, he will remember the extra pain you caused him. And he will know you can do it again, or worse. When you return to continue fighting for what you believe in, you will find him and his colleagues more gracious and more willing.

As the late Everett Dirkson said, "When I feel the heat, I see the light."

Winning in the End

There is a great deal more I could tell you.

- How to recruit for your grassroots organization.
- How best to communicate with politicians.
- The differences between offensive and defensive legislative strategies.
- Choosing a leader who is an elected official.
- When and how to use the media.

But what I would like to close with is the importance of taking a long-term approach to ending the public school monopoly, or whatever fight you step forward to lead.

If you remember from the beginning of this article, I said the good news is that the system works.

I hope by now you see what I mean. Namely, that politicians are still subservient to the people who elect them . . . to you and me.

However, most of the time, a fight really to make a difference may take years. This is especially true the further from local politics you go.

It's true Mike Farris won the battle for home schoolers in the U.S. Congress in just a couple of weeks as described above (and elsewhere in this book is an article by Mike); but Mike Farris spent years building an organization of home schoolers. More importantly, as I noted, there was little or no opposition to the mobilized home schooling force. You can be sure if the fight were for a tax credit for home schooling, the result would be different.

When you first start out, expect not to be taken seriously, especially if you insist upon principle and refuse to compromise or to be bought off.

The key will be for you and your grassroots activists to aggressively make politicians pay a price for their failure to pay attention to their constituents (you and your group). Every year, every session of the legislature, you must return pushing for your principles.

At the same time, you should be continually recruiting more members and expanding the areas in which you are active.

By doing this, you will win.

Good luck.

Honor Roll

(Honoring grassroots organizations that have made a difference for the better in their communities.)

Pennsylvania Parents Commission

P.O. Box 73
Johnstown, PA 15907

The Pennsylvania Parents Commission was established to give parents and families an effective voice in shaping the education of their children. We believe that families (i.e., a household of persons related by blood, marriage, or adoption) provide the single best unit in which to nurture children. We believe that schools and other social service agencies should support parents and parental rights. Because of these strong beliefs, we acknowledge that it is the fundamental right and responsibility of parents and families to direct the rearing and education of their own children. Therefore, we will assist parents and families in reaffirming this fundamental right and responsibility by: researching federal and state education issues, analyzing current education legislation, and disseminating this research and analysis.

PA Parents Commission publishes a bi-monthly newsletter, *The Parents Perspective.* We make available resources on current education issues, including videos, books, booklets, and packets. To receive a list of available resources, please write to PA Parents Commission, P.O. Box 73, Johnstown, PA 15907, or call (814) 255-1719. Eunice Evans or Anne Barbera will be very happy to help you network or find data on a specific education issue.

5

Digging

Psssst! Want to know a little secret? Freedom of Information or Open Records or Sunshine laws are not special perks for the press.

They give homemakers, blue-collar workers, and professionals just as much right to see government documents as we ink-stained wretches of the journalistic world.

That is something to keep in mind if you are starting to investigate a school policy like OBE and your local educrats are clamming up when asked simple, direct questions—questions such as: How much will this cost? Where's the research to show it works? Who are the outside consultants being used? What assessments are you going to use for your Outcomes?

Check out your state Freedom of Information Act (FOIA) and see what your rights are. You ought to be able to find a copy of the State Code in your local library. Typically, lawmakers will have granted their fellow "public servants" in the social bureaucracies a number of exemptions from required disclosure; but you should find a large volume of material that your public agencies have no business shielding from public view.

Information-gathering is essential to citizens' having an impact on an essentially surreptitious policy like OBE, with all of its hidden agendas. But ask politely for documents (such as budgets, learner outcomes, assessment plans) before you invoke the FOIA. You should receive them: After all, you are footing the bill with your tax dollars and/or sending your children to the school system that wants to make them experiments in a "new paradigm." Your money, and even more importantly, your children, are at stake—so you have rights.

If you are refused documents and straight answers, consider exercising your legal rights under FOIA. Ideally, if parents are being stonewalled, a local media outlet will go to bat for them and file a FOIA request. Even though the media have no greater privileges than the common man, a media filing may prod a nervous bureaucrat to speedy and complete compliance—lest unfavorable publicity ensue. But given that so many news organizations nowadays seem content to accept agency handouts without digging deeper, citizen activists may have to do the job themselves. They may even need to create their own "media"—i.e. newsletters or shows on public-access TV—to get the word out.

All sorts of revealing information may be available as records open to public inspection. In Montgomery, Texas, parent Joy Southard asked for lesson plans used in some of her daughter's past classes. The school district's Campus Improvement Plan stipulates that Student Exit Outcomes are supposed to be reflected in lesson plans. Mrs. Southard wanted to see how OBE played out in daily practice—a not unreasonable request from a parent exercising rightful authority over her child's schooling. School officials denied the request on the grounds that these were exempted confidential papers. However, on June 27, 1994, state Attorney General Dan Morales held that the lesson plans indeed were subject to disclosure under the Texas Open Records Act.

Stipulations and interpretations will differ from state to state. Citizens should be aware that their state law may give an agency the right to bill the person making the FOIA request for costs of reproducing documents or employee time in amassing the material. In Virginia, the agency is supposed to notify the petitioner of any cost in advance of complying. (Unfortunately, some bureaucrats jack up the price tag of compliance to deter critics from pursuing FOIA requests.) If you have in your group a lawyer interested in school reform—one of those noble souls willing to work *pro bono* —it would be a good idea to have him check out the legalese before you go the FOIA route.

In digging for facts about education and related issues, I have used the FOIA to good effect to elicit information from a local school system, state department of education, and the U.S. Department of Labor. Perhaps a quick review of my experiences would be helpful:

Local: The letter from the nearby Chesterfield suburban school system, long considered one of the state's best, had come in signed, "A Concerned Teacher." No name was affixed. The object of concern was a new social studies curriculum on the multicultural/OBE model about to go into effect. It was designed, said the curriculum committee, "to enhance students' self-worth and their appreciation of a diverse and ever-changing world." Fifth-graders, for example, would study the America of the 20th Century by concentrating on just three persons: Cesar Chavez, Eleanor Roosevelt, and Colin Powell, a trifecta of diversity.

The curriculum, wrote the Concerned Teacher, "is clearly a disaster in the making, and we, as teachers, have fought to no avail to have the program reconsidered. You need to know that."

I have received many other letters, phone calls, and visits from teachers who are fearful of letting me publish their name. It is regrettable that so much intimidation should exist in a field dedicated to cultivation of the intellect. Teachers, most of whom really care about what happens to their pupils, should feel free to speak their minds publicly about what works best in the classroom. Tenure apparently is not all it is cracked up to be as a protector of academic freedom, at least in elementary and secondary schools.

Enclosed were purported letters of dissent from social studies teachers in all the county's high schools.

Now, I could not accept the validity of all this material on the word of one anonymous person I had no way of contacting. So in search of vertification, I filed a FOIA with the school administration asking for copies of all letters from faculty members on the issue of the social studies curriculum. To its credit, the school administration replied promptly and fully.

The official documents confirmed everything Concerned Teacher had told me. Overwhelmingly, teachers were disgusted with a curriculum that elevated "globalism" over the teaching of basic civics and geography. The entire social studies faculties of some schools sent in strongly worded protests. Some of the objections were: The radically different new approach has nowhere been tested; students will be harmed by a de-emphasis on the teaching of U.S. government; the lack of textbooks will make cohesion difficult; the concept of "global citizenship" will confuse young children who lack a base of knowledge. One school's faculty wrote, "Our students need more structure. The conservative community in which we teach does not support such radical change. Many of our parents are veterans and expect that geography and government be taught in recognizable courses."

Yet despite the near-unanimous opposition of teachers, the school administration was going full-speed-ahead to implement the curriculum. As much as anything else, these facts gleaned from a Freedom of Information request opened my eyes to the way the OBE philosophy was being railroaded into school systems. When so many subject-matter teachers raise so many valid objections only to be totally ignored, something has to be out of whack.

State: When I first began looking into OBE, the State Department of Education readily supplied drafts of the "Common Core of Learning," a new assessment system, and other documents. However, as I wrote columns questioning the wisdom of making slippery outcomes (such as "appreciating diversity") the new graduation requirements, the department went into its disinformation mode.

The department consistently ducked the cost issue. State Superintendent Joe Spagnolo took heated exception to the Virginia Taxpayers

Association's extrapolating a rough estimate of a $500 million initial price tag, using figures I had cited from Pennsylvania's early experiments with OBE. But Spagnolo never said what the costs might run in Virginia, other than blandly conceding there would be "associated costs." And the official line was that this was grassroots, pure Virginia reform—as Virginia as Smithfield ham—not a carbon copy or a package bought off some national consultant's shelf.

Since by then I had seen outcomes from other states and noticed their eerie similarity to Virginia's (see state-by-state comparison in the Appendix), I was skeptical of the department's information, to say the least. In an op-ed article, Spagnolo had claimed "factual inaccuracies" in my commentary—without citing a single specific example. So, finally, in an attempt to spread more facts on the public record, I filed the following Freedom of Information request:

April 27, 1993

Joseph A. Spagnolo, Jr., Ed.D.
Superintendent of Public Instruction
Department of Education
P.O. Box 6-Q
Richmond, VA 23216–2060

Dear Dr. Spagnolo:

Pursuant to Section 2.1–342 of the State Code of Virginia, specifically the Freedom of Information Act, I hereby request all documents, working papers, and correspondence on the following topics related to the Department of Education's World Class Education Initiative:

1. Cost estimates, preliminary or otherwise, for implementing World Class Education statewide. This would include one-time, start-up expenses, as well as projected costs over a phase-in period.

2. A listing of compensation paid to all consultants—or obligated to be paid—in developing the proposed "Common Core of Learning."

3. An accounting of all personnel costs already incurred, or those projected, for the World Class Education Initiative. This would include costs of retraining teachers and administrators, and new positions within the Department of Education.

4. Preliminary cost estimates for adopting so-called "performance-based testing," or any other new pupil assessment system, to include the use of consultants.

5. Projected costs or estimated costs of mandatory enrollment of

all 4-year-olds in the state as part of the World Class Education design.

6. A copy of all research that formed the basis of your statement in an April 21, Richmond *Times-Dispatch,* Op/Ed article that "every dollar spent in quality early childhood programs results in saving $5 to $6 in reduced social, welfare, and prison costs."

Thank you for your attention to this matter. I understand that under provisions of the FOIA, I can expected a response within a week.

This isn't presented necessarily as a model FOIA letter. It probably *is* good to begin the letter by citing the Code section under which you are making your request and to have a reminder of the legal deadline in the final paragraph. But in the body of the letter, you should make your request for information as specific as possible—with dates, places, names of documents you seek (if you have some inkling of them). My letter cast a wide net and sometimes you haul in a lot of eel and jellyfish with your catch when you do that.

Sure enough, the department responded by leaving a humongous box at my office door (*sans* ribbon). It was big enough to contain Jimmy Hoffa's long-lost remains. Instead it was crammed full of so many copies of contracts, correspondence, and working papers that you would have sworn DOE must be conducting spring housecleaning.

A little later came a cryptic letter stating that the cost of supplying me with this cornucopia of paper exceeded $1,000, and DOE officials should have billed me for it, but since they forgot to give me the required advance notice, well . . . just forget it and enjoy.

I figured that was a little warning that the next time I filed a broad-based FOIA request, they would make me pay.

Anyway, the documents did help me do more than engage in "Truth by Trivial Pursuit." Although there was still no overall cost figure for the OBE plan, the box was a treasure trove of information about key players and programs. I found, for example, that. . . .

• Sociologist William Spady, head of the High Success Network in Colorado, was indeed the lead consultant for Virginia's program. He had been paid $2,000 a day to dispense his wisdom about how to mold the New American Child. In explaining why Spady had been selected without competitive bidding, a DOE bureaucrat wrote, "Dr. Spady was selected to work with the Common Core of Learning Team as {sic} he is a leader in Transformational Outcome-Based Education, one of three design models being implemented across the nation in the area of Outcome-Based Education." But little more than a month later, Virginia Secretary of Education, James Dyke, denied in a television appearance with me that Virginia's plan had anything to do with transformational OBE. Incredible, simply incredible!

From the department's working papers, I also learned that Spady had contracts in 30 states and several Canadian provinces which helped explain why so many of the attitudinal outcomes were practically identical from state to state.

• Spady was the top gun, but the state was also paying more than 50 other consultants for their wisdom on such OBE topics as "authentic assessment." The director of something called the Starshine Foundation in Del Mar, California, was pulling down $1,641 a day, plus travel expenses for her and her husband/assistant. Their gig included some kind of musical skit. Her contract was for 60 days which meant the state was on the hook for almost $100,000 in honoraria.

If the state had that much excess money, why wasn't it handing some out to classroom teachers as merit bonuses for exemplary teaching?

• Although Spagnolo denied having a bottom-line price tag, some of the components looked to add up to real money. The department wanted to spend $7.3 million to open a Center for Staff Development to retrain teachers, and $41 million for a strategic plan to use computer technology to support OBE restructuring.

The box also contained a real gemstone I had not asked for or expected: a set of working papers from The New Standards Project at the University of Pittsburgh, a joint project of Pitt's Learning Research and Development Center, and the National Center on Education and the Economy. Virginia was one of 17 participating states whose taxpayers were helping to subsidize the NSP.[1] (It has subsequently severed its ties with the NSP.) A proposal for the NSP, 1992–95, stated the explicit objective of developing "a radically new approach to the assessment of student progress that would drive fundamental changes in what is taught and learned. . . ." The system would be based on OBE/Mastery Learning: students would take the test as many times as they needed to pass it, and the achievement gap between best and worst performers would be closed. All would be "equal."

I wonder what other horrors might lie in the innards of the state education bureaucracy. But state and local officials are models of clarity and gracious compliance with requests for information compared with the behemoth in Washington. . . .

Federal: The Labor Department began playing an ever heavier hand in the schools during the Clinton administration. Labor Secretary Robert Reich and Education Secretary Richard Riley jointly introduced the

President's Goals 2000: Educate America Act in April, 1993. Through the School to Work Act, Labor is pushing for a vocationalized curriculum, and through the SCANS reports DOL is spreading the notion of workplace correctness—that education biz should be all about producing well-socialized, group-thinking workers for big biz.

These developments do not bode well for what remains of liberal education. Labor is not an agency with a good track record for honesty. In May, 1990, I discovered—with the help of an informant—a secret scheme hatched in the DOL a decade earlier for scoring job-seeking test takers according to wildly disparate standards—depending solely on their racial or ethnic self-identification.[2] The scam was called "race-norming"—the scoring of test takers against norm groups composed entirely of members of their own race. The scheme could have come right out of apartheid. In fact, it could be called the liberals' apartheid.

My columns exposing race-norming caused quite a stir in Washington, and on July 24, 1990, Labor Secretary Elizabeth Dole published a proposal in the Federal Register to suspend for two years the test in question, the "General Aptitude Test Battery," during which time it would be retooled.[3] According to standard procedure, there would be a period for "public comment." At the end of that period, I asked to see a copy of the comments, thinking the reactions of business and labor to race-norming would be interesting. No dice. I was told I couldn't see them. So I filed a FOIA request. What happened next speaks volumes about the attitude of Imperial Washington to challenges from the little people beyond the Beltway:

First, the DOL's Employment Service waited a good six weeks even to reply to my letter, even though federal law requires a response within 10 days. Then the agency's director rejected my request because, he said, "pre-decisional" release "would be detrimental to our decision-making process." Understand, these were **public** comments; but how can they truly be public if they are kept private? And why such a proprietary interest in **our** decision-making? Don't these decisions affect us all?

Finally, after two more months had passed, the Employment Service director got back to me and said the newspaper could have the documents after all. But there would be a $465 charge for copies. My newspaper filed an appeal citing FOIA provisions for waiving the fee when disclosure would contribute to public understanding of government activities; but the director delivered a beaut of a rejection. Because race-norming "has been publicized extensively by the news media, including your newspaper," there is essentially nothing more to be contributed to public understanding. So here was a federal bureaucrat presuming to decide what was newsworthy about his own domain.

Finally, my paper forked over the money, and, seven months after the information had been requested, a 25-pound box of public documents arrived at my office. And, yes, there was quite a bit more to be learned from the contents—including the extent to which the government itself had manufactured responses to create the appearance of significant support for its scam. Hundreds of the letters of endorsements were duplicates, the obvious product of an internal campaign to make the testing scam seem indispensable to American commerce.[4]

One lesson to draw from all this may be that the higher you go in your quest for information, the colder and more arrogant the attitude you may expect to encounter. There is a lot to be said for the idea that the best and most humane government is that government closest to the people. My experience has been that local and state officials—even when they have disagreed with me on policy—usually have complied on deadline with FOIA requests, and have done so courteously. My experiences with the federal government have been quite different; and some people have encountered far worse. In some cases, federal compliance with lawful requests has taken not months, but years.

I cite these cases not to suggest that every citizen group ought to rush out and file FOIA requests. Probably relatively few will. I do recommend, however, that you seriously dig for all the facts you can obtain. Documentation well may be your most potent weapon. Whether you use the FOIA or not, you ought to have a FOIA attitude—that public information belongs to the public, and that you have a right to have access to it. I am not suggesting that you be brash or arrogant in your pursuits, only that you be determined.

One of the best ways to begin amassing a solid background is to request help from reputable organizations that have been on top of the issue for a long time. For your convenience, there is a listing of some of those organizations in the Appendix. And if you are serious about pursuing the FOIA route against a resistant bureaucracy, I highly recommened the chapter on the Freedom of Information Act in a 1994 book, *The Citizen's Guide to Fighting Government*, by Senator Steve Symms and Larry Grupp.[5] The authors stress that federal agencies, in particular, "would rather eat barbed wire than give out information they consider to be private, or to have their routine disrupted with FOIA requests. They will try a whole bag of standard tricks to avoid compliance." Symms and Grupp, however, offer resources for foiling those tricks. One of the best sources of knowledge on FOIAs across the land is the Freedom of Information Center, Box 858, Columbia, Missouri, 65205.

Happy digging!

Gathering the Facts and Presenting Them to Policymakers

By Carolyn Steinke
California

The mandatory AIDS curriculum became our next area of involvement. Our concern increased upon a health teacher's observation that 30 students in our local high school were HIV-infected. Not knowing the facts about how this disease is spread—and if, in fact, condoms are a barrier to transmission—but knowing the statistics on teenage promiscuity, we were determined to do something.

With the assistance of AIDS experts—and using the Freedom of Information Act—we obtained documents from the Centers for Disease Control (CDC). We discovered, to our amazement, that the public was being lied to—**Condoms were not safe!**

Condom pores were anywhere from five microns to 70 microns in size. An HIV particle is .1 micron in size. A ratio of .1 microns to 5 microns is like shooting a BB through a tennis net. A document from the Food and Drug Administration showed in a simulated use study that one out of three condoms leaked the viruses. (The study did not take motion into account.)

With our facts documented, we went to Sacramento to meet with the directors of the Healthy Kids, Healthy California program. They refused to consider our documentation, even though we had obtained it from the CDC.

In 1992, California was developing a seven-year matrix for its Health Framework. Upon receiving the first draft we couldn't believe our eyes. Homosexual sex was to be discussed as normal and healthy. Children were to celebrate this diversity and to demonstrate tolerance of all lifestyles.

Once again, we moms flew to Sacramento and sat in on the hearing of a 13-member task force, composed of at least six persons who were pro-homosexual-rights. The room was filled with gay rights activists, book publishers, IBM, General Electric, etc., but to our amazement the only people who had come to represent traditional family interests on behalf of the children of the state were . . . we three moms.

As the task force reviewed the Framework line by line, we had our first exposure to the terms "one-stop shopping," and "Schools: the hub of the community." Social services, mental health, and school-based clinics now were to be wedded to the school under inter-agency agreement. We learned that the California legislature by joint resolution had changed the legal definition of "family" to be "any group that gathers together for in-depth sharing, constitute a family." The reason for the redefinition became abundantly clear: The term was being used to describe the "school family."

A state task force member, and mental health director, contended that all children should be introduced to the concepts of homosexuality and same-sex partners in marriage. She also believed in introducing the subject whenever it came up, as early as kindergarten. Previously she had promoted a program called Outer-Course, involving such practices as masturbation, group masturbation, and body licking—presented as safe alternatives to sexual intercourse.

It was almost impossible to contain ourselves and just take notes, especially when we heard the task force discuss state waivers to individual school sites for the purpose of dispensing Medi-Cal cards to students without the prior knowledge of the parent or guardian. We returned home determined to wage a war against this Framework adoption.

Hundreds of us flew to Sacramento to testify at public hearings. Our campaign was a total shock to the State Board of Education. Never before had the board experienced this magnitude of opposition to a state Framework adoption.

We were assured that nothing would be passed that did not address our issues. We were told we had until mid-January to lobby for our changes—that nothing would be done until after the holidays.

On December 18, the board passed the final draft, which was worse than the first. Little did we know then that this Framework was the very picture of Outcome-Based Education.

6

Town Meetings

On July 16, 1993, at the suburban Mills E. Godwin High School in Henrico County—a suburb of Richmond (Virginia's state capital)—I saw one of the most amazing phenomena I have ever witnessed.

It was a sweltering night. There were baseball games in town, neighborhood pools beckoned, and, of course, it was the peak of the beach-or-mountains vacation season. It would have been a good night just to sit out front in a rocking chair with a tall, cool beverage in hand.

And yet this high school's auditorium seating 800 was completely filled, and there were people standing everywhere.

Now, I once served as PTA program chairman for my children's public school and I know that if you can lure 50 people out for an evening's presentation on an education or family issue you have done a bang-up job. And that's during the school year.

The topic that July night was the state's transformational OBE plan. To say that the issue had crashed through any apathy barrier and captured the public's interest would be an understatement.

No established organization was sponsoring the town meeting. Instead, just two Moms—Gayle Graham and Dr. Karie E. Dawkins—had decided to hold a town meeting for informational purposes. Originally, they had thought they would get a small group together in a school library, but then interest mushroomed. Karie takes up the story in her personal statement at the end of this chapter, so I'll leave that part to her.

Another strange thing happened. I had gone simply to observe, with the thought that the meeting might provide fodder for next week's column. (I had been discovering enough fresh outrages in the OBE movement to write columns about it almost every week.) But then Lee Graham, Gayle's husband (who was moderating the meeting) asked me to stand up in the audience and be recognized. Suddenly, practically the entire audience was standing and cheering. I was being given a standing ovation!

Talk about weird: We media types rank in public esteem even lower than politicians and used-car salesmen—and we earn our ranking. I know my opinion columns attract bricks along with bouquets (and in my trade you expect the mixed reaction). So what I deduced from the first standing "O" I'd ever received in my life was that an awful lot of citizens appreciated the fact that someone was trying to get OBE out front and center for them to consider, before it was a *fait accompli* for their children. (Why so many in the news media fail to cover issues like OBE in depth is a topic with which I will struggle in Chapter Eight.)

During the panel discussion, the state education department's representative, Dr. Ernie Martin, made a strong effort to assuage public concerns. He said that the state wanted to communicate with citizens; that nothing was set in concrete yet (even though the State Board of Education had adopted its "Outcomes" Framework); that "rigorous academic standards" would be developed to attach to the outcomes; that there would be public hearings next year after the standards were presented; that the State Chamber of Commerce, Business Council, and Manufacturers Association all endorsed the Common Core of Learning, along with the state NEA affiliate and other education groups; that the focus would be not on having winners and losers but making all children winners—a "revolutionary thought," he said, but "why not?"

The audience received Dr. Martin's comments politely, but it was clear during the ensuing public comment period that the state had gained few converts. Parents and teachers paraded to the microphone to express, overwhelmingly, their discontent. Remarks went along these lines: It's just another experiment, a fad, that will encroach on teaching time. It tramples parental rights. And from a young high school math teacher: "There can be no accurate way to measure OBE outcomes; OBE will not produce all winners; it will produce all losers."

One of the most perceptive comments of the night—given the big biz backing for OBE—came from parent Catherine Davis (an African-American woman who quipped that she was speaking up to add "the spice of diversity" to the mostly white gathering). Referring to the metastasizing of industry's Total Quality Management into education policy, she noted that TQM is supposed to take into account how the customer feels. But as to a reform that undermines parental authority, she said, "I'm not a happy customer."

"If you're truly into TQM, you should be asking me what outcomes I want," she said, to thunderous applause.

At the end of August, a second town meeting—this time at majority-black Huguenot High School in the city—would be held, and Mrs. Davis would not be only a dash of diversity. The audience included many African-American parents who considered OBE a giant step backward for education; and among the members of an eloquent panel of Moms who took on the state's representatives was Eileen Hunt, president of N-PAC, a black women's organization. So now it was becoming clearer that opposition to state-mandated OBE crossed racial, political, economic, and social—as well as ideological—boundaries. (And this audience, too, gave me a standing "O" when I was introduced as a panelist!) The education establishment's portrayal of the opposition as radical-right yahoos wouldn't stick.

Our experiences in Virginia were being repeated all over the country. I commend to you Chris Helm's moving account at the end of this chapter as to the Cuban emigrés who came to her with tears in their eyes after one of Ohio's town meetings.

The beauty of citizen-organized town meetings, as astute activist Wayne Sullivan has pointed out, is that they shift the balance of power in the citizens' favor. Public hearings at the State Capitol almost always favor the agency bureaucrats. They are held on the bureaucrats' home field, before audiences typically packed with special interests having a stake in perpetuation of the nanny-state. But when citizens organize the meeting and invite the speaking participants, the whole psychology changes. Now the government representatives are having to account to the people they are supposed to be serving. You could call this a paradigm shift if you are interested in talking like an OBE guru.

Town meetings also are a useful counter to the increasingly common practice of government agencies using professional "facilitators" to manipulate the outcomes of public meetings. In her two books, Beverly Eakman of the Education Policy Consortium in Maryland has extensively documented how this works.[1] Typically, facilitators use "selective hearing" in the public meetings. Writes Ms. Eakman: "Words or expressions that express the facilitator's own preconceived ideas, or biases, are immediately placed into discussion, while words or concepts that go against the facilitator's biases are ignored." Some use the Delphi Technique, which entails deliberately escalating tension within a group, "pitting one faction against the other so as to make one viewpoint appear ridiculous and the other sensible."

Government money actually has funded training manuals for these "change agents," or facilitators, as Ms. Eakman also documents. This is an ominous trend for representative government in America, but revival of true town meetings—*sans* government facilitators—can reinvigorate the Republic.

By no means should town meetings be held to berate or bully the other side. Organizers should stress civility and common courtesy.

The purpose is to get the facts on the table, and hear all sides. Strongly-worded position papers can come later.

Not surprisingly, folks from the government may realize that citizen-organized town meetings change the terms of the debate, and try to shun them. Lil Tuttle suggests one way to counter that . . .

"Some town hall meetings adopted a debate format with proponents (state officials) and opponents . . . going head to head. State officials realized they could neither control the debate nor defend their plan effectively, and they began refusing to attend. By the end of August (1993), the only way our local group could force state officials' attendance was first to arrange for local TV, radio, and newspaper personalities to act as moderator and questioners. State officials could either show up or see their empty chairs on the evening news shows. . . ."

That's called playing hardball, ladies and gentlemen. Sometimes you need to haul out those Louisville Sluggers.

Citizen Participation Through Town Meetings: A Case Study

By Wayne L. Sullivan
Virginia

In September, 1993, Virginia Governor Wilder ordered the State Superintendent of Public Instruction to cancel Outcome-Based Education—the core education initiative of his administration. After more than two years of high-pressured sales effort, the State Department of Education had not convinced Virginians that OBE was the solution to our education crisis.

This was a MAJOR victory. But the war is not over. It is just a "speed-bump" in the continuing contest with the education elitists who have repeatedly stolen the power of the ballot as well as the rights of the customer (parents/students).

Elsewhere in this volume, the key leaders in this battle tell their story. That shows a bit of righteous use of raw political power at the grassroots level. It is our prayer that this victory be repeated over and over again and that our schools once again become the source of pride in every neighborhood in America.

I first became aware that a major program was planned by the Virginia State Department of Education when I saw four ads for facilitators in a give-away "newspaper." The salary would attract very experienced and effective group control specialists.

Further investigation revealed that Virginia's former First Lady had been appointed chairman of the "World Class Education Initiative" with a symbolic board of directors of the usual suspects acting as industry, finance, and civic representatives. (The State Department would later object to allowing politics to be any part of education reform decisions.)

A check with some of the battle-scarred veterans of past skirmishes with the State Department of Education proved that, in fact, OBE was being "sold" to Virginia. They were holding information sessions; and parents, new to the fray, were universally astounded. How could anyone consider such a major change, which could only result in a "dumbing-down" process?

It was not enough that test scores of American children had fallen to last place among all industrialized nations. Now, we had to eliminate testing and core curriculum so that no test comparisons would be possible.

From the past education reform battles, we had come to know and appreciate a number of activists across the state. But many had dropped out, utterly overwhelmed and discouraged by the bureaucratic barriers to parental involvement. So what should we do?

It would be wrong to upset parents without immediately directing them to worthy battle strategies. But, if we played by the State Department of Education's rules, as in the past, how could we expect a different result?

It was an election year in Virginia, with all the state executive offices (Governor, Lieutenant Governor, and Attorney General) and all 100 seats in the House of Delegates up for election. Certainly, education reform should be a likely campaign issue. A quick survey confirmed this and resulted in several position papers opposing the current administration's implementation of OBE.

A series of citizens' town meetings was scheduled. The format was to have balanced presentations of all sides of the Outcome-Based Education proposal and to allow open discussion. The overall plan was as follows:

1. Several town meetings were scheduled in each metropolitan area.

    a. Each education activist group in the area was enlisted to take a turn at sponsoring a town meeting.

    b. Education activist/leaders from adjacent areas were invited to attend so that they could organize town meetings in their own area on a coordinated schedule.

2. A member of the World Class Education Speakers Bureau was invited to give a 20-minute presentation along with three or four other knowledgeable participants.

3. Early commitments were obtained from key officials and candidates.

    a. Town meeting organizers would select among them for a speaker or speakers on their panels.

    b. Others were recognized for a short statement.

    c. Position papers were distributed whenever available.

4. Obtaining answers to parents' questions was the main objective.

    a. Questions from panel members to each other to ensure a clear understanding of the issues.

    b. Questions from a panel of newspaper reporters, talk-show hosts, and television news reporters to sharpen the focus and identify the substantive changes proposed.

c. Questions from the audience usually on 3×5 cards and delivered by the moderator or reporter panel to highlight their very real concerns and determination.

5. Distribution of literature was unrestricted and diverse.
6. These town meetings were aggressively promoted.

a. Handbills were distributed to homes, athletic events, and playgrounds.

b. Public service announcements were fully utilized.

c. Talk radio was "hustled" to center stage in an all-on-one (activists versus the bureaucrats) contest.

d. Letters to the editor were coming from everywhere.

e. Op-Ed pieces and columns (particularly Bob Holland's) provided the joining of the issue and carried the arguments forward to the public.

7. Requests ballooned for speakers for small church, library, or kitchen table meetings and they continued throughout the program.

These town meetings put enormous pressure on the State Board of Education. Their professional (and costly) team was no match for the parents. Over 850 attended the first major town meeting. This total exceeded that for an entire month of programs planned by the State Department of Education, most of which were in-house staff sessions.

Because of this and future successes, each town meeting became more difficult to schedule. The Education Department was unwilling to assign anyone to represent them. This was at a time when, according to our plan, many meetings were being planned in a number of cities.

Some of the reasons given are particularly significant.

First, they would not participate on any more panels with any political candidate. So we tried it both ways—that is, with a candidate and an empty chair for the Education Department; and with an Education Department representative and no candidate. Both were extremely successful, but, frankly, the latter was more devastating to the Education Department. It seemed that the more the bureaucrats tried to explain, the more the parents objected.

Then, the Education Department said we could not have Bob Holland on the questioning panel, because he, reportedly, had written incorrectly about OBE. They withdrew this request when no one would agree with them.

The Education Department arranged to have the co-sponsorship by PTA groups withdrawn. This resulted in cancellation of several reservations at schools with insufficient time left to reapply. In each case, alternate meeting places or schedules were worked out.

In another case, the PTA representatives refused all conditions and scheduled two meetings, one non-political and one political, both with full sponsorship of the PTA. The actual meetings never were held because OBE was canceled before the scheduled events. However, this diverse interest was particularly decisive.

The political connection, as a potent weapon, had been made early in the town meeting plan. Elsewhere in this reference book, a master political strategist's "short course" details the potential impact of a relatively small percentage of eligible voters. The demonstrated convictions of hundreds of parents at these town meetings in many localities resulted in both the elected and bureaucratic leaders deciding to stop immediately the introduction of OBE. Their statements, which are included, confirm the impact of these meetings. In addition, many of the leaders of these citizens' town meetings have been called to reform education by serving on local school boards, Blue-Ribbon Committees, and on the State Board of Education. This is the basis for the real victory—saving this generation from the lifetime handicap of an inferior education.

The key to this war is: "Who is in charge?" Do we serve the government or does the government serve us? Or, more specifically, who uses the power? The answer is: Those who make the rules. I believe we proved that in this victory over Outcome-Based Education in Virginia, the people can make the rules, and then they can use their power.

Grassroots Organizing Makes an Impact

By Dr. Karie Dawkins
Virginia

The Virginia Department of Education (DOE) had developed a $1.5 million marketing strategy to convince legislators, businessmen, and other citizen groups that the "Common Core of Learning" (CCL)—the centerpiece of OBE—was an excellent program. Although strong opposition in Pennsylvania had not been totally successful in getting rid of OBE, that did not mean that parents in Virginia should give up. Many knew that getting the truth out to parents about OBE was critical.

An unorganized, grassroots phenomenon of concerned parents that had individually researched OBE and the CCL began informing people at their churches and civic groups. Some parents, upon doing their own research of OBE, became so concerned that they started inviting other parents to home and library meetings to share informations about the dangers of CCL/OBE. As the numbers of informed parents grew, people across Virginia soon started networking. The networking was augmented by the Virginia Family Foundation and several individuals. Later, many parents groups were formed to help keep abreast of the information and to disseminate documentation to other concerned parents.

The most exciting development was the planning and positive attendance of a town meeting at a local high school to inform the public about OBE/CCL. Originally, only some neighbors and nearby legislators were invited to meet at a local library. Having legislators understand the high cost to implement the CCL and that academic scores would decrease was considered important because they only tended to hear the OBE hype from educrats. Because of the impending state elections, potential candidates were also invited to come and learn more about OBE. The campaign office of Mike Farris (candidate for Lieutenant Governor of Virginia) was called to see if someone could represent Mr. Farris because of his strong background in education, constitutional law, and knowledge of the national impact of OBE. When Mr. Farris himself agreed to come to the meeting, the location was changed to the local high school.

Getting the word out about the meeting initially seemed to be impossible, with only two weeks available for the parents to secure the location, print and distribute flyers, and advertise. Parents were enlisted to distribute flyers. The most successful form of advertising was the use of flyers half the size of an 8.5 x 11 inch sheet of paper. They were the perfect size to be placed in mailboxes and as handouts or bulletin inserts. An individual who had experience distributing sales flyers for various local companies showed everyone how to place flyers on mailboxes legally (e.g., federal law prohibits placing anything in or on the mailbox that would interfere with mail delivery; however, flyers may be placed on the mailbox stand or under the mailbox). The local map was divided into regions and families were assigned neighborhoods for flyer delivery.

Newspapers, TV, and radio stations were notified. School board members, principals, political leaders, and the local school superintendent were personally invited by telephone to the meeting. Knowing that the local school superintendent was out of town, everyone was surprised and pleased when he arrived at the meeting. His support was greatly appreciated.

Considering that this meeting was planned (and took place within a two week period) by parents with no previous experience in this kind of "activism", the success of the meeting was overwhelming. More than **800** people attended.

The meeting began with parent/researcher giving a brief introductory talk about CCL/OBE, explaining some of the terminology and sharing his concerns with parents in our community. Then a panel discussion was held, allowing a certain amount of time for each participant to speak. Besides Mike Farris, the panel consisted of a representative of Academics First, a self-described liberal, a high school government teacher and member of the county's Board of Supervisors, and an official representative from the DOE. The inclusion of an official was in stark contrast to DOE's practice of **not** inviting opposition to be on their "panel discussions" for OBE, CCL, Developmentally Appropriate Practice, or the School to Work initiative.

Representatives of the DOE brought copies of the CCL, and other literature. They were surprised at the strong concern expressed by parents who attended. DOE officials were not consistent with their facts, with **their** "facts" being in serious conflict with indisputable documentation available at the meeting that was brought by parents that had researched the subject. There was no "smoking" such a well-informed and prepared group of parents. Many participants wondered if the DOE was just flustered, untruthful, or unaware of the negative impact OBE had had in other states. The indoctrination of officials and teachers with misinformation disseminated from within the educational establishment had become all too apparent by those who genuinely sought out the facts.

At the meeting, copies of the CCL, the CCL Vision Statement, and other pertinent brochures from the DOE were available. In addition, copies of CCL critiques were made available. Local businesses helped defray printing costs. At the end of the meeting, donations were made that **exactly** covered the cost of the facility and the rest of the printing.

Although the major news media did not accurately report the meeting's significance, Op-Ed columnist Robert Holland and radio talk show host, Blanquita Cullum **did** accurately inform their audience about the meeting.

The then governor of Virginia "publicly" took the CCL off the active implementation track to cool the rapidly spreading grassroots opposition during the election campaign. However, the fight continues in Virginia because many of the OBE-related programs started by the former state superintendent of education area still in effect. Goals 2000 and the School to Work Initiative that passed federally are direct attempts to implement OBE nationally and to have federally run school systems. Because younger teachers have only been taught behavioral modification and "progressive" methods of teaching, the only way to fight OBE is to continue to fight at the grassroots level.

"Let's Give Them Something to Talk About"

By Chris Helm
Ohio

Debbie continued to bring me documents and spent hours guiding me through the educationese that had become my life. A friend asked us to speak at her church and to inform people about OBE.

That was the first of more than 50 speaking engagements. People would hear us speak and ask us to come to their community. We spoke in church basements, schools, and libraries. Our calendars now had names of the next town we were going to, alongside our children's little league schedules. The size of audiences ranged from 20 persons to hundreds. Two housewives making overheads of state and federal documents, kissing our husbands goodbye, and pointing the mini-van toward towns that neither of us had even been to before. We were a strange pair and had different ways of dealing with the upcoming meeting. I would be singing all of my favorite songs that got me charged up for the meeting ahead: "Let's Give Em Something to Talk About," by Bonnie Raitt, "Against the Grain," by Garth Brooks, and "Brick in the Wall," by Pink Floyd, to name a few. Debbie would be shuffling through the documents that she had read 100 times before.

Parents weren't the only people who turned out at these meetings. School personnel were notorious for showing up and attempting to interrupt. The same questions would fly at us. "What group are you with?" "Who funds you?" "What are your credentials?" Our answers were always the same. "We don't belong to any group." "We fund ourselves" (we always refused money), and "Our credentials are unimportant. We are not the ones setting education policy for this nation." Many of the parents who had arranged these town meetings paid a dear price for them. Some were hassled to the point that they could no longer leave their children in the public schools.

One meeting stands out in particular. There was a group of women that approached me after a meeting with tears in their eyes. One of them took my hand and said, "We are from Cuba. We escaped from that country to come here for freedom. Don't people see that with Goals 2000 and OBE this country will be just like Cuba?" My stomach felt queasy.

Our objective in these meetings was to expose what was going on and convince parents to write to the Governor, State Legislators, and Congressmen. As a result, thousands of letters poured in from the citizens of Ohio. We were driving to the State House once a month and hand-delivering mass mailings to every representative exposing OBE and Goals 2000. When we first started these deliveries the "keepers" of the statehouse floors were friendly. After a while our mail was being opened and okayed before they would let us deliver it. Soon, we no longer were allowed to deliver them from floor to floor. We were forced to take them down to the mail room. One day, as we were waiting to have our mail okayed, I stood looking at a picture on the wall in the State House. The secretary ordered me to sit down! I realized at that point that I was standing next to an open door leading to a room where she had taken one of our mailings. The person in the office was discussing the content of the mail over the phone with someone. They were worried.

The mass mailings, parents' letters, phone calls, and personal testimony at hearings resulted in the Education Reform package being rejected by the legislature. OBE had been brought to a screeching halt. But it would be a short-lived victory.

Town Meetings, the Luksik Video, and Embarrassed Officialdom

By Anne M. Barbera
Pennsylvania

We knew we had to get more people involved. Our group, as did many others, started a newsletter. This gets information out, but does not get it to the people as quickly as is often necessary. Telephone trees were started, and the umbrella coalition sent first-class mail updates to leaders in the state. The way we reached, educated, and recruited the most people, however, was through town meetings. All the leaders in the state who were willing went on the speaking circuit. We reached many people who could not attend the meetings because, generally speaking, the news media gave us great coverage. The speakers received many invitations to appear on radio talk shows.

Citizens throughout the state set up the meetings. Some town meetings were hosted by pre-existing activist groups and others by legislators, PTA, churches, groups of parents or taxpayers, etc. These meetings were held in schools, firehalls, church buildings, hotels, and community centers. The number in attendance ranged from a few to five hundred, depending on the sponsor, location, weather, etc. As a rule, one of the leaders in the state was invited to speak, and afterwards, was followed by a question-and-answer period.

Some town meetings were debates between citizen activists and bureaucrats from the Department of Education. The citizens always came prepared with briefcases full of documents, files of Department of Education correspondence, state contracts, and the like. The bureaucrats came with nothing and asked the audience to trust them; they were the authority; they had the best interest of the children at heart. The citizens were always able to document the errors in the bureaucrats' statements. Those trusty brief cases held all the right documents to show the bureaucrats could not state accurate information. It wasn't long before the Department of Education refused to debate us; they could not handle the embarrassment.

Unable to get the Department to debate, one taxpayers' group invited a pro-OBE superintendent from a neighboring county to speak in favor of OBE. This gentleman was trying to refute our position that OBE, as set down in the new regulations, takes away local control. The superintendent explained that their strategic planning committee had given the parents on the committee the task of writing the mission statement for the district. The mission of the school then would meet local standards. He was very emphatic in stating that the parents, alone, wrote the wonderful mission statement for the district, and he proceeded to put it on the overhead projector so we could read along as he read it aloud. From our trusty little briefcase came a copy of the state's mission plan taken from the new regulations, section 5.202 (f). We read directly from the regulations and, lo and behold, the state's "mission of public education" was word for word the same as the mission statement supposedly drawn up by the parents. Is it any wonder we find it difficult to have faith in the OBE proponents?

I was involved in town meetings in various ways. In my own community, I hosted a meeting, with the chairman of the Pennsylvania Parents Commission, Peg Luksik, as the speaker. I rented a hotel conference room at a discounted price, arranged for informational material to be duplicated so everyone would have a large packet of information to study, drew up a flyer and then had them distributed to churches, schools, and public pamphlet racks. Approximately 200 persons turned out to hear the program. There was high interest as was evident from the questions fielded. Money received in the donation can on the literature table helped to defray the costs. Some of those in attendance later arranged for meetings in their own small communities.

As the battle heated up, it became evident that more speakers were needed. The requests were coming in from all over the state. Then Peg Luksik had a brilliant idea. She had her local town meeting professionally videotaped. She was truly inspired that night. Her talk was dynamic and insightful. At many meetings throughout the state where sponsors were unable to get a speaker, they showed this tape, "Who Controls the Children?," and then answered questions as best they could.

As I drove Peg to town meetings and debates from one end of the state to the other, I had the opportunity to observe first-hand the deception and arrogance of the education bureaucrats. They must consider the parents and taxpayers to be very ignorant people. They definitely feel they know what is best for our children. At the literature tables I manned, I heard so many sad stories from parents. Parents want high academic standards and less socialization of their children. OBE gives them just the opposite.

Having learned first-hand what our state really had planned for our children and having heard so many stories of what is happening in the schools, I felt obligated to go on the speaking trail to get the message out. I spoke at schools, firehalls, and churches throughout my own county and in all the neighboring counties. People were eager to hear the truth about the regulations and to receive materials. They truly wanted to become more knowledgeable on the subject.

At one such meeting, I had a fun experience. The meeting was billed as a showing of the video, "Who Controls the Children?," followed by a presentation from both sides and then a question and answer period. Little did I know that my opponent would be the Governor's adviser on education. She had not only been the president of the state teachers' union but the national teachers' union. Needless to say, she was very upset and put out by having to watch the video. She wanted the sponsors to show only 15 minutes of the 58-minute video, but they had to follow their advertised program. During her presentation, she made several erroneous statements. Digging through my files of materials, I was able to produce Department of Education memos and documents that refuted the facts she had given the public. Neither she nor her husband left in a pleasant mood. Once again we were made aware of the purposeful cover-up of the true facts surrounding OBE—mainly the lowering of academic standards and the loss of local control.

7

Dumbing Down

After writing columns about OBE for several months, I came to a basic realization one bleary-eyed morn at 2 a.m. while trying to keep a tight time schedule. And this is it . . .

One word summarizes OBE's fatal contradiction—**deadlines.**

The advocates of pure OBE want to do away with them. Children are to be allowed to take a test over and over again—as many times as they need or want—until all have reached a common standard of mastery. Failure is to be abolished from the vocabulary. No one fails; all will succeed. Competition is out; cooperation is in.

At the same time, OBE's proponents claim to favor education that is geared to a "real-life" context of work and relevant social issues. They contend that their new approach (which is actually Progressive Education recycled) will prepare children to succeed as workers in the 21st-Century global marketplace.

Sorry, but that doesn't add up. It's nonsense.

Deadlines are a part of daily existence—and not just in column-writing but in lines of work all across the economy. A farmer must meet deadlines to get his crop to the market. A junior executive must prepare a report in time for its presentation at a board meeting. A lawyer must prepare a brief in time for it to be filed in court on behalf of his client. A physician's deadlines for expeditious treatment may make the difference between life and death.

This is nothing more than common sense. A parents' group in San Marcos, Texas, was on the mark in criticizing the bright idea of OBE guru Bill Spady that timed tests should give way entirely to "complex role performances"[1]:

"One need not reflect long to see that real-life role performances are time-based. A system that wants to model the real world cannot free itself from the constraints of time, though it in no way follows that student learning must be based on a rigid and inflexible pattern. However inconvenient for those of us who might prefer it otherwise, the real world is based on clocks, calendars, and deadlines. Any educational system that fails to prepare students for this aspect of life, especially students at the secondary level, has failed them miserably."

Hear, hear! In fact, a school system that imposes no time limits whatsoever ought to be charged with education malpractice. There is nothing "real world" about schooling that eliminates all deadlines—and all consequences of missed deadlines. Children in Japan and the European Economic Community are not being taught to hold hands, hug trees, and feel good about themselves. They are learning science, mathematics, and language—hard subjects that will prepare them for the reality of global economic competition.

The corrosive effect on **academics** is one of the Big Two concerns I have detected about OBE as I have talked to people across America. The other is the manipulation of socio-political **attitudes**—behavior modification, indoctrination, brainwashing—discussed in Chapter Two. The concerns are related, but either one standing alone would be enough to raise warning flags about what OBE would mean for children's future.

Another key concept in OBE's flabby academic approach is **self-esteem,** which began infiltrating education from California's touchy-feely, self-esteem movement a decade ago. How youngsters feel about themselves is supposed to be of over-riding importance. For that reason, grades are eliminated or replaced with euphemisms (like "not yet" or "emerging") designed to sugarcoat the reality of work that fails to meet a minimum standard.

But, here again, a basic contradiction arises. In real life, most people receive boosts to their ego because they have a done a task well. Conversely, most have to deal with occasional failures in business or in personal relationships—and find that success in life often means acknowledging failure, then moving on and rising above it. OBE doesn't prepare children for the real world when it seeks to insulate them from failure. Indeed, it denies them the authentic self-esteem that comes from real achievement.

Few persons have had a better opportunity than Minnesota native Cheri Pierson Yecke to see the academic folly of OBE up close and personal. A teacher of English and history who is currently pursuing graduate studies in education, Ms. Yecke was the 1988 Teacher of the Year in Stafford County, Virginia, and in 1991 a finalist for the Agnes Meyer Outstanding Teacher Award given by *The Washington Post*. Cheri was one of several outstanding teachers who were willing to let me quote them on the follies of OBE. When you can find such authoritative witnesses, by all means use them.

In 1991, the Yeckes moved back to Minnesota and enrolled their children in the Cottage Grove schools, which they had attended from 1982 to 1984. But they returned to find that the district had been implementing OBE during the seven years they had been away. Amazingly, they found that, academically, their daughters had progressed while in Virginia "light years" ahead of their peers in Minnesota.

Ms. Yecke recalled that her younger daughter, Tiffany, who had always loved school, was "in a matter of days begging to stay home."[2] The reason? "The work was far too easy, but what was worse was that any display of intelligence was ridiculed in a cruel and demeaning way by many of the other students. Hard work and self-discipline are looked down upon, and status is often achieved by poor performance."

Indeed, students learn to live up—or down—to what is expected of them very quickly. If there are tricks to the trade, count on the school-savvy kid to learn them. Recounted Ms. Yecke:

"The prevailing attitude among many students is, 'Why study? They can't fail me, so who cares?' What sort of work ethic is this producing in these children? No one fails, regardless of how little they do. Instead, they receive "incompletes," which can be made up at any time.

"The kids have the system figured out. When there is a football game or show on TV the night before a test, a common comment is, 'Why study? I'll just take the test and fail it. I can always take the retest later.'"

Incomplete could be the Grade of Choice in an OBE system. In the Yeckes' Minnesota district, there were 15,500 Incompletes at the end of a semester, or approximately one-half of all grades awarded. In a 1987 study, "Mastery Learning Reconsidered," Johns Hopkins University researcher Robert Slavin found that one reason for the disappointing academic yield from Mastery Learning was that multiple opportunities to complete work and pass tests provide no incentive to do work on time and well.[3] He also found that group projects led by the highest-level students contributed to mediocre academic performance by stealing time from subjects in which the students excelled and investing that time on areas in which they had little interest, such as art or environmental awareness. The expropriation of gifted students to act as peer tutors has been called, aptly, a Robin Hood approach to education.

Commenting on this robbing from the gifted, researchers at the Independence Institute in Golden, Colorado, asked: "What kind of system turns an excellent math or science scholar into a bored, mediocre student by denying him time to pursue his academic interests so he can become a successful, if very average, artist?" The answer: "Mastery Learning/OBE."[4]Dr. Slavin has protested that his research pertains only to Mastery Learning, and is being misapplied to OBE. Yet Mastery Learning and OBE employ similar techniques, especially with regard to testing. "While most would agree that outcome-based education and mastery learning are not synonymous, the two concepts have much in common," wrote James M. Towers, associate dean of the school of education at St. Mary's College (Winona, Minnesota). "In my opinion, the important connection between OBE and mastery learning lies in the fact that mastery learning techniques are generally employed by teachers professing to have implemented outcome-based learning environments. In essence, mastery learning is oftentimes the engine that propels OBE programs."

Writing in the *Phi Delta Kappan*, Towers made as his main point the inadvisability of extending OBE to teacher education. From working for a semester in an OBE approach, he concluded, "remediation seemed to take priority over enrichment activities, particularly in terms of time devoted to each. Those students who mastered the material the first time seemed to be 'treading water,' with very little incentive to work beyond the minimum level they had already attained. With OBE—or all our noble efforts to make sure that 'all students can succeed'—I fear we might be ignoring and even boring those students with the potential to be tomorrow's intellectual and social leaders in education . . . ." His concerns about OBE/mastery learning in teacher education mirror those of many as to this concept's use with America's schoolchildren.

And hear OBE guru Bill Spady himself, on the connection between OBE and mastery learning:

"In January of 1980 we convened a meeting of 42 people to form the Network for Outcome-Based Schools. Most of the people who were there—Jim Block, John Champlin—had a strong background in mastery learning, since it was what OBE was called at that time. But I pleaded with the group not to use the name 'mastery learning' in the network's new name, because the word 'mastery' had already been destroyed through poor implementation. I argued that we had about five years before they destroyed the term 'outcomes,' but at least we could get a start and pursue a clear vision of an idea. Well, I was wrong; it took 10 years instead. Now anything that moves is called an outcome."[5]

Call it OBE or Mastery Learning or something else: When the primary message to students is that sloth and irresponsibility will have no negative consequences for them, schools fail to prepare children for real life. Given the documented failures of mastery learning, where is the evidence that the megamillions spent to implement OBE would increase the quality of education?

Teachers are among the most effective witnesses to OBE's folly. Imagine Cheri Yecke's chagrin upon moving back to Virginia only to find that the state was attempting to mandate OBE in all schools. Her voice of experience carried much weight at the town meetings.

Teachers see the consequences of ill-advised theories being pushed into the classrooms from central administrations or itinerant (albeit affluent) consultants. Given OBE's utopian embrace of absolute equality of outcome, it is no wonder that all forms of **ability-grouping** are under attack by the education establishment. Vern Williams, the 1990 Teacher of the Year in populous Fairfax County, Virginia,—part of the Washington, D.C., metro area—has seen the drive to end ability-grouping come round and round as an administrative fad during his 20 years in teaching. But the force behind the current dogma makes him worry about the impact on, particularly, the teaching of mathematics—his subject.[6]

Throwing a large number of pupils of widely divergent abilities into one math class, says Williams, guarantees a mixture of (1) "very bored" and (2) "very frustrated" pupils—the faster and slower math students.

And Williams was bold enough to write a lengthy letter to the County School Board making his practical points from classroom experience. Would that more independent-minded teachers could be encouraged to muster the courage to do likewise.

Wrote Williams:

"We have been told recently that low-ability students will gain just by being exposed to higher-level concepts. We are told that they probably will not learn many of the concepts, but that's okay because they will still be better off. Well, we do more than expose our students to concepts. We teach! Putting students of all abilities together in seventh-grade math will force us to abandon any serious teaching."

Dr. Sylvia Kraemer found that the state proponents of OBE were selectively reciting "research" in an attempt to make the case that heterogeneous (mixed-ability) grouping results in better academic results for all children.[7] Their favorite sources were Jeannie Oakes' "Keeping Track: How Schools Structure Inequality," along with Robert Slavin, who advocates cooperative learning. But the educrats failed to cite James A. and Chen-Lin Kulik of the University of Michigan who, after closely examining the total body of research on ability-grouping (including Oakes' and Slavin's), found that:

- Higher aptitude students usually benefit from ability-grouping.
- Benefits are greater in special classes for high-aptitude learners.
- Contrary to conventional wisdom, grouping programs usually have only small effects on pupil self-esteem.
- The Oakes' conclusions were "based on her own selective and idiosyncratic review of older summaries of the literature and on her

uncontrolled classroom observations. Objective analysis of findings from controlled studies provides little support for her speculations. Whereas Oakes believes that grouping programs are unnecessary, ineffective, and unfair, the opposite appears to be true. American education would be harmed by the elimination of programs that tailor instruction to the aptitude, achievement, and interests of groups with special educational needs."[8]

The termination of ability grouping (or de-tracking) is part of an ideological agenda that meshes with the OBE egalitarian philosophy. The notion of intellectual leveling—that no matter what our individual prowess in, say, algebra, that we should be in one big classroom working on politically correct group projects—may make ideologues feel good. But children are academically cheated. As the Kuliks write, "Both higher and lower aptitude students would suffer academically from such de-tracking. But the damage would be truly profound if, in the name of de-tracking, schools eliminated enriched or accelerated classes for their brightest learners. The achievement level of such students would fall dramatically if they were required to move at the common pace. No one can be certain that there would be a way to repair the harm that would be done."

Some critics believe a subtle form of racism plays into the movement to dumb-down the curriculum and trash honors classes. Faced with growing numbers of African-American and other non-Caucausian students, some school administrations are despairing of the possibility of maintaining competitive, academically rigorous systems in which students sort themselves out according to achievement. For one thing, they are afraid of political criticism if minority students wind up too heavily in the lower-achieving groups. Or maybe they are closet believers in an innate, fixed intelligence that locks in blacks to the lowest rung. So in the name of "equity" and "multiculturalism," they are going to the OBE feel-good model. The problem with that racialist mindset is that it sells all students short. Hurt most of all, perhaps, are minority students who are being told that they are not expected to meet academically demanding standards, which means that they should not aspire to go to college and graduate school and to learn a profession. They should settle for being a well-socialized, other-directed worker in the local factory.

The theory of **multiple intelligences**, developed a decade ago by Harvard psychologist Howard Gardner, works nicely for OBE schools looking for excuses not to challenge students intellectually. In his book, "Frames of Mind," Gardner argued that the traditional idea of intelligence as being verbal and logical/mathematical is too narrow.[9] He theorized that there actually are seven forms of intelligence, the other five being: spatial; bodily-kinesthetic, musical, interpersonal, and intrapersonal. Some teachers use the theory to promote thematic projects in which students are able to apply their particular kind of high intelligence (it being assumed that we are all smart in some way). For example, a student might be assumed unable to comprehend "The Right Stuff" for a project on space travel, but, not to worry, he could simulate walking on the moon. Gardner has cautioned that the intelligences work in concert, not in isolation; nevertheless, his theory is rich in dumbing-down possibilities.

"Watching schools implement untested theories about 'kinesthetic,' or other intelligences when they can't teach reading looks suspiciously like one more fad," said Denis Doyle, a senior fellow at the Hudson Institute.[10] "The hard truth is that today's youngsters, as never before, must hone their academic skills. Knowledge pays and pays handsomely; ignorance costs more than we can afford, individually or socially. Schools may want to teach English, mathematics, or physics by using music, dance, or football, but they cannot be permitted to lose sight of their academic mission."

Doyle warned of working a "cruel hoax" on disadvantaged youngsters who lack an old-boy network to sustain them. "Of all our citizens, they have the most riding on a good education. To propose that they have a different "set" of intelligences—and cannot perform academically—comes perilously close to asserting that they can't learn what we expect of a well-educated citizen in a modern democracy. That's not only wrong, it's dangerous."

Yet the OBE school is not terribly concerned about teaching the **basic skills of reading, writing, and computing,** which are in fact derided as "lower order thinking" according to Bloom's Taxonomy. The words "reading" and "writing" (and for that matter "mathematics") appeared not once in the original draft of Virginia's OBE framework, the so-called Common Core of Learning. In fact, the very idea that pupils should be required to memorize anything, or engage in any sort of structured drill, is not consistent with the OBE ideology.

The original version of the Elementary and Secondary Education Act reauthorization (HR6), which resulted from a Clinton administration study on how to reinvent education along OBE lines, contained this dead giveaway of intentions under a section pretentiously entitled "What Has Been Learned":

"The disproven theory that children must first learn basic skills before engaging in more complex tasks continues to dominate strategies for classroom instruction, resulting in emphasis on repetitive drill and practice at the expense of content-rich instruction, accelerated curricula, and effective teaching to high standards."[11]

That's like saying you can put the roof on your house before you build the foundation. It's just as nonsensical as saying you can prepare children for real life by eliminating deadlines, failure, and competition. This section of HR6 was rewritten before final passage to reduce the blarney quotient. This, however, is typical of the ideology that is driving phonics out of primary schools—even though massive research studies by Harvard's J. S. Chall and others have shown phonetic decoding to be the most effective and cost-efficient way of teaching children to read.[12] In phonics' stead comes the "whole language" approach, which encourages pupils to invent their own spellings—the important thing being that they feel good about learning.

The OBEish ancillary philosophy in the primary grades is something the educrats have labeled "developmentally appropriate practice"(DAP), a term plainly meant to end all debate because, after all, who wants to defend something that is "developmentally inappropriate?" This, however, turns out to be a unilateral treatise of the National Association for the Education of Young Children[13]: It is now "appropriate" to let children in grades K-3 meander from one multi-age, cut-and-paste learning center to another, picking up reading and other basic skills by osmosis while exercising their "higher order thinking skills." When a child decides he wants to know how to spell or sound out a word, if ever, he will ask the teacher—and not before. Teachers no longer direct the learning show; they are bit players called facilitators. The children are the stars.

Amazingly enough, the Southern Regional Education Board—an Atlanta-based outfit bankrolled by tax money from 15 Southern states—issued a report in the fall of 1994 stating that "all schools should implement developmentally appropriate curriculum, instruction, and assessment practices in kindergarten and grades 1–3."[14] The SREB further stated, in typically OBEish prescriptive fashion, that the success of DAP "will require school administrators, teachers, and parents to change their behaviors and their expectations of both children and schools." But more than ed-school jargon about "behaviors" is involved here. England tried DAP as Progressive Education and recently abandoned it as an abysmal failure. And DAP essentially is a revival of America's Open Classroom, which briefly flowered in the post-Vietnam era, then fast wilted.[15] It is outrageous that members of the tax-funded Systemic-Change Gang like the SREB are trying to foist a failed model on all schools.

Thomas Sowell has made a trenchant observation about the folly of de-emphasizing in the early grades the intellectual exercise that memory is:

"It is hard to imagine how a small child, first learning the alphabet, can appreciate the full implications of learning these particular 26 abstract symbols in an arbitrarily fixed order. Yet this lifelong access to the intellectual treasures of centuries depends on his mastery of these symbols. His ability to organize and retrieve innumerable kinds of information, from sources ranging from encyclopedias to computers, depends on his memorizing that purely arbitrary order."[16]

So-called "authentic testing" or assessment is what in many respects drives the whole OBE movement. In essence, the hand that controls the tests will control the whole of American education. That certainly is the explicit hope of the founders of the New Standards Project, which is developing the instruments of so-called "authentic" assessment, which is supposed to replace objective, knowledge-based testing.

Ruth Herman, a testing expert at UCLA, has observed in a federal research paper that "rather than measuring lower-level skills and rote memory," authentic tests measure such things as "metacognitive processes and attitudes" and immerse children in tasks having "real-world applications."[17] Lauren Resnick, co-director of NSP, has stated that the "heart of the New Standards assessment system will be student portfolios," which will contain three kinds of work: (1) that chosen by the school, teacher, or pupil, (2) assigned projects, or (3) responses generated by NSP "matrix examination tasks."[18]

An example of a NSP exam is "The Amusement Park Task," which has been tried out in Pittsburgh schools. Children are told they are going to an amusement park and each fourth grader will have a second grader as a buddy. That part of the task, say Resnick and the NSP's Director of Equity Initiatives, Warren Simmons, has "a social dimension. Students are asked to consider the needs of a younger buddy." Pupils are asked to do some math to figure how to budget their money and time to enjoy the day at the park. But typically the emphasis is on social outcomes, not exactness in doing math, which becomes "open-ended." Furthermore, the NSP bigwigs say that because test "equity" is a major concern, whole-and small-group discussions of the task are "designed in part to level the playing field for students from different backgrounds." FairTest, a Cambridge Massachusetts, advocacy group dedicated to the abolition of standardized testing (particularly of the multiple-choice variety), has gone so far as to propose that, in the name of equity, questions that elicit the least difference in passing rates between majority and minority test-takers should be given priority in the final preparation of a test. Here is yet another example of how concern for equal outcomes is driving down the ideal of educational excellence.[19]

The rhetoric of reform is all about standards that are high, indeed "world-class." But Gregory J. Cizek, an assistant professor of educational research and measurement at the University of Toledo, has perceptively observed that standards in reality are fast disappearing from American life. Why? Because we insist on having standards that do violence to no one—that everyone can pass. These then become either dumbed-down or doctored standards. Ways are found to "cloud the issue"—one being the obfuscation of "psychometrics." Cizek cites the hullabaloo that ensued when thousands of teachers repeatedly failed competence tests in the 1970s and 1980s. The solution? "Psychometrically, the standard was 'adjusted statistically with reference to measurement-error variance.' Everyone passed. . . . On a national scale, when we have a collective angst that public school students aren't measuring up, we re-analyze the data. Ah! A psychometrician assures us that it—educational failure—is 'the big lie.' Mental measurement to the rescue! More self-esteem salvaged."[20]

If academic excellence were the main goal, an analysis by Daniel L. Singal in the November, 1991, issue of The Atlantic Monthly should have ended the debate long ago.[21] Professor Singal closely examined the relatively few schools that did not—repeat not—experience the 80-point plunge in SAT verbal scores that occurred in schools generally from 1963 to 1980. His analysis demonstrated that those consistently high-performing schools shared these qualities in common:

- The schools maintained a philosophy that academics must take precedence over all other concerns. No Affective Ed for these schools.
- They never abandoned a traditional liberal arts curriculum to chase Sixties' fads like "relevance" (now being revived in OBE). They continued to stress English grammar and vocabulary, as well as rigorous (and precise) math.
- They also continued to group students by ability in as many disciplines as possible. "The contrast was stark: schools that had 'severely declining test scores' had 'moved determinedly toward heterogeneous group (that is, mixed students of differing ability levels in the same classes), while the 'schools {that} have maintained good SAT scores' tended 'to prefer homogeneous grouping.' "

Yet, the OBE philosophy would head the nation's schools in exactly the opposite direction: away from the liberal arts and toward a thematic hodge-podge of social concerns; away from classical learning and toward "relevance;" away from grouping by intellectual ability and toward use of gifted students as peer tutors in mixed-ability classes.

The dumbing-down of America started before there was a philosophy called OBE. But OBE loads all the pernicious trends on one bandwagon. The question is whether citizens can stop it now and recapture their schools as institutions to train the intellect and transmit the American heritage. The first step is to understand the nature of the beast, and to appreciate the stakes involved. The following observations of our citizen-activists indicate that they see and know with great clarity. . . .

Kentucky Now Leads the Nation—In Defections from Public Schools

By Donna Shedd
Kentucky

The two greatest concerns about OBE for us in Kentucky are the narrowing of the curriculum—what a lot of people refer to as "dumbing down"—and the totalitarian aspect of inculcating politically correct attitudes in our children. The belief that they can engineer a utopian planned society is consistent with the philosophies of the KERAtistas. They become quite enraptured, almost giddy, when they speak of no more failure, all children succeeding at high levels, all coming to school ready to learn, all healthy, all happy.

They take relativism to new heights, or rather new lows. They are opposed to absolutes—absolutely. I asked one of the PhD's who put together our outcomes about the outcome stating, "All students will make sense of what they read." I told her that sounded vague and relative to the individual. How could you measure such an outcome? What about objective and measurable skills such as discerning the author's purpose? She responded that an author's purpose is not always clear, and, besides, many authors are dead—so who knows? I bit my tongue.

With the narrowing of the curriculum, the "less is more" philosophy is flourishing in Kentucky. Once teachers taught students as much as they could pack into a semester or a year. The tests were a sampling of all that was covered. Now the students are taught only the sampling. Many teachers are instructed by their superiors to allot a certain amount of time each day to teach the test. Why? Our tests are high-stakes tests. Even though the state is comparing test scores from this year's eighth graders with the scores of the eighth graders from two years ago, if the schools don't show improvement continuously until they reach "perfection," the state will impose sanctions and take them over. Teachers' jobs are dependent on how their students do on these state tests. The Commissioner says (in print) that the law requires our tests to "reflect the learning and behavior we seek," and that will enable "our educators to concentrate on producing Zero Defect students." And he wants teacher support?

Children are taught less content for a practical reason. There is a need to make room for more process, of course—and then there are all those sociopolitical attitudes to instill. More time to spend on environmentalism, feminism, globalism, and egalitarianism. That works out well in Kentucky. Our tests are full of all the **isms**. The tests are based on our valued outcomes (which were re-named learner outcomes, then learner standards, now academic expectations, although nothing changed but the name). The outcomes were re-worded in the spring of 1994 and condensed to just 57, but there's been no change. They were making them "clearer." They are very clear about that. One of our colleagues testified that in the original outcomes "knowledge was ignored in ambiguous language. Now it's ignored in clear language."

The outcomes were reviewed by a group hired by the Department of Education and their report called the outcomes "almost content free." They said that, likewise, the tests were very low on content. Most of the content was in the multiple choice questions; therefore the state board of education has decided not to have multiple choice questions anymore. Now the students won't have to know much of anything before taking the test, except, of course, how they feel about things.

The test will be all open-response questions, or what we once called short answer essay. They are the antithesis of objectivity. Fourth graders are asked to solve the problem of the homeless. Eighth graders are to address the problem of the disappearing rain forest. Scoring guides from the Department of Education indicate a pronounced bias toward political correctness. Those scoring guides tell the teachers what scorers will be looking for in the students' responses and thus what he/she must teach to remain employed.

The KERAtistas know how critical it is that the teachers support the restructuring. What a dilemma they have. They want the teachers to support a program that not only is academically depleted and morally relative but also will drive teachers from their jobs—if not sooner, then a little later. The solution to controlling teachers was House Bill 182, passed in 1992, when teachers were waking up to what was in store for them. The bill (though worded with the usual legalese) says that any school board member, superintendent, or staff member who engages in a practice that hinders implementation of KERA will be reprimanded on the first offense and fired on the second. The law was extended in 1994 to include parent members of the site-based councils. Although the Department denies that this law restricts teachers' freedom of speech, the bottom line is that it is being used as a threat at faculty meetings. Teachers are told they can only say positive things about KERA, and they are intimidated into silence. We have become a voice for teachers and administrators. I wish I had a dollar for every time one had said to me, "Thank you for saying what we cannot say."

I pulled my three young children out of public school after the first round of the KERA tests in the Spring of 1992. The private school where my children are now enrolled has 172 new students this year, an increase of 28 percent. Our county had a homeschooler increase this year alone of 500, or 147 percent. Private school enrollment is up all over the state. Many new private schools have been formed since KERA. This summer, the public schools in Montgomery County, Kentucky, ran ads in their local newspaper in an effort to recruit students. Parents would rather pay the tuition on top of their property taxes than let their children go to public schools under KERA. (Watch out for legislation against home-schooling and for regulation of private schools.) According to the 1994 National Report Card, Kentucky leads the nation in declining public school enrollment in 1994. Yet all other measurables are up—more per-pupil spending, smaller classrooms, the types of features that attract parents. Make that, **usually** attract parents.

The OBE Philosophy Is Engrained In Education Establishment

By Lil Tuttle
Virginia

Public education was, and is, in serious trouble. Despite increased financial and human resources given to schools, U.S. students aren't being well educated. Statistical data from international tests performed in 1988 showed that average Japanese students achieved higher scores than the top five percent of U.S. students taking college preparatory mathematics (functions and calculus). Since these students represent the "pool from which most of tomorrow's mathematicians, engineers, and scientists will emerge" (IEA, "The Underachieving Curriculum"), the numbers make tomorrow look pretty bleak for American kids. Clearly, something must be done to make schools accountable for both the quality of education they deliver to students and the use of taxpayers' money.

The idea of outcome-based education was born out of the desire to do just that. Some wanted to see schools measured by Outcomes—the depth and breadth of knowledge and scholastic skills students had acquired when they came out of schools—rather than by inputs—the money, books, computers, personnel, etc., taxpayers put into the schools. Such a system might have put educators' feet to the fire by providing parents, taxpayers, and lawmakers with an independent means of judging which schools were actually educating children well and which were not.

Unfortunately, OBE was thoroughly corrupted by sociologists, educational psychologists, and the education interest groups with anti-intellectual, anti-achievement, anti-direct instruction, and anti-accountability agendas. Theirs was a different vision. They managed to co-opt the outcome-based language and poison the concept before it could be clearly defined in academic terms.

Today, fighting the most egregious OBE-type school practices is only the immediate and urgent goal. Citizens' long-range goal must be to wrestle control from an education establishment whose collective judgment can no longer be trusted. Parents and taxpayers can and should force a public debate on how and what children are taught, how efficiently schools use the time and money given to them, and who ultimately controls the lives of the children.

When all the rhetoric is stripped away, there are basically two approaches to educating children: progressive/child-centered and traditional/teacher-directed.

• **Progressive/child-centered/affective:** Extensively tried in England ("progressive education") and in the U.S. during the 1970s ("open education"), child-centered education is being reintroduced to U.S. schools as Developmentally Appropriate Practice (DAP) through efforts by state departments of education and the National Association for the Education of Young Children. One education journal called it the U.S.'s "quasi-national education policy," and most parents associate the approach with OBE.

The basic tenets of the child-centered model are that children learn through free-play, and learning should not be inhibited by adult-established ideas of competition, achievement, and failure. Child-centered proponents advocate the use of whole language in reading; non-graded or mixed-age classroom organization; ungraded (no A-B-C-D-F) work; mixed-ability (heterogeneous) grouping; integrated curricula (a blending of disciplines into themes); and the elimination of standardized testing. Self-esteem is to be taught as a prerequisite to learning.

Each student ("self") is encouraged to discover or construct his own knowledge and "truth" (sense of right and wrong). Teachers are non-directive facilitators, helping students find and use information. Students are responsible for their own learning, and academic knowledge and skills are taught as needed through real-world projects in cooperative learning groups or mini-learning centers. Student peer groups are used to control the school environment and mediate conflicts.

England abolished the child-centered approach as national policy in 1992, claiming it was primarily responsible for the two-decade decline in student achievement.

Traditional/teacher-directed/academic: This approach puts teachers in control of the learning process and the classroom. It assumes that adults have a body of knowledge worth transmitting to the next generation and that children are capable of scholastic achievement when taught directly and explicitly. Both students and teachers are held accountable in this model.

Teacher-directed proponents advocate phonics to teach beginning reading; serious traditional courses of English, math, history, geography, civics, and the sciences; letter grades on work performed; homogeneous (similar ability) groupings within academic subjects; and standardized or norm-references testing to monitor achievement. Self-esteem is expected to be earned through individual achievement.

In this model, the teacher takes control of the learning process, deciding what will be taught to and learned by the students, and the classroom, defining the rules to which students must adhere (i.e., what is "right and wrong"). Carefully structured, sequenced instruction in the traditional subjects, methodically moves students from naive learners to proficiency.

As James Davison Hunter, author of "Culture Wars: The Struggle to Define America," points out, activists "who actually hold strongly traditionalist or strongly progressive positions are in the minority (perhaps 20 percent at each end.)" Yet these activists are irreconcilable. The 60 percent of the population in the middle is joining forces with the traditionalists because they, too, are increasingly dissatisfied with public education. According to the Southwest Education Development Lab, "the public is no longer willing to assume that educators "know best" about learning and teaching."

Clearly, the "one size fits all" public school no longer fits all students in this diverse society. It only guarantees one group or the other will be angry. The only means of changing the education system is through politicians who oversee education at the federal, state, and local levels. The Democratic Party seems firmly wedded to the NEA and others promoting the full implementation of the child-centered model. Although some Republicans are responding to appeals from traditionalists, the party's commitment to breaking the chains of the education establishment is still questionable.

The battle over education policy and practices will continue until parents have the personal and financial freedom to choose the school for their children. Goals 2000, designed to give parents less control, surely will escalate the battle.

Train your sights on the politicians, get commitments, and hold them accountable.

Note: In January 1995, Virginia Governor, George Allen named Lil Tuttle to the State Board of Education.

Victory Over CLAS in California—Or Only a Reprieve?

By Carolyn Steinke
California

Experience is the best teacher. By 1993, we were done trusting the system. It was at a Constitutional Coalition Convention in St. Louis that the lights went on for several of us. The picture became clear: The monster was called Outcome-Based Education, and it was everywhere. Now we understood. What we had been fighting were only the tentacles of the beast. We also came to understand that it originated at the federal level, was promoted through federal carrots (dollars), and was mandated by state legislation.

It was a river of legislation parents knew nothing about.

We returned home with a new resolve to obtain documentation of California Authentic Performance-base testing, the CAP, as it was then called.

First, we obtained the 1991 California legislation, SB1274 (California's Education Reform Act), which contained "waiver" language that made it possible for the Department of Education and the State Board to waive any Education Code, State Law, or District Policy "when it interfered with the restructuring plan."

Next, we procured copies of the CAP test—and we could hardly believe our eyes. The first 1992 CAP test I read, for eighth-grade language arts, was astounding. It was entitled, "My Mother, Rachel West." The family in the story was pondering the death of their mother, examining their ambivalent feelings, wondering if the life force that had so overwhelmed their exercise of free will was now a greater loss than relief.

The prompt question to which a child was to respond in essay form: "Recall a time when a member of your family did or said something that made you see them in a different light, and write about it." Next, children, during the test, broke into groups for the purpose of in-depth sharing of experiences based on the question, finishing the test by completing a second essay, which we were told was never graded.

Negative themes were found in the stories in the CAP Language Arts assessments and subsequent tests, which portrayed parents in very negative stereotypes and promoted discussion on how marriage inhibits freedom, and how children abandoned by their parents made it in the streets.

In a story, "Just Lather, That's All," a barber contemplates, in graphic depiction, slitting the throat of an officer in his chair. How the blood would gush in great spurts, covering him, the chair, and virtually running out of the front door of his establishment—thereby signaling to others his act of violence.

Other tests portrayed God as impotent. Issues of gun control were presented so as to promote the conclusion that the student was to write to their legislators urging them to ban guns in order to prevent needless killing of little children.

Language Arts assessment was not the only point of contention in the state testing. The Math assessments required solutions to math problems in essay form. Math no longer demanded a right answer; calculators were the substitute for memory.

This testing format could never in a million years give parents and teachers an accurate measure of a student's mastery of building-block skills in math.

In 1993, the Department of Education purposely misled the public into believing that the old CAP test was being replaced with the new CLAS (California Learning Assessment System) because the CAP was based on outdated multiple-choice testing while the CLAS was an authentic performance-based test measuring students' "higher-order thinking skills."

It wasn't until teachers began sending us copies of the new CLAS test that we realized the only difference between CAP and CLAS was the name. In pilot tests, California children had been tested in this manner since 1987—all in direct violation of California Education Code 60650, which states as follows:

personal beliefs— no test, questionnaire, survey, or examination containing any questions about the pupil's personal beliefs or practices in sex, family life, morality, and religion, or any questions about his parents' or guardians' beliefs and practices in sex, family life, morality, and religion, shall be administered to any pupil in kindergarten or grade one through grade twelve, inclusive, unless the parent or guardian of the pupil is notified in writing that such test, questionnaire, survey, or examination is to be administered and the parent or guardian of the pupil gives written permission for the pupil to take such test, questionnaire, survey, or examination.

This was a psychological test! It measured nothing academic. When examined by licensed psychologists and psychiatrists, the testing was declared "potentially dangerous when administered by non-professionals." Liberal professor Richard Paul, Ph.D., and other experts on critical thinking, held a press conference on the Capitol steps to condemn CLAS as "educational malpractice."

The old CAP and the new CLAS did achieve one purpose: They enabled the education establishment to evade accountability by replacing objective testing with this form of assessment.

Throughout 1994, California waged a battle to wring the truth from the education establishment and stop CLAS. At one point, an Assembly Education Chairwoman threatened that anyone who would disseminate copies of the CLAS test "would not leave the hearing room without being slapped with subpoenas."

It pays to know your rights: According to federal copyright laws, it is permissible to copy materials that have been in multiple use in a classroom; are open for criticism and evaluation; and are not being reproduced for profit.

We instructed the marshal to deliver to the Committee members highlighted copies of the CAP and CLAS tests. That's when the real fireworks began.

First, Department of Education officials denied the authenticity of our copies of the tests. When members asked to see "actual" copies they were told they could not because the committee might disclose the contents to the public.

What transpired next was sheer delight. Our prepared questions enabled committee members to see the foolishness and incompetence of the test and its proponents. The press was obliged to come on board, and, with media attention, we were off and running.

For the next four months, a handful of us began speaking at town meetings and debating the experts up and down the state of California. Some weeks we were out five nights and then attended seminars all day on Saturday.

The United States Justice Foundation and the Rutherford Institute began championing parents by filing suits in local school districts claiming parents' rights violations.

We targeted school board meetings and many districts took a stand for local control by opposing the Department of Education edict to prohibit parental "opt-out" of the test. Some local boards took it a step further and began opening up the "top-secret" tests.

Then truly courageous boards voted not to administer the test at all. They were stunned to find out their state funds were being threatened. Individual board members were slapped with lawsuits and threatened with removal from their elected positions. So much for local control! Parents grew all the madder and by now our town meetings moved to auditoriums and large churches.

California Senator Gary Hart submitted a series of amendments that would have hit hard at educators or parents who objected to CLAS (for example, by removing teachers' credentials if they discussed or shared the test; removing the rights of parents to opt out of the test; and subjecting anyone accused of "subverting" or attempting to subvert the test to a $10,000 fine, one year in jail, and damages up to $1 million.

By now, our only hope of stopping this test and the legislation rested with Governor Pete Wilson, because the liberal legislators had ignored the strong protests of California parents.

Past State Board of Education presidents Joe Stein and Joe Carribino publicly joined with us in our veto plea to Governor Wilson.

On September 27, 1994, Governor Wilson did veto CLAS testing.

It came as no surprise. One week earlier, we had received an urgent call from the Governor's Office crying "uncle, uncle, please tell your parents to stop jamming our direct phone lines." Apparently citizens had logged more than 20,000 calls of protest that week.

Sometimes experience is a tough teacher, but we are learning well. The CLAS veto is not a victory, but only a short reprieve. This test is coming back with a new name—CCTP (California Comprehensive Testing Program). The legislation for the Education Reform is on a fast track—but so are we.

Parents Involved in Education (P.I.E.) was born out of this battle, and it was about time. Even though government has succeeded in stripping away our parental rights, we **will** take them back. We **will** take back local control of our schools. We **will** ensure that our tax dollars go to a public system to educate and equip children academically in basic skills, not in behavior modification and mind control. We **will** only accept validated curriculum. Our schools are not laboratories and our children are not guinea pigs.

There is no issue closer to the hearts of American parents than our children and our children's children, and if it takes our last breath, we will not stop until these wrongs are righted.

The Networking Must Continue— For the Children's Sake

By Anne M. Barbera
Pennsylvania

Many teachers—especially the older ones and those who have successfully raised a family—are outraged by the problems OBE creates. They see very clearly the dumbing-down of academics and the interference in private family matters. These are the ones you can get to help you—not openly, but anonymously. Many of these teachers have taken early retirement; they will not be part of this academically corrupt experiment.

Others are very good, well-meaning teachers, blind to the dangers of OBE, and brainwashed into thinking they must solve society's social ills. These teachers you can work with and help them understand that because some children have problems, it does not follow that all children need counseling and psychological help. If children dwell on problems all day, they are imprisoned in their unhappy or unsafe environment. Children need the real tools of escape: They need to be able to read well so they become culturally literate, and they need to have their minds expanded through knowledge obtained in academic subjects.

The last group of teachers are those who firmly believe they should raise your child because you are not capable. It is these teachers who are dangerous for our children.

As the state of Pennsylvania continued its battle to prevent the revision of our education regulations (which more accurately should be called the restructuring of an educational system), we gained notoriety across the nation. Because the PA Parents Commission was in the forefront of our state battle, we began to get requests for help and advice from across the nation. Our mailing list expanded to include subscribers from many of the 50 states. Our video, plus the many informational booklets we had put together, have helped citizen groups throughout the country. We continue to work diligently to help educate the public on the issue of the restructuring of education.

OBE, or whatever it is called in each state, is detrimental to our children and a serious cause of family problems. The primary purpose of education is the development and broadening of our children's minds by exposing them to all academic subjects and requiring them to memorize facts, as well as teaching them the application of this knowledge. This type of education is what has made our nation great. This type of education is what brought a cure for many diseases, a vaccine for polio, put a ship in space, enabled a man to walk on the moon. None of these likely would have occurred if education only had required students to be exposed to supposedly "relevant" information and skills—the concept that is being expounded under the guide of OBE (or Compact for Learning, etc.).

The most important aspect of learning that is being denied our children is the tool necessary to read well. When a child cannot read well, he cannot fully participate in education, because he cannot read directions or follow manuals. Children become embarrassed, bored, and troublesome, and many eventually drop out of school. In Pennsylvania, about one-fourth of the students do not complete their education.

I saw first-hand the problems caused by the whole language method of teaching reading. My oldest son was taught by this method back in the first grade. Needless to say, he could not read any book other than his reader. Overriding his objections, his mother taught him phonics and then transferred him to a new parochial school. He excelled throughout school and higher education. I shudder to think what could have happened if I had not been aware of the problem. Now, 30 years later, I have witnessed the same grave error with my grandchildren. Only this time is much worse, because the child is not corrected for misspelled words, punctuation, capitalization, correct sentence order, and recognition of words. Today anything goes, and the child is supposed to feel good about him/herself when others cannot read what they wrote or when they cannot read their textbooks, library books, or even comic books.

One mother chose an outstanding second-grade teacher for her children, knowing they would continue to receive excellent phonetic skills. What a shock it was for her when she realized her third child was being schooled with the new curriculum. The teacher had been trained in seminars, was now a lead teacher for the new program, and no longer stressed phonics or responsibility in following instructions. The child's journal is unreadable and only partially answered, often with incorrect responses. The child received no corrections but a high grade for this work.

Even though our battle was hard-fought, the state bureaucrats won when they put the new education regulations into effect. Our time was well-spent and the war for our children's minds is not over. People have been awakened, parents are keeping close tabs on what their children are being exposed to. Parents are taking their complaints to teachers, administrators, school boards, and legislators. They are constantly being chastised and rebuked, but the PA Parents Commission, under my chairmanship, is still here aiding and educating in any way we can. We are continuing our research, putting together new informational booklets, and trying our best to answer people's specific questions with documented material if it is available. We believe networking is of the utmost importance because there is strength in numbers. For this reason, when we receive calls of desperation from people throughout the country, we try our best to hook them up with someone in their state who can lend support. Pennsylvania is once again gearing up to get legislation passed that will enable us to retain control of our children.

Even though I am tired of the battle, want to quit and just be a wife and grandma, I am committed to stay involved and fight. My grandchildren and all other children are too valuable to hand over to the state or federal government. They are our children, our gifts, and our responsibility.

8

Breaking the Media Silence

Those who favor **freedom**-based—as opposed to state-prescribed **outcome**-based—school reform have large disadvantages to overcome in waging war through the media to win the minds of the citizenry. To crack the barrier, they may have to use alternative media—talk radio, computer networking, and community newspapers—or create their own media, through newsletters, fax machines, flyers, or other grass-roots techniques.

We'll look at the possibilities later. First, why are the media an obstacle to free and balanced discussion of this issue?

Part of the problem is that major news media have shown themselves too lazy, preoccupied, or politically correct to cover an education debate with huge implications for the country's future. Even stories written by reporters exhibiting a blatant liberal bias would have been preferable to no coverage at all. But the silence has been eerie. Consider:

• When Goals 2000 passed the House of Representatives, not a line of coverage appeared the next day in *The Washington Post*, the favorite rag of the federal establishment. Yet Goals 2000 was the legislative linchpin of the whole national effort to restructure American education according to the OBE philosophy.

• Not until the School-to-Work Opportunities Act was being signed into law did it receive a few lines of coverage—and then there was nothing about the profound shift toward a work-based curricula it seeks to impose. Instead, we got Labor Secretary Robert Reich exulting and cracking jokes on a late-night show.

• Only when amendments dealing with prayer or condom distribution were proposed did the mammoth reauthorization of the Elementary and Secondary Education Act rate much wire-service coverage. Yet in the thousand-page bill were many provisions consolidating Big Government power over education, such as "corrective action" subjecting local school boards and superintendents to federally mandated dismissal if they fail to abide by the New Standards.[1] But after passage, news reports typically spouted Washington's party line that the reauthorized law accords localities "new flexibility" in improving the schools.

And look at these lead paragraphs from The Associated Press on the other two key pieces of the federal power grab in education:

"WASHINGTON (AP)—The Clinton administration won Senate approval Tuesday (February 8. 1994) of school-to-work legislation aimed at ensuring that students are adequately prepared for the "jobs of tomorrow."

The Senate scheduled an evening vote on the broad Goals 2000 education bill, which would implement voluntary, national education goals."

Accounts like this simply pass along dutifully the distorted version of the truth peddled by government propagandists. In truth, there is nothing "voluntary" about Goals 2000—not if states take federal education funds. And School-to-Work has the objective of radically transforming the curricula of every school along a work-based model favored by business interests. (It could be called the **School to Work—Or Else!** law.) The national media looked no deeper than the surface of government hype.

This is the second part of the problem: the gigantic propaganda machine that government and the business and education establishments have put together to market the top/down, statist OBE reform. Unfortunately, with media types inclined to lead cheers for social agencies, these horn-tooters gain undeserved credibility.

In my home state, the State Board of Education had held no public hearing on its OBE plan. Yet an organization of political and business big shots called Virginians for World-Class Education had raised private money to sell the plan. Meanwhile, the State Department of Education was using public money to market OBE to "target populations" as though it were a new brand of toothpaste.[2] I understand that this approach was common in many other states: Propaganda first, public hearings only after the transformation was a *fait accompli*.

The state marketing plan contemplated, among other things:

- Regular surveys of the target populations (school administrators, teachers, parents, lawmakers, civic groups, religious leaders, the press, even the Department of Education's own staff) to measure the impact of the OBE sales pitches.
- By-invitation-only promotional sessions with small groups of business and community leaders, (but no department-sponsored mass meetings for just average parents and folks.)
- Lobbying of legislators.
- Letters to the editor that business leaders need only sign and send to their local paper, canned articles for business newsletters, and a

video featuring Superintendent of Public Instruction, Joseph Spagnolo, and corporate executives touting OBE.

• "Ecumenical lunches" with selected "key" religious leaders. The Religious Left, perhaps?

• Employment of a communications specialist to develop a "consistent response strategy." Response to what? To any and all criticism, which Ed-Central did not accept with equanimity. At one point, insiders told me, the strategy was to respond to any column I wrote, whether a rebuttal was pertinent or not.

The state's OBE brigade even planned to take to the Virginia State Fair to distribute bumper sticks and pencils touting the cause. In a way, it was too bad Governor Doug Wilder pulled the plug on the "Common Core of Learning"—the framework containing the learner Outcomes—before the Fair opened. It would have been fun to see what stickers the state came up with, and how citizens countered the ticky-tacky tactic, (perhaps copying the state's famous tourist slogan, "Virginia is for Outcome-Based Education Lovers—NOT.)"

This campaign was small potatoes, however, compared with what the National Education Goals Panel has assembled to propagandize the joys of Goals 2000 in each and every community across the USA. Late in 1994, the Panel, an all-politicians' group assembled in Washington under the Goals 2000 law, was preparing to distribute a Community Action Tool Kit developed by the U.S. Department of Education and its tax-funded regional laboratories, which have been incubators of education experimentation.[3] This Tool Kit consists of five pounds of brightly colored manuals printed on expensive glossy paper. The government's agents tried hard not to overlook a single item the well-equipped Goals 2000 activist might need: Heck, even sign-up and reminder sheets are printed on the high-quality slick paper.

These are some of the items in the Let-Government-Do-It-For-You Tool Kit:

• Not only canned letters to the editor, but also op-ed pieces, feature stories, radio spots, and entire speeches endorsing the federal power grab in education. This is Connect-the-Dots grassroots support. The government has done all your thinking and writing for you; only your signature is required.

The lack of widespread media outrage over this elaborate and shameless attempt by government to manipulate the media suggests that a midnight tolling for freedom's demise is closer than we might think in America.

• A Troubleshooting Guide for dealing with opponents, a.k.a., The Resistance. Advise the Kit-makers: Identify your opponents; list their resources. This sounds ominously like something out of one of Chairman Mao's tool kits for the Red Guards during the Cultural Revolution.

• Detailed case histories showing how opponents may be co-opted in order to implement radical curricular change. For instance, educrats in Edmonds, Washington, deliberately published multiple drafts of the district's OBE plan, because "it gives the message that you are open to change."

• Step-by-step plans for manufacturing community support through the use of so-called facilitators and change agents. Those are people who steer public meetings toward a phony, government-approved consensus. The kit's Community Organizing Guide offers this advice: "An organized discussion about education reform will not happen spontaneously." In other words, ordinary rubes cannot be trusted to reach the "correct" conclusion. Their meetings must be facilitated. It would be hard to imagine any more vivid demonstration of the government elite's contempt for public opinion.

Beverly Eakman has documented extensively in her two books how the regional education labs, formed under the 1965 ESEA (now reauthorized for five years) long ago contracted with behavioral scientists to develop this manipulative tool for imposing state-desired "innovation."[4] There is even a training manual for "change agents" written by Ronald and Mary Havelock at the University of Michigan's Institute of Social Research.[5]

Ironic, isn't it? Even as parents across the nation object to restructuring plans that have more to do with manipulating their children's sociopolitical attitudes than with teaching them to read, the government has adults in its gunsights for attitude adjustment as well.

"Only by changing the attitudes and behavior of community members," the Tool Kit states, "will it be possible to reach the National Education Goals." But that wasn't just a sudden brainstorm from within the budding bureaucracy of the National Education Goals Panel (one of three new bureaucracies Goals 2000 establishes). No, that kind of didactic prattle is common to members of the Systemic-Change Gang pushing OBE. As the National Center on Education and the Economy (a Carnegie creation that has become a virtual adjunct of the Clinton Education Department) declared in a 1992 funding proposal . . .

"If we are to succeed in radically transforming schools, we must alter attitudes outside the schoolhouse door."[6]

The center's panjandrums added that it would be necessary to use "all the techniques of the modern media strategist as well as the proven methods of community organizing," One of its Change-Gang partners, the Public Agenda Foundation, already has "been successful in designing and orchestrating citizen education campaigns" in five communities.

The media manipulation multiplies.

And it is spreading to cyberspace, where censorship of citizen dissent to systemic restructuring is beginning to become an ugly reality. An incident growing out of the appearance of Secretary of Education Richard Riley as a guest on the Education Bulletin Board of the Prodigy Interactive Computer Services in September, 1994, demonstrated Washington's reluctance to engage in free and open discussion with opponents of systemic (OBE) reform.

Karen Iacovelli, executive director of the Long Island-based National Parents Alliance and at the time a coordinator of Prodigy guests, had arranged for Secretary Riley to make an appearance on Prodigy in September to answer at least selected questions on-line. Writing in the March, 1995, issue of *Crisis* magazine, Ms. Iacovelli explained that Prodigy's Education Bulletin Boards have become "exercises in raw freedom," with networks of community leaders posting pertinent information on education practices and reforms. Riley's appearance was a "major coup" for Prodigy, and drew a record number of posted questions from members. Many of the queries indicated either skepticism or hostility to the federal government's role in pushing top/down school reform. In the middle of his appearance, Riley's office announced a delay in responding to the questions because the Secretary had to undergo emergency prostate surgery. Bulletin Board participants responded sympathetically, posting prayers for his recovery, and awaited the Secretary's return.

"In mid-October," Ms. Iacovelli wrote, "Riley reappeared on the service. Instead of responding to questions, he asked participants their opinions on the role the federal government should assume in setting standards to advance education, It was a 'loaded question' and not readily accepted by members. Another torrent of participant response followed. By mid-November, with questions piling up, Riley had still failed to respond. This was uncharacteristic and unprecedented guest behavior. . . ." (After Ms. Iacovelli's article appeared, Riley did answer selected questions.)

In an attempt to expand the debate by having a guest opposed to government involvement in education, Ms. Iacovelli invited George Roche, president of Hillsdale College. He accepted, and even wrote a special article that was to be presented to Prodigy members on the consequences of government control over education; however, a Prodigy bulletin board manager ordered her to cancel the invitation without offering an explanation to President Roche. Ms. Iacovelli was told that several board participants had objected that the guest program was not "broad-based" (an ironic complaint, given that she had arranged for George Roche, an opponent of government involvement in education, partly to balance out the appearance of Richard Riley, a powerful advocate of government involvement).

Earlier in 1994, the American Federation of Teachers had entered an agreement with Prodigy whereby an exclusive bulletin board was created for union teachers. Many citizen participants on the Education Bulletin Board fear that this special arrangement opens the door for Prodigy to cater to the whims of its paid editorial sponsors. The possibility exists that the education establishment will try to squelch citizen networking and dissent on the online services, although there was no direct evidence of AFT involvement in the Riley/Roche fiasco.

As Ms. Iacovelli wrote, "That one of the country's leading educators {Roche} was not extended the courtesy of an explanation and that I was explicitly instructed to cancel his appearance, confirmed to me that online dialogue is vulnerable to First Amendment abuses. It remains unclear if Dr. Roche was rejected by the {Prodigy official} or a pressure group now acting upon Prodigy."

Instead of Roche, Prodigy offered as special Education Bulletin Board guests in January, 1995, Drs. Maryann and Gary Manning, who are advocates for invented spelling and whole language in reading instruction. Many of the parents on the board vehemently oppose those techniques, while many union teachers strongly support them.

Citizens who dare to oppose OBE—preferring a different model of reform—also face the real possibility of being portrayed as Religious Right "fanatics" by the education establishment's propaganda organs. One of the Educationist Left's favorite authors has been Dr. Janet L. Jones, an Oregon guidance counselor and consultant, who wrote a resource manual, "What's Left After The Right?", for the Washington Education Association with funding from the National Education Association. Among those she characterized as leaders of the "Far Right" movement were President Ronald Reagan and neoconservative William Bennett, recent author of *The Book of Virtues*. That's casting the net for villains rather widely.

In an April, 1993, article for The American School Board Journal, Dr. Jones reported darkly that in several states "religious right activists and groups have begun to work against outcome-based education, which sets specific achievement levels students must reach in each subject before graduation."[7] She mentioned Pennsylvania, New Mexico, Colorado, Florida, Iowa, New York, Ohio, Virginia, Kansas, and Minnesota. Having had contact with hundreds of concerned parents and teachers, especially those from Virginia, I wonder how Dr. Jones presumed to know the religious backgrounds of the OBE opponents. I never asked in my own conversations—and besides would membership in a church or Sunday School (or synagogue or mosque) disqualify a citizen from speaking out on education issues? Surely not, in a nation founded by settlers seeking refuge from religious persecution.

To be sure, the proponents of systemic change often target particular activist groups led by religious figures, and the Rev. Bob Simonds of the California-based Citizens for Excellence in Education (CEE) seems to be a special bogeyman for those who wail about an amorphous Radical Religious Right. But irony of ironies, Simonds and an associate, Professor Arnie Burron of Colorado, were in the summer of 1994 negotiating a "compromise" with OBE guru William Spady by which they supposedly would go forth and market somewhat differing versions of outcome-based education.[8] That news was causing a certain amount of consternation in both pro- and anti-OBE camps. I am under the impression that a great many parents—whether they profess a religious faith or not—don't want "outcomes" for their children's schooling written by Bob Simonds any more than they want Bill Spady's paradigm shifts. They want local autonomy, parental rights, and good, solid basic education. They'd like both the assorted gurus and the government to get out of their face.

As for the Big Media, there is a reason most reporters are unlikely to leap to the aid of mainstream Americans being unfairly tarred as religious fruitcakes. And, furthermore, there is a reason for media silence in the face of arrogant attempts by education elitists to remake public attitudes. The reasons are: (1) The media elite shares the philosophical disposition of the government elitists, and (2) the media elite is becoming ever more enamored of the idea that it, too, has a (shall we say?) calling to change public attitudes.

The 1986 work, aptly entitled *The Media Elite*, by Robert Lichter, Stanley Rothman, and Linda Lichter, compellingly made the case, with solid research, for the pervasive liberal bias of the media.[9] A survey of 238 journalists at America's national news organs (ABC, CBS, NBC, PBS, *Time, Newsweek, U.S. News & World Report, The New York Times, The Washington Post,* and *The Wall Street Journal*) showed striking differences between the mediacrats and the general public.

For example, on the question of religious faith: 86 percent of the public respondents said their religious beliefs were "very" or "fairly" important to them, while an identical 86 percent of the elite journalists said they seldom or never attended church. On politics, the survey found a ratio of more than three liberal journalists for every conservative, which Professor Ted J. Smith, III, noted in a *National Review* article "contrasts sharply with the distribution among the American public:

every relevant poll conducted in the decade from 1975 to 1985 found conservatives outnumbering liberals in the electorate, often by a ratio of three to two or more."[10] Even more dramatic, as Professor Smith of Virginia Commonwealth University's communications school tells it, "Among elite journalists who voted for a major party candidate, support for the more liberal Democratic contender ranged from 81 percent for McGovern and Carter, to 87 percent for Humphrey, to a high of 94 percent for Johnson."

In an attempt to get a clue to the disposition of the new generation of mediacrats, the authors also surveyed students at Columbia University's Graduate School of Journalism, the prep school for many of tomorrow's media elitists. They found that while the students were more diverse according to race and sex than their predecessors, they showed even less diversity of opinion: Liberals outnumbered conservatives 85 percent to 11 percent, or more than eight to one.

In a close look at the new journalists coming out of communications schools and heading to jobs often landed in places where they have no roots, New York writer Stephanie Gutmann found the breed to be notably imbued with a Change-the-World philosophy. They, in fact, have much in common with Big Education's change agents. They believe journalism has become a tool for implementing social change, whether it happens to be the change the locals want or not. This new self-righteousness contrasts with the old ethos that the reporter's job was to present the facts in a balanced way and let people make up their minds for themselves.

Concludes Ms. Gutmann:

"Like schools of social work and schools of education, schools of journalism transplant rarefied, elitist, city-folk concerns like multicultural education and condoms for six-year-olds to the heartland. The daily newspaper, once a simple voice—a neighbor talking to neighbors—becomes a hectoring superego, the voice of the cultural elite."[11]

Speaking of which, listen to the editor of *The Wichita Eagle*—fresh from foundation-funded deep thinking at journalists' conclaves—lecturing to his readers on the glories of the so-called Public Journalism, by which newspapers now are supposed to become full-fledged players on the civic stage, rather than mere reporters and commentators:

"Public journalism's effort to help public life go better," Davis Merritt, Jr., wrote in a modest full op-ed page presentation,[12] "cannot succeed in a vacuum. When journalists decide to substitute for chronic cynicism something more useful; to modify traditional detachment by becoming fair-minded participants; to open their minds and newspapers' columns to fresh views, you are also asked to change—to take up the identify of 'conscientious citizen.''

''The art of being the conscientious citizen requires, for most of us, a change in attitude similar to the change public journalism asks of journalists.''

Basically, this is OBE journalism, which is found also in collaborative projects with a predetermined slant by reporters for media organizations that once considered themselves tough competitors. It should help explain why citizens who believe OBE's anti-competitive approach to be a disaster in the making for education receive so little sympathetic coverage from the major media. And it helps explain something else, too: why newspapers, alas, are losing readers faster than the magnificent Cape Hatteras national seashore loses sand during a nor'easter. As Forbes editor James W. Michaels notes, ''If newspapers hope to survive, they would do well to be less concerned with a liberal social agenda and more with the lives, hopes, and fears of their potential readers.''[13]

The electronic media are even worse, sometimes giving the appearance of being in the pocket of the very social agencies they cover. Consider this revealing advice in a SCANS document as to how a School to Work project in the Hoosier State could obtain glowing ''news'' coverage:

''Whenever a school-to-work project like IndianaPLUS is adopted in any locale, a strong push should be made to involve the local ABC television affiliate and/or the Public Broadcasting Service (PBS) station in the area. While no one can guarantee in advance that a station will participate, it is highly unlikely that both the ABC and PBS stations will decline. The project is a good local story and is directly linked to the schools, the business community, and other important station constituencies.''

So much for media watchdog. Evidently ABC and PBS have chosen to be media lapdogs for the Systemic Change Gang. That's not surprising for an outfit directly on the government dole like PBS, but ABC owes its viewers an explanation if it has chosen to be a PR agency for Big Government.

But despite all this, the worst thing a citizen activist can do is to whine and rail about ''media bias.'' Once the nature of the beast is understood, there are smart ways to attack the problem.

I commend, especially, the article by Donna Shedd of Kentucky at the end of this chapter. Rather than fret about the unwillingness of the state's largest newspaper to give her side of the argument a fair break, she began distributing her articles to the small, community newspapers around the state. While some of the smaller papers are skittish about controversy, at least they tend not to be infected with the virus of liberal elitism. After more and more of the smaller papers ran her pieces, Ms. Shedd finally was contacted by the big-city journalists. Once a story is out there and being told in many community publications, it becomes harder for Big Media to ignore.

Also, verify your documentation independently. Have your facts straight when dealing with the media, and be calm and professional. Cathy Reid of North Carolina tells how her group got stuck with being characterized as Religious Right because a member cited just one piece of information out of a CEE newsletter.

By no means should all newspaper or television reporters be written off as ideological enemies. Many try to report the news in a fair and impartial manner, regardless of their personal feelings or background. Certainly reporters who do play it down the middle have access to a wider range of story fodder than do the obnoxiously one-sided types; and some are known, suspected, or closet conservatives more eager than you might imagine to report news about preserving basic education and wholesome values. It is wise to keep an open line of communication with the press—if nothing else, to show journalists that you are not the ranting crazies their left-wing, J-school professors warned them about.

An emerging means of alternative communication is the computer network. Cindy Duckett of Kansas, one of the pioneers in becoming your own mediaperson online, tells about the possibilities on the Information Superhighway.

Finally, there's talk radio, which sometimes seems to be the keeper of the flame of American freedom. Sure the medium is rough and tumble, and sometimes callers or hosts let loose with comments that play fast and loose with the facts. But this is a forum for Americans to say what's on their minds—and statist school reform has been among the hottest topics. In making guest appearances on talk shows from Washington State to Chicago to Texas to Connecticut (including also Richmond's Lou Dean of WRVA and Blanquita Cullum of WLEE) I found the hosts to be well-informed about OBE issues—to have done their homework. Talk radio is not just the province of national superstars like Rush Limbaugh and G. Gordon Liddy (who has been a real stalwart in the OBE fight). Almost every community has a local talk radio program nowadays, and hosts typically are receptive to concerns of the community. They don't protect sacred cows.

When national talk-show host Michael Reagan—son of the former President—attended a recent National Conference of Editorial Writers' meeting in Phoenix, he faced many media elitists who sneer at talk radio.[14] But as Edwin Feulner of The Heritage Foundation recounted, Reagan turned the tables when he asked a show of hands as to how many of the 150 or so editorial writers had read the Clintons' 1,342-page health-care reform plan. Only one hand went up. He next asked how many had assigned a staff member to read the plan. Only a dozen had.

By contrast, Feulner noted, "Michael Reagan's unique contribution to the national debate has been to read the Clinton plan's legislative language to the listeners of his show. To do that, he has read the plan—from front to back—twice."

If only Congressmen and members of the media elite would read the contents of mammoth pieces of social legislation, the propagandists for statist solutions would have far diminished chance of success. Maybe that's the role of the citizen-activist: actually to read and study these proposals and to get out the word via radio, fax, newsletter, modem, television, newspaper, hand-delivered flyers, carrier pigeon, or whatever form of communication can be devised by the mind of man.

Create your own media? With the modem and the fax, the tools are available for citizen-activists to do it. No government-funded Community Action Tool Kits are necessary.

Patience May Be Rewarded With Media Fairness

By Cindy Duckett
Kansas

The daily debate and discussion that takes place on Prodigy has increased my knowledge of educational issues, bolstered my confidence in dealing with them in a public, and sometimes hostile setting, and has given me many good ideas from the experiences of others. I have put that knowledge, confidence, and many of the ideas to use in my local community.

I pass a lot of the information I gather on the bulletin board along to my friend Ruth to use in putting together her monthly newsletter. With the assistance of several friends and neighbors, I have targeted several key elected officials to educate on a regular basis with small, regular mailings that deal with specific issues of concern. We take turns doing the mailings and the follow-up calls to make them aware that at least some portion of their constituency is concerned about the direction that education is taking in our district and state. I have also made contact with several people in the local TV, radio, and newspaper media and have shared my concerns and my documents with them. I got to know the education reporter at our local newspaper and have provided resources on numerous occasions for a variety of articles and I stay in touch with local talk radio.

I have found the impact on media people and legislators to be slow—sometimes frustratingly so. Over time, though, I have seen that it does make a difference. Several years ago, one of the editorial writers at our local newspaper wrote a scathing editorial entitled, "Let's buy the religious right out of the public schools." I was angered when I read that article. If it had been directed at any other group in our society, the public outcry would have gone on for months. But on reflection I realized two things: First, that he must have seen religious folks as a threat of some kind or he never would have felt compelled to write such a piece; second, that parents needed to communicate more clearly that what they were dealing with was not a religious issue, but rather a civil rights issue. The central point was that every child has a right to a solid academic education and that every parent and student has a right to privacy—and that both of those were imperiled by our state reform plan. It was then that I decided to establish some regular communication with these writers, and today, though they still are not dealing with many of the issues that I wish they would, we haven't seen any more of the "anti-religious-right" comment in some time. And they are beginning to deal with some of the substantive issues in a fair and appropriate manner.

TV Reporter Jayna Davis Focused the Public's Attention

By Walt Larsen
Oklahoma

In the fall of 1992, the State Superintendent of Public Instruction of Oklahoma proudly, and loudly, announced that "this is the year we attain full implementation of OBE." Ms. Garrett went on to say that this reform was not a back-to-basics approach but a complete *paradigm shift* in a movement that would sweep the country. We were to be early entries to the 21st Century. She had forgotten the minor detail of telling us when we had started this journey and was now announcing our arrival.

I had voted for Ms. Garrett based on her "common sense and accountability" campaign. I had even, reluctantly, supported the largest tax increase/school reform in state history, because it was sold as a much-needed pay raise for our teachers and improvement in the schools.

In early January 1993, during a School Board meeting, I witnessed the first shots fired in the "Battle of the Bilge" as a silver-tongued junior administrator from my district explained (with reverence) the miracle of **OBE.** This young man threw numbers around faster and looser than a commodities broker—this percentage increase in this positive factor, that percentage decrease in that negative factor. In short, it was a canned/planned sales pitch designed to baffle if not dazzle.

I was later to find that he has been parroting the pitch of a sociologist, William Spady, and had not bothered to check out any of Spady's claims. One success story was about a school that had been closed for 10 years; another about an inner-city school whose changes had to do with a complete demographic remake of the school and nothing to do with OBE. Other numbers were just plain bogus and the address of "success" was always changing.

The next three months were a blur of meetings with angry parents, phone calls until 1 a.m., meetings with evasive, scared, pompous, defensive educators—and the forming of PRIDE, our parent/patron activist group. All of this culminated in a presentation by a former teacher, Mrs. Carol Bond, before more than 1,500 angry parents, curious taxpayers, and a few teachers. The television coverage alone guaranteed the issue would not soon fade away.

A local television reporter, Jayna Davis, kept the public's attention focused with timely reports and pointed interviews—in particular a revealing on-camera shot with our senior state education officer, Ms. Garrett, saying she didn't know of a successful implementation of OBE. By April, 1993, Ms. Garrett was saying she didn't even know what OBE was and asked if anyone did; she "clarified" the state position that OBE was strictly voluntary. Our 7,000 state-mandated "Learner Outcomes" were transformed to 1,136 "Priority Skills," which were nothing more than a *Reader's Digest* version of the same outcomes. Several large district school boards openly rejected the reform movement in "NO OBE" votes. Although we know those votes really didn't stop anything, they were encouraging.

We have not defeated OBE in Oklahoma, but we have caused some strategic withdrawals. The battle continues to expel Values Clarification, Affective Ed., Mastery Learning, Cooperative Learning, Sex Ed. for 12 grades, and watered-down, or non-existent, academic standards.

The real villain now, however, is lurking deeper in existing and pending legislation requiring teachers to be indoctrinated and in Parents as Teachers programs just beginning to rear their ugly heads. It is becoming clearer that reformers have gone underground and are getting better at camouflaging their movements—scattershooting bits and pieces of the agenda in this regulation, that policy statement, and those pieces of legislation. Those dedicated to stopping these unworthy reforms must now become speed readers and legislative activists gleaning these fragments from bills before the whole piece of legislation passes.

This is not the time to shrink from the task. Too many have lost the zeal. We are winning skirmishes and need all the forces we can muster to win the war.

Beware the Misleading Language Of School Restructuring

By Dr. Karie Dawkins
Virginia

Parents researching and learning the truth about OBE learned a very important basic lesson. To make OBE more acceptable to the general public, many traditional education terms are used by OBE proponents, but the terms have been secretly redefined. For example, when educrats talked about the "New Basics," they were not talking about academics such as reading, writing, and arithmetic, but attitudes and outcomes determined by a closed group of self-styled clitists intent on social manipulation and power. The term "cognitive" traditionally has referred to thought processes and thinking skills; however, as used in OBE, cognitive refers to "a belief system." In other words, the public is intentionally being deceived to believe that one thing will be done based on the traditional understanding of ther terms used, while the developers of the curricula intend to implement an entirely different program based on their personal definitions of the terminology used. That the term "academics" may also be privately redefined by OBE proponents and educrats would also come as no surprise. Therefore, being alert and diligently challenging and determining the **true** meaning of what is being proposed, carefully examining each **detail** of **any** educational program and the **specifics** of what is to be taught and tested, are critical necessities. The time of **blindly** accepting what is presented and **blindly** trusting the educational establishment is past. The technique of privately changing standard definitions of words so as to purposely mislead parents and the public is pervasive, often goes unrecognized, is unforgivable, and must never be tolerated.

The Splashy Coverage Is Reserved For the OBE Proponents

By Joe Gwynn
Virginia

It would not be fair to say that we were ignored by the local media. We called in to radio talk shows and were interviewed by local TV stations, even if only for a minute or two. To say that we were frustrated by having to express our problems with OBE in short "sound bites" is an understatement; but we reasoned that something was better than nothing. Likewise, some of the letters to the editor we wrote were printed in the Norfolk *Virginian-Pilot*. We also observed, however, that stories about our activities were usually buried in some obscure part of the paper. Not so, however, with the proponents of OBE. Articles about their classroom innovations and ideas were placed in prominent places in the newspaper. There were large color photos of happy students in their classrooms. It was clear to us that our local media people were either opposed to our ideas or unwilling to investigate OBE for themselves. Thus, the great majority of busy parents still do not understand what transformational OBE is, or why there is controversy surrounding it. Many of the teachers we talked to do not know what OBE is either, even though they're using it in their classrooms.

And They Call This PUBLIC Television?

By Sharon Thompson
Virginia

I was very concerned that most parents were still hugely unaware of the unfolding drama in education. I innocently called our local "public television station," thinking that they, too, would be concerned and would want to get the word out to the public. They were interested and aware. Later I was to learn that they were most concerned about serving as a public relations tool for the Department of Education. Still, they led us on with "planning meetings" for a while. The plan was a televised discussion of the pros and cons of OBE between us and Dr. Joseph Spagnolo, State Superintendent of Public Instruction. Excuse after excuse was offered to postpone that event. Dr. Spagnolo wound up on public TV by himself fielding obviously canned questions from the person who had supposedly been planning the joint appearance.

There was no question that our time had been wasted, except that we had met and worked with several members of the Department of Education. Those meetings led to me getting more information and several of us attending State School Board meetings. The information that we got there was priceless and became a large part of new and improved presentations for town meetings. The School-Board meetings also gave us valuable insights into mainstream media. We could hear first-hand what was said at meetings and then see what was reported. The biases in the reporting were startling and helped us realize that we could not count on TV or newspapers.

Radio, on the other hand, proved more helpful. Blanquita Cullum in Richmond was especially helpful in getting the word out to the population. Another radio announcer (whom I regret I cannot name because I did not hear it myself) put out a free plug for one of our town meetings without our even asking him to do so. After the initial meeting, however, we mostly relied on word-of-mouth and would get several hundred people with that method.

We believed that school officials and teachers also needed to know about the Common Core of Learning, and we invited them with phone calls and personal visits. The reaction from them was less than satisfying, however, because most had the attitude that the government was always doing something and this was just another fad. We were always happy when an educator came to our meetings and were very happy that more were coming before the "Common Core of Learning" was killed.

Why were we so concerned? We saw that the "Common Core of Learning" was based mostly on values and attitudes rather than academics. We felt that any curriculum that led to such outcomes would bring our children through indoctrination that could run counter to their family's values as well as leave them less than well prepared academically. The values and attitudes in the school would, of course, be political. Public education would be subverted for political goals rather than concentrating on the most noble goals of education for the sake of our children.

Of course, our research brought to light much more in the schools that justified grave concerns about psychotherapeutic and new age practices in guidance programs; values clarification; kids being taught to determine their own values in family life, guidance, and drug abuse prevention programs; the use of a reading program (whole language) that had proven to be a failure where it had already been used for several years; globalism; and beliefs most clearly associated with socialism. There was (and still is) much work to be done, but our most immediate goal had to be the "Common Core of Learning."

Start With the Small Newspapers, And the Big Ones Will Follow

By Donna Shedd
Kentucky

In January, 1991, I filed to run for the office of State Superintendent of Public Instruction. Not because it was a great job: KERA had stripped the office because the people got to vote for it and have a say in the education of their children with their tax dollars. To replace it, KERA created the office of Commissioner of Education. Our Commissioner was imported from California and makes twice the governor's salary. And he is appointed. I ran for the remains of the Superintendent's position because it would get me invitations to speak all over the state—on education. I could also collect names and addresses for a mailing list. That I did.

Since my campaign of 1991, I have spoken around the state and done radio and TV talk shows whenever I was invited. There are others who speak publicly, as well. We usually speak at organization meetings, church groups, citizens' groups, etc. The Family Foundation, which joined with us fairly early in the battle, has held some town meetings and at least one debate in west Kentucky. The Department of Education's memos now advise their officials not to debate us.

In the spring of 1993, I began to send articles to a small monthly Christian newspaper here in Louisville, having long since given up on the Louisville *Courier-Journal*, the big one. When I had four articles written and had gotten some response, I decided to send them to all the other daily newspapers in the state. There are 22 of them. Two weeks later, I got a telephone call from far eastern Kentucky. A woman whose friend had sent her a clipping of one of my articles asked if I would send it to their local weekly paper. She said, "Ninety-five percent of our teachers hate KERA and all of our administration hates it, but our parents don't know." So I sent the articles. The newspaper called me long distance to thank me. Then it finally dawned on me: We had been neglecting a very important medium. If the small newspapers are printing information about a topic that concerns people the way education does, the big newspapers almost have to acknowledge an opposing view is out there. And they have.

On December 5, 1993, the Louisville *Courier-Journal*, KERA's biggest cheerleader up to that time, shot itself in the foot by announcing the newspaper was no longer going to sponsor the state spelling bee because it promoted academic competition, which was not in the spirit of KERA. It was the story of the year. Rush Limbaugh discussed it and used the story's "pull" quote in his "Stupid Quotes" column in his newsletter. The cat was now out of the bag—and what an offensive feline she was. Liberals and conservatives alike were alarmed that KERA held academic competition in disdain. Local talk radio shows were inundated with calls. No one wanted to talk about anything else. Somewhere an editor had to be castigating himself.

Before Christmas we were called by the education reporter for the Courier. He was doing a story on Outcome-Based Education and KERA. It ran on January 2, 1994, front page, and not just "above the fold," but top story right under the banner. In it, the Commissioner denied that Kentucky had Outcome-Based Education but admitted that there were people in the Department who had a fascination for OBE and felt that KERA was an example of it.

A rally was held on January 13, 1994, on the Capitol steps in Frankfort. In spite of the fact that it was a weekday at noon, and in spite of a cold drizzling rain and fog in the mountains of eastern Kentucky, we had 973 people show up with signs. Of course, the media printed numbers much lower, and the Commissioner reportedly told the Department that there were only 150. The important thing was that legislators were inside the Capitol looking out the windows.

Once the media recognize your existence, you wear a bullseye. One of the revered liberal columnists in the Lexington paper got a bit hysterical and called me the "chief whipper upper" of the rally, which he described as "a gaggle of hot-eyed citizenry." Opponents of KERA are frequently charged with being the religious right by the liberal left and the Department of Education. The Department sent out articles to counter ours. They have sent memos to administrators to warn them of our "tactics." One memo claims the Department has a database on KERA critics and asks schools please to send the Department any information they have on us (toll-free number provided, paid for with tax dollars). This memo was accompanied by some articles on the religious right. One article cited explanations for people being part of the religious right, such as certain personality characteristics based on the Freudian concept of projection (of aggression, resentment, and inadequacies). It said that some Christian Right behaviors might "constitute evidence of personality defects such as dogmatism, distrust of others, and excessive nostalgia." The Department, when called to account, denied having a database (we have the memo that says they do). They said they merely have a file of newspaper clippings and reports (we have that, too).

KERA opponents have been called a whole lot worse than religious right, although that is the most oft-repeated charge. We've heard "lunatic fringe," and, once, "bull-goose crazies." The name-calling comes primarily from editorial writers in the big newspapers, Commissioner Boysen and his crew, and the Pritchard Committee, a group that claims to support academic excellence, but that received a grant of $250,000 from the Carnegie Foundation to promote and monitor KERA. They set up watchdog groups across the state to ensure that changes were made. If the school is naughty and resists KERA, they tell. The executive director is currently at Harvard University teaching a course on education reform.

I was asked to do an article for the liberal *Kentucky Journal* last summer. The editor said he was doing an issue on religion in Kentucky and wondered if I would do something on the religious objections to KERA. I sent him a piece explaining that objections to KERA aren't necessarily religious and perpetrating that fallacious argument simply serves to waste time that children don't have to spare. He printed it.

Lately the charge is that we are against public education and have a hidden agenda to get vouchers for our children in private schools. I'm sure other states have encountered this accusation. It is an attempt not only to take the spotlight off the real issue, but also to drive a wedge between us and the teachers. They have always relied on the divide and conquer strategy. But they're getting transparent. Or, we're wising up. We now cultivate relationships. We build bridges. You never know when a bridge could be useful to get where you want to go.

A video production company has made a video with representatives from each of five different anti-KERA organizations. We were wary at first but decided it was worth risking. The company did a nice job and treated us quite fairly. The video is being used by educators.

On October 5, 1994, we rolled out our fall campaign at a press conference in the Capitol rotunda. We released a new brochure that portrays a sad Shakespeare who is feeling left out of Kentucky state outcomes. Inside the brochure, we put our teaching standards beside the state outcomes. The contrast is revealing. The back side of the brochure lists five changes that we would like to see in KERA. We are currently working with a state Senator on the bill request that makes these changes and he will pre-file it when we are finished revising it. Many legislators already have asked to be included as sponsors of the bill.

The big newspapers have said that the fate of KERA hangs at the polls. There are many anti-KERA candidates. But the media need to realize that many of our sitting legislators are gravitating our direction. They are listening and realizing that KERA is not the program that was sold to them in 1990.

It's a defective product.

Honor Roll

(Honoring grassroots organizations that have made a difference for the better in their communities.)

Project Educate

14401 E. Willowbend Circle
Wichita, KS 67230
(316) 942-4545/FAX: (316) 942-6424/ Internet e-mail: chpx25b@prodigy.com
Cindy Duckett, President; Dr. Chuck Kriel, Spokesman
(316) 733-5968/FAX: (316) 733-8370

Project Educate was organized in 1994 in the belief that a city-wide, nonpartisan group should be established where transmisison of information could be accomplished and where constructive suggestions, ideas for improvement, and objections to specific portions of school programs could be heard and made politically effective if agreed upon. Our main purpose is to get the facts on any given subject, get them as impartially as possible, make them available to the public, and pursue, through the school board and the elective process, changes believed necessary.

We support classes where basic subjects, taught thoroughly and individually, make up the bulk of activity. We believe that grades are the best measure of pupil achievement and should be maintained in as objective a manner as possible. We believe in standardized nationwide proficiency tests to empower parents to compare their school with others in the state and other schools nationwide. We support the publication of these test results on an aggregate basis by school. We believe that every student and family has a fundamental right to privacy. We oppose the use of personal questions in classroom assignments, surveys, or tests. We believe that parental permission must be obtained before student-identifiable information may be transferred to any individual or entity. We stand firm in our support of a parental rights amendment to the state constitution to ensure that parents are guaranteed the right to direct the education and upbringing of their children.

We accept no inferior status for parents in conferring with school authorities on the education of our children. We believe that education needs not only our dollars, but also our principles, and our personal time and interest, and we intend to provide that through this group.

9

Big Biz and Ed Biz

Finally, after about a year of investigation, I came to this painful conclusion:

The scariest and strangest aspect of the monolithic movement to restructure American education according to an OBE philosophy is not the participation of the federal government. (After all, voters still have a shot at influencing Washington's official policy through the political process.) Rather, it is the effort by big business—more specifically, the Business Roundtable (BRT), an organization of the CEOs of the 200 largest corporations—to impose its own model of reform on schools across the nation. It is a model hawked relentlessly by David Hornbeck—until recently the BRT's superconsultant—and it is premised on children's being malleable "human capital" for the emerging technological, global workplace of the 21st Century.

The spiritual presence behind the corporate offensive is W. Edwards Deming, the guru of Total Quality Management who died recently at the age of 93. Deming was credited with being the brains behind Japan's post-war economic surge and TQM has been a useful model for restructuring some American businesses, such as Xerox, Motorola, and Ford. But in Deming's declining years, "total" took on the look of "totalitarian" as he espoused a cooperative "way of life" in which all competition and merit systems would be abolished.

"In place of competition for high rating, high grades, to be Number One," Deming asserted in *The New Economics*, "there will be cooperation on problems of common interest between people, divisions, companies, competitors, governments, countries. . . . There will be joy in work, joy in learning . . . Everyone will win; no losers."[1] Deming's increasingly prescriptive ideas about society at large may have been impractical at best, if not downright destructive, but few in the corporate culture seemed inclined to challenge them. Rather, as Leon Wieseltier wrote in The New Republic, TQM has become "Zen for CEOs."[2] And the absolutist idea of remaking society also appealed to social democrats like Hillary Rodham Clinton, who played a pivotal role in assembling the components of a statist reform for New World Order schools.

Aspects of Deming's utopian vision when applied to education can be seen, for example, in the Kentucky school system, which (beginning with a court order in 1990) was restructured according to the BRT model provided by Hornbeck—a Carnegie fellow who is the current superintendent of Philadelphia schools, with degrees in law and theology. Some of the anti-competitive manifestations: The State Spelling Bee has been abolished because there were winners and losers; social studies questions on the state assessment are open-ended, with bonus points for political correctness; and math no longer demands right and wrong answers, only an understanding of process.

It may be that we should be worrying about the Deming-down of American education rather than dumbing-down *per se*, although the two may be synonymous. To build a high-skilled, high-wage workforce for the 21st Century, the word from on high is that schools need to concentrate less on knowledge and literacy, and more on process and attitudes. Because Frederick Taylor's 80-year-old model of the industrial assembly line is supposed to be giving way to Deming's TQM model, it is supposed to follow that a primary mission of schools is to instill social skills in workers for front-line cooperative work. In calling for a focus on assessing and certifying students' workplace skills, Arnold Packer, the executive director of the Secretary's Commission on Achieving Necessary Skills (SCANS), asserted:

"Standardized pencil-and-paper, multiple-choice tests cannot be the basis for these certificates. After all, such tests can't tell much about how well an individual works in a group."[3]

Now, wait a minute. Just who decided that being a good group-socialized worker bee is more important in an individual's education than acquiring knowledge about, say, the rise of Western civilization?

The powerful push from TQM-infatuated corporate boardrooms raises some basic questions, namely . . .

- **What is the primary purpose of education?**

(a) To enable students to develop their intellects to the utmost of their capacity and to become independent-thinking individuals in a free society, or . . .

(b) To train youngsters to be competent, well-socialized, customer-serving workers in the high-performance workplace—in other words, to meet the needs of big business?

- **Who decides whether Shakespeare or Systems Thinking—liberal arts or workplace indoctrination—is the most important priority for the local high school's curriculum?**

(a) Patrons of the school, who pay the taxes and provide the children, or . . .

(b) Corporate chiefs heeding their high priests of TQM and

OBE, issuing *pronunciamentos* on restructuring, and bankrolling Madison Avenue campaigns for nationalized education and elitist coalitions to squelch the opposition?

If you answered (a) to both questions, go to the head of the class (if there still is an honors chair in your Deming-downed school). But the BRT push suggests a significant segment of the big business world favors (b).

The bull-headedness behind this monolithic push is maddening. I say that out of sadness, not an anti-business animus. I have always been—and still am—pro-business, because free enterprise is a system in which the individual can go as far as his ingenuity and energy will take him. In fact, the OBE/TQM misadventure makes me think of Bill Bailey and starts me humming to myself, "Won't you come home, big business? Won't you come home? You've been a long time gone!"

Gone, that is, down a road of state-directed, centralized education that is not appropriate to this blessed Republic of free individuals. And considering the natural "home" of business to be the free market, I wonder why corporate moguls want economic choice for themselves but a dictated model for less privileged families. (I wonder also if these millionaire executives have in mind OBE public schools for their own children, or, instead, elite private schools where liberal learning still prevails.) In Connecticut, for example, the Business Roundtable opposed a parental choice bill, while pushing for its OBE plan, which ultimately was defeated in the legislature. BRT representatives often sneer at statements that they are pro-OBE, but everywhere David Hornbeck has gone with BRT backing (more than a dozen states), OBE plans have followed.

Some business leaders, by contrast, have exhibited altruistic motives in advancing family choice. Patrick Rooney of The Golden Rule Insurance Company in Indianapolis, for instance, has awarded millions of dollars of scholarships to enable children from low-income homes to have the option of attending private schools. And in New Orleans, Patrick F. Taylor of the Taylor Energy Company is one of a growing number of business leaders who help out disadvantaged children who stick to their plan to go to college. His Project New Orleans awards $1,000 per year to each student who qualifies for a Pell Grant and goes to a Louisiana college. The money goes toward such quickly accumulating college expenses as books, transportation, clothing, and lab fees. These are just two examples of thousands of ways civic-minded U.S. business leaders help children and education.[4]

Many business people tell me they do not agree with the idea that outcomes like "working cooperatively in a group" ought to replace literacy as the basic aim of education. In fact, one of the letters I have received during the OBE wars of which I am proudest came from W. O. Jones, III, president and CEO of Kjellstrom and Lee, Incorporated. Mr. Jones wrote, in part:

"As a businessman I can assure you that what we need is more attention to the basics of education, not less. We need stricter, not easier, performance evaluation procedures. We need to continue to push individuals to strive to be the best that they can be, not 'on a par with everybody else.' If OBE happens to get ensconced in our system, we may have lost all opportunity to return to the concept upon which our society was founded . . . individual responsibility and achievement."

Unfortunately, OBE took root as big-business' school reform of choice when President Bush and the nation's Governors launched the America 2000 program in 1989. The language computed: "Outcomes" lent the veneer of a no-nonsense, bottom-line approach. And who could argue with them that the old way of measuring education strictly by its "inputs" (per-pupil ratio, number of books in the library, teachers with master's degrees, etc.) was flawed? Alan L. Wurtzel, chairman of the well-run and highly successful Circuit City Stores, Inc., noted that although per-capita spending on schools almost doubled between 1960 and 1990, student achievement was stagnant between 1970 and 1990.

"We developed the current input-based system in the 19th Century," observed Wurtzel (in one of his op-ed responses to my columns), "to meet the demands of an agricultural economy. We adapted it in the early 20th Century to meet the requirements of a factory-based industrial economy. It is increasingly unsuited to the post-industrial economy based on computers, communications, and global competition. It is also out of sync with our society, in which increasingly large numbers (up to 40 percent) of our children grow up in poverty, often with only one parent who is frequently a child herself, who dropped out of school."[5]

Wurtzel said business, government, and increasingly the American public agree that Total Quality Management is essential for America to compete in the world. And he pointed out, "Outcome-Based Education is the school version of TQM."

"As with TQM," he continued, "Outcome-Based Education starts by defining the 'product' it seeks to produce: Children educated to World Class standards. It benchmarks the quality of competitors' 'products'—in this case, the children of Europe and Japan. It seeks to eliminate 'defects' early in the process by delegating responsibility to front-line workers (in this case, teachers and school-level administrators) and by providing them the training (staff development) and incentives (bonuses for success, help for lack of success, and the possibility of dismissal for clear and persistent failure). It also provides the modern tools (much improved technology, especially computers) necessary to do the job."

Wurtzel and other leaders of big business reasonably diagnosed some major ills in American education. But their prescription of a large dose of industrial TQM strikes many as too simplistic and mechanistic—not to mention susceptible to the piggybacking of assorted agendas destructive of education rigor and individual rights. (President Clinton has appointed Wurtzel to the National Skills Standards Board that is being set up under Goals 2000.)

Professor Leila Christenbury, editor of *The English Journal*, reminded the OBE/TQM proponents that, "the education of a human being cannot be reduced to input and output, and firmly resists a business/factory model. While it may seem a helpful simplification, students are not raw material moving in a school assembly line of classes and credits. Input and output are, ultimately, meaningless terms in education. So many hours in school rarely equal so much learning: The equation is never so clean. Further, teachers are not workers who have total control over their raw material, the students; as teachers will tell you, the relationship between the two groups does not resemble roles of shaper and shapee. Finally, the end result of the process, education, is vastly more idiosyncratic than the production of a perfectly baked cookie or a shiny new car."[6]

But in 1989, with a Republican administration joining with the business interests, the initiative looked attractive to some conservatives. From the start, The Business Roundtable has insisted on the following nine "essential components of a successful education system":[7]

1. The new system is committed to four operating assumptions:

- **All students can learn at significantly higher levels.**
- **We know how to teach all students successfully.**
- **Curriculum content must reflect high expectations for all students, but instructional time and strategies may vary to ensure success.**
- **Every child must have an advocate.**

2. The new system is performance- or outcome-based.

3. Assessment strategies must be as strong and rich as the outcomes.

4. School success is rewarded and school failure penalized.

5. School-based staff have a major role in making instructional decisions.

6. Major emphasis is placed on staff development.

7. A high-quality, pre-kindergarten program is established, at least for all disadvantaged students.

8. Health and other social services are sufficient to reduce significant barriers to learning.

9. Technology is used to raise student and teacher productivity and to expand access to learning.

The lingo is easily identifiable as being from the OBE/TQM school. Look at point No. 1's repeated reference to "all children," as opposed to "each child." The plan is out of the group-think model, as opposed to one based on individual merit.

The BRT's 1994 Education Initiative for the State of New Jersey put flesh on the barebones principles.[8] It asserted that "the State should establish standards that all students should achieve. These standards should articulate what all students should know and be able to do, and include skills such as critical thinking, problem solving, and those recommended by the (Labor) Secretary's Commission on Achieving Necessary Skills (SCANS)." SCANS directed that schools teach such "workplace competencies" as "interpersonal skills," defined this way: "They can work on teams, teach others, serve customers, lead, negotiate, and work well with people from culturally diverse backgrounds."

That's more Deming-down. The purpose of education is to train simpletons to be compliant TQM munchkins for big business. As for assessment "as strong and rich as the outcomes" (more boilerplate OBE), the BRT said this means performance exams testing the student's application of skills and knowledge "in either a live performance or an end product": portfolios—a collection of the student's work over time; and "project exams," which would evaluate "extended participation in a task that has meaning in the world." How's that? As opposed to having meaning on Jupiter? Or having no meaning in the world?

Upon passage of the Clintons' Goals 2000, the BRT declared in a rededication to its OBE agenda that, "All (teachers, administrators, and aides) will have to adjust to the idea that the work of schools is governed by a commitment to standards of achievement, not by rules about how long or how hard students and teachers must work."[9] Words like "will have to" and "must" permeate BRT manifestos, leaving no room for disagreement, or any leeway for local parents. (A thought: If OBE schools must eliminate rules about getting class work in on time, will OBE-loving businesses eliminate their deadlines, too?)

Until 1993, the BRT Education Task Force was run by IBM's John Anderson, who has taken over the New American School Development Corporation, which was established under Bush's America 2000 to open so-called "Break the Mold" schools. As of July, 1994, the BRT

Education Task Force was chaired by Joe Gorman, CEO of TRW. Among other key players are Frank Shrontz, chairman and CEO of Boeing, and Robert Kennedy of Union Carbide. In addition the CEOs of the following corporations were on the task force promoting OBE:

BellSouth, Xerox, K-mart, Gannett, McGraw-Hill, Springs Industries, Morgan Stanley & Co., Amoco, Ashland Oil, the Perkin-Elmer Corporation, Colgate-Palmolive, United Parcel Service, ARA Services, Aluminum Company of America, UNUM Corporation, the Kroger Co., MCI Communications, Cummins Engine, Circuit City Stores, CPC International, Marsh & McLennan, Bell Atlantic, Manville, J.P. Morgan & Co., Whirlpool, and United Air Lines.

By no means are those are the only corporate players. In 1991, the Committee for Economic Development, a New York-based group of 225 corporate leaders and educators, issued a report called, "The Unfinished Agenda: A New Vision for Child Development and Education," that echoed regular Carnegie Foundation calls for vastly expanding social programs in the early childhood and into regular school.[10] The report called on business leaders to get communities to support "a comprehensive and coordinated strategy of human investment"—beginning at birth and covering all aspects of development and growth. The CED said $10.23 billion in additional public spending would be required to ensure that all children arrive at school physically, emotionally, and mentally ready for school.

Said James J. Renier, chairman and CEO of Honeywell, Inc., who led the group that drafted the report: School reformers "have a tendency to speak of the problem as academic in nature—improving math and science achievement, and that sort of thing. They haven't been as focused on the social agenda." True to the CED's wishes, Goals 2000 and the ESEA reauthorization have a heavy social agenda, including turning schools into one-stop shopping centers for social services (see Chapter 10).

But the crux of the industrial/education complex's agenda lies in the third, and least noticed, of the school reform bills passed by Congress in 1994: the School-to-Work Opportunities Act. This measure has the teeth to enforce a work-based learning model on American schools, in keeping with the design propounded in the 1990 Ira Magaziner/Hillary Clinton report, "America's Choice: High Skills or Low Wages!," and the series of elaborate blueprints published as a follow-up by SCANS, under the chairmanship of a former (Republican) Labor Secretary, William Brock.

Goals 2000 sets up under the wing of the Labor Department (where Secretary Robert Reich is a long time OBE/Deming-down advocate) a National Skills Standards Board that is to define the skills necessary for every job in the country. But School-to-Work goes even further: Through federally approved state plans, it will specify how the schools are to inculcate and certify those workplace competencies in all children. And it sets up a system for tracking children early on through "career majors" toward employment in specific industries. Counseling would begin "at the earliest possible age, but not later than the seventh grade." (Title I, Sec. 101.)[11]

Were this merely an effort to keep education abreast of workplace changes in a technological era and to enhance student's career options (as an exercise of their own free will), there might be much to commend in School to Work. Unfortunately, however, there is a strong element of paternalism. Section 6103 mandates "a coherent sequence of courses that (provide) the students . . . with strong experience in and understanding of all aspects of the industry the students *are planning to enter.* (Emphasis added)." But many young people don't decide on a field of work, much less a specific industry, while they are still in high school. School to Work seems to anticipate forcing them to make an early choice, or somehow making it for them. Section 6146 indicates the extent to which education is to be coupled with economic forces. It calls for designing of model curricula "to integrate academic, vocational, and occupational learning, school-based and work-based learning, and secondary and postsecondary education for *all* students in the State." (Emphasis added.)

In essence, School to Work resolves by Big Brotherly fiat a long-standing debate between the liberal arts and applied education. Workplace "competencies" replace Cardinal Newman's idea of knowledge as a valuable end in itself. Somehow the objective of producing workers for a high-performance technological workplace has supplanted the ideal of preparing Americans to think for themselves by drawing on a solid base of knowledge as opposed to sheer emotion.

The SCANS reports flesh all this out.[12] Unfortunately, SCANS is not just another government commission the reports of which turn into dust collectors; its prescriptions are being put into the directed systemic change from coast to coast—from Florida to Oregon, two of the first states with gung-ho SCANS implementation. A key recommendation in the April, 1992, SCANS report "Learning a Living," was that the high school diploma be replaced with a Certificate of Initial Mastery (CIM) pegged to mastering the SCANS competencies. The commission's idea was that most students would earn their CIM by age 16—then to be forced into a choice of work, work training, or college.[13] But, true to the principles of Mastery Learning, "Students may take as long as they need, and the schools will be obliged to provide education that enables students to acquire the certificate, and to provide the services necessary for students of any age, both in-school and out-of-school, to meet this goal. Thus, the system is not 'pass/fail' but 'ready/try again.' " (And again and again and again.)[14]

Sure enough, by Spring 1994, the Carnegie-spawned National Center on Education and the Economy, which sponsored the Magaziner/H. R. Clinton pro-OBE report, was unveiling its design for a CIM. Marc Tucker and Boeing's Frank Shrontz were touting the CIM as a replacement for the traditional high school diploma, which they derisively pictured as measuring nothing but time spent in a seat. (That may be news to students who struggled to pass trig and English literature to earn their honors diplomas.) But what of value would the CIM measure? The SCANS commissioners conceded that civil rights laws would prevent businesses from using the attainment of CIM as a criterion in hiring. (And besides if **everybody** gets a "world-class" CIM, what distinctions are to be made about ability anyway?) But they added that employers could review for hiring purposes all the information on the SCANS resume that is supposed to replace the traditional report card.

Ah, yes, the student resume. Beginning in middle school, it would be a cumulative resume containing data about "courses taken, projects completed, and proficiency levels attained in each competency," and a student who had shown enough stuff on his resume would win a CIM, the SCANS report stated. But the sample SCANS resume was a good bit more revealing than that. It contained a place for the student's Social Security number and home address, and called for ratings not only of the "workplace competencies" (resources, interpersonal skills, information, technology, and systems) but also the SCANS "personal qualities" of responsibility, self-esteem, sociability, self-management, and integrity/honesty.[15]

Moreover, these largely subjective evaluations of a student's persona would go into a big computer and receive heavy use. The report stated that the Educational Testing Service, the nation's major publisher of tests, was preparing an "employer-friendly system called WORKLINK through which these assessments of a student's personal qualities could be shared electronically with businesses. Somehow that doesn't seem very little-guy-friendly. Sure enough, the National Institute of Business Management's October, 1993, newsletter reported that, "New Jersey is pilot-testing WORKLINK statewide. Once in place, it will let a firm access information on high school grads by phone, fax, or computer, thus eliminating at least some of the guessy aspects of the hiring process.'[16] (Not to mention some of the gutsy aspects of personal privacy.)

As incredible as it may seem, the industrial/education bigwigs pushing what they are pleased to call "systemic reform" of education are not really seeking to raise literacy levels. Ponder carefully the statement of Thomas B. Sticht, an associate director for basic skills of the National Institute of Education at the time he joined industrialists on SCANS:

"Many companies have moved operations to places with cheap, relatively poorly-educated labor. What may be crucial, they say, is the dependability of a labor force and how well it can be managed and trained, not its general educational level, although a small cadre of highly educated creative people is essential to innovation and growth. Ending discrimination and changing values are probably more important than reading in moving low-income families into the middle class."[17]

And hear the words of a major government educationist in the restructuring movement, Dr. Shirley McCune, senior director of the federally funded, Mid-continent Regional Education Laboratory, keynoting a Kansas education summit in 1989:

"Curriculum is not simply putting some facts in kids' minds and it isn't teaching them the past {sic} history of the world . . . but we also have to prepare them with the range of knowledge and skills that they're going to need for their personal, psychological well-being, their self-esteem, their ethics, their ability to give and care for others, with group organizational skills working with people who are different than they are. We're going to have to provide them with Career Development skills. All of those are clearly part of what has to be a part of the curriculum."[18]

That sort of reasoning may be expected from someone who has spent too much time in the company of ed-school graduates. But I never thought I would see the day that supposedly clear-thinking business leaders were buying into such edubabble. OBEist David Hornbeck has held sway with the BRT and business councils around the country. Most recently, he prepared an OBE plan for Alabama that enjoyed business establishment backing. And Hornbeck, with Lester Salamon, actually suggest in their co-edited book, "Human Capital and America's Future," that it may be counter-productive—from the business perspective—to educate students to too-high a level:

"What is more, employer beliefs about the superior capabilities of educated employees turned out not to be confirmed in practice; educated employees have higher turnover rates, lower job satisfaction, and poorer promotion records than less educated employees." And Salamon added this thought regarding employers training their own employees: "One final complication arises from the fact that, unlike physical capital, human capital cannot be owned by someone else."[19]

(Well, yes, not since the days of slavery anyway—and surely the plan isn't to take the servile arts to that extreme.)

Big business has made the serious mistake of misidentifying its needs for minimally educated entry-level workers with what is best for Americans as a whole. There is more to life than workplace competencies. Reading and appreciating Thoreau's reflections on nature or Longfellow's poetry may have little, if any, application to business. But the ability to read, to survey the sweep of history for what lessons it may impart, and to plumb the mysteries of pure science are all part of what it means to be human. Not someone's human capital, mind you, just an individual human.

Business also errs in presuming that it has some sort of right to impose its utilitarian scheme on communities across the nation. In January, 1995, a BRT spokesman told me the organization was still committed to implementing its brand of reform in every state in the nation.

What can citizens do to make their displeasure known in corporate boardrooms? Well, they could write to the CEOs and invite them to come out to the grassroots and talk to some real people about schools—as opposed to their staffers and pricey consultants. Or if that doesn't work, they could buy a share of stock, go to the stockholders' meetings, and inquire as to why the management has taken leave of its senses.

How Strange the Gullibility Of the Big Business Community

By Lil Tuttle Virginia

Information was essential. We had to know what the scope of the state's plan was and how it fit into the national restructuring efforts. Armed with little more than telephones, fax machines, computer modems, and contacts, we began to gather state and national documents. Each document led us to more sources. We needed to know who was involved in this restructuring, and we found some pretty heavy hitters: the Business Roundtable, federal and state Departments of Education, several Regional Education Laboratories, the Carnegie Foundation, the National Education Association, the Children's Defense Fund, the National Association for the Education of Young Children, People for the American Way, the National Center on Education and the Economy, the National Association of School Boards, the National Association of State Boards of Education, to name a few.

We had to know why this was gaining such momentum. The motivations were varied: to acquire money and power; to avoid accountability; to further a liberal/progressive political agenda. Some knew exactly where they were headed, and others were duped. The gullibility of the big business community was most surprising. Not one of those corporate executives would have invested in an untested, multibillion-dollar plan put forth by a business entity with a 30-year track record of failure—yet they bought and sold the DOE's plan. Unbelievable!

Although education was a hot topic at the grassroots level, press coverage was generally shallow and often limited to the official rhetoric provided by the State (much the way coverage of Goals 2000 and other federal education legislation has been lately.) Rarely was any substance of the State's plan reported or evaluated. If the content of the plan was to reach the general public, it wouldn't be through the mainstream press.

10

Federal Social Agendas

Citizens can battle OBE and related education quackery in their own communities, but to be fully effective they also must be aware of the genesis of many of the wrong-headed policies at the national level. They have to understand that the statists' agenda goes far beyond a traditional education in the Three Rs and morality. And they need to make their influence felt in Washington.

For a time, I found that practically every column on OBE I wrote for my paper in Richmond, Virginia, would draw a heated letter to the editor from one of the bigwigs on the national Systemic Change Gang. U.S. Secretary of Education, Richard Riley, wrote four himself. His public affairs director dutifully penned another one. Marc Tucker, the big enchilada from the National Center on Education and the Economy, sent a letter that was critical of me and my work; and so did William H. Kolberg, president and CEO of the National Alliance of Business.

This flattering attention given one politically incorrect editor in the South speaks volumes about just how "voluntary" the agenda behind restructured education is to be.

In a September, 1993, presentation to a conference of state Chapter 1, ESEA directors, Secretary Riley proclaimed that Goals 2000 "would create a national partnership for educational excellence." He called the measure "the legislative framework for all of our reform proposals."[1]

At the same gathering, Undersecretary Marshall Smith said that "content-based systemic reform" was Washington's objective.[2]

And to complete the hype, Thomas Payzant, the Assistant Secretary for Elementary and Secondary Education, gushed that in reauthorizing the ESEA and passing Goals 2000, "We want to create an 'ethic of learning' across America. This ethic begins and ends with a straightforward premise: high standards will replace minimum standards—high standards for **all** children."[3]

Content? Excellence? Ethic of learning? High academic standards and accountability have been the sales pitch; but the reality of the heavy federal incursion into elementary and secondary education is quite different.

To begin, how does encouraging youngsters to play basketball half the night prepare them to pursue high academic standards the next morning? Remember federally subsidized midnight basketball, and the hullabaloo in Congress over whether it would be kept in the crime bill? Well, Goals 2000 had already been passed by Congress and signed by the President, with Part D of it being the Midnight Basketball League Training and Partnership Act. That's right—Congress had already provided handsomely for midnight basketball (with grants of up to $130,000 for small leagues and more for those with more than 80 players) in the education bill even as the politicos were haggling further over the matter.

This is an example of redundant social legislating. A program seeded in several mammoth bills stands a better chance of survival than if it were planted in only one. And it also shows that with so many huge bills of a thousand pages or more, many Congressmen haven't been aware of all that they were passing. Let's hope the new Republican-controlled Congress (which promises to be more wary of Big Government) will do a better job. But here is a service that alert citizens groups can perform: Obtain copies of legislation and read and analyze the contents. Then fax information to lawmakers and other concerned people about key sections. The Pennsylvania Parents Commission (P.O. Box 73, Johnstown, PA, 15907)—Anne Barbera, chairman—has done a particularly outstanding job of bird-dogging federal legislation.

The strange case of Johnson City, New York, is a prime example of how the feds and their allies have been attempting to push one model of change—the OBE model—on all schools in America. Johnson City is a blue-collar school district of fewer than 3,000 pupils, with only one high school. In no way could it be characterized as America in microcosm. Yet the U.S. Department of Education, through its National Diffusion Network, has been providing Johnson City's school system $100,000 a year to tout the educational Nirvana that has supposedly been attained there since OBE began to be installed 20 years ago. Here is that shining OBE school district on the hill, where failure has been abolished and "high self-esteem" is a graduation requirement. Pupils don't receive Fs for poor work—only "Incompletes" and then retest after retest after retest. Johnson City school administrators, past and present, have proclaimed these schools far and wide to be glittering successes.

When, during a televised discussion in 1993, I asked Virginia Secretary of Education, James Dyke, for an example of where OBE had worked, he responded "Johnson City." Since then, I have found that citizens across the nation have been fed the same pap by their own official OBE shills: Johnson City is the success story that "proves" OBE should be instituted in local schools.

There's just one problem: This is either ideological fantasy or outright deception. Johnson City's academic record is strictly mediocre. Printouts of State Regents Exam data from the New York State Department of Education (as of February, 1994) show that Johnson City isn't even an exemplar for its own metropolitan area. Johnson City is one of 12 school districts in Broome County, New York. Just look at how its academic results stack up:

- On the most important subject of all—reading—Johnson City's third graders ranked dead last among the dozen districts and its sixth-graders eleventh.
- On high school graduation tests, Johnson City's scores ranked in the lower half of the county in English, history, global studies, math I and II, and Spanish. Overall, the district was in the middle of the pack, tied for sixth and seventh.
- Its students averaged eighth of the 12 districts in reading, writing, science, and social studies in the lower grades.
- In not a single subject did Johnson City rank higher than fourth within Broome County. And its teacher turnover and student dropout rates were the worst in the county.

This is the model for the nation? What kind of Department of Education would spend tax money to propagate that claim across America? Answer: The same Education Department that would put out a Community Action Tool Kit to assist change agents and facilitators in molding "correct" attitudes toward school reform in every community.

There is a way, however, for OBE school districts like Johnson City's to declare themselves unequivocal successes. That would be by redefining success. No wonder the high priests of OBE are so anxious to do away with standardized testing and to replace it with squishy assessments. Scrapping the tests eliminates all basis of comparison with other school districts. For good reason, Johnson City has applied to New York State for an exemption from Regents' testing in all subjects. Like other OBE districts, it much prefers the subjective method of assessing portfolios of student projects. That would be more conducive to perpetuating the image of excellence in which Johnson City and the OBE hucksters are so heavily vested.

Clearly also the recent federal enactments on education are laden with social agendas that have only the most tenuous connection, if any at all, to academics. Midnight basketball is only a small example.

The school-based or school-linked health clinic is a major example. Provisions for such clinics will be found in every piece of what the Clintons and their sycophants call their "human capital and lifelong learning" scheme. The idea is that one-stop shopping for social services should be available for pupils and their families in every school. Teachers are asked to be less transmitters of knowledge than social workers.

A glimpse at what the Clintonites envisioned for school-based clinics (SBCs) as a part of systemic education reform might be had from a lengthy white paper prepared for the Council of Chief State School Officers in 1993 by then-Surgeon General Joycelyn Elders and Jennifer Hui, a planning specialist with the Arkansas Department of Health.[4] At the time, Dr. Elders was taking the lead in spelling out the social side of education reform. It's true that, post-1994 election (with President Clinton possibly looking for scapegoats), she was fired for making a controversial remark in a United Nations forum about the desirability of teaching schoolchildren about masturbation. But Dr. Elders had made many even more inflammatory statements before and had never been disciplined. She had advocated the dispensing of condoms to children as young as eight, for example, while declaring that children should be taught that sex is a "healthy part of our being, whether it is homosexual or heterosexual." While Elders' shoot-from-the-hip style became impolitic for a President hoping for re-election, there's no evidence the policies she espoused have been shelved.

Her formal paper used language that was more clinical—but perhaps in its own way more revealing—than the off-the-cuff comments. Dr. Elders contended that "social-health-economic" concerns must take priority over "religious-moral values"—and that educators should concentrate less on teaching the 3Rs and more on whether children "are physically, emotionally, and psychologically fit for learning." Then, in breathtaking detail, she outlined the Clinton plans for a "comprehensive school health program."

Consider the range of counseling sessions contemplated for SBCs set up under Goals 2000 and the ESEA. Pupils would be counseled on:

- sexuality
- contraceptive methods (condoms dispensed of course)
- sexually-transmitted diseases
- nutrition and weight reduction
- stress management
- alcohol and drug abuse prevention
- safety (seat belts, helmets)
- parenting

- suicide prevention
- family life
- "psychosocial" concerns (whatever those might be)
- jobs
- pregnancy (referrals for abortions)
- breast self-exam
- testicular self-exam
- welfare benefits
- child abuse

With such additional intrusions on classroom time (already severely crimped by non-academic activities), does anyone believe SAT scores would ever emerge from the pits? And would parents be given an absolute right to decide if a children would participate in such activities, some of them quite personal? Parents who have discovered that their children have been subjected to "self-esteem" counseling in elementary school without their knowledge or permission know the answer to that question.

The SBC Plan had this to say about parents: "So many of our social problems are worsened by parents' uninformed attitudes toward health and inappropriate behavior toward their children. Instruction, counsel, and peer discussion ought to be available." That sets the stage for the Parents as Teachers programs that are to be funded under Goals 2000. The idea is that parents should be taught by the state how to be good parents—the state having done such a brilliant job of handling other responsibilities. This could be the precursor of state licensing of parents. It opens wide the possibility for participating parents to have their children turned over to the tender mercies of the Child Protective Services if they violate some tenet of state-prescribed child-rearing (that children should never be spanked, for example).

Clearly, propagating the myth of total family collapse in America is critical to the promoters of the OBE model of systemic reform. And Joycelyn Elders was far from being the only trumpet for that viewpoint. Consider this canned article that the Virginia Department of Education distributed for suggested use in staff or parent newsletters to plug OBE:

"World Class Education is far more than a slogan, and those involved in education need to know a few things about it.

In the United States, public education consumes more than $200 billion each year. Virginia this year will spend in excess of $4.5 billion for kindergarten through grade 12. Despite these financial commitments, there is growing evidence that our schools are in trouble. Dropout rates remain too high; graduates both at college

and in the workplace lack the ability to compete with their counterparts in Western Europe and the Pacific Rim.

We need to acknowledge at the outset that the problems in public education in our country are not because principals and teachers do not care, or are not trying their utmost to help students learn. The reality is that schools today face many complex societal problems.

By the time a young person graduates from high school, he or she has spent just nine percent of his or her life in school. Teachers have to combat the stark reality of the other 91 percent. According to statistics from the Children's Defense Fund, today in America:

- **every 26 seconds, a child runs away from home;**
- **every 46 seconds, a child is abused or neglected;**
- **every 64 seconds, a teenager has a baby;**
- **every 14 hours, a child younger than five is murdered, and**
- **every seven minutes, a child is arrested for a drug offense.**

The non-school environment of a child in the last decade of the 20th century is vastly different from that of earlier generations. . . .[5]

The Children's Defense Fund, a left-wing group with which Hillary Clinton is closely associated, was the source of the only quantifiable data in that bleak diatribe about the "stark reality" of home life. And the CDF is hardly an objective source, given its vested interested in perpetuating dependency on the state. Dr. Sylvia Kraemer, a political liberal who actively opposes OBE, went to the trouble of cranking in data from under-18 children as a whole from the 1990 U.S. census, and found that the CDF scare figures used to promote "World Class Education" could be put in a quite different light:

- **every year less than 2% of our children run away from home;**
- **every year only 1% of our children are abused or neglected;**
- **every year only .7% of our teenagers have babies (and many of these will be 18 and 19 year olds, a 'normal' age for first marriages and births less than a century ago);**
- **every year .003% of the 18.3 million children under 5 years are murdered;**
- **every year .1% of our children are arrested for a drug offense."**[6]

Of course, as Dr. Kraemer notes, everyone should be concerned for the small group of children to which such horrible things happen. "But we ought not to distort the educational mission of schools to address the needs of this tiny minority of students. The vast majority of students go to school to learn, not to find a surrogate family."

The bottom line is that ideology is driving education policy. In an in-depth analysis of "The Failure of Sex Education" in *The Atlantic Monthly*, Barbara Dafoe Whitehead wrote of the utter lack of evidence that comprehensive sex education is working. Teenage pregnancy and the incidence of sexually-transmitted disease are soaring despite mandated sex-ed from kindergarten through high school. Yet, the lack of empirical support does not deter or discomfit the advocates. "Up and down the sex-education ranks, from the Surgeon General to local advocates, there has been little effort to make a reasoned case for comprehensive sex education. Challenged, the sex educators simply crank up their rhetoric: Criticize sex education, they say, and you contribute to the deaths of teen-agers from AIDS."[7]

Added Ms. Whitehead:

"The underlying core of comprehensive sex education is not intellectual but ideological. Its mission is to defend and extend the freedoms of the sexual revolution, and its architects are called forth from a variety of pursuits to advance this cause. At least in New Jersey {one of the first states to mandate sex-ed}, the sex-education leaders are not researchers or policy analysts or child-development experts but public-sector entrepreneurs: advocates, independent consultants, family planners, freelance curriculum writers, specialty publishers, and diversity educators. However dedicated and high-minded they may be, their principal task is not to serve the public or schoolchildren but to promote their ideology."

Related social agendas permeate the laws that are supposed to improve the quality of schooling. A prime example is the Women's Educational Equity Act of 1994, which was inserted in the ESEA reauthorization. By way of advancing the radical-feminist mindset that all girls are victims, this law sets up the federal government in the business of passing judgment on teaching methods and textbooks.

The Women's Equity Act (an interesting title implying equity is for one sex only) claims that "teaching and learning practices . . . are frequently inequitable" for women and girls; that "classroom textbooks and other educational materials do not sufficiently reflect the experiences, achievements, or concerns of women and, in most cases, are not written by women or persons of color;" that girls do not take as many mathematics and science courses as boys, girls lose confidence in their mathematics and science ability as girls move through adolescence, and there are few women role models in the sciences."[8] It authorized $5 million in Fiscal Year 1995 and at least that much in FYs 1996 through 1999 for "gender equitable teaching." That mixed bag would include the creation of new "curricula, textbooks, software, and other educational materials to ensure the absence of gender stereotyping and bias."

Commenting on that, the Washington-based Independent Women's Forum stated: "Congress has now required that your children be brainwashed with the new feminist agenda: that girls are oppressed beginning in nursery school and boys are natural-born victimizers and predators."[9]

The feminist agenda was advanced through some highly dubious education "research." The American Association of University Women released a study, based on interviews with 3,000 boys and girls, supposedly showing that schools systematically destroy the self-esteem of girls. Between the ages of 11 and 16, girls supposedly suffered a 31-percent drop in self-esteem, and boys a 23 percent drop. The AAUW surmised that this feeling-good "gap" was hurting girls' academic achievement. Basically, the AAUW asked the boys and girls about their happiness—a method said by independent reviewers to be a fallacious basis for making self-esteem ratings. Other researchers have said their studies have shown little, if any, difference between girls' and boys' self-esteem. The AAUW declined to release its data for objective review.

"The truth about girls and education," said the Independent Women's Forum, "is much different than the propaganda. Girls are succeeding in school at **higher** rates than boys. Girls get better grades. More girls than boys graduate from high school. Women make up 55 percent of college enrollment. More women than men pursue post-graduate degrees. While boys continue to lag far behind girls on achievement scores in reading and writing, girls are catching up to boys in science and math."[10]

The Forum called the Women's Equity Act "feminist pork." The act "ensures that feminist ideologues—whose day jobs are researchers and educators—will get millions of federal dollars to build an educational establishment dedicated to 'gender equitable teaching.' In the meantime, they will be delivering an insidious message to our boys and girls: Girls can't succeed on their own; they need legal or institutional help."

A pervasive agenda—as mentioned in previous chapters—is that of the Progressive Educators, or the neoprogressivist OBE advocates. HR6 contained a dead giveaway to the intentions of the OBEists when it make the follows audacious assertion under a didactic "What Has Been Learned" section:

"The disproven theory that children must first learn basic skills before engaging in more complex tasks continues to dominate strategies for classroom instruction, resulting in emphasis on repetitive drill and practice at the expense of content-rich instruction, accelerated curricula, and effective teaching to high standards."[11]

Disproven theory? What bogus research could be advanced to "prove" that children need not have a foundation in the basics before proceeding to solve the problems of the world? In true Orwellian fashion, that provision stood truth on its head. What actually has been learned in more than 125 research studies—including comprehensive surveys by Jeanne Chall of the Harvard Graduate School of Education—is that phonetic decoding is the most effective and cost-efficient way to teach children to read.[12] Any rational person (which may not include OBE's most ardent fans) knows that reading is the key to higher learning. The "disproven theory" dictum was a dagger pointed at what phonetic programs remain in public schools, because phonics necessarily entails some degree of drill and repetition (which need not be synonymous with drudgery, as the use of music in the successful commercial program, "Hooked on Phonics," shows). The OBEists favor whole language, which is basically a repackaged version of the look-say method favored by yesterday's progressivists.

The National Right to Read Foundation, which is directed by former Education and Justice Department official Robert Sweet, led a successful campaign to have the blatantly anti-phonics language changed. Nevertheless, the original language was a tip-off to the mindset of the bureaucrats who will be writing the regulations for the new education laws.

Finally, power is an agenda unto itself, While TQM-style, site-based management lends the appearance of increased local flexibility, the ESEA obliges states to take drastic actions against local school systems adjudged to be out of compliance with OBE standards.[13] "Corrective action" must be taken, which may include:

- the withholding of funds;
- reconstitution of school district personnel (mass firings);
- removal of particular schools from the jurisdiction of the local educational agency and establishment of alternative arrangements for public governance and supervision of such schools;
- implementation of the opportunity-to-learn standards or strategies developed by such State under the Goals 2000: Educate America Act;
- appointment by the state educational agency of a receiver or trustee to administer the affairs of the local educational agency in place of the superintendent and the school board;
- the abolition or restructuring of the local educational agency;
- transfers of students; or
- some unspecified joint state/local remedial plan.

Or as one school board association official put it, "I don't think any {corrective action} is left off that list short of a nuclear attack on the school districts." Even the liberal leadership of the National School Boards Association, which otherwise supported Goals 2000, protested this unprecedented federal threat against the autonomy of local school boards.[14] (And school boards are endangered in other ways: In Pennsylvania, newly elected conservative board members were fending off attempts to force them into compulsory indoctrination by the state bureaucracy.)

Bruno Manno, a senior fellow at the Hudson Institute and a proponent of education reform based strictly on academic outcomes, wrote in a paper alleging the "hijacking" of OBE by educationists that the Clinton administration, through Goals 2000, "has abetted the effort to shift the focus from what our children learn to what education bureaucrats spend."[15] Manno said the 19-member National Education Standards and Improvement Council (NESIC) "will certify education standards (on 'content, performance, and opportunity to learn') that states 'voluntarily' submit to it. In reality, it will be a sort of national school board whose members will be the usual education-establishment suspects—experts in school finance and equity and the long laundry list of educators, activists, and interest-group representatives. Goals 2000 will make these bureaucrats more powerful than, for example, the National Governors' Association's Education Goals Panel. For this reason, the NGA withheld (its) endorsement of the final Goals 2000 legislation."

Furthermore, Manno observed, "Goals 2000 creates NESIC-sanctioned national delivery or opportunity-to-learn standards. The latter term is simply the new educational jargon for inputs and services. These standards will measure whether there is an 'adequate' supply of money, programs, and other human and physical resources in every school, every district, and every state. These are standards for schools, not for students. Moreover, these standards will certainly provide the impetus for new lawsuits aiming to force states to redistribute resources among various schools and districts."

Summing up the impact of all the federal legislation, he wrote, "None of this will provide our students with an enhanced opportunity to learn. It will, however, provide education bureaucrats with expanded opportunities to spend, litigate, and regulate."

An inkling of the kind of content standards that might be coming down from the national school board came with the release of proposed national standards for teaching American history, developed by the National Center for History in the Schools at UCLA. The standards are politically correct to a fault, giving blanket coverage to such warts on America as the KKK and Joe McCarthy, but scant mention of George Washington and none at all of General Robert E. Lee. The Great Depression is a major topic, but the development and tenets of the Constitution receive little attention. For OBE-style performances, students are asked to do such things as, "Analyze the impact of the Great Depression on the American family and gender roles. (Consider multiple perspectives)," and "Explain the impact of the Great Depression on African-Americans, Mexican-Americans, and Native Americans (Consider multiple perspectives)."

Lynne Cheney, chairman of the National Endowment for the Humanities when the NEH made the grant to develop the history standards, was appalled at the direction they took—so much so that she played the key role in blowing the whistle on their PC content, and in calling for an end to the politicized process of writing national curricular standards.[16]

What about you? If the agendas being advanced through the maze of legislation and regulation are not your agendas, what can you do about it? That will be the subject of the final two chapters.

Here's How To Lobby Your Elected Representatives

By Anne Barbera
Pennsylvania

When lobbying regarding the federal bills Goals 2000 and ESEA (the "Improving America's Schools Act"), we first ordered copies of the bills. When our Congressmen or Senators would not send us a copy, we obtained it directly from the Senate Document Room. We also obtained critiques of the bills from various national pro-family organizations such as the Family Research Council. In reviewing those critiques, it made us more sensitive to certain issues when we read and critiqued the bills ourselves.

In order to be effective in lobbying, you must be very familiar with the bill you are discussing. We found that most often we knew more about the bill than the legislative aides we met with. Very, very few lawmakers or their assistants read the bills. They are prepped by the lobbying forces of the Departments—in this case, the Department of Education. You must challenge them to read the bill themselves by pointing out specific sections and what is actually said in them.

First, learn your material well. Set a goal to educate on specific sections of the bill, know the wording of these sections—what they say and what they do not say. Often legislators have been led to believe the bill will accomplish something not contained therein. Do not back down, if the wording is not in the bill.

Second, put your arguments in outline form, quoting or citing the specific sections of the bill. If possible, find back-up material to substantiate your position. Make copies of these plus any other short articles pertinent to the subject. Make packets for each legislator you will visit.

Third, remember the legislators and their staff are busy and will only give you a short time. They will not read any lengthy material; therefore, only short, thorough, and well-documented critiques are valuable. Your knowledge of the subject, polite mannerisms, and genuine concern will be the key to whether they even read the material. Emotionalism does not win the battle. Try to get a commitment from the legislator.

Fourth, set up an appointment, get the date, time, and the contact person to whom you spoke to make the appointment. We found some legislative staff denied we had an appointment, but we stuck to our guns and did meet with the education staff person. From now on, I will always have the date and the staff member who made the appointment. We wanted to lobby all one hundred Senators and as many Congressmen as possible. We contacted pro-family people in all the states. If they were unable to travel to Washington, we requested them to make an appointment with their own legislators. We then kept the appointment for them, telling the legislative staff member that they had requested we visit them, as indeed they had.

Fifth, divide up the appointments among those who do show up to lobby. Give each the name of the legislator, their building and room number, the appointment time, the name of their constituent for whom you are lobbying, the date and name of the staff member who made the appointment, packets of material for each legislator with any specific instructions on the legislation. Additional packets could be left with other legislative staff, with whom you did not have appointments. Plan for the lobbyist to return pertinent information to you. Prepare a sheet with the information needed, such as name of the legislator visited, their reaction, pertinent comments, commitment, etc. Have these faxed or mailed to you as quickly as possible. Get back to the people in your state and other states to let them know what additional work needs to be done with their legislator.

All in all, we must remember that the majority of the staff members in Congress are young, recent graduates of our ultraliberal universities and are idealistic, not realistic. They actually do not know the real world and yet they are the ones writing the bills, gathering the information, and advising the legislators. We must always treat them with respect, build up their ego, and then from knowledge and logic let them have the facts about the legislation at hand. We must dress and act professionally, because appearance is quite important to this young generation. Wear comfortable shoes; the halls of Congress are long and offices are in many buildings.

National talk radio shows are of utmost importance in fighting federal legislation. For some people, it is their only knowledge of the subject. We sent our critiques of the bills to as many talk radio shows as possible. Some of the hosts invited us to be guests by way of telephone hook-up. Christian radio stations will also give out news that is not heard in the general media. Conservative newspaper columnists are another very important vehicle to use. Not only should we send all of these a critique of the proposed legislation but also any material that verifies our claims.

National pro-family organizations are of the utmost importance.

They will put information in their national newsletters, and assist you in getting information out through their local and state chapters. Concerned Women for America was most helpful in keeping us updated on the progress of bills in Congress. Their chapters close to the District of Columbia helped in the lobbying effort.

Tremendous support came from the Eagle Forum, a national group of very dedicated and well-informed activists. They have had tremendous experience in fighting and winning national battles such as the one over ratification of the Equal Rights Amendment. Phyllis Schlafly puts out two monthly publications, which are always thorough and easy to understand. *The Education Reporter* publishes accounts of education battles and successes nationwide—quoting from the materials in question, state legislation, etc., and giving detailed accounts of how the battle was fought. Many of the Eagle Forum's state chapters have telephone chains as well as their own newsletters. Today they have more expertise in the education arena. Other groups offered their own critiques—some of which were helpful, but some of which lacked sufficient documentation, such as citations of the sections of legislation.

Freedom Works: Ask the Home Schoolers

By Michael P. Farris
President,
Home School Legal Defense Association

In 1993, Virginia saw one of the greatest evidences of the power of grassroots activism on educational issues. We killed the state mandate for Outcome-Based Education through a variety of activities that arose from a heart-driven concern for children, academics, and freedom. That story is told in this book by one of the principal architects of that victory.

One might wonder whether other parents in other venues fighting similar issues can ever have a realistic hope to succeed. I believe they can, because just months after our OBE victory, I was called on again to participate in another battle for educational freedom. This time the venue was Congress. And this time the parents were parents from home schools and private schools who wanted to preserve their right to educate their children.

How did we do?

Well, for eight days in February, the home schoolers of this nation gave Congress a lesson on the power of grassroots politics it is not likely to forget.

It began when Congressman George Miller (D CA-7) introduced an amendment to H.R. 6, an enormous education reauthorization bill, which would have required all teachers in America to be certified in each and every course they teach. This provision would have hampered public schools—especially small public high schools. It would have seriously interfered with America's private schools. But for home schools, the Miller provision was the political equivalent of a nuclear attack. America's home schoolers astonished Congress with a political counter-strike that was quick, effective, massive, and decisive.

Added shortly before the Education and Labor Committee was to return the bill to the House, the Miller amendment *(Section 2124 (e))* stated:

"ASSURANCE.—*Each state applying for funds under this title shall provide the Secretary with the assurance that after July 1, 1998, it will require each local educational agency within the State to certify that each full time teacher in schools under the jurisdiction of the agency is certified to teach in the subject area to which he or she is assigned."*

This amendment alone would have raised serious concerns for home schoolers. But coupled with the new definition of schools, it was deadly. The word "nonprofit" had been added to the definition of schools in H.R. 6, changing the definition for the first time since the Elementary and Secondary Education ACT (ESEA) was enacted in 1965.

"§ 9101 (11) The term 'elementary school' means a non-profit day or residential school that provides elementary education, as determined under State law."

"§ 9101 (20) The term 'secondary school' means a non-profit day or residential school that provides secondary education, as determined under State law, except that it does not include any education beyond grade 12."

The addition of the word "non-profit" to each of these definitions eliminates any ambiguity as to whether private and home schools were included in the definition of school.

Concerned by the implications of the Miller amendment and the new definitional language, Representative Dick Armey (R TX-26) offered an amendment to protect home and private schools from the certification requirement. Armey's amendment read:

"Nothing in this title shall be construed to authorize or encourage Federal control over the curriculum or practices of any private, religious, or home school."

This amendment was rejected in committee.

It was at this point, on February 14, 1994, that Representative Armey's office contacted HSLDA for our analysis of the Miller amendment.

Based upon review of the Miller amendment, the definitional language, and our 11 years of defending home schools against legal challenges from local education agencies, we knew that it was imperative to add protective language to the bill. It is beyond dispute that local school authorities believe that home schools and private schools are under their jurisdiction.

The danger was seriously exacerbated when the Education Committee rejected Dick Armey's original amendment. If the intent of Congress was directed exclusively at public schools, what was the justification for rejecting Armey's original amendment? By doing so, Congress created a legal presumption that it intended to force home schools and private schools to adhere to the standards in this legislation.

We immediately contacted Representative Miller's office to express our concern and ask for clarifying language. However, Mr. Miller's staff told us flatly that he would not agree to any amendment to

§ 2124(e). With a vote only nine days away, we had no choice but to contact our members.

By the evening of February 16, 1994, "Urgent Alert" letters had been mailed to HSLDA's entire membership list of 37,000 families. The letter summarized the situation and outlined a six-step plan of action for contacting Congress and spreading the alert to friends and neighbors. Also contained in the mailing was a list of the Representatives whose offices did not need to be contacted because they had already assured HSLDA of their support for the protective language.

People were amazed by the ability of the home-schooling community to respond quickly and in massive numbers to the threat posed by H.R. 6. There are three central reasons the home-schooling community was able to respond in this manner:

1. HOME SCHOOLS WERE ORGANIZED

The day after Bill Clinton was elected, we started getting an enormous number of calls from people who were panicked that Clinton would work to revoke home-schooling freedoms. Our response was: "This is not a time for panic but a time for preparation."

Frankly, the greatest danger posed by a liberal President is not the actions that are likely to be undertaken by his administration. The greatest danger is that one or more Congressmen will be emboldened by the atmosphere created by such a presidency to attempt legislative maneuvers that would be unthinkable with another in the White House.

We wanted to be prepared for any attack coming from the education establishment and their friends in government. So in January, 1993, we created the Congressional Action Program (CAP) to assist in the event a federal legislative emergency arose.

But the real preparation and organization work has been done over the past 10 years by state and local home school groups that have worked to advance the cause of home-schooling freedom. The Home School Legal Defense Association and the National Center for Home Education simply built a "federal response network" to function effectively with the existing state and local home school groups. The decade of preparation that preceded this alert was essential in our collective ability to respond quickly and effectively.

2. HOME SCHOOLERS WERE EDUCATED.

If we had been required to spend a long time explaining to the home-schooling community why teacher certification was a bad idea, we would have been dead in the water. The first major threat ever to endanger the home school movement came from the laws in a number of states that required all teachers (including home school parents) to be certified.

One by one the states removed these laws. The last three states to relinquish certification laws created home-schooling legends. North Dakota, Iowa, and Michigan were the famous triumvirate of evil for their steadfast insistence on teacher certification laws. Nationally, almost all home schoolers closely followed the Bismarck Tea Party, the *Dejonge* case in Michigan, and the multiple tribulations faced by parents in Iowa.

Fighting these battles not only served to educate home schoolers on the substance of the teacher certification issue, it also gave them valuable experience in the intricacies of the political process. For example, home schoolers were well-schooled in the principle that all calls and letters must be polite. The overwhelming feedback we have received from Congress is that home schoolers were incredibly polite, yet very firm.

Moreover, most home schoolers were sufficiently politically sophisticated to refuse to be misled by the tactics of Congressmen Miller, Ford, and Kildee. These and many other congressional offices tried to convince callers that the threat to home schooling was non-existent.

The reality is that Congress had conducted no hearings on the Miller provision. There was no evidence that a federal teacher certification rule was a good idea for public schools. It is probable that Miller and others never thought about how their language would affect home schools and private schools, but their absence of subjective sinister intentions was wholly irrelevant. What mattered was the legal meaning of the words employed in the Act.

In all of the cases challenging teacher certification laws that we have handled, there has never been a law that was originally written to apply to home schooling. In every case, a law written generally to apply to all teachers ended up forcing home schoolers into compliance. There are often unintended consequences to legislation. And most home schoolers were smart enough not to be misled by condescending assurances.

Moreover, many of the Congressmen making these assertions had not read the relevant provisions, not had they read the corresponding definitional sections, nor did they have any understanding of the home school law in their states. Indeed, Congressman Ford called home schoolers in Michigan "truants" in his speech on the floor of the House. (He later corrected the printed text merely to say that home schoolers were violating the compulsory attendance law.) Most home schoolers knew better than to be led astray by the assurances of "intent" made by people who publicly decry home schooling as nothing more than truancy.

3. HOME SCHOOLERS ACTED ON THEIR BELIEFS.

Tens of millions of people were concerned about homosexuals in the military. Likewise, millions held strong views about NAFTA. Every American was directly affected by the Clinton budget and tax increases. Yet, according to some Congressmen, many congressional offices received more calls on H.R. 6 than on those other three issues combined.

Many other people called on H.R. 6 besides home schoolers. But everyone recognized that the lion's share of the activity came from home schoolers.

Most Americans complain about various proposals in Congress. However, until those complaints are directed into meaningful political action, very little will be accomplished.

But I must confess that I long for the day in which freedom-loving Americans, affronted by the continual erosion of their liberties in other arenas, will demonstrate the same degree of seriousness displayed by home schoolers protecting their educational liberty. It is my belief that those of us who believe in parent-directed education in the public schools have not because we ask not.

Mandated Family Life Education Was the Wake-Up Call

By Joe Gwynn
Virginia

As a husband and father of three children, and pastor of a small congregation in Virginia Beach, I never would have guessed that I would find myself embroiled in a major controversy over public schooling. Neither would I have imagined that I would help organize a group with a mailing list of more than 1,600 concerned parents. But that was before Family Life/Sex Education, Outcome-Based Education, Goals 2000, and World-Class Education. With three children enrolled in public schools, not to mention the children in my congregation, I could not justify remaining a bystander. It is presumptuous to think that an hour or two per week of Sunday School and Church, no matter how well done, can counterbalance the 35–40 hours per week our children spend in their classrooms.

In early 1989, the parents of Virginia were hit with a "Family Life/Sex Education" mandate by the Virginia General Assembly with several disturbing components. As I went through channels to voice my concerns, and was "stonewalled" at every turn, I became even more disturbed. I discovered that special-interest groups had been pushing Virginia legislators for mandated sex education a long time before we knew it was in the wind.

We quickly organized a group called Citizens for Better Education and did what we could to stop it. We added to our mailing lists every person who spoke at public hearings, or wrote an informed letter to the editor. Our list included Protestants, Catholics, Jews, Mormons, and some parents who did not attend church at all. We are white, black, Filipino, Asian, and Pacific Islander. What unites us is our common belief that parents' rights are inalienable, and that civil government in America was instituted to serve people, not vice-versa.

When more than a thousand parents showed up at a special School Board hearing to voice their opposition to family-life education, they made the front-page of the Norfolk *Virginian-Pilot*.. It was clear that the only people who wanted sex-ed in Virginia Beach were the people who had written it and those who planned to teach it. But it was approved anyway. The hearing was a sham. That experience with sex education was my "wake-up" call.

After that, I began to question *everything* the schools were doing. In hindsight, I had been quite naive. I still thought guidance counselors were in public schools to advise students about which courses to take. I had no idea that psychological counseling was being foisted upon elementary school children, with neither the consent nor knowledge of their parents. I had never head of Duso or Pumsey—psychological counseling techniques that most parents find offensive. The more I uncovered, the more determined I was to change things. I rarely missed a school board meeting. I also spoke out against what I saw was wrong, and wrote letters to local newspapers. Virginia was the only state in the Union still appointing all school board members, but we fought for and won the right to elect them.

Honor Roll

(Honoring grassroots organizations that have made a difference for the better in their communities.)

Citizens for Better Education

4916 Gulfstream Circle
Virginia Beach, Virginia, 23464

Joseph L. Gwynn, President, (804) 495-1600
Fran Faatz, Vice President, (804) 427-3031

Citizens for Better Education is a network of concerned citizens which consists mostly of the parents of public school children in Virginia Beach organized to monitor and improve the quality of public education. We believe it to be the God-given role of parents, not the state, to be the primary educators of our children. Likewise, American civil government exists to serve the people, not vice versa. We intend, therefore, to employ every lawful means to resist the supplanting of our parental rights and prerogatives by elitist educators and statist teachers' unions. We support those practices that foster traditional, American, Judaeo-Christian values and that provide mechanisms for meaningful parental involvement. In terms of curricula, we support the sound and proven and oppose the unsound and experimental.

11

Positive Alternatives

If you believe with all your heart and soul that a new dogma about to be forced on schools is wrong-headed and dangerous—and if you therefore oppose it in public debate as strongly as you know how—you probably will hear yourself categorized by the dogmatists as an "aginner" who favors a mediocre *status quo* in education.

I had that experience after I had sounded the alarm about OBE in my weekly newspaper column. One of the big business backers of OBE cited dropout rates and other statistical evidence of public schooling's shortcomings and charged that I had no ideas for constructive change—that I was just a naysayer. His implicit point was that the choice was between OBE and an unsatisfactory *status quo*.

His charge bothered me because it was unfair and untrue. In my 25 years of opinion writing—going way back before I'd ever heard of OBE—I must have written hundreds of columns advocating improvements in education. To cite a few examples, I had favored:

• Parental choice, both within the public school system and including private schools through tuition tax credits.

• Alternative certification of teachers, bypassing the ed-school Mickey Mouse courses.

• Phonics-based reading instruction.

• Merit pay for teachers.

• Beefed-up academic requirements for high school graduation.

• Distance learning, using technology to reach remote schools in the state, and to reduce educational disparity.

And so on.

But my critic did me a favor. He made me realize that the OBE gang was seizing the initiative by defining "reform" on its own terms (and never mind that OBE in many respects is just a throwback to failed ideologies like Life Adjustment and Progressive Education). He made me realize that in a great debate such as this one, it is critical to state not only what you are **against** but what you are **for**—even if you are reiterating your long-standing beliefs.

Why should the idea of school reform be limited to government-mandated, **outcome-based**? There are, after all, opposing models for reform, which could be called **freedom-based** or **opportunity-based** education.

This idea is by no means original with me. Some of the citizens battling OBE plans across the nation have been aggressively pursuing positive alternatives.

In Alabama, a grassroots effort involving teachers and other educators sprang up to promote a reform plan ("Score 100")—countering point by point an OBE plan (Alabama First) developed by ubiquitous consultant David Hornbeck and pushed by segments of Alabama big business and Governor Jim Folsom. The OBE plan was developed in the wake of a judge's ruling in an equity lawsuit that the state must restructure education.

The Eagle Forum of Alabama was one of the groups that worked especially hard for Score 100, which was presented as "opportunity-based" education.[1] Score 100 proved to be tough competition for OBE. Although the final "outcome" was uncertain as this was written, Folsom lost his bid for re-election (to Fob James) and numerous other OBE supporters in Alabama also went down to defeat in the 1994 elections.

The presentation of a positive alternative made possible a side-by-side comparison that was not flattering to the establishment's OBE scheme. Here is an example:

Score 100	**Alabama First**
Academics	
High standards through *proven* methodology and renewed emphasis on rigorous core curriculum of traditional subjects, crowded out over the years.	Experimental methodology based on vague "outcomes." No success story anywhere to support high hopes and expectations.
Accountability	
To parents and taxpayers for local goals.	To a new bureaucracy for state-mandated goals.
Bureaucracy	
Shrinks, with greater percentage of money going directly to the classroom.	Swells, with 21 new commissions, task forces, and programs.
Testing	
Nationally normed standardized tests evaluate school for	Subjective assessment replace nationally normed standardized

accountability. Teachers may use project assessment and portfolios to evaluate student progress.	tests. Portfolios and projects evaluate schools.
Methodology	
Local systems choose methodology.	Mandates only Performance-Based/Outcome-Based Education
Teachers	
Treats teachers as professionals who are free to use traditional methods to cover broad subject matter.	Retraining all teachers is required to implement the philosophy of reform that focuses on limited outcomes. Increased paperwork and sanctions experienced in other states.
Taxes	
Minimal, if any, increase. Capital improvements, textbooks, and teacher salary increases offset by trimming bureaucracy and competitive bidding for non-instructional services.	Drastic increases to fund an extra $942 million per year in five years. Approximates $1,000 annually in increased taxes for family of four.
Parents	
Upholds parental rights.	All schools must provide parent education training.
Choice	
Dissatisfied parents may send child to another public school on space-available basis.	None. Students are locked into a failing school even when it is declared a "school in crisis."
Reading	
Proven phonics and word attack methodology must be taught in classrooms and schools of education in addition to other methods.	No change. Anticipating failure in current whole language approach, remediation offered for children and adults.
Discipline	
Strong.	Strong.

Alabama's Score 100 was refined from an Education Improvement Act of 1991 that was never implemented, noted the Eagle Forum's 6th District Chairman, Gay Jones. Having a positive proposal is obviously more effective than simply saying no to OBE.

Another exemplary approach is that of the Connecticut grassroots campaign—the Committee to Save Our Schools (CT:SOS). These citizens believe that the best defense against the "back door" introduction of OBE will be a strong offense—by which they mean building on their success at halting OBE by proposing "positive (and much-needed) reforms." I commend to you a reading of their 10-Point Plan at the end of this chapter.

Just a few words here about the diversity of those seeking alternatives to OBE. The stock put-down from the education establishment is that opposition to OBE comes only from very conservative groups, which they label "Religious Right." But consider the backgrounds of the three leaders from Connecticut who have contributed their thoughts to this book:

- **Jeff Satinover**, M.D., is a practicing psychiatrist who also graduated with the Ed.M. degree from Harvard's Graduate School of Education. He was a fellow of the Yale Child Study Center.
- **Kay Wall** was executive vice president of a market research firm and also has run her own company. Altogether, she has 22 years' experience in the business world. She "retired" a few years ago to raise her son, who is a student in a Greenwich public school. Kay currently serves on the Greenwich PTA Council.
- **Ken Von Kohorn** received a B.S. from Yale in 1968 and an M.B.A. from Stanford University Graduate School of Business in 1972. He worked for a West Coast investment counsel firm from 1972 to 1976 and then moved East to found Von Kohorn Research & Advisory, an investment firm that manages two hedge funds in addition to some individual accounts. His business is in its 19th year.

They don't exactly fit the stereotype, do they?

The Connecticut plan could be called freedom-based reform. It would expand the freedom of teachers to teach and families to know about school programs and to be able to choose among them. Some of the points your own reform group might agree with, and some not. That's freedom-based education in a larger sense: What Connecticut citizens want as an approach to education might not be precisely what citizens of Alabama want, or vice versa. That is the strength of America's system of federalism, under which, according to the 10th Amendment, powers not specifically given to the federal government are reserved to the states, and the people. That is supposed to include education, which is not one of the federal government's enumerated powers in the Constitution.

Sometimes a positive must begin with a negative, however, and it is worthy of note that CT: SOS's Point No. 1 calls for other states to emulate Governor George Allen of Virginia who has said the state will forgo federal education dollars if the federal controls are detrimental to children.

At a meeting of the Republican Governors Conference in Williamsburg following the voters' resounding repudiation of Big Government in the November 1994 mid-term elections, Allen gathered support for a "Common Agenda of Reform,"[2] whereby states agreed to go to court to enforce the 10th Amendment when the federal government oversteps its constitutional bounds. They also made plans to convene a Conference of the States to consider possible constitutional changes to make the states full partners once again in a system based on dual sovereignty.

In the Williamsburg Resolves, the Governors stated, in part:

"The hallmark of self-determination is government that is responsive and accountable to the people. The appetite for power on the part of Federal institutions has allowed a centralized government to operate often without the support of the people and in disregard of their will. This has undermined the very premise of representative government.

Citizens possess little or no control over the actions of Federal courts and the Federal bureaucracy, both of which have assumed dramatically broadened policy-making roles in recent decades. In the recent elections, Americans signaled their determination to reassert control over the Congress, which has long been largely insulated from accountability to the voters by reason of procedure, perquisite, and distance.

The problem is not that the Federal government invariably pursues the wrong aims or invariably fails to attain those aims which it pursues. Examples abound in our history where the exercise of Federal power has been wise and unwise, effective and ineffective, constructive and destructive.

The problem, fundamentally, in a country of this size and diversity, is the inherent unaccountability of a *national* legislature and bureaucracy. Governments at all levels can and do make mistakes that call for correction. Such corrections, however, are more easily accomplished at the State and local levels, where voters can more easily hold the responsible decision-makers accountable. When decision are made at the Federal level, the actions that aggrieve people in one State typically are made by officials elected from other States,

or by officers who are not elected at all, and over which the affected citizens thus have no real political influence."

The Governors' notion of dual sovereignty may be a debatable concept; and the possibility of a Conference of States becoming a runaway vehicle for rewriting the Constitution makes some citizens nervous. Nevertheless, the basic idea of re-energing the Tenth Amendment has merit. By enacting Goals 2000, the 103rd Congress and the Clinton administration clearly collaborated to strip education from local accountability and to consolidate power over school policies at the national level. No less a constitutional scholar than Stephen Arons, professor of legal studies at the University of Massachusetts (Amherst), has written that. . . .

"The Goals 2000 act adopts a top-down, authoritarian, and systematized model of schooling, and it ought probably to be rejected by teachers, students, families, and subcultures on educational grounds alone. But by moving control of the goals of education and the content of schooling ever further from individuals, and by linking performance testing of all students to national content requirements, the act also raises serious constitutional issues."[3]

Establishment of a national curriculum, Professor Arons observed, is "inconsistent with the principles of constitutional democracy," which hold that "if political majorities are empowered to manipulate the content of communication or to regulate the individual freedom to form and express opinions, majority rule itself, and the 'just consent of the governed' it is supposed to express, would be rendered meaningless."

Of course, the Clintonites and the congressional sponsors of Goals 2000 (and related legislation) protest that all of the content, performance, and opportunity-to-learn standards are "voluntary." Doesn't the act use that word about 75 times? Yes, but as Professor Arons sagely warns, "these assurances ought to be given no more credence now than Americans in 1789 gave to the argument that the new U.S. Constitution contained sufficient checks and balances to make a Bill of Rights unnecessary for protecting individual freedom. There is no education 'bill of rights' in the Goals 2000 attempt to reconstitute schooling in the United States." (The Grassley Amendment, discussed in Chapter Two offers only limited protection from invasive surveys.)

The 104th Congress came to power in January, 1995, with an overwhelming mandate to stop the steady intrusion of the federal government into Americans' daily lives. The best favor the Congress could do for Americans who seek the best schools for their children would be to repeal Goals 2000 and related acts. The next-best would be for

Congress to strip out of those laws the provisions most detrimental to liberty.

In a report requested by new House Speaker Newt Gingrich, the Heritage Foundation recommended termination of NESIC (the *de facto* national school board), as well as the National Education Goals Panel (sponsor of the "Community Action Tool Kit") and Robert Reich's National Skills Standards Board. Under its recommendations, the 1,000-page Goals 2000 bill would be reduced to just 10 pages, in which federal aid would enable states to do education reform their own way. In addition, Heritage proposed a five-year plan for dismantling the U.S. Department of Education and transferring its responsibilities to the states.

Were such changes to come about, they would enable freedom-based reforms to take root in local soil and to thrive. And then local citizens would have much greater ability to shape schools in the way they wanted.

In Birmingham, Margaret Brown, research analyst for the Eagle Forum of Alabama (4200 Stone River Circle, Birmingham, 35213), has done a superb job in preparing a Resource Guide for Real Reform, entitled "Regaining Excellence in Education." The agenda in her guide may or may not jibe exactly with what you want for your schools. But the detailed guidance on preparing legislation would be applicable to other school reforms needing state lawmakers' action.

Ms. Brown divides the reform drive into four positive parts (with a-pox-on-OBE subtitles): Producing Academic Excellence (Preventing the OBE Dumbdown); Protecting Parents' and Students' Rights (Tying the Hands of OBE's Big Brother); Making School Systems Accountable to Local Citizens (Preventing the OBE Power Grab); and Getting the Dollars to the Classroom (Bursting the OBE Bureaucracy Balloon).

Her guide is far from being a polemic or a theoretical document. It provides a wealth of practical advice, and, where appropriate, sample legislation to put a positive agenda into action through state and local governments. For example, Ms. Brown offers something akin to a Bill of Rights for Parents and Students. It calls at a minimum for these protections:

- **Ensure parent access to all curricular information and materials, including teachers' manuals and supplementary materials.**
- **Permit parents to have their child excused from nonacademic tests; instruction or assignments that conflict with their religious beliefs; sex education, health education, family living, or parenting classes; and counseling programs. Exemption from such instruction, tests, or assignments should be permitted based on the religious beliefs of the parent or on the right of parents to direct the education**

of their children. Students should be provided an alternative learning experience using materials acceptable to the parent and must not be penalized by reason of the exemption.

• Require schools to make parent conferences available at a time working parents can attend.

• Require that state education personnel comply with the provisions of the federal Family Educational Rights and Privacy Act in all programs, regardless of the source of funding.

• Prohibit any policy, program, or activity that interferes with open communication between parent and child. (Amazingly enough, in some school counseling sessions, students are encouraged to share their feelings and problems with those in the group, but no one outside—parents included.)

• Prohibit the use of standard induction techniques of hypnosis, guided imagery, TM, or yoga.

• Require prior written permission of parents for psychological or psychiatric testing or treatment.

• Require prior written consent for medical examinations, treatment, testing, or referrals. Absolutely prohibit distribution of condoms or other birth control devices and provision of abortion or birth control counseling or referrals at any school or school-related center.

• Require school personnel to foster and encourage the values, attitudes, and standards of behavior inherent in our laws and founding documents and prohibit them from presenting illegal conduct as an option for students to consider.

• Require prior written consent for the release of student records to anyone other than the student or his parents or guardian.

• Provide a procedure to challenge the content of student records and have corrections made.

• Require that policies on students' and parents' rights be displayed in a prominent place in each school and that all school personnel and parents are informed of the policies.

• Provide for disciplinary action against violators of parents' and students' rights to ensure future compliance.

This is only a small example from a 56-page manual for citizen action. There are also sample bills to require the use of phonics in teaching reading, provide for alternative certification of teachers outside the usual education-school track, create Parent Advisory Councils, and channel more money into classrooms as opposed to the school bureaucracy. This manual would be a valuable source of ideas for any citizens' group seeking better and more accountable schools.

To reiterate, the agenda of these Alabamans may not be precisely your agenda. The role of choice among competing schools is a major consideration in preparing a reform plan. It so happens that this group did not go beyond the concept that if a family is dissatisfied with its assigned public school, it ought to be a able to transfer to another public school on a space-available basis. Personally, I long have favored the concept of parental choice among a wide range of schools, both public and private, including schools with a religious orientation. In my ideal system, this would be accomplished through tuition tax credits, without government dictation of curriculum, teaching methods, or teacher credentials. Another possibility is the creation of so-called charter schools—independent public schools organized by parents, teachers, or even universities or entrepreneurs, and issued a charter by the school board.

Some opponents of OBE fear that choice plans may become a subterfuge to pull private schools into the deadly whirlpool of government regulation. Especially with vouchers, they see statist controls following the money. That could happen if care isn't taken in how choice plans are structured; however, an in-depth discussion of the pros and cons of choice is beyond the scope of this book. The basic point is that citizens should decide specifically what they stand for, then present as united a front as possible, and make a plan to achieve their objectives.

The CT: SOS 10-Point Plan

By Dr. Jeffrey Satinover, Ken Von Kohorn, and Kay Wall Connecticut

1. **Reject Federal Interference.** Connecticut should follow the example of Governor George Allen of Virginia, who says that rather than cave in to the "dictates of some bureaucrat," he will give up federal education funds. He says, "We'll forgo the money if it's contrary to what we think is best for Virginia's students."

2. **Relieve Teachers From Certification.** Certified teachers receive training at Teacher Colleges steeped in the "progressive"/OBE education philosophy. The alternative route opens up teaching to those who can meet high academic competency requirements set by the General Assembly—without having to attend Teacher Ed schools.

3. **Inject the Free Market.** School choice as a local option would provide parents the ability to select the program best suited for their children. Charter schools should also be allowed (essentially public schools with fewer state controls).

4. **Prune State Mandates.** We should eliminate the state mandates that reduce to below 80 percent the amount of classroom time that can be spent on core academic subjects, which include Language Arts, Math, Science, History, Geography, Foreign Languages, and the Fine Arts. The non-academic mandates diminish local control as well as take time away from teaching core academic subjects.

5. **Enact a "Sunshine" Provision.** It is vital to open up for public inspection all state tests and associated scoring keys and rubrics two years after their use. This will inhibit the state or federal impetus toward political correctness, because the scoring methodologies in areas such as writing samples would be exposed to public scrutiny.

6. **Require Standardized Tests.** We need to continue to use standard nationwide academic proficiency tests and to publish the results on an aggregate basis by school. This will enable parents to compare their school work with others in the state and with schools nationwide.

7. **Provide for Disruptive Students.** We recommend expanding the Connecticut pilot program to create special Charter schools with a low student/teacher ratio to deal with persistently disruptive students. This will benefit the students who need more focused attention, and

it will also provide relief to students and teachers in the classrooms that were being adversely affected.

8. **Protect Student Privacy.** Increasingly, schools survey students to determine their beliefs, attitudes, and values. As a result of numerous examples of surveys having been sent to Washington by groups all over the country, including Save Our Schools, the Congress recently enacted a "Protection of Pupil Rights" amendment to the Goals 2000 legislation. This act protects children's privacy in federally-financed school programs, and our recommendation of a Connecticut version would protect students' privacy in state-financed programs. The federal privacy protections cover such areas as political affiliations, sexual behaviors or attitudes, legally-recognized relationships such as with lawyers, doctors, or ministers, and surveys about family income.

9. **Reduce Overhead.** In Connecticut, the staff/pupil ratio has increased from 6 percent in 1971 to 13 percent in 1990. We should cut the number of administrators relative to pupils, both as a cost-saving measure and to reduce unnecessary interference with classroom teachers.

10. **Identify the Reading Curriculum.** We should seek that all public schools report their K-2 reading instruction methodology and curriculum to the local board of ed. Because of the decades-long controversy between the "phonics-first" and "whole language" methods of reading, it is vital that parents and board of ed members possess explicit, current information on how the local schools are teaching students to read.

Through a process similar to the one we used to combat OBE, we will be promoting our 10-point Plan as an alternative to the top-down, heavily bureaucratic "reform" models. Asserting a credible alternative should help us maintain momentum and motivate local chapters with positive reform objectives.

Honor Roll

(Honoring grassroots organizations that have made a difference for the better in their communities.)

Committee to Save Our Schools (CT:SOS)

P.O. Box 5222, Westport, CT 06881
Phone: 454-7283; Fax: 226-1636

The Committee to Save Our Schools (CT:SOS) announced its formation at a Hartford press conference January 10, 1994. Founded by Dr. Jeffrey Satinover, Ken Von Kohorn, and Kay Wall, its purpose is to promote positive education reform in Connecticut through research, networking, communication, educational forums, and involvement in the political process. Eighty communities throughout the state have formed chapters.

CT in May, 1994, successfully opposed an education "reform" bill backed by then–Governor Lowell Weicker. The "reform" bill would have turned over to the State Board of Education authority to impose Outcome–Based Education and to dictate student assessments throughout the state.

CT:SOS will continue to work on behalf of true education reform. A newsletter was planned to begin publication in May, 1995.

12

Do's and Don'ts

This chapter belongs principally to those who have survived the initial battles of the OBE war. I am a war correspondent; they are the brave soldiers. They have a world of useful advice to pass along from experience at the front, and they deserve to have the final words.

From my observer's outpost, I offer one main "do" and one "don't" that summarize my advice:

Do:

• **Be smart.** Find out when your local and state school boards meet, and go to all the meetings. Gather all the documents you can, and verify your facts. Start small, network like crazy, and, when you're organized, hold a town meeting and invite both sides to present their cases. Get the bureaucrats off their turf and onto yours. Invite political leaders, candidates, and future candidates, and try to get them to go on the record. Be polite, be patient, but be persistent.

Don't:

• **Be Shrill.** Screaming about some elaborate "conspiracy" is only going to squander your credibility. Don't go into a public meeting impugning the motives of every player on the other side. You will make no allies—and you might lose some. It may be hard to keep your temper, especially when the other side is slamming you and your background, but if you stay calm and stick to verifiable facts—using original documents and quoting them liberally—you will gain the support of other parents who want the best for their children.

Do you wonder sometimes if everyday parents can have an effect on such a powerful Juggernaut? Well, listen to OBE guru William Spady, speaking in exasperated tones before a public forum at his own High Success Network Conference in Vail, Colorado, in the summer of 1994:

"And so it goes from state to state to state . . . they shut OBE down in Oklahoma in three weeks. Three years of effort gone in three weeks! . . . They shut Connecticut down over the issue of academic standards. . . ."

The Vail conference was part of an initiative aimed at reaching a compromise with certain OBE opponents, notably Bob Simonds' Citizens for Excellence in Education (CEE), a national Christian organization considered (at least until this conference) to be one of the OBE's movement's most implacable foes. One question the activists in the various states need to decide early is the extent to which they might compromise with the pro-OBE side. Do they believe OBE is an insidious philosophy gnawing away at the fiber of American schools and society? If so, it is doubtful they would want to strike a bargain. On the other hand, do they believe there are elements in OBE that might be adapted to some schools or some students' needs—and that might be offered a choice plan? Again, I am suggesting a question, not the answer. It's the kind of question that citizens in an activist group ought to decide early, rather than facing dissension in the ranks late in the game—thus allowing the OBE proponents to play divide and conquer.

Meet a stalwart activist—Anne M. Barbera, a Pennsylvania grandmom of 20 whose activism goes back to the White House Conference on Families in 1980—when she discovered a pervasive effort by statist nannies to restructure families as well as society. In the 1980s, Anne had success in alerting the community to the real agendas behind compulsory sex education. She did this by attending statewide teacher workshops and getting copies of the material that was to be taught. The next task was to get that objective information to the people. The upshot, she said, is that, "Vile sex education remained out of our school for 10 years."

"Throughout the 1980s," said Mrs. Barbera, "we tried to gather support in fighting the non-academic invasion of our education but the problems had not sufficiently surfaced for us to be able to rally the people. The general public believed the educational system was still the same as when they attended school. It's like an alcoholic; they usually have to hit bottom before they will admit they need help. Today (1995), problems in education have hit rock bottom."

But the earlier battles have taught some valuable lessons, she believes, for the war against OBE. This is her advice, in her words:

• **First, educate ourselves**—not only studying pro-family literature but reading the manuals, periodicals, and Department of Education material that the teachers and education establishment use. Analyze these, highlight them, and use them when explaining to others. Their own material is the most damaging and the best to quote from in letters to the editor, and the like. Attend seminars, conferences, etc., given by the education establishment. You will have your eyes opened very wide. You will be in painful shock.

• **Second, educate others.** The truth must get out. Remember, most people know only what they read or hear from the local media, which is definitely biased. After all, the media only print or announce material handed to them from the education establishment. Use every source available to you: **newspaper,** through friendly reporters and columnists and letters to the editor; **radio,** through announcements of events and guests or call-ins on radio talk shows; invite news people to your events, give them updates on current issues, quoting facts from the establishment's own material; **television,** invite the local station to any events you may host or participate in, make good use of cable access channels, showing pro-family educational videos and take advantage of the free announcements for your events, and **local county flyers** or **advertising handouts.**

• At neighborhood get-togethers, have coffee and doughnuts and show a film, give out literature and discuss local issues and how you might tackle them. Donate pro-family books to the libraries to counter those typically on the must-buy list of the liberal American Library Association.

• **Third, take action.** Testify at state and district education hearings. Lobby the legislators, either in person or by mail. Attend local school board meetings on a regular basis to learn what they have planned for our children.

• **Fourth, join a local group,** and if none exists, **form a group**—either a chapter of a state or national group or just a new local group. If a new group, decide on a name, how extensive and what direction your actions will take; then elect officers, write simple by-laws, set up committees, and decide how you will raise funds for any necessary expenditures. Establish a way to keep current on the issues you intend to tackle—such as subscribing to particular journals and newsletters. Make contact with local teachers who share your concerns and have them feed you material from their school districts. This they can do anonymously to protect confidentiality. The same process can work at the county, regional, and state levels.

Set up committees, giving each member a responsibility. You will need a legislative committee to monitor all pertinent legislation at the state and federal levels. You may get copies of the bills through the Document Offices at the state capital and the Document Room, United States Senate, Washington, D.C., 20510. If you intend to lobby, you will need a lobbying committee that will get to know your state and its federal legislators. Their job will be to contact them on issues and direct letter-writing campaigns when specific bills come up. A publicity committee is very important, because it will be the main link to the general public. Committee members must supply the news media with current alerts and information, notices of meetings and events, summary of speakers' topics, and help with letters to the editor.

Anne Barbera and her Pennsylvania Parents Commission have been in the forefront of the OBE fight. Others like her have risen to the task in other states, as the Juggernaut just rolls along. Here are some thoughts from them on what you should and shouldn't do. . . .

Don't Forget a Sense of Humor— And Never Give Up

By Cindy Duckett
Kansas

• **Get your priorities straight.** These can be overwhelming issues to deal with at times and many of us who have been at this for a while have found that once we have committed, our lives were forever changed. There are always new documents to read, more meetings to attend, and the telephone begins to ring constantly as others "wake up" and need information. Balance is the key and it's important to make sure that your own families are taken care of first. For many, that has meant pulling our children out of the public school system, learning to let an answering machine catch the phone during the dinner hour and family time, and turning down important meetings to be able to help our own children with homework or to plan a birthday party and other important family events. If education and family are truly the important motivators that we say they are, we must be prepared to lead by example.

• **Deal with documents.** It's easy to go out and make any claim you want about your state or district's reform plans, but rest assured that at some point you will be challenged on your statements by those with a vested interest in seeing these plans through to their fruition. Be prepared to back up every claim you make with documentable proof. Your credibility will make the difference between being taken seriously or being labeled a "nut."

• **Keep a strong sense of humor.** If you don't have one, work on developing one because you'll need it. When you realize the possibility of the human tragedy that could result from some of these plans, it is easy to become both cynical and depressed. I have found no other factor that reduces my own effectiveness more than to give in to these emotions. Surrounding yourself with positive, energetic people really helps.

• **Be prepared to stay with this over the long haul if you hope to make any real impact.** These plans did not crop up overnight. They took years of planning and implementation. They are not going to go away overnight either.

• **Realize that many of the people you will work with are proba-**

bly very well-meaning people, even if they do seem at times to be misguided. Name-calling and personal accusations are counter-productive. The best thing you have to fight with are the facts and your own personal integrity. Treat your opposition with the same courtesy you expect for yourself and in time you may find that you have made some unexpected allies, though others probably will never agree with you.

• **Be considerate when dealing with legislators, media people, and school officials.** All of them have busy schedules. Keep in contact just often enough to keep the dialogue flowing but not so often that they come to look at you as a pest. Keep your visits and phone calls short and to the point, and, whenever possible, communicate thoughts through the mail to give them the opportunity to deal with your information at a time that is convenient for them.

• **Know what you are "for" as well as what you are "against."** I think that the vast majority of people would agree that education does, indeed, need reforming. Throwing out one bad plan is all well and good, but little is gained if you don't have some idea of what changes should be implemented to bring about true educational excellence for our students. Personally, I favor: tuition tax credits, return of true local control of education, alternative certification of teachers, and a parents' bill of rights.

• **Decide from the beginning whether you are willing to compromise.** If so, know where you will compromise and how much. Personally, I see no compromise possible on OBE. The plan was devised by the same established people who helped get education in the mess that it is in today, and I have no faith in their ability to produce a plan that will result in real student achievement.

• **Don't get discouraged when you talk to people and they don't come around immediately.** I have found that when I make a new contact and begin educating that person, it typically takes about nine months for them to begin to understand and share my concerns. Some never do, but for most, I've found this time frame to be average, and thus have come to think of the process as akin to giving birth to a baby. These people need time for the seeds you plant in your initial contact to sprout and grow. They need time to absorb all you have told them and many of them need to see some of the things you've told them about actually happening in their own schools, and to their own children.

• **Finally, never, never give up!** This battle is for the future of our children and our nation. It is a battle that we cannot afford to lose, for if we do, I can see nothing that will be left that will matter.

Do Your Homework With Care—It Will Pay Off Handsomely

By Dr. Jeffrey Satinover, Ken Von Kohorn, and Kay Wall
Connecticut

1. We assembled video tapes and packets of information from around the country. The videos and prepackaged OBE information made an excellent introduction for newcomers to education "reform." We suggest starting with more balanced, less obviously ideological material to avoid alienating those who haven't yet decided which side of the debate they agree with. For example, the NBC affiliate in Oklahoma City produced a televised news report on that state's experience with OBE, and it makes for a good introduction (some skeptics here scoffed that "Oklahoma is not Connecticut," but others recognized the national implications of different states experimenting with nearly identical "reforms"). Once your audience has caught on to the disturbing facts of OBE, more dramatic material (as long as it remains factually correct) can be used.

2. After a few months of independent work, we found it essential to form an organization. We decided that it should have a simple name (don't worry too much about cute acronyms). Once we felt ready to announce our existence to the state, we held a press conference—a friendly legislator made arrangements to make sure that the press actually would be there to cover our statement. At press conferences, we recommend that you keep your comments short (no more than two or three minutes per speaker) and allow plenty of time for questions.

3. Only a small percentage of interested people will be willing to get heavily involved. Of these only a few will be capable of doing the necessary work. Expect growing support and encouragement from many, but also expect that much of the burden will be carried by few.

4. When you're small, don't try to work directly with your opponents (i.e., trying to convince them that their ideas aren't very good ones or that there is substantial opposition, etc.). It's a waste of time unless you're better at maneuvering key pieces of information out of them than they are at extracting what they'd like to know from you.

5. Legislators respond primarily to voters. They respect constituent pressure, and at the beginning you don't have any to exert. You aren't a "player"—yet. So don't waste too much time lobbying individual representatives.

6. It is essential, however, to identify one or key legislators who wholeheartedly agree with you—and who are interested in sound ideas. Such legislators exist. Find them, and work closely with them. They may not be the current leadership, and may instead be younger (or newer) up-and-comers looking for an issue to raise them above the herd. They will make useful suggestions and help you arrange key actions that can leverage your smallness (*e.g.*, timely news conferences that put both you and them before the public eye). They will keep you informed of the shifting tide among their colleagues, and about which political districts are critical for success. For example, we had strong upper-middle-class Republican support from the beginning; but at the end, it was the blue-collar Democrats who were our strongest, and most numerous, allies—and for good reason: It would be the future of **their** kids that would be most damaged by further corrosion of public education.

7. Use the media. Go on every talk radio show that will have you (and education is a "hot" issue these days); put letters and Op-Eds in every small-town paper you can. Then photocopy the published pieces for further dissemination. Soon the larger media outlets will become interested (it doesn't hurt to encourage them with phone calls and news releases). Find key talk-show hosts or editors who are on your side—they'll create opportunities for you. Hardly a week went by when one of us wasn't on the air with a sympathetic talk show host, issuing challenges to the CEEC (it could just as easily have been the department of education) to debate us. Soon, the public caught on that the CEEC didn't want public airing of the issues. For them, it was a "done deal." They buried themselves in their own superiority.

8. Challenge your opponents to debate you at every step of the way. They usually won't accept—but that's okay. The CEEC wouldn't debate us until the very last minute—in the vain hope that by not talking to us publicly, they wouldn't lend credence to us as "legitimate." They seemed never to want to talk substance, but instead to label us and therefore discredit us. Resist the labeling. It won't work as long as you . . .

9. Talk substance at every opportunity. Many of the reformers think that they need not clearly explain their proposals to concerned parents, and they tend to couch their ideas in education jargon. They don't recognize how hollow their slogans sound to most thoughtful parents. Educate yourself to the facts; don't be afraid of being specific and of quoting sources. Honor your listeners and their intelligence and they'll honor your appeals. It's a longer, tougher row to hoe than sound-bites and catchy one-liners, but unless you own a television station it's the best way to go (and more satisfying, too).

10. Arrange to hold public forums in as many towns as you can. They should be organized by local citizens. We would usually have two or more hours, in the evening, to present and field questions. Our radio shows usually ran an hour or so. Between these two types of outreach, the three of us spent one or more evenings every week, for the six months prior to the vote, barnstorming around the state. **That's what turned the tide.** The people who showed up were self-selecting and highly motivated. Once they knew what was going on, they put the pressure—**very effective pressure**—on all the legislators we wouldn't have been able to convince by ourselves. Legislators had their arms twisted in the first place to support OBE-type "reform" by Big Education and by Big Business; but it was the parents who voted them into office who untwisted their arms. And virtually the only phone calls, faxes, or letters legislators were getting came from irate voters who were opposed to the CEEC's recommendations. Since "education reform" is a top/down plan, what support there is for it among voters tends to be tepid at best. Lukewarm supporters don't bother contacting their legislators.

11. Create a package of audiovisual materials—e.g., something simple, like overheads. Your speakers can each contribute and use selections from the package when they go and speak. Carry your own overhead projectors and screen—a small detail, but one that may prove crucial if you go to places that aren't well organized or aren't accustomed to arranging their own public events.

12. Who will arrange the forums? Talk to individuals who have some knowledge and concern about OBE already (there are plenty). In every town there will be one or two "movers." Have them organize a presentation and advertise it (local papers, flyers at schools, etc.). Every forum will attract people from nearby towns who will then want you to talk to them. It soon snowballs.

13. Have one person willing to attend meetings of the state "reformers" (such as our CEEC) and obtain all the available public documentation. All of the nonsense the CEEC discussed was right there in black and white for anybody to see. It's just that hardly any normal person wants to waste time keeping up with it. Yet nothing was more effective than putting their own paperwork up on an overhead, and showing a gathering of parents just what the CEEC members themselves actually said about what they were doing—as opposed to their PR firm's sound-bites and billboards. We had a key person willing to do this—for two years. Because of her, we had the ammunition to kill them—namely their own words.

14. Have at least one computer-savvy person hooked into the Prodigy (Interactive Service) education bulletin board. It is a terrific source of information, battle-plans, early-warnings, and encouragement. Whatever dilemmas you may run into, you can be sure that people in other states have, too. Ask and you will receive.

15. Every time you have a forum, get names and addresses and phone numbers. Compile a statewide database of supporters. Urge the activists in each community to set up a "chapter" in what is a loose, statewide affiliation, as we did with Committee to Save Our Schools.

CT: SOS's efforts were rewarded in the spring of 1994 when the Connecticut General Assembly rejected OBE by a 105–45 vote in party caucuses. We now have over 80 chapters all over the state—hard-working people whom we can quickly bring up to speed on issues as they arise. The battle is far from over. The state department of education has announced it will be pushing OBE-type "reforms" anyway, evidently unmoved by any noticeable respect for the democratic process.

Keep the Focus on Academics and Use Original Documents

By Sharon Thompson
Virginia

In retrospect, I believe that we did at least two things correctly, mostly upon the advice of activists from Pennsylvania who had gone this route before us.

No. 1: We kept the debate and the voicing of our concern away from values and on the lack of academics in the "Common Core of Learning." We knew that there would be every attempt to label us "right-wing, religious nuts" so that we could be discredited and dismissed. No matter what our concerns politically and religiously, we kept those to ourselves. Our public stance was that the "Common Core of Learning" was not academic enough in its orientation. This did two things for us: It gave them nothing with which to discredit us, and it made the "Common Core" an issue that people of all religious and political persuasions felt comfortable in opposing.

No. 2: We used "their" documents as much as possible in all public presentations. We did not present our opinions. We brought the actual documents to the public, something the State Department of Education had somehow failed to do. People could not argue that we were wrong when they were looking at the actual documents. It was a shock to many to get these insights into our educational bureaucracy.

In addition, we were greatly helped by the fact that 1993 was an election year for the Governor of Virginia. In the end Governor Wilder (Democrat), whose administration had started the ball rolling with Virginia's "Common Core," killed the document, agreeing with us that it was not academic enough and too values-based. It was a major victory in one battle in the war. (The war itself, alas, does indeed still continue with concerned parents fighting for the state to maintain control of education rather than give control to the Feds, a move that will put us right back where we were with the "Common Core.") Although we objected to politics in education, it was the fact that the Democrat candidate for governor, Mary Sue Terry, was slipping so badly in the polls that, I believe, led Governor Wilder to kill the CCL.

George Allen had said "No OBE," a statement that won him many votes. We're still waiting for that promise to remove the elements of

OBE that have already infiltrated Virginia's school system and to prevent the federal government from taking over the state's public schools. The "Common Core of Learning" was just a list of exit outcomes. There is much more to the woes of public education than that. Governor Allen, are you listening?

Escape the Comfort Zone and Be Active

By Cathy Reid
North Carolina

First, inform yourself; then do what you can to keep the public informed. Use all means available to you. Concerning the media: They can be your friend or your enemy. Be brief when speaking with them, and always make sure you can back up anything you say. Correct any discrepancies through letters to the editor if you can't get them corrected any other way.

Don't wait until you are in the midst of controversy; head off the problem before it starts, if possible. Get on the mailing list for your local school board's agenda, and attend the meetings. Know where school money is coming from, and know where it's going. Above all, be an informed voter; find out what a candidate stands for and get behind the candidates of your choice. I refuse to believe that returning our schools to being academic institutions is unattainable. We just need to get out of our comfort zone and do something.

The Virginia OBE Controversy From the Other Side

By James P. Jones
President, State Board of Education

When Joe Spagnolo, the State Superintendent of Public Instruction, first showed me in 1992 a draft of his OBE framework called the "Virginia Common Core of Learning (CCL)," I sensed that it was going to be controversial, although I did not imagine then the firestorm of opposition that would ultimately lead to its total repudiation after only a brief life.

School board members are always dependent in some degree upon professional educators, and this is particularly true in Virginia, where the State Board of Education has no independent staff and relies upon the superintendent and his subordinates in the Department of Education as its primary professional advisers. The board has no independent funding to hire experts of its own, and local teachers and administrators seem reluctant to go over the head of the superintendent to communicate directly with board members.

Perhaps for these reasons, the board did not know in the beginning of the problems faced by Outcome-Based Education in other states. To the board, like many parents and teachers in Virginia, OBE seemed a brand-new invention. What was clear, however, was that the "Common Core of Learning" was a break from traditional educational policy. The idea of depending on "outcomes" rather than "inputs" seemed sensible enough, but the CCL itself was put together with language that did not look like a normal school curriculum. The board did, however, agree with the basic assumption that lay behind Spagnolo's efforts—that our public schools were not doing the job that needed to be done and that halfway reform measures were not going to make a difference. Ironically, it was on this point that Spagnolo and OBE opponents agreed. While many in the education establishment did not accept the fundamental idea that our public schools needed to be changed, pro-and anti-OBEers alike agreed that our schools were in a downward spiral and dramatic changes needed to be made.

During late 1992 and early 1993, the board hammered on Dr. Spagnolo to revise the CCL to make it more precise and understandable. As president of the board, I felt a special responsibility to involve the board as much as possible in the process. I scheduled special meetings devoted only to the CCL. These meetings, particularly one held in February 1993, were often contentious. A news reporter who attended the February meeting reported that members of the board were "posturing to oppose or at least water down the plan."

Spagnolo agreed to many of the changes proposed by board members in the CCL and in the face of opposition, he continued to be conciliatory so long as he could retain the essence of his approach. With each new draft, however, the public became more confused. Even though later drafts were more precise and traditional in their presentations of the outcomes, the earlier drafts were widely circulated and made it only more difficult to explain what the essence of the program was.

It finally seemed to me that further tinkering was only going to make matters worse and that it was time to decide upon some fixed formulation of Spagnolo's proposal that could be presented to the public for comment and hearing, where it would either make or not in the marketplace of public ideas. Continuing to describe the Common Core of Learning as a "work in progress" or "only a draft" gave its critics more ammunition and exposed the program as a *tabula rosa* on which could be projected the many criticisms of public education. It was clear to me that the CCL was seen as a prime example of everything that people perceived as wrong with our schools. From "whole language" teaching to guidance counseling to lack of discipline, the CCL was seen to encompass all of the real or imagined ills of modern education. OBE was criticized on the one hand as being a too radical break with the past and on the other as a continuation of what had been going on in our public schools for years. In either event, it was held out as the epitome of everything that was wrong.

While Spagnolo made the point that the CCL was only a "framework" and that individual standards and assessments would come later, it seemed to me important that we tie down the form so that some public decision could be made on it. Accordingly, I scheduled a presentation and vote at the board's regular meeting in late May, 1993. At that meeting, in spite of public comment overwhelmingly hostile to the CCL, the board unanimously approved it.

Dr. Spagnolo and his staff were obviously pleased with this milestone, but it did nothing to dampen the criticism. Members of the legislature were now receiving complaints from their constituents concerning the CCL, and Spagnolo and board members began to hear from concerned legislators on a routine basis. In July, only about six weeks after the board had tentatively approved the Common Core of Learning, I went with Spagnolo to a meeting of the Northern Virginia legislative delegation. That delegation, the largest and most cohesive in the legislature, met regularly to discuss matters of interest and scheduled an entire meeting on the CCL. Spagnolo made a spirited defense of his proposal at the meeting and the legislators were thoughtful and asked intelligent questions. It was clear to me, however, that almost all of the legislators, both Republicans and Democrats, were, if not in outright opposition, certainly leaning that way.

To me, the most telling remark came from State Senator Richard Saslaw of Fairfax County. I had served in the State Senate myself for five years and had been a close friend of Saslaw, a businessman and moderate Democrat with the reputation of being able to get to the essence of things. At the end of Spagnolo's presentation, he told Spagnolo, "Well, in spite of what you say, all of these people opposed to OBE can't be wrong. I don't think you could get two votes out of 15 in the Senate education committee right now." I knew then that the CCL was in desperate trouble. For the next several weeks, I mulled over what the board ought to do in the face of the mounting opposition. Dr. Spagnolo tried a public relations counter attack, but it seemed to me that the Department of Education's public relations machinery was simply not equipped to deal effectively with an issue such as this. I doubted the ability of the proponents of the CCL to turn public opinion around.

I attempted to conduct my own unscientific sampling of opinion whenever I could. I remember being seated next to a Norfolk businessman at a dinner unrelated to education. We began talking, and I told him that I served on the State Board of Education. He expressed interest in improving our public schools and I asked him if he had heard about "OBE" or the CCL. He replied that he thought that he had. I asked him what he thought it was and he responded simply, "It means dumbing down, doesn't it?"

In mid-August of 1993, after talking with several other board members informally, I told Spagnolo that I had decided that the CCL was insupportable and that we ought to withdraw it and move on to other areas of education reform. Spagnolo asked for an opportunity to work with his staff to come up with alternatives that might allow us to keep the OBE approach. After about 10 days of this work, Spagnolo and I met, and he presented me with his proposals. All of them involved keeping the CCL, although with changes. I told him frankly that I did not think that these changes, which would be viewed as cosmetic, would make any fundamental difference.

Finally, in early September I decided to act. I drafted a press release in which I would announce that I was recommending to the board that the CCL be withdrawn. I canvassed fellow board members and felt certain that I had at least five of the nine members committed to vote to drop OBE. I did not want to surprise Dr. Spagnolo, however, and I told him what I was going to do. I also sent to him and to the Governor's office copies of the press release that I planned to issue later that week. Much to my surprise, two days later, without talking to me, Governor Douglas Wilder issued his own press release in which he announced that he was going to direct Spagnolo to withdraw the CCL. Obviously, Governor Wilder, a skillful politician, had been making his own judgment of the public reaction to the CCL and did not want to let anyone else take credit for stopping OBE in Virginia. While constitutionally the Governor probably had no power to change a matter of education policy set by the Board of Education, his unilateral action did produce a more clear-cut conclusion than if it had been made merely by the board. At the regular monthly meeting held a week or so later, without mentioning the Governor, the board formally adopted a resolution putting an end to Virginia's OBE experiment.

I believe that the opposition to the Common Core of Learning in Virginia succeeded for two principal reasons. The first was Robert Holland's series of newspaper columns in opposition. Holland's work was carefully researched and therefore tremendously effective. In fact, Spagnolo told me at one point that he felt that "Bob Holland knows more about OBE than anyone else." In the second place, the public's widespread distrust of government and of public school officials as representatives of that government, translated into effective political pressure that caused all of the principal policy players in the State to be either indifferent or hostile to OBE. For example, the education establishment, while it showed some early enthusiasm for the CCL, later turned exceedingly cool. The Virginia teachers union and the State PTA council both voiced at various times during the controversy either opposition or inconsistent support of Spagnolo's proposal. Elected officials were even more clearly influenced by letters and contacts from constituents.

While the opponents of OBE were victorious, their tactics raised for me some troubling questions. Many of the activists, for instance, showed an ideological opposition to anything relating to the public schools. Some of them at least implied that their preferred solution was to abolish the public school system. While private school choice may eventually become a reality, I believe that reliance on it alone as a solution will hamper intermediate efforts to improve our schools.

The anger of some of the opponents also made the OBE controversy more prolonged and bitter than it might otherwise have been. While many of the opponents spoke and wrote in rational opposition, others tended to personalize their attacks. Robert Holland's columns, while never personal, supported the view that those who were pro-OBE were of that persuasion only because of financial self-interest or desire for bureaucratic power. For some anti-OBE activists, this was their first foray into public policy, and it seemed difficult for them to recognize that such questions often involve matters in which well-intentioned people of equal intelligence simply arrive at different conclusions. When I became president of the board, shortly before the OBE controversy started, I instituted a public comment period for Board of Education meetings, something that had not been the practice in the past. I felt it was important for board members to hear from citizens in some regular way. As the anti-OBE dispute intensified, the public comment period was filled increasingly by OBE activists. Many of them were insulting or hostile, or both, which only served to reinforce the board members' notion that those opposed to OBE were irrational or extreme.

There were certainly different approaches, however. One prime example was Kerri Vailati, a cheerful homemaker from Hampton, Virginia, who, while she home-schooled her own children, had developed a keen interest in the public schools and OBE. Kerri endeared herself to me and other board members by explaining to us that her last name rhymed with "spaghetti" and proceeding to carefully tell us from a parent's point of view what she saw wrong with the direction the board was taking. Testimony from her and from others like her were effective, although they were frequently drowned out by shriller voices. One critic accused us of conspiring to indoctrinate school children with un-American ideas and capture "resisters" on a nationwide computer data base. Another speaker told us that Virginia citizens would soon rise up and "squash us like bugs" if we continued with OBE and there were even worse letters and messages.

In fact, between board members and the anti-OBE public, there was the common belief that our public schools did need to be dramatically improved. To put the issue on the basis of "them" versus "us," while likely effective in energizing the movement, has unfortunate long-range implications. There ought to be enough common ground to solve education problems on a consensus basis. To divide into ideological camps, particularly with a view of the opposition as evil or irrational, or both, does not easily lead to solutions. I found most of the anti-OBE activists I met to be well meaning, intelligent, and concerned. While I did not agree with everything they said, I shared with them, more than I did with many in the education establishment, a conviction that we did need to change things.

While it may be necessary for effective mass movements to generate support through exaggerated conflict, I think that more lasting change can be created by efforts to find common ground. Regardless of the merits of OBE, the lasting success of the Virginia controversy will likely be that it caused thousands of parents and citizens to become more involved in improving education. Keeping that involvement alive should the prime goal for all of us.

Honor Roll

(Honoring grassroots organizations that have made a difference for the better in their communities.

Kansas Education Watch Network

P.O. Box 483
Wichita, KS, 67201

(316) 685-5664; Fax: (316) 685-8597
Jim McDavitt, Executive Director

Kansas Education Watch Network (KEW–NET) was created in 1991 in response to education restructuring in Kansas after understanding that the state's system of education was employing Outcome-Based Education (OBE).

Business leaders, taxpayers, parents, and educators saw the direction of education as a detriment to academic success for Kansas children and reacted by organizing in opposition.

Since its inception, KEW–NET representatives have spoken before thousands of Kansas citizens, have interviewed many authorities and presented information on national and local media outlets about the deterioration of education, and have published hundreds of papers on efforts to bring reason and truth to our public schools.

KEW–NET intends to continue to stand in the path of educational dishonesty and fraud while offering those charged by The Creator with the educational responsibility of children a combination of the truth about educational agendas and the alternatives and tools with which to succeed in spite of those agendas.

Appendix A

Comparison of Diversity/ Group Skills Outcomes

Alaska: Be a responsible citizen; have the knowledge, skills, and attitudes to be a citizen of the world who accepts and respects differences in peoples' cultures.

Colorado (Aurora): Demonstrate consideration for individual differences. **(Weld Co.)**: Demonstrate respect and cooperation within a community of individual and cultural differences.

Connecticut: Connecticut public school students will respect and appreciate diversity; respect the humanity they share with other people and live and work in harmony with others; acquire and apply an understanding and appreciation of the values and achievements of their own cultures; and show understanding of international issues {that} affect life on our planet and demonstrate skills needed to participate in a global society.

Florida: Florida students appreciate their own culture and the culture of others, understand the concerns and perspectives of members of other ethnic and gender groups, reject the stereotyping of themselves and others, and seek out and utilize the views of persons from diverse ethnic, social, and educational backgrounds while completing individual and group projects.

Georgia (Gwinnett Co.): Collaborative contributor who cooperates effectively in a variety of settings and with a diversity of people; cooperates effectively with a diversity of people.

Illinois: Each student will demonstrate the ability to solve problems and perform tasks needed to succeed in a diverse society.

Indiana: Enculturation; pursuit of illuminations and assimilation of the norms, values, traditions, languages, and aesthetic contributions of one's own society and civilization; emotional and physical well-being; pursuit of competencies and practices allowing for realistic assessment and acceptance of self and others and for adjustments in coping with physical, psychological, and social changes.

Iowa: All learners respect diversity and promote equity for all.

Kansas: Students work effectively both independently and in groups in order to love, learn, and work in a global society.

Kentucky: Demonstrate an understanding of, and appreciation for, sensitivity to a multicultural world view; demonstrate an open mind to alternative perspectives.

Maine: By the year 1997, every school will be measured on the following outcomes: schools will achieve gender, race, and socioeconomic equity in every measure of student achievement.

Minnesota: The Minnesota graduate performs as a community contributor who appreciates and understands diversity and the interdependence of people in local and global communities; demonstrates a respect for human differences.

Missouri: Graduates will be effective members of society who possess a sense of personal and cultural heritage combined with a curiosity about the understanding of people whose traditions are different from their own.

Nebraska: Acquire knowledge which is of long-term significance to themselves and our multicultural international society.

New Hampshire (draft): Students will demonstrate an increasing ability to appreciate the universality of human experience and gain a better appreciation of themselves and others; self-respect, respect for others, integrity, human worth, responsibility to self and others.

New York: All students will demonstrate commitment to the history and culture of the major groups which comprise American society and the world.

New Jersey (suggested): Each student must be able to demonstrate in personal work, and learning situations the ability to: use effective interpersonal skills (e.g., working on a team, leading others, negotiating, interacting with people from diverse backgrounds.) Each student must: demonstrate respect for racial, cultural, ethnic, and religious diversity.

North Carolina (Odyssey Project): Value the cultural pluralism of the United States, while understanding the special problems faced by a pluralistic society.

Ohio: Respect individual differences, points of view, and work of others. Function effectively within multicultural environments.

Oklahoma: Students work effectively both independently and in groups in order to live, learn, and work in the 21st Century.

Pennsylvania: Each student shall gain knowledge of various cultures in order to foster an appreciation of the dignity, worth, contributions, and equal rights of all people.

Virginia: Understand the diversity of our society and respect the civil and human rights of others; communicate and cooperate with people of varied backgrounds; understand the views and needs of others.

Washington: Function as caring and responsible individuals and contributing members of families, work groups, and communities.

Wisconsin: Students will demonstrate the knowledge and attitudes necessary to understand, respect, and appreciate individual, societal, and global diversity and to work cooperatively with people of different values and backgrounds.

Wyoming (Hot Springs County): Collaborative contributors who use effective leadership and group skills to foster, develop, and sustain supportive relationships with and between others in culturally diverse work, community, and family settings.

A Comparison of Communication Outcomes

Alaska: Communicate effectively; talk about feelings, ideas, and concepts with clarity; appreciate the value of reading as a lifelong activity.

Colorado (district): Demonstrates interactive communication.

Connecticut: Connecticut public school students will learn to communicate effectively in speech and writing; listen, view and read with understanding.

Florida: Florida students communicate in English and other languages using information, concepts, prose, symbols, reports, audio and video recordings, speeches, graphic displays, and computer-based programs.

Georgia (Gwinnett Co.): Effective communicator who informs, expresses self, and persuades by sending and receiving verbal and non-verbal languages; writes to communicate personal feelings, attitudes, and ideas; writes to communicate technical information and/or judgments; uses oral and non-verbal language to communicate in both formal and informal settings; actively listens, interprets, and responds to verbal messages and other auditory cues.

Illinois: All state residents will be literate, lifelong learners knowledgeable of their rights and able to contribute to society.

Indiana (district): Attainment of interpersonal understandings; pursuit of comprehensions and applications of family and group communications functions, and relationships in various social, cultural, and ethnic settings.

Kansas: Students have the communication skills necessary to live, learn, and work in a global society.

Kentucky: Students are able to apply basic communication and math skills in situations similar to what they will experience in real life.

Iowa: All learners communicate in various ways with diverse audiences.

Minnesota: A Minnesota graduate performs as an effective communicator who receives and interprets the communication of others.

Missouri: Missouri graduates will be literate communicators who: present ideas effectively in a variety of contexts for a variety of purposes using appropriate technologies; keep themselves informed about issues at home, in their communities and in the world; listen carefully to others, anticipating their frames of reference, interests, questions and concerns, responding with sensitivity and insight.

Nebraska: Demonstrate strong, basic and advanced thinking skills supported by observation, communication, computation, reflection, and problem solving, including those needed to be productively employed.

New York: All children will read, write, compute, and use the thinking skills they need to continue learning by the time they are in the fourth grade or its equivalent.

North Carolina (Odyssey Project): Odyssey learners are: communicators who express ideas, information, intent, and feelings verbally, written, and symbolically.

Ohio: Demonstrate effective listening and communication skills.

Oklahoma: Students have the communication skills necessary to live, learn, and work in the 21st Century.

Pennsylvania: Communications: Each student shall become proficient in reading, composition, listening, speech, understanding, interpreting, analyzing, and synthesizing information.

Vermont: Vermonters will see to it that everty child becomes a competent, caring, productive, responsible individual and citizen who is committed to continued learning throughout life. Measures of success will include: effective communication through reading, writing, speaking, and listening.

Washington: Communicate effectively and responsibly in a variety of settings.

Wisconsin: Students will develop a command of the thinking processes of analysis, creative thinking, problem-solving, decision-making, visualization, and concept development which permit them to interpret and apply the knowledge base. Communication processes (listening, speaking, reading, writing, viewing, image-making, and other symbolizing) enable them to communicate thoughts with others.

A Comparison of Life Management Outcomes

Kansas: Students have the physical and emotional well-being necessary to live, learn, and work in a global society.

Oklahoma: Students have the physical and emotional well-being necessary to live, learn, and work in the 21st Century.

* * *

Alaska: Be a responsible citizen; be committed to health and fitness; accept personal responsibility for sustaining oneself economically; know parenting skills, respond positively to life's social, environmental, and physical changes; recognize how doing well in school relates to one's future; have positive self-esteem; know how to set and achieve personal goals; be confident and flexible; form satisfying relationships with others based on respect, trust, cooperation, and compassion.

Arkansas: Students will exhibit/demonstrate attitudes and attributes which will promote mental, physical, and emotional health; exhibit positive self-concept and a sense of self-worth and individual uniqueness; exhibit personal adapatability to change; demonstrate qualities of self-control and self-discipline; demonstrate respect and appreciation for individual and cultural differences; maintain healthy family relationships; function as an informed consumer; manage money and personal resources; work effectively with diverse individuals and groups.

Colorado (district): Demonstrate personal, social, civic and environmental responsibility; be self-directed learners who are adaptable to change; set priorities and achievable goals; evaluate and manage own progress toward goals; creates options for self; takes responsibility for actions; creates a positive vision for self and future.

Connecticut: As adults, students will be challenged to function successfully in multiple roles—as citizen, family member, parent, worker, and consumer. Connecticut public school students will demonstrate the ability to undertake the responsibilities of citizenship in their communities, in the state, in the nation, and the world; understand human growth and development, the functions of the body, human sexuality, and the lifelong value of physical fitness; understand and develop personal goals and aspirations.

Florida: Florida students display responsibility, self-esteem, sociability, self-management, integrity, and honesty; Florida students establish credibility with their colleagues through competence and integrity, and help their peers to achieve their goals by communicating their feelings and ideas to justify or successfully negotiate a position which advances global attainment.

Georgia: (Gwinnett Co.): Self-directed achiever who develops self-respect by accomplishing personal goals based on high standards; manages time, money, and resources effectively; assesses and modifies personal skills and abilities to maintain a positive view of self and to recognize one's impact on others; involved citizen who accepts responsibility for contributing time and talent toward community and global affairs to enhance the quality of life for all; identifies personal and community values; demonstrates integrity by choosing and applying responsible and ethical courses of action.

Illinois: Each child will receive support services necessary to enter school ready to learn. The school system shall lead in seeking coordinated health, human, and social services for children and their families.

Indiana: Moral and ethical character enhancement; pursuit of judgments and behaviors portraying personal and social commitments to principles reflecting truth and goodness.

Indiana (Draft): Pursuit of judgments and behaviors portraying personal and social commitments to principles reflecting truth and goodness; pursuit of competencies and practices allowing for realistic assessment and acceptance of self and others and for adjustments in coping with physical, psychological, and social changes; pursuit of attitudes and capabilities to produce socially and personally needed products and services; pursuit of abilities to know one's self, search for meaning in one's activities, make purposeful and responsible decisions, develop a philosophy of one's existence, and select lifelong learning goals.

Iowa: All learners manage life to promote personal and interpersonal well-being.

Kentucky: Students shall develop their abilities to become self-sufficient individuals; students shall develop their ability to become responsible members of a family, work group, or community; students shall develop their ability to solve both problems in school and in a variety of situations similar to what they will encounter in life; demonstrate healthy lifestyles; demonstrate self-control and self discipline; demonstrate ability to make decisions on ethical values; demonstrate caring, responsive, consistent behavior; demonstrate an open mind to alternative perspectives; use critical thinking skills in life.

Maine: By the year 1998, child and family services will be delivered through a system with the following characteristics: in each community, children's readiness to learn will be assessed by research-based standards of emotional, social, and physical well-being; communities will be accountable through their school boards for improving the emotional, social, and physical well-being of their children through the coordinated uses of local, state, and federal resources.

Minnesota: The Minnesota graduate performs as a community contributor who makes informed decisions and exercises leadership on behalf of the common good.

Missouri: Missouri graduates will be self-sufficient individuals who: cultivate the knowledge, skills, and confidence needed to assume responsibility for their own intellectual, emotional, and physical well-being and that of others who depend on them; possess an inquisitiveness that stimulates creative thought and expression in a continuous quest to enhance the quality of life for themselves and for others; use reasoned principles to set goals and the self-discipline to pursue their goals effectively, monitoring their progress and reassessing the goals as needs arise.

Nebraska: Nurture their own physical and mental health and hold on to their initial excitement and interest in learning; identifying, defining, and productively addressing the important problems facing them, their work place, their society, and the world at large.

New Hampshire (draft): Students will demonstrate an increasing ability to appreciate the universality of human experience and gain a better appreciation of themselves and others.

New Jersey (suggested): Each student must: act as a responsible member of a family, community, and society (e.g., commitment to democratic principles, respect for environment, adherence to moral and ethical principles); show a positive view of self as a learner, a worker, and a family member (e.g., self-management, individual responsibility, self-esteem, sense of personal efficacy).

New York: All students will demonstrate commitment to the core values of our democratic society and knowledge of the history and culture of the major groups that comprise American society and the world.

North Carolina (Odyssey Project): Odyssey learners are: concerned and confident citizens who carefully consider and commit to local, national, and global stewardship.

Ohio: Maintain physical, emotional, and social well-being; function as a responsible family member; manage personal resources to attain goals; establish priorities to balance multiple life roles; demonstrate appropriate interpersonal skills.

Oklahoma: Students have the physical and emotional well-being necessary to live, learn, and work in the 21st Century.

Pennsylvania: Each student shall acquire and use ther knowledge, skills, and habits necessary to promote individual, family, and community health and wellness; each student shall acquire the use of knowledge, skills, and attitudes needed for successful personal, family, and community living.

Vermont: Vermonters will see to it that every child becomes a competent, caring, productive, responsible individual and citizen who is committed to continued learning throughout life. Measures of success will include: physical and mental health and fitness; students' development of self-respect; acquisition of skills necessary for the common personal and business transactions of life; knowlegeable exercise of rights, duties, and responsibilities of citizenship; students' acceptance of responsibility for their own learning, behavior, character, and health.

Virginia: Exhibit truthfulness, fairness, integrity, and respect for self and others; contribute to their own health, safety, and physical fitness; understand the views and needs of others.

Washington: Function as caring and responsible individuals and contributing members of families, work groups and communities. Know and apply the core concepts and principles of mathematics; social, physical and life sciences; arts; humanities; and health and fitness.

Wyoming (Hot Springs County): Self-directed achievers who formulate positive core values in order to create a vision for their future, set priorities and goals; collaborative contributors who use effective leadership and group skills to foster, develop, and sustain supportive relationships with and between others in culturally diverse work, community, and family settings; involved citizens who take the initiative to contribute their time, energies, and talents to improve the welfare of themselves and others and the quality of life in their local and global environments.

—Compiled by Cindy Duckett

Appendix B

The Myth of Local Control, or They Told Us This Was Wichita, But It Looks A Lot Like Tulsa to Me!

Sources:

Kansas Quality Performance Accreditation: A Plan for Living, Learning, and Working in a Global Society, Kansas Board of Education, March 12, 1991,

and

Oklahoma Outcomes for Educational Excellence Accreditation: A Plan for Living, Learning, and Working in the Twenty-First Century (draft), Oklahoma Board of Education

Outcome 1

Kansas: Teachers establish high expectations for learning and monitor student achievement through multiple assessment techniques.

Oklahoma: Teachers establish high expectations for learning and monitor student achievement through multiple assessment techniques.

Outcome 2

Kansas: Schools have a basic mission which prepares the learners to live, learn, and work in a global society.

Oklahoma: Schools have a basic mission which prepares the learners to live, learn, and work in a global society.

Outcome 3

Kansas: Schools provide planned learning activities within an orderly and safe environment which is conducive to learning.

Oklahoma: Schools provide planned learning activities within an orderly and safe environment which is conducive to learning.

Outcome 4

Kansas: Schools provide instructional leadership which results in improved student performance in an effective school environment.

Oklahoma: Schools provide instructional leadership which results in improved student performance in an effective school environment.

Outcome 5

Kansas: Students have the communications skills necessary to live, learn, and work in a global society.
Oklahoma: Students have the communication skills necessary to live, learn, and work in a global society.

Outcome 6

Kansas: Students think creatively and problem-solve in order to love, learn, and work in a global society.
Oklahoma: Students think creatively and problem solve in order to live, learn, and work in the 21st Century.

Outcome 7

Kansas: Students work effectively both independently and in groups in order to live, learn, and work in the 21st Century.
Oklahoma: Students work effectively both independently and in groups in order to live, learn, and work in the 21st Century.

Outcome 8

Kansas: Students have the physical and emotional well-being necessary to live, learn, and work in a global society.
Oklahoma: Students have the physical and emotional well-being necessary to live, learn, and work in the 21st Century.

Outcome 9

Kansas: All staff engage in ongoing professional development based on the outcomes identified in the school improvement plan.
Oklahoma: All staff engage in ongoing professional development based on the outcomes identified in the school improvement plan.

Outcome 10

Kansas: Students participate in lifelong learning.
Oklahoma: Students participate in lifelong learning as contributing members of a community of learners.

Appendix C

(Note: A Michigan parents' group compiled what it found to be the symptoms of OBE and circulated the list widely. It has popped up as a reprint in diverse places, ranging from meetings of educators pooh-poohing its contents to anti-OBE tomes. It is reprinted here by permission not to suggest that each factor from A to Z necessarily proves that a school system "has" full-blown OBE, but rather to illustrate how these parents had been paying close attention to all the telltale buzzwords coming out of their school bureaucracies.)

The ABC's of OBE
Does Your School Have OBE?
It Does If:

A. You have a mission or belief statement which includes "All Children Can Learn."

B. You have a three-to-five-year Improvement Plan.

C. An Annual Report is issued at district and building level.

D. You have Site-Based Management. Have your teachers and parents been empowered by serving on hand-picked committees to develop a mission statement or a 3–5 year Improvement Plan?

E. You have Cooperative Learning or Peer Tutoring.

F. You have multi-age level grouping, having eliminated grades K–3 to start with.

G. You have replaced Carnegie Units (specified course requirements for graduation) with Outcomes (or Benchmarks) that must be achieved or demonstrated.

H. You have replaced Carnegie Units (specified course requirements for graduation) with Outcomes (or Benchmarks) that must be achieved or demonstrated.

I. You have inclusive Education (mainstreaming of Special Education and Juvenile Delinquents into regular classrooms).

J. You have extended school day, year (200 days or more) to year-round school.

K. You have Thematic Teaching (all classes teach to the same theme over a certain length of time).

L. You have Team Teaching.

M. You have removed competition by cooperative learning and group grades, as well as by elimination of valedictorian or salutatorian.

N. You have eliminated rote memorization of facts and knowledge (content) and replaced it with what is perceived as realistic and relevant teaching.

O. Your teachers are referred to as facilitators, coaches, or interactive participants.

P. Your teaching staff is continually involved in professional development to train them in consensus building and collaboration.

Q. If you frequently hear references to Spady, Hornbeck, Sizer, Goodlad, etc.

R. You have been accredited by the North Central Association or another Accreditation program, or are in the process of being accredited. Both systems are outcome-based models (schools are required to target their evaluation efforts by measuring changes in students' behaviors). "It is now the rule that the government must supervise accreditation; it cannot be just a private enterprise." (Dr. Ralph W. Tyler, "The History of School Evaluation in America," *Create Newsletter*, Feb., 1992.)

S. You have Individualized Education Plans (IEPs) or Child-Centered Education.

T. You have continual assessment of Growth and Development.

U. You have collaboration and consensus as a goal of all committees.

V. You have portfolios.

W. You stress higher order thinking skills (HOTS) or critical thinking (focuses on deciding what to believe or do) and the use of Bloom's Taxonomy (used to inculcate a prescribed set of values).

X. You have partnerships between parents and the school, the community, and the school, business, and the school, and have established Foundations to help the school be more innovative.

Y. You have a school nurse, school counselor, school psychologist, school social worker, or the Student Assistance Program, linking the schools with all community service agencies with the goal of becoming a "one-stop, service provider."

Z. You hear reference to Mastery Learning, Performance Based Education, Glasser's Reality Therapy, Management by Objectives (MBO), Planning Programming Budgeting Systems (PPBS), Total Quality Management (TQM), Accelerated Schools, Effective Schools, Comer Schools, Johnson City schools, Schools for the 21st Century, Sizer's Coalition of Essential Schools, Professional Development Schools,

Outcomes-Driven, Developmental Model (ODDM), all of which are Outcomes-Based Education.

—Prepared and researched by
Michigan Alliance of Families
P. O. Box 241
Flushing, MI 48433

Honor Roll

(Honoring grassroots organizations that have made a difference for the better in their communities.)

Schoolhouse News

824 E. 77th Street
Newport News, VA 23605

(804) 838-4592
Terrie Harper, Director

Terrie Harper from Newport News, Virginia found that there was a need and an interest in getting information out to the families within her community. Terrie started and hosts a television show called Schoolhouse News which airs on her local cable access channel.

Schoolhouse News is about "education reform and how the changing face of education will affect you and your family". Terrie states that she has several simple goals: (1) to inform, (2) to bring on guests who are "out there at the meetings, writing the letters"...informing the audience of what is happening at the federal, state or local levels and (3) most importantly, getting folks involved...showing them how one person standing in the gap can make a difference.

Her first guest was Kerri Vailati, another grassroots worker. In addition, Terrie has had on her first show teachers, community leaders, parents (imagine that!), local school board members, state school board members, national education speakers and on and on.

According to Terrie, the really great thing about her television show is that anyone can do the same thing. Usually local public access television shows only require that you fill out simple forms. Production costs are minimal to free. You can tape your own series or rebroadcast tapes that Terrie has already produced. Terrie is also interested in broadcasting interviews you might send to her. For more information, you can write Terrie and Schoolhouse News at 824 77th Street, Newport News, VA 23605 or call (804) 838-4592.

Appendix D

OBE: DOA

A sampler of headlines from around the country

OBE: DOA
Richmond (Va.) *Times-Dispatch*, September 16, 1993.

In Littleton, Colo., Voters Expel Education Faddists
The Wall Street Journal, Nov. 17, 1993.

Board Tosses Out O.B.E. (Montgomery, Texas)
Education Week, June 15, 1994.

Minn. District Scraps O.B.E. Experiment Seen as Model,
Rosemont-Apple Valley-Eagan, Minnesota
Education Week, June 1, 1994.

Public Opposition Kills Reform Plan in Conn. Legislature,
Education Week, May 11, 1994.

OBE Strictly Local Option, Garrett (State Superintendent of Schools) Says,
The Daily Oklahoman, April 23, 1993.

Victory in Alabama! OBE Put on Hold,
Education Reporter, June, 1994.

Pa. House rejects proposal to teach attitudes in school,
The Washington Times, February 10, 1993.

After three strikes—Is OBE out? In Pennsylvania? In South Dakota? In North Carolina?
Education Reporter, April, 1994.

Honor Roll

(Honoring grassroots organizations that have made a difference for the better in their communities.)

Eagle Forum

VIRGINIA	**NATIONAL**
3128 N. 17th Street	**68 Fairmount**
Arlington, VA 22201	**Alton, IL 62002**
(703) 243-7660	**(618) 462-5415**
Helen Blackwell, State Director	**Phyllis Schlalfly, Founder and President**

Eagle Forum, America's first national pro-family organization, was founded by Phyllis Schlalfly in 1972 to meet the need for a bold voice on behalf of the traditional family at the state and local level.

Phyllis Schlalfly brought the growing problem in the schools to national attention in 1984 with the publication of *Child Abuse in the Classroom*. This widely distributed paperback contained testimony given in seven regional hearings held throughout the country by the U.S. Department of Education, in which parents were allowed to describe a shocking plethora of psychological tests and games, role-playing, mind-altering activities, hypnotic techniques and other abuses having nothing to do with genuine education or learning, which had been experienced by their children in public schools, almost entirely without the parents' knowledge or permission.

It was Mrs. Schlalfly herself who had persistently urged and finally persuaded the Reagan administration to hold the hearings, against vigorous resistance from the educational establishment.

The distribution of *Child Abuse in the Classroom* awakened the nation to these inexcusable practices, as many readers recognized techniques that were being used in their own local schools and being forced upon their own children. The book helped to focus national attention upon such programs as "Values Clarification" and discredit them.

In 1986 Eagle Forum began publishing a monthly tabloid newsletter, the *Education Reporter*, to share news about the battles over education cropping up everywhere, but ignored by the liberal news media. The *Reporter* became a valuable source of information to public officials as well as parents, and a networking tool for the valiant education warriors in almost every state.

The Eagle Forum office became a clearinghouse for information on the subject, fielded hundreds of thousands of inquiries, and referred many newly awakened citizens to Eagle Forum leaders in their respective state or locality. While some states were already in its grip, others, like Alabama and Virginia, were able to turn it away.

Alabama Eagle Forum mounted an extensive campaign, including proposing their own alternative to OBE, providing genuine education reform.

Appendix E

THE VIRGINIA COMMON CORE OF LEARNING

(excerpts)

DRAFT
October 20, 1992

Virginia Department of Education
P. O. Box 2120
Richmond, Virginia 23216-2120

Personal Well-Being and Accomplishment

Growth and improvement begin and end with the individual—with one's inner self; one's personal dispositions and beliefs; one's individual assumption of responsibility for attitudes, thoughts, choices, and actions. This dimension embraces the physical, mental, emotional, and spiritual aspects of life that provide the foundation for personal fulfillment.

Life Context

An increasingly complex, changing environment that creates a high degree of personal and public uncertainty. • Global interrelationships that will strongly influence educational and productivity standards for Virginia's citizens. • A social environment marked by increasing ethnic, economic, and age-related diversity and the danger of polarization • Increasingly complex issues and problems relating to health care • A diversity of values and information influencing personal choices.

Life Role for Personal Well-Being and Accomplishment

A fulfilled individual who has a good sense of his/her abilities and needs, and uses that knowledge consistently to make choices likely to lead to a healthy, productive, and fulfilling life.

Student Outcomes

A student who is becoming a fulfilled individual uses the Fundamental Skills of Thinking, Problem Solving, Communicating, Quantifying, and Collaborating to:

- Analyze personal strengths and limitations to improve behaviors, capabilities, and plans.
- Implement and manage personal, educational, and career plans and revise those plans according to changing circumstances.
- Exhibit behaviors that contribute to wellness, safety, and physical fitness.
- Balance intellectual, emotional, physical, artistic, and material goals and activities.
- Manage personal needs without ignoring the needs and rights of others.
- Critique and verify information necessary for making important life decisions.

Interpersonal Relationships

In our complex world the skills required for human relationships are becoming more and more important; people must be able to live in harmony. This dimension embodies the range of family, personal, community, business, or international associations that each individual encounters in life.

Life Context

Cultural diversity among the people with whom we must live and work • Need to work collaboratively to produce high-quality products and services and compete successfully in the global marketplace

• Rapid and extensive changes in communication and emerging technologies that will affect life roles and human relationships.

Life Role for Interpersonal Relationships

A supportive person who values associations with other people, and builds and maintains a variety of beneficial human relationships.

Student Outcomes

A student who is becoming a supportive person uses the Fundamental Skills of Thinking, Problem Solving, Communicating, Quantifying, and Collaborating to:

- Build and support friendships.
- Exhibit principles of truthfulness, respect, fairness, and integrity.
- Analyze conflict to discover methods of cooperative resolution.
- Encourage and support the views and needs of family members, other members of the community, and work-related associates as appropriate.
- Explore other cultures in order to understand, communicate with, and cooperate with people of other communities and nations.

Life-Long Learning

Today's students, educators, and citizens should not think of learning as something that occurs only, or even primarily, in a school. This dimension reflects the reality that new challenges, ideas, information, and opportunities present themselves both in and outside of the classroom, and long after the years of formal schooling have been completed.

Life Context

An information age created and accelerated by advanced technologies • Knowledge increasing at an exponential rate • High expectations for quality products and services • Unequal distribution of resources for education • Social and cultural diversity stimulating increased global interdependence • Better understanding of how people learn

Life Role for Life-Long Learning

A self-directed learner who continually gains in knowledge and in the ability to respond to a changing environment.

Student Outcomes

A student who is becoming a self-directed learner uses the Fundamental Skills of Thinking, Problem Solving, Communicating, Quantifying, and Collaborating to:

- Anticipate new situations and probable needs, and use the knowledge that these circumstances require.
- Use information, organizations, and persons as learning resources.
- Demonstrate confidence in using knowledge and skills to think, to solve problems, to communicate ideas, and to model collaborative learning strategies in various settings.
- Use efficient learning techniques to acquire and apply new knowledge and skills.
- Modify information sources and learning strategies as the situation or need demands.

Cultural and Creative Endeavors

Life can be enhanced through an understanding and appreciation of one's own culture and that of others. This dimension includes the range of activities and personal contributions that give expression, meaning, and enhancement to both the individual and the community.

Life Context

The proliferation of multicultural contacts and relationships • Demands for cultural and artistic activities and programs in an environment of shrinking funds, facilities, and resources • An increasing use of complex technology for creating and sharing cultural products and services • A growing need for outlets for individual expression to counter and to balance demands for standardization and for the depersonalization of many human activities

Life Role for Cultural and Creative Endeavors

An expressive contributor who appreciates and enjoys cultural and creative activities, participates in them, and grasps important ways in which culture defines both the individual and society.

Student Outcomes

A student who is becoming an expressive contributor uses the Fundamental Skills of Thinking, Problem Solving, Communicating, Quantifying, and Collaborating to:

- Investigate and participate in various cultural and creative endeavors.
- Express insights, feelings, and perceptions through a variety of creative performances or products.
- Explore a variety of leisure activities.
- Analyze how cultures, technology, and the arts transform human perceptions.
- Examine ways that culture and the arts reflect the aesthetics, history, beliefs, values, and traditions of people in present and past societies.

Work and Economic Well-Being

The well-being and vitality of a community depend heavily upon the productivity of all of its members. This dimension encompasses the range of skills, abilities, and attitudes necessary to produce, market, and deliver quality services and products.

Life Context

A workplace where frontline workers are responsible for problem solving and managing the production process • A need for employee retraining programs that enable persons to adapt to changing technology and production methods • The changing nature of work to include various technologies • A work environment that may not value investment in human resources as a key to success in a global economy • A demand for people who can perform a variety of tasks and serve as effective team members and leaders

Life Role for Work and Economic Well-Being

An efficient producer who takes responsibility for consistently producing high-quality products or services.

Student Outcomes

A student who is becoming a quality producer uses the Fundamental Skills of Thinking, Problem Solving, Communicating, Quantifying, and Collaborating to:

• Create quality products and/or services.
• Collaborate effectively in planning, producing, and delivering products and/or services.
• Support and encourage accountability for individual contributions within the group process.
• Recognize and adapt to changes in work methods as needed.
• Use merging technologies and resources to meet the demands of competition in a global marketplace.

Local and Global Civic Participation

The involvement of all members of society is especially important in periods of rapid change. This dimension encompasses the diversity of political, economic, and social rights and responsibilities of citizenship, both in the local and international community.

Life Context

A growing disparity in the distribution of wealth and resources worldwide • A world characterized by increasing interaction of racial, ethnic, and cultural groups • Worldwide communication that provides a limited view of social, political, and economic realities • An increasing population of individuals needing assistance in caring for themselves • An increasingly mobile population resulting in reduced involvement in local government • Increasing globalization of industry, coupled with a lack of understanding among consumers as to how foreign markers and economies affect personal economic decisions and circumstances.

Life Role for Local and Global Civic Participation

An involved citizen who is well informed about the history, political structure, and needs of his/her community, and is involved in local, national, and international issues.

Student Outcomes

A student who is becoming an involved citizen uses the Fundamental Skills of Thinking, Problem Solving, Communicating, Quantifying, and Collaborating to:
• Identify community problems and negotiate solutions contributing to the public good.

- Explore the history and culture of, and communicate with, people from a variety of social, ethnic, linguistic, and national groups.
- Cooperate with individuals and groups in seeking social, political, and economic stability and improvement.
- Support and defend civil and human rights worldwide.
- Analyze the meaning and effects of significant events, ideas, and public documents.
- Exhibit responsibilities of citizenship within a democratic society.
- Participate in and support community service activities.

Environmental Stewardship

Our long-term health and survival depend on our ability to understand the environment and act to protect, manage, and enhance its resources. This dimension concerns all aspects of living in, using, and preserving the natural world.

Life Context

Expanding imbalance resulting in irreversible changes within the natural environment • A rapidly growing world population • Steadily diminishing natural resources such as fresh water, fossil fuel, and endangered species • Accelerated conflict between the consumption of natural resources and the need to protect the environment • Proliferation of national and international efforts to preserve the environment.

Life Role for Environmental Stewardship

A responsible steward who comprehends the interrelationships and essential workings of the natural world, appreciates their vital importance, and uses resources both effectively and responsibly.

Student Outcomes

A student who is becoming a responsible steward uses the Fundamental Skills of Thinking, Problem Solving, Communicating, Quantifying, and Collaborating to:

- Investigate the structure and dynamics of the physical and living environment to provide a basis for responsible stewardship.
- User the environment responsibly, and encourage others to do so to improve the human condition.

• Appreciate the aesthetics and diversity within the environment, and their relationship to people's physical, social, and economic well-being.

• Predict the effects of human actions and the results of natural events on the environment.

• Develop plans and perform actions that protect and nurture balance within the environment.

Appendix F

The following are selected columns by Robert Holland that appeared in the Richmond (Va.) *Times-Dispatch*:

* * *

December 23, 1992

Look Inside Common Core: Less a New Paradigm Than Old Pablum

By Robert Holland

Brother, can you paradigm? Paradigm, paradigm, everyone's touting a new paradigm these days. Politicians, pundits, futurists, columnists, assorted other cranks—all God's chilluns got paradigms.

And now the State Board of Education is boasting that its draft of a Common Core of Learning for Virginia's public schools is "based on a new paradigm, that of transformational outcome-based education." This is supposed to be the centerpiece of the long-promised World-Class Education.

Paradigm is nothing but a prissy word for model or example. The central bureaucracy in Richmond is unveiling a New Model for public education.

Goodness knows, the old model needs more than a tuneup. But Virginians should follow the sound principle of "buyer beware." They should make sure they are not taking delivery on a lemon. They should kick the tires and get behind the wheel and see how this baby handles.

Copies of the 40-page document should be circulated in every school and parents and other interested citizens should be brought fully into the review loop before the Core's scheduled 1996 phase-in. The education department's Common Core "Team Leader," Harvey Carmichael, says that 4,000 copies of a rough draft have gone out to school officials, but that there needs to be "much cleaning up" of language before a public "marketing" campaign kicks in. I say forget the PR and let parents in on the ground floor.

Change is not the issue. Radical change—such as Baltimore's turning nine inner-city schools over to a private contractor, or Milwaukee's voucher experiment—might benefit education. The question is whether proposed changes are for the better—indeed, if they are genuine change.

The draft asserts that "relevancy" is the most pressing issue for education today. (Anyone else hear echoes from the "relevant" '60s when education standards went into a nosedive?) It knocks the old ideas of knowledge for knowledge's sake, distinct academic disciplines, paper-and-pencil testing, and competition at which some pupils succeed and some fail. Instead, the school of the New Paradigm should be geared to problem-solving in "real-life" situations.

The Common Core consists of 38 "student outcomes categorized within seven Dimensions of Living." Let me try to make a little of this real to you:

One Dimension of Living is "Environmental Stewardship." The "Life Context" includes such assertions as these: "expanding imbalance resulting in irreversible changes within the natural environment . . . . a rapidly growing world population . . . . steadily diminishing natural resources such as fresh water, fossil fuel, and endangered species."

The desired "Student Outcome" looks to be the production of little greenies who will buy wholly into that gloom-and-doom scenario. How is such blatant propaganda supposed to encourage higher-order thinking?

Some other Dimensions of Living are "Local and Global Civic Participation," "Interpersonal Relationships," and "Cultural and Creative Endeavors." There are repeated references to "unequal distribution of resources" (both globally and within the United States), to "cultural diversity" and "multicultural contact," and to being, yes, a good citizen of the world. It all sounds New World Orderish. And vaguely ominous.

At the back of the document, a few examples are helpfully provided. There is an instructional unit for 8-year-old students—8-year-olds!—on homelessness. The students are supposed to sally forth into the community to research this issue. No doubt it is old-fashioned to believe the youngsters' time would be better spent in class reading the classics of children's literature—notably, regarding the homeless, Dickens.

The designers of the Common Core anticipate children as young as 4 and 5 being immersed in community activism—indeed, early childhood education would lead the phase-in in '96. One problem: Public education is not yet compulsory for those ages. Does part of the master plan remain to be told?

Is all this "real-life" education truly a New Paradigm? In a history of Virginia public schools, J.L. Blair Buck wrote of a core curriculum plan implemented by the state in 1932 that:

". . . Instead of continuing the conventional requirements of social studies, science, and English for all pupils, it was proposed to allot about the same amount of time to challenging social problems . . . . The problems were of a kind about which both the pupil and the community might be really concerned: problems of health, of conservation, of community improvement, and beautification. The proposed way of studying these problems was to set the stage for cooperation rather than competition, initiative and self-control rather than discipline under duress. . . ."

That pitch 60 years ago sounds an awfully lot like what has again become the central bureaucracy's idea of revolutionary reform. In earlier days the real-life or holistic model traded under the name of "progressivism." To the extent that strains of that sappy philosophy are found in modern education, intellectual rigor suffers. (Buck did write that by 1942 the attempt in Virginia to organize instruction around "social and economic problems found very little acceptance.")

The State Board of Education means well but it ought to re-examine the assumptions behind its Common Core of Learning, which is supposed to undergird all learning in local schools. Attempts to impose this kind of scheme do not have a happy history: There's not a paradigm's worth of difference in utopias concocted by central planners. Better that the board looked to making teachers, principals, and parents freer to innovate at the classroom level.

Nor should competition and failure be viewed as dirty words. One learns from failure. And students will have to compete when they leave the unreal world inside schooling's cocoon.

* * *

January 27, 1993

Outcome-Based Education Seeks to Mold the New Virginia Child

By Robert Holland

Watch out. The Education Establishment is beating the tom-toms for a monolithic version of school reform—something trading under the deceptively benign name of Outcome-Based Education (OBE).

The National Education Association, through its Center for Innovation, is gaga over OBE, as are many pedagogues in education schools, think tanks, and state departments of education. Many big businesses—lured by the promise of job-worthy graduates—also are uncritically embracing OBE. The America 2000 program, launched by former President Bush and the nation's governors (new President Clinton prominent among them), is hep on the OBE paradigm, too.

Now OBE may be coming to Virginia. The opening shot is a bill in the current General Assembly to make kindergarten attendance (public or private) mandatory for all 5-year-olds, beginning in 1994. An effort to require enrollment of 4-year-olds will follow in a year or two, because the OBE game plan being developed in the State Department of Education anticipates massive state intervention in early childhood.

Concerning all this, I offer three pieces of free advice to parents and taxpayers: (1) Guard your wallets. (2) Weigh carefully the educrats' words, because—as with Orwellian Newspeak—they often mean the opposite of plain language. (3) Beware of behavior modification masquerading as solid academics.

OBE begins from an unassailable premise—that schools should be judged by "learner outcomes" rather than, say, the numbers of books in the library or teachers with master's degrees. But OBE would not make schools directly accountable to parents for concrete academic outcomes. OBE actually is the polar opposite of parental choice among a wide variety of competing schools. Parents are out of the loop.

Central bureaucracies predetermine the desired "outcomes," which have far less to do with whether Johnny can comprehend the Federalist Papers or place the Civil War in the correct half-century than with his acquisition of politically correct attitudes toward such matters as global resource inequality, multiculturalism, homelessness, alternative lifestyles, and environmentalism.

Many of the concepts and much of the jargon in a draft of Virginia's proposed Common Core of Learning are found in OBE programs in other states. In Pennsylvania, a storm of controversy has enveloped state educrats' dogged efforts to replace Carnegie units and standardized tests with 51 non-competitive "learning outcomes," such as these:

- All students relate (to current problems) in writing, speech, or other media, the history and nature of various forms of prejudice. . . .
- All students develop skills of communicating and negotiating with others to solve interpersonal problems and conflicts.

Thousands of Pennsylvania parents have turned out for meetings protesting OBE; the state's House of Representatives voted 170 to 24 against an environmental education component; and Governor Robert Casey, a liberal Democrat, urged that all sections on manipulating attitudes be stripped from OBE. No matter. The state's board of education arrogantly voted this month to forge full speed ahead.

Virginia's Common Core—not yet given final State Board of Education approval—similarly lays out 38 student outcomes within seven "Dimensions of Living." Color it all warm and fuzzy.

One Dimension is "Local and Global Civic Participation," encompassing "the diversity of political, economic, and social rights and responsibilities that individuals have as citizens of their locality, their nation, and the world." Typical student outcomes under this section are: "Identify community problems and negotiate solutions contributing to the public good," and "support and defend civil and human rights worldwide." Environmentalism constitutes another Dimension.

These aren't independent-study projects for high school seniors, mind you. They are the kind of "real-life" immersion that the state's schools would expect beginning in early childhood. (Ah, those carefree years—whatever happened to them?) Years away from a rudimentary understanding of basic science or history, children are supposed to have the answers to world problems. To be sure, they would discover them in "negotiating" groups, not as independent-thinking individuals, because OBE is predicated on cooperation, not competition. All pupils succeed; failure and retention are passe. Students teach other students.

The potential for indoctrination is enormous—and even if that is not the state's intention, NEA activists will take it as an engraved invitation. (To its great credit, the Virginia Education Association has not rushed to embrace OBE. Its leaders want more information.)

In fairness, Virginia's board does not appear to be in the headlong rush to implementation that Pennsylvania's is. The first draft of the Common Core is undergoing revision, and, if it passes legislative muster, a phase-in would not begin until 1996. So there is time—if anyone out there cares—to wrench the focus back to the basics of learning.

What about cost?

The Wharton School of Economics estimated a $16 million fiscal impact of OBE in just five Pennsylvania school districts. Spread over the entire state, the added expense would exceed $1 billion. In Virginia, the costs of mandatory schooling for 4- and 5-year-olds alone would be enormous. Yet no fiscal impact statement has been forthcoming.

Surely Virginians deserve to know the price tag in taxes for this statist vision of molding a New Virginia Child.

Moreover, they deserve to know what research suggests they would get for their money. Early OBE experiments in places like Chicago and Bill Clinton's Arkansas have shown that reading, math, and other achievement scores have declined. No doubt, however, self-esteem is sky-high.

Strangely enough, Virginia's Education Department has said parental choice plans are a no-go because of a lack of proven results. Yet the educrats would impose their Common Core vision statewide without a single pilot study or demonstration of success—just as, indeed, the state's "safe sex" curriculum was pushed into place several years ago.

* * *

February 21, 1993

(Part One of a Four-Part Series)
Re-Education, the Multicultural Way

By Robert Holland

Los Angeles—Go West, young man, go West. So why were the good folks at the Foundation Endowment in Alexandria passing along Horace Greeley's advice to me? Because opportunity beckoned in La-La Land: I could attend a four-day strategy session of the grand high poohbahs of multiculturalism, a movement that is gaining momentum in American education.

So it was that I came to Tinseltown as a registered conferee of the National Association for Multicultural Education, along with more than 700 educators from schools in every state. And from 7:45 each morning until well into the evening—from February 11 through a sweetheartless Valentine's Day—I went to small-group workshops on such weighty topics as "From Christopher Columbus to Rodney King: Power and Inequality in the U.S.," and "Instructional Activities for Fostering Multicultural Diversity Competence."

This total immersion in diversity-speak (which might be compared to Chinese water torture, multiculturally speaking) may have been just punishment for all my sins of 50 years—as well as my ancestors' for several hundred years before. I tried to blend in—as well as a white Southern male heterosexual and member of the oppressor class could.

Today I outline my main observations. Over the next three days I will go into particulars:

- Multicultural activists seek to reprogram children who are reared in politically incorrect homes.

Lily Wong Fillmore, a language professor at the University of California at Berkeley, stated that objective with astonishing bluntness. "When you consider the kinds of things I am proposing as necessary additions to the school curriculum for a multicultural society," she said, "there will be some definite clashes with the practices, beliefs, and attitudes that are taught in many homes. In fact, that is precisely why such curricular changes are needed and why the changes have to be for all children, not just those we serve."

Sadly, she said, there are parents who don't recognize that "differences are just differences," and some who "act as if they own the Earth and can do with it whatever they please. . . . [Therefore] no matter what their parents and families think about others or the environment . . . we are going to have to inculcate in our children the rules that form a credo that will work for a multicultural 21st Century. . . ."

• Parental resistance doesn't faze them.

Public revulsion over a "Children of the Rainbow" curriculum that glorified homosexual parenting ended in Joseph Fernandez's ouster as New York City's school chancellor the week he was to have spoken here. Never mind. His director of multiculturalism, Leslie Agart-Jones, came here conceding no mistakes and blaming the whole flap on distortion by parent and media critics.

A re-education workshop on how to "successfully influence behavior and attitude change in resistant groups" tipped off what multiculturalists have in mind for recalcitrants. Officials of a federally funded University of Michigan sensitivity clinic recommended a matriarchal game in which white males are not allowed to speak—the better, said Tasha Lebow, that "they get the first feel of what it is like for so many of us in society."

• For all the rhetoric about love and inclusion, this brand of multiculturalism tends to be hateful and limited.

Some within the movement do have benign intentions of teaching people to get along and of melding the best elements of diverse cultures. But that is not the primary focus.

Instead, disparate cultures are to be celebrated unabashedly—and uncritically—except for the dominant Anglo-Saxon culture that gave America its framework of constitutionalism. The duty of Eurocentrists is not only to learn about minority cultures but also to hang their heads in shame for the racism, sexism, classism, heterosexism, and environmental pillage their kind—beginning with Christopher Columbus—have inflicted on this land the past 500 years.

A teacher in a workshop put PC thinking into action. A white child had asked her why the class couldn't lay aside negativism and simply study Columbus within the context of an age of exploration. To which she had replied, "That would be like a Jew celebrating Hitler because he had a dream." So much for that pupil's cultural self-esteem.

• Americanism yields to multiculturalism.

"Creating the effective multicultural, multi-ethnic, multi-lingual society is a great social experiment," said Steve Lilly, education dean at California State University. "However, on the outcome of that experiment hinges the future of the United States—not as we know it, but as we need to know it."

One workshop's participants decided they did not like hyphenated

American names (African-American, Asian-American, etc.) But what they proposed to drop was, yes, the American suffix. They ridiculed the concept of a common culture. The multiculturalists would have us revert to our tribal associations. In schools, all immigrant languages—more than 100 in L.A.—would have parity with English. In Detroit, host city for next year's NAME conference, multiculturalists have removed American flags from their classrooms.

A nation without unifying ideals, or even a national language—there's a word for that, as well as a proper name:

Anarchy, thy name was Yugoslavia.

* * *

February 22, 1993

(Part Two of Four Part Series)
History Bent by Hateful Ideology

By Robert Holland

Los Angeles—When fads are running in education, the big publishing houses are sure to be close behind, if not actually in the lead. Thus it was no surprise to find three dozen publishers displaying their multicultural wares at the third annual conference of the trendy National Association for Multicultural Education (NAME) here this month.

Among the brightly colored books, posters, and audio-visual materials arrayed around a large room were works that could supplement traditional textbooks in positive ways—biographies of Thurgood Marshall, Simon Bolivar, and Indira Gandhi; the papers of Dr. Martin Luther King, Jr.; stories about many American Indian tribes, to cite only random examples.

Unfortunately, just as is the case with NAME itself, the baggage is exceedingly heavy: Gross historical revisionism in the service of a vindictive political ideology is overpowering efforts of well-intended people to teach about cultural diversity within a framework of national unity. Oppression pops up between covers that look deceptively benign—for example, in a "Let's Talk About Racism" book for third-graders published by Gloucester Press of London and hawked here by a representative of Children's Press of Chicago.

Inquiring young minds are told that racism is an invention of Europeans who "invaded the Americas, Africa, and Asia" over the past 500 years. "Black Africans were brought to America and sold to rich white farmers to plant and harvest the crops," the primer continues. Although a "terrible civil war" enabled them to regain their freedom, "today many people who have black skin must still fight the racism that came about so long ago."

Slavery was an ugly reality, but accounts like this are maliciously imbalanced. There's no mention of slavery that dates to ancient times, and that has been practiced in many non-Western cultures. Or any indication that a slave trade brought Africans to these shores—and that the traders on the other end were African lords selling their own people into bondage. Or any acknowledgment that the United States, while imperfect, has come closer to the ideal of racial equality than any pluralistic society in history.

Leading multiculturalists are plugged into the gospel of victimhood. They find it expedient to pretend that minority cultures are flawless (and sometimes to embellish their accomplishments—i.e., Egypt as the black cradle of civilization from which the Greeks pilfered all their ideas). Meanwhile, they condemn those of European ancestry—specifically, white males—for all oppression in the world.

How this plays out in an activist classroom became apparent during a workshop conducted for NAME by Jesus Nieto, a teacher educator at San Diego State, a state-supported California university. Drawing on pop literature like The Book of Racist and Sexist Quotes and The Peoples' History of the United States, Nieto launched his lecture with the profound observation that "we honor a slaveowner (George Washington) on our dollar bill"—one of which he waved overhead. As far as this workshop leader was concerned, the Father of Our Country had no redeeming qualities.

Nieto proceeded to tell a rapt audience that: Runaway slaves routinely were burned to death with green (slow-burning) firewood in New York state; the U.S. is in Somalia not to feed starving people but to protect Rockefeller/Big Oil interests; the capitalist system is defined by the robber barons; the Scholastic Aptitude and Stanford-Binet tests were devised by racists; the CIA and Green Berets are of Nazi origin; 60,000 people starve daily because greedy U.S. corporations have pushed them off their land; and so forth, ad nauseam.

Nieto concluded that "sexism, racism, classism, and environmental destruction" define the United States, and that "if [authorities] don't have a[n FBI] file on you, why not?"

To anyone who values reason, it cannot be reassuring that NAME devoted many its workshops—held at the rate of 15 an hour for 700 educators from all 50 states—to shaping the thinking of those who teach the schoolteachers. Most alarming was the teachers' docility: They were swallowing baloney whole. After Nieto's presentation, they flocked around to take his handouts, with tips on oppression-studies materials they could use in their own classrooms. Could anyone be that gullible?

James Banks, a University of Washington professor and leading multiculturalist author, bashed liberal historian Arthur Schlesinger, Jr. for arguing that the movement is "disuniting" the West. NAME's objective, he said, is simply "to get the West to tell the truth and to realize its ideals." And to do that, it is necessary "to construct knowledge based on our own lived experiences."

This construction—or reconstruction (or deconstruction)—begins with Columbus, who is being transformed from a visionary explorer into the most odious monster who ever walked the Earth. Never mind contrary evidence that neither Columbus nor the Spaniards sought to wipe out the native population (though mistreatment occurred) but rather to blend Christianity into their cultures.

For Nieto, the New Truth poses a bit of a problem, given what he acknowledges as his conquistador ancestry. But that only enables him to add guilt to anger, which makes him a double-barrelled multiculturalist on a mission.

* * *

February 23, 1993

(Part Three of a Four-Part Series)
All Aboard the Multicultural Express

By Robert Holland

Los Angeles—Multiculturalism means celebrating cultures in a grand profusion—reveling in all the diversity and not being "judgmental" about minority cultures.

Great, say homosexual activists; we want in on this multicultural education. We want schools to teach "gay culture," not simply the gay sexuality discussed in sex-ed or family life classes.

As became clear from attending a strategy session of the National Association for Multicultural Education here February 11–14, not all multiculturalists appreciate the gay-rights crowd's company.

During one small-group discussion, a black woman angrily denounced homosexual activists for "blending your cause with that of people of color. People died struggling for their voting rights. That is not the same as political activism on behalf of a sexual preference; that is not part of the multicultural expression." A black man rose to second her sentiments, only with "an even greater sense of resentment."

A woman identifying herself as a Latino lesbian tearfully retorted that her six adopted children "have gone through Hell because of the homophobia of people of color." She said it was time to change that.

These were tense moments. This discussion took place a few blocks from the scene of the bloody rioting last spring, and the possibility of more color-coded violence during the media-hyped Rodney King saga is never far from anyone's mind.

But the confrontation passed. And despite this flare-up the issue is moot: Gay and lesbian activism already is entrenched in the multicultural movement. How could it be otherwise among diversity-worshipers? Wouldn't it be elitist to deny admission to any group that deems itself a culture? How could suburbanite feminists be catered to in their every whim, but not homosexuals?

Publishers are offering a whole line of "anti-homophobia" materials, including books such as Annie on My Mind for ages 12 and up. It is described in a Global Village catalogue as follows:

"A fictional love story about two young women. A well written and touching story of how Liza and Annie fall in love when they meet at the school they go to [sic]. Liza tells us the story as she looks back on the year and remembers."

NAME conducted sessions on how educators (700 attended from all 50 states) could work homosexuality into the curriculum more thoroughly. Lesbian activist Denise Berro of California State University at Sacramento—liberally citing the research of University of Virginia lesbian activist Charlotte Patterson, a psychology professor—laid out a comprehensive plan of action. It included:

• A ban on "heterosexist language" in the classroom. Example: A teacher should never, ever say, "Take this home to your mommy and daddy" because the child may have two mommies or two daddies. Instead, say, "Take this home to the adults in your home," advised Ms. Berro.

• "Gay role models" for children in schoolbooks and on the teaching force.

• A teaching unit on gay culture, to include "fashions, speech mannerisms, and other distinct ways of being in the world."

• Use of supplementary materials to quell discrimination against homosexuals. She commended works of the National Education Association and the Anti-Defamation League.

There's no reason to believe that such a comprehensive homosexual agenda will be pushed with any less ardor just because the New York Board of Education voted 4–3 to dump one of the gay-culturists' most visible promoters within public education—schools chancellor Joseph Fernandez. In fact, NAME vowed to keep up the fight for Fernandez, who was ousted just two days before he was to have addressed the NAME conference.

Fernandez' "Children of the Rainbow" curriculum would have

begun teaching in the first grade that homosexual activity—including child-rearing—is perfectly normal behavior and an alternative lifestyle worth touting. It recommended books like Heather Has Two Mommies and Daddy's Roommate, the latter about a father taking a male lover after his wife leaves him.

In dismissing a community school board in Queens, Fernandez tried to ride roughshod over parents who objected to gay glorification for moral reasons—or simply because they wished schools to be teaching literacy, not lunacy. And that was his downfall. But many more battles are sure to come across the nation.

Clearly, the multiculturalists' strategy—as expanded on repeatedly during NAME's four days here—is to override unacceptable parental attitudes wherever found and to shape children into sensitive, global citizens who think the "right" thoughts about diversity, tolerance, equality, the environment, and such.

Ultimately what the diversity-cultists want, you see, is not diversity at all, but conformity of thought.

* * *

February 24, 1993

(Part Four of a Four-Part Series)
Multiculturalism Tucks Into Education 'Reform'

By Robert Holland

Los Angeles—Were the multiculturalists who caucused out here for four days to plot strategy to transform American education just a bunch of balmy radicals? Will they have no more lasting effect on society than, say, goldfish-swallowing—or a '60s love-in?

As a participant in National Association for Multicultural Education (NAME) workshops, I listened to ideas that once seemed too goofy ever to be accepted into middle-American classrooms:

Instruction about the culture of homosexuality. Rejection of American symbols of unity—July 4 celebrations soon may go the way of Columbus Day—in favor of a rainbow of exalted Third World cultures. A relentless search-and-destroy mission against serious literary works that offend members of the victimhood. And a determined effort to reshape children's attitudes in ways contrary to parental teachings.

But as comforting as it would be to dismiss these people as flighty intellectuals, they are gaining dominance. Indeed, as David Horowitz suggests, roles already may have flip-flopped, with conservatives now constituting the counter-culture. Writes Horowitz, a reformed 1960s-style leftist, in his pungently anti-PC Heterodoxy:

"We [conservatives] are the 'revolutionaries' demanding a universalist standard of one right, one law, one nation for all; we are the champions of tolerance, the opponents of group privilege, and of communal division; we are the proponents of a common ground that is color-blind, gender-equitable (in both directions), and ethnically inclusive. . . ."

How mainstream is multiculturalism? Well, in just its third year, NAME attracted educators from every state to a meeting at a ritzy hotel in downtown L.A. Although no attendance list was released, I counted participants from Virginia Commonwealth, Old Dominion, George Mason, and Hampton universities, and several Virginia public-school systems.

Theirs also is, remember, the party in power. NAME leaders could barely contain their ebullience. They reveled in the prospect that Bill Clinton will be the "diversity President"—a reasonable expectation given his use of color-and-sex quotas to fill his Cabinet.

NAME plans to move quickly: Clinton will be asked to hold a White House Conference on Multiculturalism. How could he refuse?

Besides leaning on friends in high places, these multiculturalists are looking at "pedagogical bonding" (as education professor Geneva Gay of the University of Washington put it) to advance their cause. The theme of the L.A. conference was a tip-off: "Creating Connections: United We Make a Difference." Declared Ms. Gay at a brainstorming, end-of-conference session: "You tie your agenda to somebody else's, and ride their tail. And that has been done to us on all kinds of occasions (notably by gay-rights activists) . . . Let's turn the tables a little bit and have some reciprocity . . .

"If we can persuasively achieve a tie between the generic principles of education, for example, and multiculturalism," Ms. Gay continued, "you almost have a captive audience, because people then realize that if they abandon multicultural education, they also have to abandon their anchor point. And that, I think, could be a strategy."

"We are winning the cultural war . . . in the trenches," exulted Ron Takaki, ethnic studies professor at the University of California, Berkeley. He cited required courses in multiculturalism.

Another education professor, Christine Sleeter of the University of Wisconsin at Madison, mentioned Outcome-Based Education as a candidate for issue-"piggybacking."

Indeed, OBE IS a wonderful match. In classroom philosophy, it is practically multiculturalism's twin. For a proposed Common Core of Learning, the Virginia Department of Education has been flirting with "transformational" OBE, which seeks to inculcate the very kinds of attitudes ("learner outcomes") sought by NAME types. Schools would expect students to acquire the politically correct outlook on maldistribution of global resources, environmental degradation, diversity of values, and multiculturalism itself.

But OBE is just one part of a larger movement in public education that dovetails with the multiculturalists' mission.

Surely there's no grand conspiracy. More likely, educrats just parrot one another's gibberish. But how is it that so many of the well-heeled foundations, the federally funded regional education labs, the education schools, publishing houses, testing services, and state education departments are singing from the same "reform" choirbook? They are moving virtually in lockstep toward replacing classroom competition (grade structure, objective tests, Carnegie units, ability grouping) with cooperative, feel-good projects that enhance self-esteem.

Suddenly, Big Education is pushing the "affective" domain—that dealing with feelings or emotions—out front of teaching basic skills. The movement is so monolithic as to create a feeling of helplessness among those who think it a dreadful mistake.

This is a curious reversion to the failed progressive education of a bygone era, and an even stranger way to be preparing American children for competition in an unforgiving world economy. But it is made to order for multiculturalism, which is more about celebrating diversity than teaching children to write a coherent paragraph in the language of national unity: English.

Here and there the resistance—the counter-culture—wins a battle. In Pennsylvania, a parents' revolt led to that state's House of Representatives voting 139–61 this month to reject OBE—an action that has at least slowed the juggernaut. And in New York City, a 4–3 vote of the School Board ousted the darling of the multiculturalists, chancellor Joseph Fernandez.

But the resistance is not well-organized. I returned from L.A. with the depressing thought that the situation is not going to get better anytime soon.

* * *

March 10, 1993

Education Invades the Affective Domain

By Robert Holland

Imagine this: A school system scuttles or downgrades tests requiring pupils to compute the area of a triangle, name the author of the Virginia Declaration of Rights, and identify the use of metaphor in writing.

"That kind of testing only rewards memorization and drill in 'lower-order' skills,'' the system's superintendent declares, after checking with trend-setters at the big foundations and ed-schools. ''We want a new kind of assessment that will test students' ability to engage in 'higher-order' thinking—to work together for a greater society: environmentally pure and culturally diverse.''

So in place of tests of achievement in reading and math comes an evaluation of 38 outcomes for pupils within seven Dimensions of Living.

A test for ''Personal Well-Being and Accomplishment,'' for example, calls for ''student completion of affective inventories.''

Huh? Here's a translation from the edubabble: ''Affective'' means emotions and feelings, as distinct from rational thought. This is a realm into which educrats are plunging pell-mell without a psychiatric license. So students spill their guts, and their innermost ruminations go into Big Brother's database.

A test for ''Interpersonal Relationships'' calls for ''teacher observations of student interactions.'' Thus, a gifted student who doesn't work well in a group must learn to mix before moving to the next level. Individualism yields to group goals.

Another test requires students ''to explore other cultures, including some aspects of language and customs.'' By ''other'' we assume that tracing the English roots of common law would not qualify.

And so this new testing scheme goes. Here, verbatim, are still more new tests:

- A student journal of his leisure activities.
- Student response to a vignette requiring the analysis of conflict and a discovery of cooperative resolution.
- Student(s') self-reporting on their responsible use of the environment.
- Teacher observation of the group process during a collaborative project.

The ''higher-order skills,'' you see, turn out to have far less to do with academic skills than with politically correct attitudes. Basically, psychological testing is replacing the basics. After pushing this for decades, the behaviorists finally have the New Age- yuppie political climate and the right-sounding jargon (''outcome-based education,'' OBE) to score big.

Unfortunately, I am not making this up. All this and more was in a draft of a ''Framework for the Virginia System of Educational Assessment,'' dated last December 9 and circulated to Virginia schools by the Department of Education.

Happily, Superintendent of Public Instruction Joe Spagnolo now says of the draft that ''we tore it up,'' because of reaction from educators statewide—reaction such as, no doubt, "how in the name of John Dewey do we measure that?"

Thank Heaven for common sense. Indeed, the last, best hope for education may be that many classroom teachers know where the latest gobbledygook from Ed-Central belongs—same place the confiscated spitballs go.

The bad news is that Spagnolo says "we are still committed to pieces of" this design and the state will be back with another draft. The December 9 version said the department wanted to get away from "one-right-answer" tests. Students should be given credit for, among other things, their "cultural strengths." A prime concern is "equity."

Pardon me, but this sounds suspiciously like a quixotic quest of equal outcomes through dumbed-down curriculum and evaluation.

A new system of assessment is supposed to be Step Two toward the World Class Education that Wilder administration officials from the Governor on down have been touting. Step One is a Common Core of Learning with all those warm-fuzzy outcomes, dimensions, life roles, and higher-order skills, but it, too, has been undergoing heavy rewrite.

World-Class Education is greatly to be desired, but you don't achieve it by decree any more than you gain altitude by standing on the roof and flapping your arms. All Virginians need to be debating far-out changes that are being obscured by a thick fog of educationese.

Do most Virginians really want to scrap well-defined Carnegie units for high school graduation (such as four years of English, three years of science, math, social studies, etc.) and replace them with 38 nebulous outcomes such as working well in groups, respecting a diversity of values, and thinking globally?

In Ed School Follies, written after a yearlong tour of teachers' colleges, Rita Kramer concluded that the goal of schooling "is not considered to be instructional, let alone intellectual, but political. . . . The school is to be made into a republic of feelings—as distinct from a republic of learning"

Virginia's education leaders ought to put all the touchy-feely junk in the shredder and insist on uncompromisingly high academic standards. Otherwise we are going to have education that is not world-class, but Third-World-Class.

* * *

March 24, 1993

Multicultural Express Rumbles Into Chesterfield

By Robert Holland

Computation is a basic skill, as is phonics. In the Brave New World Order of education restructuring, such old-fashioned basics rank way below politically correct attitudes, multiculturalism, and pupil self-esteem on the priority scale.

Still, one simple two-step calculation is entirely in order for the so-called Outcome-Based Education that Virginia's Department of Education is so determined to spread across the Commonwealth:

(1) How much is this massive makeover going to cost?

(2) What return can taxpayers expect on their, ahem, "investment"?

Extrapolating figures from a Wharton School of Economics study in Pennsylvania, the Virginia Taxpayers Association last week estimated that OBE could increase education costs across the state as much as $500 million. Is that figure off? Would the actual cost of teacher retraining, new textbooks, new tests, etc., be less than that? More? Wouldn't OBE drain money from other education projects? Or is the stage being set for a tax increase of Clintonesque proportions?

Mum's the word from DOE. Before the state goes one step further with OBE, a.k.a. World-Class Education, its leaders should have to talk cost, honestly.

As for return on the dollar, the shocking truth is that OBE—which is largely about inculcating the kinds of attitudes that infest National Education Association conclaves—is entirely experimental. There are no data to show that it advances learning. There is, in fact, evidence to the contrary. In Chicago, for instance, black parents sued educrats for malpractice, charging that OBE (then called Mastery Learning) had turned their elementary school into a "factory of failure." The district school board later dropped OBE after confirmation that test scores had plunged.

Meanwhile, Virginia educrats—with compatriots in 30 other states—are working up a full head of steam despite their claims that everything's in draft form and nothing's final. Yesterday DOE held the latest in a series of public TV workshops on OBE—this one on, uh-huh, "Overcoming Barriers to School Restructuring." And it has distributed $1.5 million for early childhood (ages 4–8) "demonstration schools" in Danville, Roanoke, Albemarle, Gloucester, Virginia Beach, Norfolk, Prince Edward, Winchester, Wise, Prince William, Stafford, and Hanover.

Chesterfield County is one of the school systems rushing to embrace the attitudinal approach ahead of the state's timetable. That's hard to figure, given the excellence the county's schools have achieved by stressing the basics. A radically revised K-12 social studies curriculum, scheduled to begin a phase-in this fall, typifies the new paradigm:

"We have designed this program," the curriculum committee proudly stated, "to enhance students' self-worth and their appreciation of a diverse and ever-changing world." The approach is "interdisciplinary" and "multicultural." Social studies used to be about basic history, geography, civics. Now, it's all about "global citizenship."

A 3-inch-thick manual lays out the New Social Studies in exquisite detail. Here is a small sampling of suggested activities:

• Fourth-graders studying "the first Americans" will be invited to make a mask and create a dance to participate in an Aztec religious ceremony (sans human sacrifice, one presumes)—this, ironically, in a school system that recently banned voluntary baccalaureate services. Evidently, religion is hunky-dory if it is "multicultural."

• Fifth-graders will study the Americas of the 20th Century by focusing on three persons: Cesar Chavez, Eleanor Roosevelt, and Colin Powell. So goes the Maya Angelou Grand Diversity Parade: a Hispanic, a woman, a black. White males like Teddy Roosevelt, Harry Truman, and Dwight Eisenhower are mere bystanders compared with such towering figures as a union boycotter of grapes and lettuce. Students will research various labor unions, including those for boilermakers, electrical workers, firefighters, mine workers . . . and teachers.

• In high school, each student will be compelled to perform 20 hours of community service annually. The teacher will decide what constitutes service. Projects with the homeless or tree-huggers are among the possibilities. Somehow I doubt that volunteering to help Concerned Educators Against Forced Unionism would cut it.

• In studying ancient Greece, ninth-graders could "write a newspaper article with the headline, 'Gloria Steinem Addresses Women's Group in Sparta.' "

The issue is not the status quo vs. reform. It is real reform vs. fake reform, education vs. political indoctrination. This is fake reform—PC junk—that profits no one except curriculum consultants peddling their wares to gullible educrats.

What works? The November, 1991, issue of *The Atlantic Monthly* examined the relatively few schools that did not—repeat, not—experience the 80-point plunge in SAT verbal scores that occurred in education generally from 1963 to 1980. The study showed that those consistently high-quality schools had these stands in common:

• They never abandoned a traditional liberal-arts curriculum to chase Sixties' fads like "relevance." They continued to stress English grammar and vocabulary, as well as rigorous math.

• They also continued to group students by ability in as many disciplines as possible. The contrast here could not have been more vivid: Schools that insisted (as OBE doctrine does) on classes of widely divergent abilities had the sharpest achievement drops. Those that maintained homogeneous grouping—thus tending to the needs of gifted and slower students alike—kept performance high.

OBE is a train wreck happening in slow motion. Must there really be another crack-up, and billions more wasted, before the bitter lesson is learned again?

* * *

April 7, 1993

OBE Express Overrunning Teachers

By Robert Holland

The letter was signed anonymously, "A Concerned Teacher." The subject was my recent column on the politically correct social studies curriculum that is supposed to go into effect in Chesterfield County this fall.

Multicultural and stuffed with globaloney, the curriculum is on the leading edge of the so-called World-Class Education the state government's education bureaucracy wishes to spread to all Virginia schools over the next few years.

The curriculum "is clearly a disaster in the making," he/she wrote, "and we, as teachers, have fought to no avail to have the program reconsidered. You need to know that."

One lesson you learn if you write long enough about education is that teachers who strongly oppose Ed-Central policy almost always fear reprisal if they give their names. That such intimidation should exist in a field dedicated to cultivation of the intellect is disturbing. Teachers, who are on the front lines, should feel free to speak their piece about what works best in the classroom.

Evidently, tenure is not all it's cracked up to be as a protector of freedom. Several other teachers, all requesting anonymity, have called or written to express concern about what's going down under the deceptive name Outcome-Based Education. Many more parents have called—and they're organizing.

An old rule of journalism is that anonymous tips are not to be accepted as fact; they must be checked out. In this case, Concerned Teacher had sent along copies of purported letters of dissent from social studies faculties of the county's high schools. To verify these, I filed a Freedom of Information request with the school administration for copies of all letters of disagreement on the curriculum issue.

The officially provided documents contained everything Concerned Teacher had sent along—and more. The level of teacher discontent with a curriculum that elevates "globalism" over teaching of basic civics and geography was staggering. From one secondary school after another—L.C. Bird, Clover Hill, Manchester, Midlothian, Monacan, Thomas Dale, Salem Middle—came strongly worded protests, some signed by entire social studies faculties. Sentiment wasn't unanimous—eight teachers at Meadowbrook favored the new curriculum—but it was lopsidedly against.

The teachers offered such thoughtful observations as these: The sweeping new approach has nowhere been tested; students will be hurt by de-emphasis on the teaching of U.S. government; the lack of a textbook will make cohesion difficult; the concept of global citizenship will confuse young students who lack a base of fundamental knowledge; the effect on Advanced Placement classes for bright students will be deleterious.

"We do not feel that our student population will benefit from the proposed approach," stated the Thomas Dale social studies faculty. "Our students need more structure. The conservative community in which we teach does not support such radical change. Many of our parents are veterans and expect that geography and government be taught in recognizable courses."

Objections overruled. Ed-Central's committee put the curriculum together over a two-week period last summer with the aid of a university consultant who was paid $6,000. (The total cost of the new curriculum is approximately $1 million.) The New Social Studies includes compulsory community service for all high-school students and more multicultural revisionism than you can shake a stick at. Cesar Chavez becomes a more historically significant (and heroic) American than, say, General Douglas MacArthur.

Chesterfield represents in microcosm the top/down approach to statewide restructuring on the OBE model. A State Department of Education memo inviting local superintendents to an April 25–28 conference in Roanoke lists a gaggle of high-powered consultants and university pedagogues who will discuss "Future Training Requirements for Teachers and Administrators for World-Class Education."

Funny thing. DOE insists there has been no formal go-ahead. Yet its fingerprints are all over the throttle. This looks suspiciously like a case of implementation first, approval later. (One hopeful note: A member of the State Board of Education swears that much of the feel-good tripe in the Common Core of Learning will be jettisoned in favor of hard academic standards before final board action next month. We'll see.)

Here's a tip-off on strategy: A politically and economically elite group has formed something called "Virginians for World-Class Education." A letter has gone out to CEO types asking for their support in selling the new paradigm to the public. It was signed by Jeannie Baliles, former First Lady; William Berry, director of Dominion Resources; Secretary of Education James Dyke; and State Board of Education President James Jones.

Having decided what's good for local schools, these worthies now want to "build grass-roots support." They've got it backward. They ought first to talk to concerned locals in places like Alexandria, where Ed-Central wants to eliminate all forms of ability-grouping (part of OBE's utopian vision)—and, of course, Chesterfield, where academic deconstruction is proceeding briskly. They also ought to talk to parents who prefer academic rigor over self-esteem and diversity pablum for their children. But everyday teachers and parents are not being empowered in this process.

Maybe it's about time they empowered themselves and recaptured these government schools.

* * *

April 28, 1993

Put Facts on the Table About Schooling Reform

By Robert Holland

Joseph A. Spagnolo, Jr., Ed.D.
Superintendent of Public Instruction
P.O. Box 6-Q
Richmond, Va., 23216–2060

Dear Joe:

Thank you for writing an Op/Ed piece last Wednesday criticizing criticisms of Outcome-Based Education, the concept that is supposed to revolutionize school curricula here and nationwide. The people will benefit from a much more extensive debate of OBE, or World Class Education, than has yet appeared in the public prints.

I confess, however, that your logic sometimes stumped me. You suggested it is wrong to draw conclusions about that OBE centerpiece—the Common Core of Learning—on the basis only of publicly distributed drafts. "How does anyone conclude anything, good or bad, about a project 'under construction?' " you asked.

Joe, that's like arguing no one should evaluate a bill as it goes through a protracted amendment process down at the General Assembly—that nothing pro or con should be said until it has become law or the Governor is on the verge of signing it. And if a gag rule applies, why not to you, State Board of Education President James Jones, and Secretary of Education James Dyke as well? After all, you three began touting this program long before the first revision was made in the first CCL draft last winter.

What was most intriguing, though, was your comment about "factual inaccuracies" in anti-OBE commentary. Because you cited no examples of factual glitches, I suspect you really are talking about incorrectness of the political kind.

But never mind. I hope we at least agree that it is important to get out to the public all the facts about this huge shift in the focus of education. To my way of thinking, it is folly to mix widely divergent abilities in one classroom, let's say, or to replace Carnegie units in well-defined subjects—math, English, and the like—with slippery, affective outcomes like being a "supportive person." But that's just my opinion.

In the interest of the facts, and nothing but, I am submitting the following request under Section 2.1–342 of the State Code, namely the Freedom of Information Act. (A formal request has been sent to your office.) Sought in particular are all documents, working papers, and correspondence related to. . . .

• Preliminary cost estimates for implementing World-Class Education statewide. This would include one-time start-up expenses as well as projected costs over a phase-in period. (You took exception to use of the Virginia Taxpayers Association's rough estimate of a $500 million price tag based on a Pennsylvania study. That figure was used, as you must know, only by way of inquiring as to the actual cost impact in Virginia. Would it be less here? More? Beyond saying there would be "associated costs," you never gave a figure, not even a hint.)

• A listing of compensation paid to all consultants—or obligated to be paid—in developing the proposed Common Core of Learning. (For instance, William Spady, head of the High Success Network in Colorado and a prime OBE guru, is listed as a consultant to the Virginia CCL team—as are several other worthies. Were they paid? How much? And how much have local consultants been paid?)

• An accounting of all personnel costs already incurred, or projected, for implementation of OBE/World Class Education. This should include costs of retraining teachers, administrators, and new hires within the department.

(ITEM: Superintendents' Memo No. 263 of last December 18 asked for each school division to recruit teachers to serve on work groups to develop standards for 38 student outcomes ("appreciating diversity," and all that good stuff). Teachers were to be paid $150 per day for each non-contract day up to 15 days.

(ITEM: Using a World-Class Education logo, DOE recently advertised for an Education Lead Specialist for Pre & Early Adolescence, salary range $43,854 to $66,958.)

• PRELIMINARY cost estimates for adopting so-called "performance-based testing," which would make assessment of pupil work more subjective by introducing such measures as work portfolios—personal journals and the like.

(According to a November 4 Education Week story, researchers "have stressed that performance-based assessments will cost considerably more than conventional tests but have not proven themselves better methods of measuring student performance." Joe, doesn't this amount to an expensive way to allow schools to duck accountability for low scores on standardized tests?)

• A list of any outside grants (from federal, foundation, or other sources) for World Class Education, along with any applicable mandates.

• Projected or estimated costs of mandatory enrollment of all 4-year-olds in the state, a move that is part of the World Class design.

• A copy of all research that formed the basis for your statement that "every dollar spent in quality early childhood programs results in saving $5 to $6 in reduced social, welfare, and prison costs."

Cost is not the only issue. OBE raises many concerns, including its potential for indoctrination and its deleterious effect on academic rigor and on opportunity for gifted children. But cost is a fundamental consideration. By all means, let's get some facts on the table.

Best wishes,
Bob Holland

* * *

May 5, 1993

Mobilized Parents Can Be Strong Force for Better Education

By Robert Holland

Parental apathy and indifference aren't universal. Contrary to conventional wisdom, there are a good many thoughtful parents who do care, and care deeply, about their children's education. And some of them who haven't been community activists before are being motivated to action—radicalized, if you will—by bizarre twists the Education Establishment is giving the school reform movement.

In New York City, a feisty grandmother, Mary Cummins, led the revolt against the multicultural, gay-glorifying "Children of the Rainbow" curriculum—a community uprising that toppled the school chancellor, Joseph Fernandez. In Pennsylvania, Peg Luksik of Johnstown leads a 22,000-member parents' coalition that has stymied the state education board's adamant push for Outcome-Based Education, the new paradigm preferred by behaviorists and self-esteem groupies.

What of Virginia? My constantly jangling telephone and growing stack of mail tell me that there's movement above ground and below—ready to erupt. The main rumblings are as a consequence of DOE's unfortunate obsession with Outcome-Based Education as a model for a Common Core of Learning (CCL) and pupil assessment.

Almost daily I hear reports of parents networking throughout the state to make their concerns known about OBE. Almost overnight, a grass-roots organization has sprung up in Chesterfield County called Concerned Virginians for Academic Excellence (Box 845, Midlothian, 23113). It is not affiliated with any political or religious group. Its members are primarily professionals and homemakers from Central Virginia, and linkage has been made with similar groups in the Northern Virginia and Tidewater areas.

The Education Establishment's strategy for dismissing the opposition to restructuring is one of the most disgusting exercises in disinformation since the KGB's heyday. The Denver-based Education Commission of the States—an entity fed by federal and state tax funds and liberal foundations like Carnegie—has led the smear campaign by distributing propaganda ascribing opposition wholly to "evangelical Christians" who seek "to take over the public school system." Just to be sure all opponents are tarred as religious fanatics, ECS says conspirators are trying to hide their agenda by concealing their true identities.

To be sure, some opposition is religiously rooted. In this week's New York school board elections, for example, the Catholic Diocese and Pat Robertson's Christian Coalition joined with black civil rights leader and mayoral candidate Roy Innis to distribute pro-family voter guides. People for the (un?)American Way may not like it, but the Constitution permits such activity. Nor, despite what the Agnostic Left would have you believe, are all religiously motivated opponents wild-eyed zealots.

Much of the opposition, however, is not religious or right-wing at all. Consider, for example, the Alexandria parents who have vigorously protested such OBE manifestations as the school systems' bid to drop an honors Western Civ course and to end all ability-grouping. Alexandria is among the more politically liberal enclaves of Virginia, and the parental OBE opponents reflect that profile. Consider, specifically, Sylvia Kraemer.

Ms. Kraemer is a self-described "left-of-center Democrat and lapsed Episcopalian." A Hollins graduate with a Ph.D. from Johns Hopkins University, she has taught American history at Vassar, Southern Methodist, and the University of Maine. She is the mother of two children in Alexandria's public schools. And she has written a 20-page analysis of the unexpurgated version of Virginia's OBE blueprint (last October's draft) that can be described only as brilliant. A few excerpts will not do it justice, but here they are nonetheless:

"Translated into the political agenda that follows from these 31 (and highly arguable) soothsayers' cliches, Virginia's public schools would be charged with training our young people to become well-adapted servants of environmentalism, multiculturalism, Total Quality Management (TQM), technological determinism, and public entitlements. . . . (This may be your political agenda, and it may be my political agenda. But it is not the business of taxpayer-funded schools to train followers for our political agendas.) . . .

"We also find buried here the Virginia Department of Education's requirement for heterogeneously grouped classrooms, and its 'Robin Hood' approach to classroom learning: Pupils who have the misfortune to be high academic achievers (to the extent that academic achievement will be noticed at all under the 'new paradigm') will be required to 'function as a teacher or mentor' for the less able or slower learners . . .

"Half of our trial attorneys can be kept busy litigating cases arising from the attempt of Virginia public schools to require high-achieving students to spend their precious in-school hours tutoring lower-achieving students. The other half will be busy litigating privacy statute violations arising from the Common Core's necessarily intrusive 'assessments' to determine whether students are acquiring the 'attitudes' and personality traits required for their 'life-roles'. . . .

"Some have argued that the kind of schooling proposed in the Virginia Common Core—a fundamentally anti-intellectual and behaviorist strategy for personality modification and group socialization—is now necessary because of the changing population of our public schools. . . . Where is it written that young Afro-Americans should not aspire to become physicians, scientists, business executives, and government leaders?"

Sylvia Kraemer expresses in a cerebral way what so many of us feel in our gut about academic deconstruction. If liberal and conservative parents buried their differences and got behind an intellectual manifesto like hers, they could be a potent force for a common core of genuine learning.

* * *

May 19, 1993

Virginia Importing School Agenda

By Robert Holland

In something of a valediction, Secretary of Education James Dyke last week assured employees of the State Department of Education that the devil theory favored by their bureaucratic brain trust really is true: All the opposition to Outcome-Based Education, a/k/a World Class Education, is attributable to an Op/Ed columnist who is distorting the program out of some malign motive, possibly "political."

And then, as if to say "nothing personal," Dyke called me up to say that he favored solid academics, not the gushy self-esteem glop, and that "we don't need some guru from California to come tell us what to do."

Fine. Then why do we need one from Colorado?

In his anxiety to assuage the education establishment's OBE blues before resigning office soon, Dyke perhaps forgot that I had filed a Freedom of Information request with Superintendent of Public Instruction Joe Spagnolo for some facts about OBE costs and implementation. Spagnolo's response arrived in a big box (no ribbon) the day before Dyke gave his pep talk at DOE.

One of the most telling FOI documents details the use of national consultants to help put together the so-called Common Core of Learning (CCL). And despite having been modestly listed as just one of 57 consultants in a document DOE distributed publicly, William Spady of the High Success Network of Eagle, Colorado, clearly has been the star of the show.

Virginia's DOE paid the High Success Network $2,000 a day to dispense Spady's wisdom at a two-day conclave in Oklahoma City last June 9–10. And then on June 19, DOE shelled Spady another $2,000 honorarium, plus travel expenses, to come to Richmond for a day to exclaim further the joys of OBE. (A DOE bureaucrat bragged about a bargain. It seems the Fairfax County public schools had paid Spady $2,500 a day.)

"Dr. Spady was selected to work with the Common Core of Learning Team as [sic] he is a leader in Transformational Outcome-Based Education, one of three design models being implemented across the nation in the area of Outcome-Based Education," DOE officials said in a document explaining why competitive bidding was not used to award him a contract.

That's true. Spady has his lucrative High Success Network perking in more than 30 states and several Canadian provinces, which explains why the attitudinal "outcomes" he favors for education are repeated almost verbatim from one state's "common core" to another's.

With Spady, a sociologist and former director of the federally funded Far West Laboratory for Educational Research and Development, comes a definite [one] world view of global resource maldistribution. His program for molding "correct" attitudes in the young is a linear successor to the behavioral modification tactics of a radical Harvard psychologist, the late B.F. Skinner, author of Beyond Freedom and Dignity.

Spady has not been Virginia's only OBE import. This spring, DOE has paraded what it describes as national experts in OBE from such places as the University of Florida, the University of Wisconsin, Cornell, and UCLA to work out standards undergirding the "outcomes" and to develop an alternative system of pupil assessment (basically, "no one fails"). For example, a Wisconsin professor was contracted to work on the CCL through August 1993 at a rate of $400 a day, or a maximum of $4,000.

National consultants are part of what will be a large OBE tab. Yet Dyke had the gall to tell DOE staffers, "We are not asking the taxpayers for more money to pay for World Class Education, nor are we seeking to establish another layer of bureaucracy." Ah, but they soon will be.

Spagnolo claimed not to have a cost estimate for the two-year budget proposal that will go to the General Assembly next year. But some pricey items are showing up on his staffers' wish-lists already—for example, $7.3 million for a Virginia Center for Staff Development to retrain local educators, and $41 million for a strategic plan for using computer technology to support OBE restructuring.

Furthermore, millions are being spent on implementation prior to formal approval of the much-revised CCL by the State Board of Education—for example, $860,000 for retraining teachers, principals, and administrators; $1.5 million for new tests; and $2.5 million for "transformational projects" around the state.

Dyke claims that editorial criticism has distorted the World Class Initiative by referring to the original draft of last October. The latest of innumerable rewrites—the April 15 version—is much better, he says.

Granted, some of the thickest jargon has been weeded, along with the most egregious examples of OBE in action, such as a study unit on homelessness for 8-year-olds. However, the new document merely camouflages more than it shows. The FOIA documents show OBE experts being paid into fall 1993 to flesh out the outcomes. And those continue to be largely "affective"—concerned, that is, with feelings.

This remains a Bill Spady/High Success production. And maybe there is a California guru as well.

A DOE insider has sent me papers from a February 22 DOE training session led by Sue Miller Hurst, director of the Starshine Foundation (Del Mar, California), which is described as "an international organization dedicated to maximizing human capacity." Together with Peter Senge of Massachusetts (yet another consultant, who was paid $9,000 for the one-day presentation), Ms. Hurst directs a project designed to transform education by "children helping children." She has worked with OBE restructuring at the early childhood level in Virginia.

My informant says my FOIA request only gives a "small glimpse" of what restructuring is costing Virginia taxpayers because it asked only about the CCL and testing, not about all the outsiders being brought in to retrain school people. As for Ms. Hurst, he/she said, "None of us has figured out what her message is yet."

It must be a powerful one to justify its price tag. Spagnolo tells me that DOE pays her $1,600 a day, plus travel expenses (usually from California), and that she has a contract not to exceed 60 days. Potentially, then, this one consultant alone could pull down almost $100,000. Wouldn't classroom teachers love to see money like that?

* * *

June 2, 1993

Test-Makers Seek to Impose Radically New Structure on Schools

By Robert Holland

The school restructuring debate has focused mainly on the correct-thinking, well-socialized students that ed biz has decided it wants to roll off the production lines.

But somehow the educrats will have to test pupils to determine that they match the specifications in the common cores of learning being adopted by Virginia and other states that are buying into Outcome-Based Education.

Rest assured that testing is far from being just an after-thought. In fact, the hand that controls the tests may well control the whole of American education.

The leaders of the New Standards Project (NSP), in which Virginia is one of 17 participating (and paying) states, have stated boldly that their aim is nothing less than "to develop a radically new approach to the assessment of student progress that would drive fundamental changes in what is taught and learned. . . ."

That statement came from NSP's working papers, which I obtained through a Freedom of Information request from the State Department of Education. DOE anticipates paying $300,000 a year through 1995–96 to participate in this project.

Located at the University of Pittsburgh's Learning Research and Development Center, NSP is a key player in the drive toward nationally prescribed standards and exams for schools, which looks like the final step to nationalization of education. Under President Clinton's Goals 2000: Educate America Act, the Department of Labor also would become more deeply involved with a new national board to set skill-certification standards for "occupational clusters" encompassing virtually every job in the country.

Up to its old tricks, DOL already is seeking to guarantee equal outcomes on a group basis on those tests. Lawrence Lorber, a Washington employment relations lawyer and former director of DOL's Office of Federal Contract Compliance Programs, says that could be done only by using different cutoff scores by group or adjusting the scores of applicants.

The latter practice is known as "(race or sex) norming," the workings of which were first exposed in this column in 1990 and which ostensibly was outlawed by the 1991 Civil Rights Act. (That no doubt is a mere technicality to DOL's numbers crunchers.)

Lorber calls the use of scoring tricks in the name of fairness or equity "social engineering masquerading as science." A review of the New Standards Project reveals a similar philosophical predisposition toward leveled outcomes—only this time the victims will be bright pupils of all races whose progress will be retarded by a dumbed-down group standard.

(Virginia bureaucracies seem to have a devilish fondness for these schemes. In the early 1980s, the Virginia Employment Commission helped DOL get the norming scam rolling. And now the Department of Education is supporting a plan to drive local curricula through national tests.) The NSP paper condemned as hopelessly elitist "a testing system designed to sort out those who would enter the elite from those who would not." So much for Thomas Jefferson's "aristocracy of merit." Under the new dispensation, we will all meet one "mastery standard" (another term for OBE), no matter how many cracks we must take at the test.

The purpose, the manifesto's authors frankly stated, "is to destroy the primary mechanisms of the sorting system in American education that have lowered expectations and limited opportunity for countless people over the years." Thus, "Having one standard for everyone requires the abolition of tracking (ability-grouping)—the assignment of students to work that is more or less challenging based on imputed intelligence."

In quest of universal mastery, they add, "we would have to explore ways to give students that fall behind more instructional time, more financial resources, a more appropriate curriculum, and better-prepared teachers." This is Robin Hood education—and the brainy (those of "imputed intelligence") possess the "riches" to be redistributed downward.

NSP's big guns are Lauren Resnick of the University of Pittsburgh and Marc Tucker, president of the National Center of Education and the Economy in Rochester, New York. As further evidence of collaboration in imposing standards from on high, consider that Tucker recently testified in Washington in favor of DOL's national job skills board.

Please note that through something called SCANS (Secretary's Commission on Achieving Necessary Skills), DOL already is wired into school restructuring. SCANS is busily churning out work orders for the New American Child. And some corporate moguls who quietly acquiesced in norming are leading cheers for this even grander egalitarian scheme.

The CEOs' disillusionment with schools that send them too many unlettered graduates who don't even show up for work on time is understandable. No doubt they hope the new system at least will give them malleable young people who can work in a group. But shouldn't it matter that this feel-good approach will penalize real intellectual achievement?

SCANS has called for replacing report cards, for example, with student resumes, which would include teacher ratings of pupils' personal qualities. Among SCANS "competencies" to be tested are "self-esteem" and "sociability."

In short, supposedly hard-nosed capitalists—gulled by government bureaucrats—are buying into the progressivist pap of Ed-School and Ed-Central. Even more frightening is the totalitarian manner in which this bogus reform is being foisted on local school systems.

* * *

June 9, 1993

Liberals Join Cry Against Outcome-Based Education

By Robert Holland

The old version of the Virginia Department of Education's regulations required a special "educational program" for gifted students.

The new version, adopted last February 25 to become effective July 1, 1994, requires "special services" for gifted children.

Scratching out education and inserting services typifies the new thinking that "educating the intellect is a socially unworthy objective; that the mission of schools is to be a service agency," said a professional educator after analyzing all the changes line by line.

"This brings the liberal welfare-state concept into the schools." And my source is . . . who? An activist emerging from last weekend's Republican convention that nominated a solidly conservative ticket of George Allen, Mike Farris, and Jim Gilmore, and that loudly cheered all calls to squelch Outcome-Based Education in Virginia? Nope. A Pat Robertson or Phyllis Schlafly fan? Quite the contrary.

This particular Virginian opposed to the prevailing Zeitgeist in education is a liberal Democrat with a strong academic background—Sylvia Kraemer of Alexandria. And she is far from alone. Among the hundreds of calls and letters of concern I have received about OBE—a group-based approach to learning that injects schools deeply into inculcation of "correct" attitudes—are many from liberals who oppose this quintessentially top/down brand of reform as strongly as do conservatives.

Is this, then, an "extremist" concern? I think not. It is a concern that candidates of all parties would be wise to address this fall. Democratic gubernatorial candidate Mary Sue Terry also has expressed reservations about what the OBE gurus call a "paradigm shift." Let's hear more.

Today let's further compare the state's old and new approaches to education of the gifted:

Old: General intellectual or specific academic ability were criteria for selection into gifted programs.

New: "Intellectual aptitude(s)"—a squishier concept—becomes the gauge, not ability. In addition, evaluators may take "leadership" into account—however they may define it.

Old: IQ tests were used for screening and identification, as well as creativity tests by trained personnel.

New: IQ testing is out but aptitude tests may be used—although there is no requirement that a pupil score at any "prescribed level." Also, such subjective measures as a teacher's "record of observation of in-classroom behavior," "assessment of appropriate student products, performance, and/or portfolio," and "individual interview" are among the criteria for qualification.

The new regs also add such requirements as these:

• That all tests be "sensitive to cultural, racial, and linguistic differences," and that "identification procedures are constructed so that they identify high potential/ability in all underserved culturally diverse, low socioeconomic, and disabled populations."

• That there be a procedure "to identify and evaluate student outcomes based on the initial and ongoing assessment of their cognitive and affective needs." (Affective has to do with feelings and emotions—the touchy feely stuff.)

• That there be "appropriately differentiated curricula" dealing with affective/cognitive needs and encouraging "higher order thinking that leads to generation of products and a focus on issues, themes, and ideas within and across areas of study."

As Ms. Kraemer notes, that thick jargon injects OBE/Common Core of Learning concepts directly into the regs. How interesting that is, given that the State Board of Education approved the gifted regs in February but didn't adopt a CCL framework until May 27.

This is just another example of how the state's agents persist in steadily implementing OBE while claiming publicly that nothing is settled.

Truly gifted pupils are in a no-man's land under the new system. Where is a place for a shy genius with a single-minded focus on knowledge not easily translated into trendy "issues" or "themes"? By dealing a blow to intelligence testing, the regs dilute gifted education in accordance with egalitarian ideology. Indeed, with the new emphasis on "services" and behavior modification, some families may clamor to take their children out of gifted programs rather than to put them in.

What of those liberal OBE opponents? On paper, Sylvia Kraemer should fit a conservative's profile of Alexandrians worthy of a good long sneer: She is a member of the federal government's Senior Executive Service. She has a PhD in history and has taught at politically correct Vassar.

But her education liberalism is of the muscular kind that recognizes the value of tough courses, hard work, high standards—the kind of equal opportunity to realize one's individual potential that thoughtful conservatives also support. As for her objection to schools getting into personal values, she opposes any encroachment from the left or right (including compulsory prayer): "The public school is the agent of the state. . . . We should fear the power of the state; any political authority that has this power has the power to coerce you."

Other liberals, like Marie Jardina, a Chesterfield resident and member of Concerned Virginians for Academic Excellence, make a similar point: While not totally opposed to OBE principles, Ms. Jardina fears that family privacy, parental rights, and personal liberty are being eroded. In particular, mandatory community service—a feature of the new social studies curriculum in Chesterfield—is potentially a "violation of civil rights," she remarked. Clearly, a part of the disinformation strategy of OBE's implementers is to slam all opposition as right-wing and religiously motivated. That just isn't so.

* * *

June 16, 1993

School Restructuring, by Hillary

By Robert Holland

So who are the movers, the shakers, behind the monolithic effort to remake public education on a nationally prescribed model?

For one, try this name, friends: Hillary Rodham Clinton. And for another, this one: Ira Magaziner.

What's that, you say? Right Social Democrats, wrong cause? Sure, I know that a national health care plan has been the First Spouse's pet project, with Magaziner as her main helper.

Ah, but I'm telling you that Dame Hillary has a national education plan, too. Even though it is barreling toward implementation in many states, discussion in the major news media has been scant—in contrast with health-care reform, which has received intensive coverage even before its unveiling. But anyone willing to spend hours in the library combing mostly obscure journals can find the Hillary (and—ouch!—Big Business/Labor Department) education connection.

Before my fan club at the Department of Education accuses me of conjuring apparitions, here are some of my references: Monthly Labor Review (July, 1991); Industry Week (August 19, 1991); Employment Relations Today (Winter, 1992–93); Educational Leadership (March, 1992); Public Management (February, 1993); and Chemical Week (March 11, 1992).

The key components of the Hillary Plan are found in the Outcome-Based Education being marketed in Virginia and elsewhere as World Class Education. Mrs. Clinton serves as co-chairman for implementation of the Commission on the Skills of the American Workforce, which laid the foundation for the Labor Department's heavy intervention in school restructuring through its ominously dubbed SCANS system, beginning in May, 1990.

Hillary also is on the governing board of the New Standards Project, in which the Virginia Department of Education is participating. Based at the University of Pittsburgh, the NSP has the explicit purpose of destroying the current testing system and replacing it with an ungraded OBE curricular approach allowing pupils to take a group mastery test as many times as they need to pass it.

In the 1992 article with Magaziner in Educational Leadership, Mrs. Clinton sought to justify her scheme in the context of national industrial policy. To meet international competition, she said, U.S. workers must be trained in a wholly new way—as members of teams that produce more. Toward that end she laid out an OBE blueprint:

There would be one standard for all American students, to be met at or around age 16. "This standard should be established nationally and benchmarked to the highest in the world," she declared. Yet states would be responsible for ensuring that "virtually all students" passed this common "world class" test. (Can you say "norming," boys and girls?)

With a Certificate of Initial Mastery in hand, students then would choose among college-prep, taking a job, or a technological certificate. Meanwhile, the Labor Department would set "voluntary" skill standards—almost surely the precursor to sharp-toothed mandates—for entry to virtually all occupations. Guess what? That is almost exactly the centralized scheme that now has come down as hubby Bill's "Goals 2000: Educate America Act." Meanwhile, with the backing of elements of Big Business, DOL's SCANS principles—extolling OBEish "higher order thinking" and downgrading basic education—are becoming staples of school restructuring. SCANS asks schools to test for such worker "competencies" and skill "foundations" as "works with others," "self-esteem," "sociability," "self-management," "integrity," and "honesty."

This emphasis on probing the psyche, educator/author Chester Finn has remarked acerbically, neglects that "factual knowledge is to thinking skills as bricks are to mortar."

In fairness, the Presidents Clinton are not solely responsible for this utilitarian push. The self-proclaimed "Education President," George Bush, set much of this in motion with America 2000. And trade journals name such corporate prime movers in OBE and SCANS as Union Carbide, Motorola, TGI Friday's, MCI, Xerox, and Gannett.

But all this is made to order for Hillary. In fact, it may be what she has in mind when she speaks modestly of aspiring to lead "a remaking of the American way of politics, government, indeed life." One of her philosophical gurus—Michael Lerner of a leftist rag called Tikkun—actually wrote the following in an essay on the "politics of meaning" (a phrase Hillary has adopted):

"The Department of Labor should create a program to train a corps of union personnel, worker representatives, and psychotherapists in the relevant skills to assist developing a new spirit of cooperation, mutual caring, and dedication to work."

That may be gibberish, but it's not far from what's actually going down.

Yes, Americans do receive too few solid results for their investment in schooling. But this ailment is certainly not the result of excessive local autonomy; rather, education standards began sliding precisely as powers were taken away from local communities and placed in the hands of central bureaucracies, beginning with LBJ's Great Society in the 1960s.

Now we are asked to believe that Hillary Clinton, the race-norming-happy Department of Labor, corporate Clintonites, OBE gurus, and central educrats have the magic for transforming the schools. Even were such institutions "effective," would everyday Moms and Dads want their children to attend and be cast in the desired Total Quality Management mold as good Organization Men and Women? And would teachers want to teach in such centers of indoctrination?

* * *

June 30, 1993

How 'Authentic' Will the New Pupil Testing Be?

By Robert Holland

In a little-noticed release the other day, the State Department of Education awarded $125,000 to each of three groups of Virginia school divisions for the purpose of creating what it called "authentic" tests of student learning for the whole state. The first batch of new tests would be for the early childhood years (defined as kindergarten through third grade), which is where DOE's 10-year World Class Education timetable logically begins.

There was much more behind this than a routine spreading of a bureaucracy's cash-green fertilizer. Citizens attempting to follow the course of school reform should be aware of the following national context:

• "Authentic" is a code word for testing that will mesh with Outcome-Based Education. OBE stresses group mastery of common outcomes, and "affective" measurements—how students feel and think about "relevant" issues, as opposed to what they know. The contrast is with something a curmudgeon might call "effective education."

• New tests are to drive a new curriculum for all schools. That's the declared objective of the New Standards Project, in which Virginia is one of 17 participating states.

• Traditional standardized testing, which has provided benchmarks for (sometimes embarrassing) comparisons among schools and school districts, has been targeted for obliteration. No lesser lights than the presidents of the Educational Testing Service and the American Federation of Teachers said so in a joint Boston appearance some time ago.

This is not to imply that all Virginia participants in the testing project necessarily buy into such an agenda. Some simply may be taking an open-minded, constructive look at alternatives to multiple-choice testing. But at higher bureaucratic echelons, where key "reform" decisions are being made, all systems are go for a radical transformation of testing.

"Authentic" assessment takes the shape of "essays, open-ended questions, demonstrations, hands-on tasks, and portfolios of work that may be accumulated over a year or more," according to Joan Herman, a UCLA testing expert.

What's wrong with those supplementary ways of evaluating student work? On the individual and classroom level, nothing at all—indeed, many of the best teachers gauge their students' work in a variety of ways besides multiple-choice and true-false tests. (Essays could be particularly rigorous were it not for the so-called "whole language" movement, which holds that students should not be penalized for incorrect spelling, grammar, or punctuation.)

The problems lie in potentially scuttling—as a common yardstick of education—one-right-answer tests requiring a command of the basics, and in shifting to the attitudinal realm. In a federal research paper, Ms. Herman wrote that the "authentic" tests, "rather than measuring lower-level skills and rote memory," measure such things as "metacognitive processes and attitudes" and immerse children in tasks having "real-world applications." What, then, of Virginia's prospective "authentic" tests for early childhood? The very term implies that tests of what pupils can recall after repeated drill are somehow fake. But is memorization really so hideous, especially at this building-block stage? As Thomas Sowell writes in his superb new book, Inside American Education:

"It is hard to imagine how a small child, first learning the alphabet, can appreciate the full implications of learning these particular 26 abstract symbols in an arbitrarily fixed order. Yet this lifelong access to the intellectual treasures of centuries depends on his mastery of these symbols. His ability to organize and retrieve innumerable kinds of information, from sources ranging from encyclopedias to computers, depends on his memorizing that purely arbitrary order."

In sum, is anything more "relevant" or "authentic" than the ABCs or the Three Rs?

Although an advocate, Ms. Herman candidly concedes potential pitfalls for "authentic" testing. One major consideration is cost. Standardized multiple-choice tests cost $1.50 per child. The new Three Ps (performance, products, portfolios) tests cost upward of $10 per child to administer and score. Multiplied by millions of pupils, that becomes real money. Furthermore, Ms. Herman adds, there is no proof that "authentic" assessment yields valid standardized results. And a single year-long "hands-on" project does not provide the variety of sampling of traditional testing.

More chilling are intimations (in documents retrieved from education databases) of a movement into the touchy-feely realm by the 800-pound gorilla of assessment, the Educational Testing Service of Princeton, New Jersey. For example, ETS lately has been compiling 1,560 "personality and affective measures," such as ratings for "coping skills," "self-esteem," and "need for affiliation." ETS' Project STACI (Systems Thinking and Curriculum Innovation) is devising computer simulations to lead students to see the "interconnectedness of human events," and its STELLA (Structural Thinking Experimental Learning Laboratory With Animation) offers Macintosh software to encourage "higher-order thinking skills" across disciplines. Writing in the Journal of Applied Developmental Psychology, an ETS associate lauds the idea of instilling "social competence" in children—or "developing systems" as he prefers to call the young folks.

Is it a stretch to see a threat to liberty and family rights in attitudinal testing? Actually, the danger is clear and present, and is well documented in Educating for the New World Order (Halcyon House, Portland, Oregon) by respected Washington writer Bev Eakman. The book tells of the long, courageous battle of one Pennsylvania parent, Anita Hoge, against the infiltration of psychological testing into schools in the guise of "affective ed."

Virginia parents clearly will be within their rights to demand that they be kept fully informed on the purpose, direction, and content of the New Testing.

* * *

July 14, 1993

To Market, To Market With OBE: Will It Sell?

By Robert Holland

By informing citizens of new policies and programs, a public agency may perform a valuable public service. For example, a health department might need to advertise the availability of a vaccine against a deadly disease. Or a public safety department might serve a purpose by announcing a crackdown on drunk drivers.

But when a department of government tries to manufacture demand for new, untested social programs, that is a different question.

It is to be expected, of course, that agency representatives will speak out in favor of their proposals before the General Assembly and in other fora in which opposing views can be heard. However, the State Department of Education's latest scheme for selling Outcome-Based ("World Class") Education over the next six months to a wide variety of "target populations"—among them state lawmakers—goes well beyond normal agency lobbying and self-promotion.

DOE'S seven-page game plan, dated June 21, includes such PR strategies as the following:

• Regular surveys of the target populations to measure the success of OBE sales pitches.

• Small-group promotional sessions with invited business and community leaders—15 to 20 at a time—in various localities.

• A speakers' bureau of 30 to 40 OBE proponents.

• Lobbying of legislators—individually and in a series of regional meetings—in an attempt to win their endorsement for decisive votes during the General Assembly budget session convening next January. Since DOE's campaign will coincide with the Governor's and House of Delegates' contests this fall, this effort could take on partisan overtones.

• Letters to the editor that "will be provided to business individuals and organizations for their use." I am certain that editors of community newspapers across Virginia will be interested to know that government-issue letters endorsing OBE—cranked out at Richmond's Ed-Central high above the James—may be headed their way.

• Canned articles for business newsletters relating the joys that OBE groupthink will bring to industrial production.

• A "summer summit" of government leaders to "discuss the benefits" of OBE/WCE. This is to be organized in collaboration with Virginians for World Class Education, an OBE advocacy group drawn from the social and economic elite. The game plan says nothing about welcoming a debate with OBE opponents, who tend to be average parents who actually send their children to public schools.

• "Ecumenical lunches" with selected "key" religious leaders. Will conservatives make DOE's cut?

• Production of a video featuring Superintendent of Public Instruction Joe Spagnolo and corporate proponents of OBE.

• A "World Class Education Voluntary Reading Review Panel." This troika will review outgoing materials "for consistency with Department of Education World Class Education definitions and interpretations."

• Part-time employment of a communications specialist to develop a "consistent response strategy." Response to what? To any and all criticism, which Ed-Central does not accept with equanimity.

What about plain old parents who see OBE as a venture in New Age reprogramming of their children's attitudes? The plan does not provide for any mass meetings for them to express their concerns.

But they can write their own invitations. Public affairs director Margaret Roberts says DOE staffers will "accept all invitations" to address citizens' groups—and that's good and proper. Judging from the many calls I receive on this subject, DOE's social schedule will be full this fall. One such parent-organized meeting will be held at 7 p.m. this Friday at Mills Godwin High School in western Henrico County.

Parents will get a brochure from DOE explaining what OBE "can do for their children." And the game plan calls for parents and others to be given that essential of all slick marketing campaigns . . . bumper stickers. (Can T-shirts be far behind?)

Yes, the Department of Education plans to do pro-OBE bumper stickers, to be distributed this fall at schools, libraries, businesses, and the State Fair. We all know what sells. So may we expect to see "Virginia Is for Outcome-Based Lovers" banners blanketing the state? This could become a hot, must-have item for all Casanovas patrolling the Southside in their pickup trucks.

By now, you doubtlessly are dying to know if you are in one of DOE's "target populations." No one wants to be excluded. Relax. There's probably a category for you. But it is interesting that "Department of Education staff" is the very first group targeted for mental massaging. That suggests OBE is not fully accepted even in DOE ranks.

Other "populations" targeted by DOE are "superintendents, principals, teachers, parents, legislators, civic/social organizations, business/industry, government officials, religious groups, non-parent groups, editorial boards, students, school boards, and the press." Between parents and non-parent groups (whatever they may be), targets appear to cover the landscape.

All of this sweaty bureaucratic exertion to mold public attitudes raises this bottom-line question:

Were OBE really "World Class" in academic content, would the Department of Education need to be waging a frenzied campaign to market it—even to its own employees—as though it were a new brand of toothpaste or underarm deodorant?

* * *

July 28, 1993

TQM for Schools: Rochester Is the Model and Results Are Dismal

By Robert Holland

Proponents concede that Outcome-Based Education is industry's Total Quality Management extended to the schools. Everyday working stiffs and parents ought to fend off the sleepiness the mere mention of TQM tends to induce and try to understand this philosophy being pushed down from the high councils of government, industry, and education.

The true believers' faith in the philosophy's curative powers is absolute. Enthusiasts like TQM consultant Henry Taylor, whose article appears on this page today, make a case for motivation more than they do for method. Those considering a radical change, however, must look at the larger picture—to wit, the full-blown experiment with TQM/OBE school reform that has been underway in Rochester, New York, since 1988. Marc Tucker, director of the Rochester-based National Center on Education and the Economy, has called Rochester's 32,000-student school system "a restructuring laboratory for the state and the nation."

That's wonderful! Lab data ought to be welcomed before Virginia buys irrevocably into OBE as the instrument of World Class Education. Let's look at some:

• In 1987, Rochester spent $4,253 per pupil in local tax dollars. By 1991, that had risen to $5,501 per pupil, and tens of millions more was being pumped in by the state (Governor Mario Cuomo is a big supporter), private corporations (Xerox and Eastman Kodak), and foundations.

• In 1987, 23 percent of Rochester's pupils earned the New York State Regents' Diploma, the most rigorous offered. By 1991, only 18 percent did.

• In 1991 more than 70 percent of the freshmen at Wilson Magnet School, generally considered the city's best, flunked the state's basic math test.

• The percentage of third-graders passing the state reading exam fell from 81 to 79 during the reform's first four years. The goal had been a 90 percent passing rate by 1991. (U.S. News & World Report, May 25, 1992).

In summary, costs have soared while academic results have plummeted. Furthermore, several newspapers have reported disenchantment among teachers, even though they were given a 40 percent raise over a three-year period as an incentive for swallowing TQM whole. Their complaint? The system is turning them into "social workers," with little time to teach.

In his 1992 book, "Thinking for a Living," (co-authored with former Labor Secretary Ray Marshall), Marc Tucker acknowledged that, "the Rochester experience demonstrates some of the complexity of the restructuring agenda in practice as well as some sense of the time it will take to implement that agenda." To say nothing of the money. And that's what OBE proponents like to say about money—nothing.

Yet Tucker hasn't slowed in his efforts to market the agenda. The University of Rochester education professor is co-director of the University of Pittsburgh-based New Standards Project (NSP), which seeks to implant OBE into curricula nationally through so-called "authentic" (essentially, no-fail) tests. Ability-grouping must be banished, because it is incompatible with the TQM ideal of happy drones working in teams.

Virginia taxpayers will be subsidizing NSP to the tune of $300,000 a year through 1995–96, if the State Department of Education has its way.

Tucker's National Center coordinated the 1990 report of the Commission on the Skills of the American Workforce, chaired by current Clinton adviser Ira Magaziner. That commission did the spadework for Clinton's Goals 2000 legislation, which seeks to yoke education to national industrial policy through Robert Reich's Labor Department.

TQM has been a useful restructuring model for some businesses, such as Xerox and Motorola. On the surface, its principles of customer service, elimination of systemic inefficiencies, and employee teamwork in implementing management objectives seem incontrovertible. But The Wall Street Journal and other publications have reported that TQM is floundering in many companies due to plans too amorphous to generate results.

Personal agendas come into play with TQM's metastasizing into spheres far removed from the production line. In the July 19 & 26 issue of the New Republic, a liberal journal, Leon Wieseltier explores in depth what he terms "Total Quality Meaning"—a spooky blending of Hillary Clinton's quest of the "politics of meaning" (see Michael Lerner's article on today's page), communitarianism, and TQM as "zen for CEOs."

Wieseltier plumbs the thinking of that guru of all TQM gurus, nonagenarian W. Edwards Deming. In "The New Economics," Deming espouses a utopian vision of a cooperative "way of life" in which all competition and merit systems will be abolished:

"In place of competition for high rating, high grades, to be Number One, there will be cooperation on problems of common interest between people, divisions, companies, competitors, governments, countries. . . . There will be joy in work, joy in learning. . . . Everyone will win; no losers." While TQM ideas and idealists may have something to offer businesses, the broader concept is taking on heavy baggage. Americans are supposed to shed their individualism and become well-socialized cogs in someone's big machine.

And the indoctrination begins in school.

* * *

September 1, 1993

A Fiscal Stick Could Discipline Education Reform

By Robert Holland

Douglas Wilder's greatest accomplishment as Governor may have come on fiscal defense. The Governor has insisted that Virginia hold the line against general tax increases while most states and the federal government were raising their rates.

Politically, that will give Wilder plenty of attack lines to use against fellow Democrat Chuck Robb in next year's battle royal for Robb's Senate seat. When it was fourth and inches in Congress for Clinton's tax-happy economic plan, Robb's support was crucial.

But in telling the General Assembly money committees last week that no state service will be sacrosanct as he seeks to balance his final budget proposal *sans* new taxes, was the Governor sending a message to—in particular—the Department of Education? The challenge, said the Governor, is to identify "those programs, activities, or services that we are prepared to do without." Then he added: "To go about this exercise in a meaningful way, just about everything needs to be put on the table for downsizing or elimination, if only for the purpose of clarifying our priorities."

So what about the much-ballyhooed World Class Education Initiative, and the expensive and unproven pedagogy of Outcome-Based Education on which it is predicated? Is it now on the table?

After spending several million in the current biennium to seed OBE in various starter projects, the State Board and the Department of Education had hoped to add about $80 million in new initiatives in the 1994–96 budget. Additionally, if their original plan to tie teacher pay raises to extra work implementing OBE were approved by the Assembly, new spending would rise to $310 million.

Remember, this is a 10-year program the department already has begun implementing in various ways, possibly in contravention of the Administrative Process Act, which requires citizen input and a fiscal-impact analysis. A full accounting of costs (beyond "initiatives") would include positions DOE has been filling based on applicants' fealty to OBE principles.

My sources are the DOE budget plans the Board of Education first considered June 24 and approved in revised form August 16. The state spends close to $5 billion per biennium on public education. On June

24, DOE reported that an increase of $359 million would be needed simply to maintain current programs. Over and above that, DOE's leadership wanted $489 million for "initiatives," mostly OBE-related. Because of what the board called "fiscal realities" (for which, thank Heaven, we can only hope for some educational ones), DOE trimmed the initiatives to $98 million, of which I identify $78 million as OBE-related.

Teacher compensation is the tricky deal. The June 24 initiatives would have given teachers a 14.3 percent pay hike over two years (costing $230 million) in return for their working an extra five hours a week on curriculum and testing to implement the "learner outcomes" in the Common Core of Learning. But the August 16 board-approved package replaces that, in essence, with an IOU—a resolution urging the legislature to find the money to reward teachers if they go the extra mile for OBE.

Good teaching is hard work. Like the rest of us, teachers have to pay their mortgage, put gas in the station wagon, and buy groceries. I wonder what teachers think about the prospect of having their pay hikes, if any, tied to Ed-Central's latest flight of theoretical fancy?

These are the state educationists' highest priority initiatives:

- Staff Development: $5.4 million. This funds the far-flung activities of a Virginia Center for Staff Development, described as "the vehicle for disseminating the products, core curricula, and reform practices developed by Department of Education efforts and the World Class Education transformation sites."
- Model schools: $3.6 million. There are already 18 of these in place to develop prototypes of the new, mandatory early childhood education the OBEists envision. This would add another 12 to start the transition to the pre- and early-adolescence level.
- Assessments: $2.8 million for Three Ps' testing—portfolios, products, performance—that OBEists prefer to objective measurements of knowledge. Particularly noteworthy is the $600,000 DOE wants to lavish on the New Standards Project, based at the University of Pittsburgh.

That hotbed of OBE is developing what may prove to be a national testing system for Clinton's Goals 2000. Because foundation money is running out, declares DOE, the 18 participating states must pick up the tab. Oh? Do Virginia taxpayers have a say in that? How does that square with Governor Wilder's tests of fiscal necessity? And if national tests are the expected "outcome," why aren't all 50 states paying?

- Class size reduction: $41 million. This would lower pupil-to-teacher ratios in the state's poorest school divisions from 25 to 1 to 18 to 1 in kindergarten through grade three. The idea is that this would help reduce disparity while also making reform work more smoothly. (Originally DOE wanted $112 million to reduce ratios in all districts.)

No doubt school systems would welcome the extra money but studies have shown that cuts in class size, while expensive, do not yield substantial gains in pupil achievement.

Governor Wilder's idea of using the budget squeeze to reassess priorities has great application for education. And the General Assembly, which holds the purse strings, must play a critical role. Western Fairfax County Delegates Jay O'Brien and Roger McClure and Senator Warren Barry have proposed that the Assembly's education committees hold hearings this fall to shed light on the OBE question.

What works? How about (from ample case studies): Phonics to teach reading. Strong leadership from principals. Rewards for excellent teaching. Discipline. Homework. Specific (and high) standards in academic subjects. And ability-grouping, targeted for obliteration by the OBEists.

Even after so much World Class hype, it still is not too late for Wilder to refocus Virginia's education debate on the basics. However, if he fails to do so, he could find OBE to be as much an albatross around his neck as taxes (and Virginia Beach, etc.) will be around Robb's next year.

* * *

August 11, 1993

Master Teachers Expose Fallacies of OBE 'Mastery' Learning

By Robert Holland

Children ought to be allowed to take a test over and over and over again—as many times as they need or want—until they all have mastered the same standard? Failure should be banished from the school vocabulary? Competition should be scrapped in favor of group collaboration on socially "relevant" projects?

Don't take the word of an ancient education writer as to how unproductive are those warmed-over progressivist dogmas of the Outcome-Based Education theorists. From among the hundreds of concerned parents and teachers I have talked to over the past six months, let me introduce you today to three who have personal insights.

• First, meet Cheri Pierson Yecke, 1988's Teacher of the Year in Stafford County and in 1991 a finalist for the Agnes Meyer Outstanding Teacher Award given by *The Washington Post*. Ms. Yecke, a teacher of

English and history, is in an unusually strong position to comment on OBE's practical effects: Her two daughters have become case studies (albeit not by the family's choosing) in before-and-after OBE experimentation.

In August, 1991, the Yeckes moved back to Minnesota (Ms. Yeckes' native state) and enrolled their children in District 833's schools. They did so without hesitation because they had lived in Cottage Grove from 1982 to 1984 and found the schools to be fine. Unknown to them, however, the district had been implementing OBE during the seven years they had been away. To their astonishment, they soon discovered that their daughters—by now in high school and junior high—had progressed academically while in Stafford "light years" ahead of their peers in Minnesota.

Younger daughter Tiffany, who had always loved school, was "in a matter of days begging to stay home." Why? "The work was far too easy," said Cheri Yecke, who taught at a Wisconsin school just over the border, "but what was worse was that any display of intelligence was ridiculed in a cruel and demeaning way by many of the other students. Hard work and self-discipline are looked down upon, and status is often achieved by non-performance.

"The prevailing attitude among many students is, 'Why study? They can't fail me, so who cares?' What sort of work ethic is this producing in these children? No one fails, regardless of how little they do. Instead, they receive 'Incompletes,' which can be made up at any time.

"The kids have the system figured out. When there is a football game or show on TV the night before a test, a common comment is: 'Why study? I'll just take the test and fail it. I can always take the retest later.' "

Indeed, "Incomplete" appears to be the grade of choice, the successor to the Gentleman's C of my generation. At semester's end in January, 1992, more than 15,500 Incompletes were recorded in District 833's grades 7–12—or about one-half of all grades awarded!

When young persons never have to meet deadlines, Ms. Yecke observes, they do not learn the consequences of sloth or irresponsibility. They lack motivation. They do not learn how to deal with life's inevitable failures.

With her husband retiring from the Marine Corps, Cheri Yecke is this month moving her family back to Stafford County. But she returns to find Virginia on the edge of the same OBE pit she just left.

Almost exactly the same, it would appear: In an interview last winter with Educational Leadership magazine, Colorado-based OBE guru

Bill Spady identified Virginia and Minnesota, along with Pennsylvania, as the national pacesetters for his "transformational" OBE, the most radical brand. In Spady's words, traditional academic subjects, such as English and history, must give way to students' grasping "significant spheres of successful living" as defined by futurists.

• Next, meet the 1990 Teacher of the Year in populous Fairfax County, Vern Williams, who shares Ms. Yecke's grave concerns about the OBE ideologues' insistence on killing all grouping of students according to ability. Williams is particularly worried about the impact of that dogma on mathematics, which he has taught in Fairfax for 20 years.

Williams says that throwing a large number of pupils of widely divergent abilities into one math class guarantees a mixture of (1) "very bored" and (2) "very frustrated" pupils.

"We have been told recently that low-ability students will gain just by being exposed to higher level concepts. We are told that they probably will not learn many of the concepts, but that's okay because they will still be better off. Well, we do more than expose our students to concepts. We teach! Putting students of all abilities together in seventh grade math will force us to abandon any serious teaching."

• Finally, meet Retha Danvers, who home-schools her children in Richmond. Ms. Danvers breaks a stereotype in at least two ways: A former university teacher of composition and rhetoric, she is a political liberal, and her reasons for home-schooling have nothing to do with religion.

Recently, she gently chided me for setting up a then-and-now dichotomy between what public education is now, and what horrors will befall it under OBE. "In actual implementation," she said, " 'then' is 'now'—in other words, your description of what the system may become is chillingly similar to what it already is. To me, close reading of OBE reveals not reform, but a justification of the same ol' same ol.' "

Retha Danvers, I cheerfully concede you half a point. Too much pablum already is being served up. But OBE would deplete the academic menu even further while filling it with what Spady terms "the affective and attitudinal dimensions of learning." Furthermore, Cheri Yecke's Stafford-to-Minnesota move suggests that Virginia is not yet as far along in academic deconstruction as some areas.

I am gladdened by the thought that liberals and conservatives might join forces in Virginia to reject OBE, and build stronger schools upon the foundation that is in place.

* * *

August 25, 1993

OBE Hive Brings a Parents' Revolt

By Robert Holland

What a wild summer this has been. Seeking refuge on the Outer Banks this week, I fully expect to encounter Outcome-Based Fishing off the Avalon Pier. OBF, you know: That's where they send down divers to hook a catch of exactly equal weight for each fisherperson so that self-esteem is enhanced to the max.

And what rich possibilities Outcome-Based Baseball presents for the pennant races. Those obstreperous Philadelphia Phillies, who have done no small damage to the psyches of my St. Louis Cardinals, should be convened in a big hand-holding group to reflect on the ills of competitive society. And in the spirit of OBB, overachievers John Kruk and Lenny Dykstra should just sit there until the Cards and all other weak sisters have caught up with them. Under OBB, you see, all divisional races must end in a tie. There must be only winners.

To say that Outcome-Based Education—with its whole attitudinal and anti-competition load—has kindled the ire of many parents and teachers this summer would be an understatement.

Recently I fled the steamy city for a few days only to return and find on my Voice Mail calls from: Alabama, Arizona, Maryland, Minnesota, Missouri, Washington, and Wisconsin—all from citizens aggrieved by OBE, folks who had received copies of my Op/Ed columns in samizdat fashion. I consider the calls less a compliment to me than a reflection of the strange reluctance of politically correct, USA-Today-ized news organizations to report on certain touchy topics in depth.

But there are honorable exceptions—notably, Charlotte Allen's article (excerpted on today's Op/Ed Page) in the August 15 Outlook section of The Washington Post wherein she chronicles the decidedly unpromising start to "thematic learning," or OBE, in Washington's schools. A suggestion for Virginia's powers-that-be: Instead of throwing hundreds of millions of tax dollars into the OBE abyss, why not let D.C. be our social laboratory? If it works there, then consider it here.

All across Virginia this hot and crazy summer, parent-organized OBE town meetings have brought out large crowds. Another major session is scheduled at Richmond's Huguenot High School from 7 p.m. to 9:30 p.m. next Tuesday. Organizers have gotten commitments from such OBE opponents as parent/educators Sylvia Kraemer of Alexandria and Cheri Yecke of Stafford County, and a conditional acceptance from State Board of Education member Alan Wurtzel, who doubles as president of the business-backed Virginians for World-Class Education. The Department of Education also has been invited to dip into its 50-member pro-OBE speakers bureau. And a newcomer to the debate will be Eileen Hunt, leader of a group of African-American women who have made fighting OBE a priority.

To say that Virginia's education establishment has been, um, linguistically impaired in responding to the groundswell of opposition also would be an understatement.

Last October, the Department of Education proudly proclaimed its allegiance to "transformational" OBE, which indeed was the brand (thick with life-adjustment mush) peddled by its chief consultant, sociologist William Spady of Colorado. But by June, Secretary of Education James Dyke was denying on Channel 8's "This Week in Richmond" that Virginia's reform was OBE at all. Then Wurtzel equated OBE for Virginia schools with industry's Total Quality Management. Finally, State Board of Education president James Jones told critics at a board meeting last week that it wasn't "transformational" OBE but traditional.

It is. It isn't. It is. It isn't. So at what public meetings were those supposed course corrections made? (In truth, some jargon may have been expunged, but the Spady influence remains in the oleaginous "outcomes" that are to be Virginia's new graduation requirements.)

Now, DOE (like a frightened doe?) is backing off its recent pledge to "accept all invitations" to speak at public meetings. The new policy, which caused Wurtzel to hedge on his Huguenot appearance, is that no candidate for political office may be on the program. Does that mean DOE will not appear with Democratic officeholders who seek to extend their political careers? DOE public affairs director Margaret Roberts couldn't say for sure.

What it means in practical terms is that DOE doesn't want parents' advocate Mike Farris, the GOP candidate for Lieutenant Governor, anywhere around to challenge official orthodoxy. Farris has stated forcefully his opposition to OBE ("it's 180 degrees in the wrong direction") and the bureaucratization of education it epitomizes.

By contrast, his opponent, Democratic incumbent Don Beyer, said the following on the Blanquita Cullum show on WLEE-Radio last week: "Outcome-Based Education is one of many things being debated now nationally and in Virginia. And I'll have an opinion when the debate is finished."

Amazing! When will we know the debate is over? Will a timekeeper sound a buzzer for Dandy Don's benefit?

Over breakfast with me last week, Wurtzel and Dyke pulled out a set of academic standards the Charlotte-Mecklenburg, North Carolina, schools are considering for their "World Class" system. They suggested that this might be an alternate model when DOE considers the standards for implementing the three dozen "outcomes" in its Common Core of Learning. To the extent Charlotte's program appears to call for rigor in traditional academic disciplines, that's encouraging.

Ah, but there's a catch. Virginia won't consider those standards until after the November 2 election, possibly in December—and public hearings won't be held until after that. Wurtzel spoke at breakfast of a desire to keep the issue out of partisan politics. Later, after consulting DOE officials, he called to say the standards can't be completed before December anyway.

The proponents' "no politics" cry rings hollow. Led by such political stalwarts as former First Lady Jeannie Baliles and Dyke, Virginians for World-Class Education has begun a well-funded political-style campaign to sell OBE. (Dyke has resigned as Education Secretary but he is considered a likely Democratic contender for Lieutenant Governor in 1997—on a ticket with Beyer, perhaps?) It is hardly fair to demand that ordinary citizens who lack such means should hold their fire until after the November elections and thereby probably forfeit their best chance to derail OBE.

* * *

September 15, 1993

As National Headmaster, Labor Wants Electronic Pupil-Dossiers

By Robert Holland

The United States Department of Labor has big plans for your local schools, not to mention your local workplaces. In fact, it has the work specs for the New American Child.

What the DOL is pushing hard through its SCANS (Secretary's Commission on Achieving Necessary Skills) manifestos looks a whole lot like the Outcome-Based Education being hawked by the education/industrial complex in Virginia and across the nation.

If you are a parent, a teacher, a student—or just an American interested in preserving individual freedom—you might want to know what's in the SCANS fine print. Perversely (if appropriately), I spent the long Labor Day weekend studying several hundred pages of SCANS documents pulled out of national data banks.

To begin with, if Labor factotums had their way, American pupils no longer would receive report cards with letter grades from A to F for their academic work. Instead, they would have cumulative resumes that would follow them throughout school—and into their working years.

On those resumes, students would be rated for "workplace competencies," such as their "interpersonal skills" and their "systems" thinking. There would be proficiency levels (but no failing grades) for academic subjects. And there also would be listings of portfolios of student work (projects on trendy topics like environmentalism), with names of teachers to contact. Portfolios are the OBEists' preferred replacement for objective testing of student knowledge.

Ever helpful, the SCANS commissioners actually provide classroom assignments to integrate SCANS competencies into the core curriculum. For example, in English class, teachers could sharpen "interpersonal skills" by having students "discuss the pros and cons of the argument that Shakespeare's Merchant of Venice is a 'racist' play and should be banned from the curriculum." So rather than studying a piece of masterful writing on its own merit, students would be invited to consider censoring it. People for the American Way, where are you?

The most intriguing "outcomes" are the students' "personal qualities" that educators would rate on the SCANS resumes: responsibility, self-esteem, sociability, self-management, integrity/honesty. Oh, yes, on those resumes, students would be identified not only by name and address but also by Social Security number.

The report further states that the Educational Testing Service is developing an "employer-friendly" system called WORKLINK through which these assessments of pupils' personal qualities could be shared with businesses electronically. Doesn't sound very little-guy-friendly.

If somewhere along the line you got on the bad side of school authorities—perhaps, say, you failed to show up for your Pumsy the Dragon self-esteem session in elementary counseling—a bad mark for integrity could dog you for the rest of your life. Talk about Big Brother abusing liberty. American Civil Liberties Union, where are you?

The DOL has some gall to judge anyone's honesty. Remember, this is the federal behemoth that for 10 years—under Democratic and Republican Presidents alike—programmed its computers to score job seekers way up or way down on employment tests, depending solely on their racial classification—and that did so without bothering to inform the victims of that official racism.

Rather than spending time in moral receivership for its intellectual bankruptcy, the DOL is back under pro-OBE Harvardite Robert Reich as a super-Cabinet agency (dwarfing Education) with a scheme that multiplies the injustices of race-norming many times. SCANS got a blessing under George Bush's America 2000 program, but now is gathering momentum under an administration that believes in government as a healer of all social ills.

In fact, an internal advisory memo to the Equal Employment Opportunity Commission gives the game away: The national job-skills certification and education assessments in Clinton's Goals 2000 legislation—now before Congress—seek to replace norming with "fuzzy" tests more likely to achieve equalized outcomes on a group basis. These subjective measurements (such as portfolios or other exhibits) "are easily questioned—so there may be an avalanche of challenges to the grading of assessment exercises," the memo warns.

The SCANSers' objectives are not modest: "The nation's school systems should make the SCANS foundation skills and workplace competencies explicit objectives of instruction at all levels." "All employers, public and private, should incorporate SCANS know-how in their human resource development efforts, employee recruitment, and training."

In "reinventing education," the SCANSers also concoct a new entitlement—to school success. Youngsters have a "right" to be educated up to an absolute standard of performance "without putting the burden of failure on the backs of students." ("Hey, Teach. You can't flunk me. I'm entitled." So much for the individual responsibility the SCANSers would presume to rate.)

It would be wrong to dismiss all this as just more psychobabble soon to fade. Several states (Florida was first) already are integrating SCANS competencies into their curricula. A careful look at the Common Core of Learning "outcomes" in OBE states like Virginia will show utilitarian strains of SCANS: "evaluating and managing one's own behavior within the functioning of the group," "plan, produce, and deliver high quality products and services," etc.

Indeed, the linkages are clear. SCANS grew out of a Labor Commission report chaired by Clinton Rhodes Scholar buddy Ira Magaziner in 1990 (and on which Virginia Board of Education member Alan Wurtzel served). Hillary Rodham Clinton was then made co-chairman for implementation with Magaziner, her ally in trying to nationalize health care. Much of that Labor report was picked up almost verbatim by Virginia's school "reformers" a few years ago. Now, SCANS is linked (as is Virginia) with the New Standards Project, which is writing national examinations on the OBE model. NSP has the stated agenda of radically transforming the school curriculum through student assessment.

Meanwhile, word from Washington last week was that 90 million Americans read, write, and compute so poorly that they have trouble holding a job. Those poor folks don't need group hand-holding and government-approved "higher-order thinking." They need structure—phonics and drill on the multiplication tables and one-on-one tutoring. The last thing they need—or their children need—is OBE.

* * *

September 22, 1993

The Ghost of OBE Past Haunts Education Still

By Robert Holland

The State Board of Education wanted to define the desirable "outcomes" of education by which children should be measured. The Department of Education brought in consultants from outside Virginia to assist in the task.

Bureaucratic brainstorming yielded dozens of learner outcomes, many of them having to do with shaping attitudes. A primary goal, said the educrats, should be "cooperation of individuals within groups . . . and cooperation of groups with other groups."

These were some of the critical attitudes they wanted to instill:

- The tendency to subordinate personal desire to the public good.
- The urge to apply critical and experimental thinking to the problems of everyday life.
- The disposition to be an economic asset.

A commentator explained that this common core of learning was devised to replace the academic disciplines of social studies, science, and English with "challenging social problems" such as the environment. Students would put their higher-order thinking skills to work in relevant ways. Studying in that fashion would "set the stage for cooperation rather than competition."

Objections to the squishy, life-role outcomes were brought to the attention of the Governor of Virginia. He agreed that education should be primarily about the basics. He ordered the Department of Education to withdraw the program immediately.

Was that the scenario for Governor Douglas Wilder's surprising strike last Wednesday at the heart of Outcome-Based Education? Pretty close. Actually, however, I'm describing Governor Tom Stanley's indignant move 37 years ago against what he considered a soft-headed and even "socialistic" curriculum.

The outcomes in the Common Core of Learning shelved last week by Wilder are remarkably similar to those above, as described in J. L. Blair Buck's 1952 history of public education in Virginia. From the May 27, 1993, CCL version that has stirred such bitter controversy across the state: Understand the views and needs of others. Communicate and cooperate with people of varied backgrounds. Use the environment responsibly. Identify community problems and negotiate solutions contributing to the public good.

This illustrates the cyclical nature of the sappy fads with which education is plagued, as well as the daunting task facing any theorists who would define education according to social goals.

The OBE specter is far more serious this time around, however. Stanley was essentially beating a dead pedagogy, while Wilder was cutting his political losses for a program developed for three years by his appointees with his knowledge. Buck wrote that the outcomes curriculum begun in 1932 on a 10-year time line never got much use; teachers massively ignored it.

Even if Wilder scrupulously upholds his vow to stop spending millions on touchy-feely experiments and to leave curriculum decisions to local communities, the big question now is whether states are going to be left alone to leave localities alone. At the federal level the Clintonites have national assessments and equalized outcomes in mind. And in an impending reauthorization, they seek to have Congress change the massive Chapter One law from a block grant program to one enforcing OBE principles as a condition of aid.

On a more hopeful note: This issue has mobilized whole battalions of parents. Contrary to what certain quote-dispensing, ivory-tower pundits have opined, Wilder's blow against OBE was not primarily a victory for the Religious Right. It was a triumph for a grassroots coalition that cut across ideological, social, and racial lines.

Much good will result if that energy is channeled in constructive ways. Wise will be the local school board that taps into it.

What are some constructive alternatives? Here are two starting points:

• Build on reading, the skill upon which all outcomes depend. Reading is the best self-esteem program. The child who can read has reason to feel good about himself.

Jeanne Chall's *Learning to Read: The Great Debate* should have ended the debate in 1975 about the best way to teach beginning reading. Ms. Chall of the Harvard Graduate School of Education reviewed essentially all research ever done on reading. Although she did not start out as a fan of phonics, she honestly reported that code-emphasis methods—teaching kids to "sound out" words (phonics)—clearly was the most effective way to teach beginning reading.

It is nothing short of scandalous that schools still buy into look-say (or guess-say) programs now peddled as "holistic" or "whole language."

• Build on the Standards of Learning, which are grade-by-grade learning objectives in each of the traditional disciplines. Former state superintendent Jack Davis, a no-nonsense educator, led in putting the SOL structure in place in 1983. There is some fluff in the SOL—it could be substantially improved— but mostly it contains solid academic objectives.

Here's an actual example: By the fifth grade the student should be able "to identify the important ideals expressed in the Declaration of Independence and the Constitution of the United States, the Virginia Declaration of Rights, and the Virginia Statute of Religious Freedom." That's just one of many outcomes in social studies and one that everyone can understand. Yet under OBE, the SOL—instead of being a starting point for school reform—would have been shunted aside.

Many parent-activists worry that the Wilder action is nothing but a political ploy and that OBE will continue to be implemented without a CCL. They have cause to be suspicious. OBE experiments such as the venture in child-directed learning at Beaverdam Elementary in Hanover County continue (with or without the backing of parents of the children who are the guinea pigs). There is no indication yet that the Governor is halting the push for more subjective testing and teacher retraining that would drive a new, feel good curriculum. Indeed, on Pat Murphy's radio talk show out of Hampton Roads last Friday, the Governor said the public relations was bad but "the concept is good and we're going back to the drawing board to try to implement it."

If it turns out that state officialdom is just engaging in more subterfuge and disinformation, the parents' revolt will grow hotter than ever.

* * *

September 29, 1993

Education's Reinventors Misled Public

By Robert Holland

When Secretary of Labor Robert Reich and Secretary of Education Richard Riley jointly introduced President Clinton's "Goals 2000: Educate America Act" last April, they said the provisions in it for curricular content and student performance standards, and for national testing, would be "voluntary."

States and localities could participate or not as they saw fit. That was just another government lie.

With the nation's attention diverted by Hillary Clinton's high-flying plan for nationalized health care, a parallel scheme to nationalize education is coming in under the radar. Last week, Riley presented to a House Education and Labor subcommittee the administration's plan to reauthorize the $10 billion Elementary and Secondary Education Act of 1965.

The reauthorization would require states to adhere to the Goals 2000 blueprint to the letter if they wanted their slice of the juicy ESEA pie—federal money on which schools, unfortunately, are hooked.

So much for "voluntary."

This is how Riley, the former South Carolina governor, rationalized the shift to statist coercion in a presentation that wowed subcommittee Democrats and (sigh!) Republicans alike:

"A common understanding of what all our children should know and be able to do should drive changes in all aspects of teaching and learning. Textbooks, teaching practices, and tests should all be geared to State content and performance standards that set forth the knowledge and skills our students need, and our diverse democracy and our complex economy demand."

Doesn't anyone in Clintonian Washington understand the danger of concentrating such power in government hands?

Goals 2000 is replete with the Outcome-Based Education favored by Reich, Hillary Clinton, and Ira Magaziner but so loathed by so many everyday Virginia citizens that Governor Wilder felt it politick to withdraw Virginia's OBE plan— if only temporarily—on September 15.

Now, no matter how intense the opposition of parents, no matter how many promises the Wilder administration makes to return education restructuring to the community (where the issue should have been from the start), the Rhodes Scholar junta in Washington wants to decide what's best for all schools.

The Virginia politician who has most closely tracked this attempted power grab is Mike Farris, the Republican candidate for Lieutenant Governor. On the day Riley presented the ESEA plans in Washington, Farris dropped by my office with the feds' 173-page (!) explanation of the changes along with the 399-page bill itself.

This maneuver is, said Farris, nothing less than "a hijacking of state and local educational prerogatives by the federal government. This is going to create detailed national control of our educational system." Farris, a Loudoun County constitutional lawyer, has made a career of defending home-schoolers and school patrons whose rights were in danger of being trampled by Big Government. He knows whereof he speaks. But if you don't like his politics, it's not necessary to take his word. Consider what many prominent public-school administrators are saying.

"It just means what everybody's been saying all along about the standards being voluntary: bull—. They're mandatory, and they're tied to money," American Association of School Administrators associate director Bruce Hunter told *Education Week*, which is not usually filled with such earthy expressions.

Of the Clintons' plan to subject non-complying school districts to "alternative governance arrangements," including possible removal of teachers, Edward Kealy, director of federal programs for the National School Boards Association, said, "I don't think any [corrective action] is left off the list short of a nuclear attack on school districts."

At a meeting last summer of the American Educational Research Association, prominent educators filled the air with alarms that the Clintons' national standards, driven by assessments, might lead to a narrowing of the curriculum, and have a harmful effect on education, as in some European countries.

Goals 2000 is a Little Shop of Horrors of educationist doctrine. It mandates equal graduation rates according to racial and ethnic group, which should be tip-off enough of what happens to individual intellectual distinction. It endorses "developmentally appropriate" early-childhood practices—a code phrase for elevating self-esteem over academic instruction. It sets up a National Education Goals Panel, consisting entirely of politicians, to review standards, curricula, and tests promulgated by, in effect, a national school board. It also gives Robert Reich's DOL power to certify skills of a national workforce.

There's much more: school-based health and social-service clinics; a "parents as teachers" program that could intrude the state ever more deeply in family life; and, of course, "opportunity-to-learn" or delivery standards. The latter provide an opening for Washington to tell each state how much it should spend per-teacher, per-pupil, or per-building in the name of "equity."

Now, Lyndon Johnson's ESEA, which was designed to provide compensatory education to help poor students improve their basic skills, is to become a big stick to enforce New Age ed across the land.

Schools are the institution closest to the heart of most neighborhoods. Local control of the education and nurturing of the young has been a cherished principle in American life. Statist control of curriculum is a pernicious trend, threatening liberty.

So why are so many people, including putative "conservatives" on Capitol Hill, sleeping through the *coup d'etat*?

* * *

October 6, 1993

DAP? It's Mush to Some, Meat to Others, a Mandate for Everyone

By Robert Holland

Meeting in Wise County out in the great Southwest last week, the State Board of Education held a quiet funeral for attitudes-laden Outcome-Based Education. Now the question is whether OBE will return as a federal mandate in the Rodham-Clinton "Goals 2000" legislation, which is expected to go to the House floor by mid-month.

Meanwhile, OBE-style self-esteem programs already are in place in many schools under other names and acronyms—DAP, for example. The concept behind those letters should be of major importance to families sending little ones off to kindergarten with the expectation they will receive a sound academic foundation in elementary school.

DAP stands for "developmentally appropriate practice" in early childhood education (ages 5–8). Here again, the education jargon is intentionally pre-emptive. After all, who can be for developmentally "inappropriate" practice—or education without "outcomes"? But it turns out that DAP is a specific term for a distinct brand of education dogma—one that not all school patrons will find agreeable.

The National Association for the Education of Young Children (NAEYC) decreed what's developmentally appropriate—and inappropriate—in primary schools in 1987. And state departments of education in such places as Oregon, Kentucky, and, yes, Virginia have signed on to DAP as a key element of school restructuring.

Last year, a requirement that local school systems adopt early-childhood programs emphasizing DAP went into the Standards of Quality as approved by a General Assembly that most likely hadn't a clue what it was endorsing. The SOQ is law. This isn't something that Doug Wilder can order off the table.

Virginians may be shocked to learn that now, by official definition, just about all traditional and structured teaching methods through third grade are deemed "inappropriate practice."

A teacher standing in front of the class leading pupils in phonic drills out of a basal textbook? Inappropriate. Teaching English, science, math as separate subjects in distinct time segments? Inappropriate. Expecting pupils to sit quietly at their desks while the teacher is giving a lesson? Inappropriate. Tests, grades, punishment for unruly pupils (such as losing out on recess)? All inappropriate, according to NAEYC gospel.

What's appropriate? Children working cooperatively in multi-age groups (5 to 7, for example) and moving from one learning center or "playful activity" to another as they wish. "Peer tutoring"—children teaching children. Subjects being taught together in themes—for example, from NAEYC's guide, "math skills are acquired through spontaneous play, projects, and situations of daily living." Teacher narratives replacing grades. No child failing or being retained—the better to bolster self-esteem.

Last year, the State Department of Education designated as a vanguard DAP school Hanover County's Beaverdam Elementary, which on its own had started an Early Childhood Developmentally Guided Education Program (EDGE) in 1990.

On a visit last spring, state schools chief Joe Spagnolo was beside himself with delight. "That's fantastic," he said. "That's what we want to create. I have yet to see anyone sitting in their seats listening to teachers talk at them."

Not all Beaverdam parents share that enthusiasm. Judy Hall and Susan Nepomuceno, who were on an EDGE design team for parental involvement, recently have voiced their concerns about academics and discipline in a child-directed environment. They told me of some "children coming home bored. They had learned to read, only to regress to shapes and colors."

To be sure, many (perhaps most) Beaverdam parents and teachers appear to support the program, which they deny is OBE or anything except a community program with the flexibility to help children succeed. In an officially arranged visit yesterday to Donna Kouri's K-1 class, I saw a blending of traditional and progressive methods. She led the whole class—seated Indian-style (since there are no desks)—in an enthusiastic discussion of number patterns and rhyming words. Then began the creative chaos of four learning centers (computers, blocks, counting, sounds) clicking simultaneously and somewhat noisily.

With dedicated teachers like Ms. Kouri, it's possible to envision good things coming from such a class. However, on the day of my visit, there were four other adults in the class (not to mention the principal and a central administrator) to monitor activities. Surely that is a lot more help than a teacher typically has. A traditional, structured environment may work better for some pupils—and teachers.

What I find outrageous is that the Hanover central school office doesn't permit objecting parents to transfer to other schools. Of course, in that respect Hanover is no different from most other Virginia school divisions.

Principal Richard Waldrop says the program is "not experimental" but instead "based on research." But not all researchers agree.

Last spring's issue of the journal *Effective School Practices*, published by the Association for Direct Instruction in Oregon, reported that DAP had been extensively implemented in England as "progressive education" and in America as the 1970s' "open classrooms." And in both cases—wrote University of Oregon researcher Bonnie Grossen—achievement plummeted. After a 25-year fling, England abandoned progressive education last year.

DAP typically relies heavily on "whole language" to teach reading, Ms. Grossen continued, despite "the weight of evidence in support of systematic phonics instruction provided by three comprehensive reviews of research on reading."

DAP will remain a state mandate unless the General Assembly modifies the SOQ next winter. It should. Teachers should be able to choose a practice that suits their style instead of having to conform to a statist model. Likewise, parents should have the right to choose among different kinds of schools.

* * *

December 29, 1993

Education and the New Economy: Educated Mind Rejects Programmed Outcomes

By Robert Holland

As we turn the page from 1993 to 1994, this may be as good a time as any to cull any useful information from all those half-read reports, curled-up faxes, and faded clippings that almost block my view to the office doorway. And then I can at last clean my desk, which will relieve an eyesore for my colleagues.

My small mountain of paper speaks, primarily, to the future of education, a subject of paramount importance. So here goes . . .

• Higher Education OBE?: The debate that rocked K-12 education in 1993 may be just warming up in higher ed. Some of the same technocrats who have demanded systemic reform, on their terms, in the grade schools are seeking higher education's restructuring also. Former Labor Secretary Bill Brock, who headed a Labor task force that defined K-12 outcomes in terms of students' "workplace competencies," recently checked in with a foundation-funded study that recommends similar entrance-and-exit assessments in higher ed.

In Virginia, Governor Wilder's proposed 1994–96 budget would require each state college to submit a restructuring plan for state approval. At James Madison University, the grand plans of President Ron Carrier for a "seamless curriculum"—praised to the skies by the state's higher-ed bureaucrats—have some professors fretting about autocratic reform that threatens to emasculate the liberal arts in favor of a vocational brand of higher ed. Maybe their fears are overblown—or maybe not.

Undeniably, technology will exert an ever more profound impact as we enter the 21st Century. My cautionary note is that we shouldn't become so enamoured of technological wizardry that we lose sight of what it truly means to be a well-educated, independent-thinking individual.

• National Curriculum: U.S. Secretary of Education Richard Riley has denied repeatedly that the Clintons' Goals 2000—due for Senate action early in 1994—will lead to a national school curriculum. Perhaps perspective increases with distance from Washington, D.C.: Eva Baker, director of the Center for the Study of Evaluation at UCLA, has said this of the feds' proposed content and performance standards:

"The 'standards' have become a code word for what we used to call curriculum. For political reasons, it's seen as inappropriate to call this entity 'curriculum' in a national context."

In other words, Washington's politicos dare not speak the truth—that the national standards amount to a national curriculum that will centralize authority (dangerously, political authority) over what American children shall be taught.

• Dumbed-Down Standards: High academic standards—set and enforced locally—are much to be desired. A major problem with the Clintonites' standards, apart from the brainwashing danger, is that they are squishy standards: subjective portfolio assessments, no ability-grouping, repeated retesting until all students supposedly master a common standard. These are the standards of national mediocrity.

• Sucking Sound, Giant: No, it comes not from NAFTA's drain of jobs to Mexico, as conjured by Ross Perot. Rather, the sound you hear is $500 million generously contributed for public education's betterment by billionaire Walter Annenberg going right down a large rathole. Annenberg, poor man, sincerely wanted to do something to stem violence in the American schoolhouse. But he has gotten horrendously bad advice. Most of his money will go to well-heeled OBE gurus, at Brown University and elsewhere, whose idea of how to make schools safer is to make them dumber. The money could better have been used for merit grants for teachers, or scholarships to enable poor children to escape failed schools, or even for law enforcement to nail punks who disrupt learning. Very little money filtered through the OBE swamis is likely ever to wind up in the classrooms.

• An Irish Perspective: Perhaps the keenest eye for OBE's fallacies comes from across the big pond. Writing last summer in the Journal of Curriculum and Supervision, Jim McKernan, dean of the faculty at the University of Limerick (Ireland), noted:

"The most fundamental criticism against OBE is that it reduces education, teaching, and learning to forms of human engineering and quasi-scientific planning procedures—procedures that view education as an instrumental means to specified ends. This . . . amounts to molding students through behavior modification. . . ."

A "truly educated" pupil, he continued, "may lead us into unexplored meaning and outcomes, into unanticipated and unpredictable directions." Is the outcome of studying Macbeth to be dictated beforehand? Of course not. "The educated mind will always achieve unique and novel interpretations because knowledge is a tool to think with. To cite the significant outcomes in advance of teaching and learning is absurd."

McKernan concluded with this timely warning: "OBE suits the technical rationality currently prevailing in the United States and other Western nations whose policies emphasize high-tech culture and the preparation of students to compete in the workplace for global economic warfare. This skills-oriented model views schools as vocational centers producing workers and rests upon the argument that skill requirements on the job change faster than do curriculum and organizational changes in schools."

This industrial model, he observes correctly, "views students as raw materials." He cited this example in a 1991 statement from the Aurora (Colorado) schools: "We will know we are accomplishing our mission when all our students are collaborative workers . . . and quality producers."

Note the remarkable similarity to these outcomes in Virginia's OBE plan, which Governor Wilder did not shelve until last September: (1) Students should learn the skill of "collaborating" to "accomplish group objectives," and (2) students should "plan, produce, and deliver high quality products and services." That's not liberal education; it's training in the servile arts.

• Finis? Ah, but isn't OBE dead in Virginia? Not really. Not with a national curriculum devised by the OBEists looming. Not with the Annenberg grants feeding the OBE monolith. Not with Virginia OBEists still determined to proceed, from kindergarten through graduate school, under new euphemisms.

The New Year, sigh, figures quickly to restore the paper mountain on my desk.

* * *

January 26, 1994

Big Media Slumber Through School Battle

By Robert Holland

Governor George Allen wasn't just tossing out an applause line last week when, in his first address to the General Assembly, he pronounced Outcome-Based Education "graveyard-dead and gone." In the context of his speech, filled with good ideas for stripping power from the leviathan state and returning it to the people, his sincerity was evident.

Indeed, Allen's education advisers have shown every intention of wiping out vestiges of OBE left after former Governor Doug Wilder's landmark decision to pull the plug on the bogus reform last September 15. That would give Allen's astute Superintendent of Public Instruction, Bill Bosher, a clean slate on which to write a comprehensive, academics-based school reform package for the 1995 General Assembly.

Unfortunately, however, OBE is still alive and well in the fever swamps above the Potomac, where it grows fat on foundation largess, and shows all the resilience of a blood-stained ghoul in a cheap horror flick. Now this oily blob—with its anti-competition, politically correct load—threatens to squish back into all 50 states as a curricular mandate in the guise of the Clintonites' "national standards" for education.

And in many states less fortunate in their leadership than Virginia, parents are trying to stave off OBE plans pushed by powerful interests like the National Governors Association, Business Roundtable, Education Commission of the States, and assorted educationist hangers-on in hot pursuit of consultants' fees.

Yesterday, as a guest of a group of concerned citizens, I was at the Downtown Club in Birmingham (a strange place for a fan of the Tennessee Volunteers to be) speaking on what lessons our OBE dust-up in Virginia might teach.

In Alabama, citizens aren't just resisting the OBE scheme, which was imported to the state by ubiquitous consultant David Hornbeck (who did a gig for the Virginia Business Council) and which is being pushed hard by Governor Jim Folsom. Commendably, they have presented to the legislature an entire alternative reform plan, SCORE 100. Among its elements: choice among public schools, phonics to teach reading, local control, and guarantees of parental rights. May the force be with them!

Since January 1, I also have received SOSes—as though I were to OBE what the Orkin man is to the creepy crawlies—from Louisiana, Texas, Ohio, Kansas, Tennessee, Georgia, and even Greenwich, Connecticut. The last particularly fascinates me because (as it was described to me) Greenwich is a liberal community, a Big Apple suburb, in which any number of network news executives are school patrons.

You'd think that if these Big Media mavens were doing their job, they would have reported thoroughly on the strange phenomenon of national OBE, so that local burghers would not have to call on some ink-stained wretch in Richmond. But in truth the Big Media coverage of this issue so critical to America's future has been shamefully skimpy—a tiny fraction of what has been devoted to the Bobbitts' tawdry domestic trials in Manassas. By contrast, the computer bulletin boards (like Prodigy, which I recently joined) are filled with citizens networking from coast to coast to stop OBE and related atrocities. And well-informed talk-radio hosts like Richmond-based Blanquita Cullum (soon to go national from her WLEE-1320 AM springboard) and G. Gordon Liddy of "Radio Free D.C." have been stalwarts in filling the information void.

But what of the big battle coming up in Washington?

After Congress' return for last night's State of the Union address, one of the first items of Senate business was to be its version of "Goals 2000: the [Mis]Educate America Act," which would set up a de facto national school board, under White House control, to certify comprehensive standards for American education. The House passed an equally abominable version last fall.

And soon both chambers will consider the companion legislation that makes a damnable lie of the Clintonites' claim that Goals 2000 is "voluntary." That's the "Improving America's School Act," which, in reauthorizing the megabillions "Chapter One" program of compensatory education for poor youngsters, would require all participating schools to buy into national standards consistent with Goals 2000 and OBE.

The likelihood of 51 Senators' acquiring enough backbone to vote against a measure labeled "education reform" may be slim, but Senate staffers, the savvy people, tell me there may be hope of killing the beast when it returns in the form of a conference report reconciling House/Senate differences. About a week of Senate debate is expected to bring a flurry of amendments.

Goals 2000 would do to education about what the Ira Magaziner/ Hillary Clinton collaboration would to do health care: in short, put the mechanisms in place to centralize control and eliminate choice. In fact,

Ira & Hillary really got the ball rolling for OBE with a thick foundation-financed tome in 1990 ("America's Choice: High Skills or Low Wages!"). It called for academically leveled education—actually, training in self-esteem and sociability—as an imperative of national industrial policy.

As a leftist nerd in the "Student Power" Sixties, Magaziner pushed through a new curriculum for Brown University that dropped required courses, gutted Western studies, and eliminated failing grades. That approach largely survives, writes Jacob Weisberg in the January 24 *New Republic*. Consequently, Brown has "become notorious for its abdication on the question of what liberal education means." Weisberg extensively documents other gassy Magaziner ventures in central planning—for Sweden, for Rhode Island, and for corporate clients. They all have ended in "disaster," to one degree or another.

So everyday Americans want their children's schools restructured by these arrogant Sixties' radicals who never outgrew their adolescent fantasies of reordering the world? Not bloody likely. From what I have heard over the past year from Seattle to Tampa, from Chicago to Dallas, citizens who have found out what's up are outraged. They want their schools back. And more are learning what's up every day, no thanks to the establishment media.

* * *

February 2, 1994

New Age Ed: Assessment Feels Sooooo Good for Test-Phobic Nation

By Robert Holland

Tests are out. Assessments are in.

In a nutshell, that is the direction the authoritarian reformers want to take American education.

Libertarian reformers, the advocates of school choice, would not be nearly so prescriptive. They would allow for back-to-basics schools with paper-and-pencil testing, for progressive schools with holistic assessment, and for all sorts of blended flavors. Families—not the government—would choose the right schools, the right approaches for particular children.

Libertarians are winning a few skirmishes. But authoritarians—the Clinton Education and Labor Departments, corporate Clintonites, and the educrat establishment—are controlling the overall direction of school reform. And assessment is central to their plans. They don't like knowledge-based tests because they sort people out—the informed from the ignorant. They advocate whole-person assessments that minimize right/wrong answers and encourage socialization, self-esteem, and "real-life" tasks.

Let's look at how that is playing out around the country:

• In Kentucky, an OBE hotbed repeatedly held up by the Clintonites as a model for the nation, the new state assessments enabled an eighth-grader to earn a "proficient" rating on a math problem despite multiplying 4 times 4 and coming up with 17. That's possible, say Kentucky educrats, because this was a word problem and the pupil was being rewarded for setting it up nicely. Never mind that the kid doesn't know his multiplication tables. Memorization is outre in the Bluegrass State. Ditto, competition. The state spelling bee has been axed.

• In Virginia, the writing section of the Literacy Passport Test for middle-school pupils assigns style and composition a value 2 to 3 times greater than sentence formation, mechanics, and usage. The result, as Spotsylvania parent Michelle Schiesser pointed out in an Op/Ed Page guest column October 20, is that a pupil can pass the LPT with writing dominated by atrocious syntax, spelling, grammar, punctuation, and capitalization. (Here is a sample from an essay that passed: "They (a pair of glasses) was neon green and they gloed in the dark . . . I could also listen to music becase, yep thats right, I also had a radio in it.")

The flip side, as parent Jeff Ludwig of Fort Lee has pointed out to me, is that a literate and intelligent pupil—an honors student, in fact—can flunk the LPT if an error-free essay is deemed insufficiently "creative" by evaluators. New Age assessment is nothing if not subjective. The penalty for such a student is disqualification from eligibility to play high school sports, a devastating loss for many vigorous young people.

• Are attitudes being assessed? You better believe it. In the recent debate on Goals 2000, Senator Charles Grassley of Iowa spread on the public record numerous privacy-invading surveys being administered to pupils without parental consent. They take up almost 20 pages in the February 4 Congressional Record. One, administered in Bettendorf, Iowa, listed 19 different ethnic groups and asked students such questions as, "Which of the above do you think would be most likely to eliminate an entire race?" And, "If you could eliminate an entire race, would you?"

So goes affective education USA. What excuse can there be for such intrusive questions?

• Now here's the latest twist: Assessments to enable "test-phobic" adults to obtain a diploma from a designated high school without ever taking a course at that school or setting foot in it.

The External Diploma Program, administered by the American Council on Education, bills itself—according to director Florence Harvey—as "a competency-based, applied performance assessment system," one that is "especially attractive to the more mature adults not attracted to traditional models of testing and instruction."

The Labor Department's SCANS competencies form the backbone of the EDP assessments. Thus, the candidates for the EDP are assessed not simply for their ability to read, write, and figure, but for their personal qualities, such as sociability, self-esteem, and integrity. And they can demonstrate their ability to read by searching for a new apartment, their proficiency at math by managing a welfare household, and their grasp of civics by registering to vote. Assessors receive $3^1/_2$ days of training to qualify them to assess EDP candidates' 65 "competencies" in private sessions. Then these assessors are assessed by other assessors during their rookie year of assessing.

Granted, self-educated people are often miles ahead of the formally educated in common sense. The EDP has the laudable objective of recognizing practical wisdom and providing a credential for it. But awarding the identical diploma that one earns by taking required courses in algebra, English literature, and chemistry, and being tested and graded on that coursework, is unfair and deceiving.

There is a respected, academic-based route to high school equivalency for adults: the demanding, $7^1/_2$ hour GED tests. But those who pass the GED are awarded a certificate, not a diploma. In effect, an EDP assessment, much of which is subjective, is being assigned a higher value than a rigorous test. The EDP is gradually gaining a foothold, having started in Fairfax, Henrico, and Prince William counties a few years ago, and soon to be adopted by a regional consortium consisting of the York, James City, Hampton, Newport News, and Poquoson school divisions. It operates in 10 states.

Ms. Harvey says the program helps those "who weren't good in school, but who are good at life." If the diploma were accurately labeled as the product of a Real-Life Assessment, there should be no problem with that.

What's really disturbing are the abundant indications EDP-style assessments are what the authoritarian reformers have in mind for all of education. The Labor Department seeks to spread the teaching and assessment of SCANS competencies to every school and every workplace. That is a matter of record. And the authoritarians have the nerve to insist that they are trashing objective testing in the cause of higher standards for all.

* * *

February 9, 1994

Hush! Takeover of Schools in Progress

By Robert Holland

Everyday Virginians fought many years for the right to elect their local school boards, their state being the only one among the 50 where such elections were verboten.

How ironic it would be if—just as the first school board elections are set for this May following a tidal wave of support in local referenda—this cherished right wereto be circumscribed by the Clinton regime in Washington.

Believe it or not, just such a power grab is in progress. It affects not just Virginia but all states and all school boards—whether elected or appointed by elected representatives.

The Clintons' complex scheme for restructuring elementary and secondary education would write into federal law a "corrective action" provision that would oblige states to oust local school board members and superintendents if they were deemed to be falling short of new federally prescribed "outcome-based" standards.

In Virginia, this would set the State Department of Education up as a more powerful entity in day-to-day school supervision than school boards, in contravention of the Virginia Constitution. Indeed, the state bureaucracy would acquire more clout than the General Assembly itself.

No, this zinger was not in the ballyhooed Goals 2000: [Mis]Educate America Act that the Senate gingerly massaged during the past week, amid many phony-baloney assurances (including revised wording sponsored by Virginia Senator Chuck Robb) that school standards promulgated by two new federal bureaucracies will not impinge on local control.

Rather, the devil is in the details of a follow-up piece of legislation that was taken up yesterday in the House Education and Labor Committee: HR 6 (originally HR 3130), euphemistically entitled the "Improving America's Schools Act."

In reauthorizing the huge Chapter 1 program for disadvantaged pupils, a $7 billion well from which virtually every school district in the country dips, HR 6 puts the hurting into enforcement of the Hillary Clinton/Ira Magaziner/Robert Reich grand plan for American education. Goals 2000 has baby teeth, but the Chapter 1 chompers are shark-sized and sharp.

Of course the liberal media have reported nothing of this. Soap-opera sagas like Skategate and the Bobbitts are much more prime-time, front-page stuff than federal usurpation of the right of local people to control the schools for which they pay and to which they send their children.

But, if only out of self-interest, the National School Boards Association (which opposes school choice and generally supports Goals 2000) clearly sees the danger.

"This provision," the NSBA's leaders said of the corrective takeover in a December 30 statement, "is heavy-handed, undemocratic, and a direct threat to local supervision of public education. It has no place in federal law." The triggering mechanism for the takeover would be a district's failure within two or three years to educate pupils up to Chapter 1 standards. But . . . get this:

These are not to be the standards of knowledge-based tests of the basics (which indeed the Clinton educrats deride as drawing too much on rote and drill). Instead, the assessments are to be geared to "cumulative portfolios" of student work and "real-life projects," according to the Clintonites' 305-page plan for reinventing Chapter 1. Under this Outcome-Based Education approach, students may know how to read and write and compute, but if they are deficient in the higher-order skills of "critical thinking"—in politically correct ways, that is—the school district may be found deficient.

And here is arrogance epitomized: The new standards have not even been formally prescribed, but the Clinton regime wants school districts yoked to them, regardless.

If a district failed to progress toward enabling "all children" to meet the prescribed performance standards, the state could take the following punitive actions (among others):

- Appoint a receiver or trustee in place of the superintendent and school board.
- Remove schools from local jurisdiction entirely and create "alternative governance procedures," such as state-imposed charter schools. (This can only be termed slick, Willie. Charter schools are supposed to be about choice, and site-based management about empowerment. But under the Clintons, these become instruments of centralized control.)
- Abolish the local school district. (This fits nicely with the philosophy of Labor Secretary Robert Reich as expressed in a 1992 article in the *American School Board Journal* when he was still a Harvard egghead. The federal government, Reich wrote, is "going to have to reorganize the size of our school districts and consolidate, creating metropolitan school districts that encompass the inner city and the suburbs. That's

going to be a political mess, but it has to happen." So sayeth the Reichmeister.)

• Mandate student transfers to other districts, with transportation provided. The shorthand for this is compulsory busing. Leave it to the Clinton claque to exhume a failed liberal experiment. Can race-norming's revival be far behind?

The hypocrisy of all this is thicker than the fog surrounding Whitewater. If schools did fail to measure up to legitimate standards, the fault might lie with local school officials—or it might not. In certain districts, for example, a failure of the federal government to enforce a rational immigration policy could leave school districts struggling to cope with sudden influxes of large numbers of unassimilated youngsters. Elsewhere, drastic cuts in state support could harm education.

In all fairness, if the principle of "corrective action" is to apply outside the realm of representative democracy, it should apply at the very top as well as to the most humble board in Middle America.

Indeed, the Republic should be able to place the White House itself in receivership whenever it is occupied by those who seek to abrogate constitutional principles to force their pet social theories on the American people.

* * *

April 6, 1994

Phonics to Teach Reading Is Politically Incorrect

By Robert Holland

Phonics vs. look-say: That's the great debate over the teaching of reading that has been raging since the introduction of the insipid Dick and Jane readers in 1930. It should have been resolved in favor of phonics long ago because all major comprehensive studies have shown conclusively that phonics—teaching children to decode words by systematically learning the sounds of the English language—works best for the vast majority of pupils.

Nevertheless, the education bureaucracy easily seduced by expensive fads just keeps going back and forth on this issue. A quick example here in Virginia:

• In 1988, State Superintendent of Public Instruction Jack Davis, a strong advocate for basic (as well as advanced) education, had a requirement that phonics be used in elementary reading instruction put into accreditation standards for the first time.

• In 1992, Davis' successor, Joe Spagnolo, a fan of Outcome-Based Education and self-esteem enhancement, had the phonics requirement stripped out. Instead he inserted a mandate in the Standards of Quality that programs in kindergarten through grade 3 be "developmentally appropriate," a loaded term that means, among other things, eschewing phonetic structure in favor of child-directed activity.

OBE proved to be as popular with Virginia parents as a colony of fireants at a Sunday School picnic. But "whole language"—essentially the look-say method of teaching reading, preferred by OBEists—remains entrenched in most schools across the state and nation.

This will be an issue with which the new state superintendent, Bill Bosher, and the Allen administration must grapple in developing their approach to school reform.

In a recent interview, Robert Sweet, president of the National Right to Read Foundation, told me something quite chilling: that the education "reform" bills now coming out of Clintonite Washington will effectively outlaw phonics in federally aided schools.

Goals 2000, which President Clinton signed into law on April Fool's Day eve, and HR6, which would use federal money to blackmail local schools into adopting OBE, constitute "a federal takeover the likes of which we've never seen in this country," said Sweet.

A dead giveaway to the intentions of the OBE swamis who are behind the Clintons' education putsch is in a section of HR6 that makes this audacious assertion: "The disproven theory that children must first learn basic skills before engaging in more complex tasks continues to dominate strategies for classroom instruction, resulting in emphasis on repetitive drill and practice at the expense of content-rich instruction, accelerated curricula, and effective teaching to high standards."

That's in a section entitled What Has Been Learned. In Orwellian fashion, it turns truth on its head. What has truly been learned, in more than 125 research studies—including massive surveys by J.S. Chall of the Harvard Graduate School of Education, among others—is that phonetic decoding is the most effective and cost-efficient way to teach children to read. And does any rational person contend that reading is not the key to higher learning? HR6 is a dagger pointed at what phonetic programs remain in public schools, because phonics necessarily entails drill and repetition (which need not be synonymous with drudgery, as the use of music in the wildly successful commercial program, "Hooked on Phonics," shows).

The OBEists want to avoid memorization and teacher-directed learning at all costs, lest some student somewhere suffer a bruised ego. Better to use "developmentally appropriate practice," which means letting children in grades K-3 meander from one multi-age, cut-and-paste learning center to another, picking up reading and other basic skills by osmosis while exercising their "higher order thinking skills."

Sweet, a former Education and Justice Department official who founded the non-profit Right to Read organization last year, has no intention of letting the feds' dumbing-down go unchallenged. The foundation recently published an alert that OBE and related exercises in behavior modification and values clarification are rapidly eroding academic standards.

Sweet's credentials for leading this battle are sterling. As an education official, he produced the landmark report, Becoming a Nation of Readers. He also worked with Marva Collins in establishing the highly successful model school in the Chicago public housing projects. It uses intensive phonics. As an administrator of juvenile justice and delinquency prevention programs he saw first-hand the bitter harvest of poor education.

"Some 85 to 90 percent of kids involved with the juvenile justice system are illiterate," he said. "That is not an excuse for their misdeeds, but when we know how to teach them and we aren't, it suggests that we are also somewhat culpable."

And why, given the research supporting phonics, does the public-school monopoly prefer whole language? The answer, in a word: greed. The average phonics program costs only about $60 per pupil while whole language programs go for $175 to $350 per. The major publishing houses "have a lot to gain" from repackaging the failed look-say programs as whole language, notes Sweet.

The Washington-based Right to Read Foundation has a national help line (1-800-468-8911) for families, and is offering at a nominal cost a simple reading test that indicates how well a person knows phonics.

It may well be private initiatives like this that keep the flame of learning alive during the coming Dark Ages of nationalized education.

* * *

June 8, 1994

By His 'Unsettling' Actions in Education, Allen Keeps His Word

By Robert Holland

"Va. Governor's Agenda Gets Mixed Reception," bugled the must-read journal of the education establishment, *Education Week*, in its June 1 edition.

The article reported grimly that "the new Governor of Virginia,"

George Allen, is "already unsettling some local educators who are wary of his views on school choice, sex education, and prayer in schools."

Already, huh?

And Allen's support of school reform based on solid academics also discombobulates boosters of the school of self-esteem enhancement.

Good.

Governor Allen should cherish all such dyspeptic mutterings from educrat-land. If he is "unsettling" the public education monopolists, he is performing a wonderful public service.

Besides, the Governor shows every sign of keeping faith with the people who voted him into office, an uncommon practice among politicians of the '90s, who more often heed statists who urge them to "grow in office."

So Allen believes parents (as opposed to agents of the state) actually should be able to choose their children's schools? That they alone should decide whether their children shall be exposed to an oxymoronic "safe-sex" curriculum? And even that students should be able voluntarily to say a prayer?

To those self-anointed elitists who favor prescription (their own) over freedom in education, that's all pretty outrageous. But the clear evidence is that most people who supply money and their children to schools like the idea of having a say.

Last summer, as the Virginia gubernatorial campaign began to warm, citizen discontent with the state education bureaucracy's scheme to impose neo-progressive, attitudinal Outcome-Based Education as the model of "reform" for all Virginia schools had grown hotter than a pepper sprout. Midsummer town meetings filled high school auditoriums to overflowing with Virginians distressed about OBE.

Allen opposed OBE flatly and put forward an alternative to stress the basics and local control. His opponent, Mary Sue Terry, wanted to change the subject to "disparity." Her reticence implied support for OBE.

Allen's administration has shown its seriousness about shifting direction in education reform in ways small and large. When citizen activists complained about impending State Department of Education sponsorship last month of a pricey OBE-related conference in Norfolk, Allen's schools chief, Bill Bosher, promptly withdrew state support of the pow-wow.

Even more significant was Allen's appointment the other day of a 49-member Commission on Champion Schools, which is to prepare a reform plan built around a toughened version of the state's Standards of Learning for the traditional academic disciplines. OBE, by contrast, sets out to break the disciplines in favor of a thematic approach to learning encouraging politically correct thinking on environmentalism, globalism, multiculturalism, and other dizzy isms.

Allen's commission isn't the Who's Who of Virginia politics and commerce such panels usually resemble. The commission is notable for its inclusion of many everyday citizens—part of no long-standing interest group—who became overnight activists because of the OBE menace. Many of them are intelligent and energetic women who come from diverse political and social backgrounds: Lil Tuttle of Midlothian, Kerri Vailati of Hampton, Eileen Hunt of Richmond, Cheri Yecke of Stafford County, and Sylvia Kraemer of Alexandria (a self-described liberal Democrat).

In his charge, Allen urged the commissioners to seek positive change. "Look at options like charter schools and other forms of school choice. Find ways to encourage competition and co-operation to ensure excellence. Enlist the assistance of a broad cross-section of our citizens, including businesses. Consider utilizing innovative technology to increase learning in rural areas. Look at public-private partnerships. And call on citizens and parents at the local level to develop new approaches to raise academic achievement."

But Allen acknowledged that Virginia's concept of academic-based education reform is not likely to mesh with the OBEish standards being pushed by the Clinton claque in Goals 2000 and the pending Elementary and Secondary Education Act rewrite (S1513). And if the two prove to be in conflict, he said, "we'll go our own way—the Virginia way—and be the better for it."

The state could forgo Goals 2000 money; or, it could go to court and challenge Washington for promulgating a national curriculum, in violation of statutory prohibitions as well as the 10th Amendment, which reserves to the states and to the people all powers (such as running a school system) not assigned to the feds by the Constitution.

Recently, I addressed a packed community college auditorium near Raleigh where Tar Heel parents had organized a Virginia-style town meeting on an OBE plan being foisted on their schools. One woman asked a question I have heard many times in Virginia and other states: "With Goals 2000 and powerful interests pushing this, are we fighting in vain at the local level? Will we have to give in eventually anyway?"

Say no to defeatism. The issue of *Education Week* that looked askance at George Allen's good work also shed tears over vanguard OBE experiments being scrapped recently in Rosemount, Minnesota, and Littleton, Colorado, as a result of citizen opposition. California Governor Pete Wilson has frozen funding of an OBE-style state assessment of students' attitudes and feelings. And Connecticut parents recently beat back an OBE plan in the state legislature.

The federal legislation is plenty horrible, all right. But the Constitution provides no basis for Washington to mandate, say, look-say over phonics, or a new New Math, or multicultural revisionism in social studies. If citizens stand for academic substance over OBE mush in communities across the land, what will the Clintonoids do: Send in the troops?

* * *

April 13, 1994

Skip the Test, Graduate Cum Laude

By Robert Holland

Let us speak today of high standards in education.

Bill & Hillary & Robert (Reich) & Richard (Riley) and all the other Clintonoids in the Imperial City say they are for them—for all children equally. And these are to be "national" standards. But the standards are also to be "voluntary"—all states must develop standards (or "strategies," as Congress provided alternatively in one of its typically meaningless compromises), but none supposedly will be forced to implement them under the Goals 2000 law.

Can you picture that? A federally directed grassroots effort, a porker with great big wings. Okay, let's see if this creature can fly.

Standards mean nothing without enforcement. If standards really are to be high—indeed, "world class"—surely local schools will be able to test students to see to it that they meet them.

Nope, not so surely.

A fortnight before President Clinton (declaring that the nation was finally getting "serious about education") signed Goals 2000 into law, his Education Department was initiating legal action against Ohio under Title VI of the 1964 Civil Rights Act.

Why? Fundamentally because that state dares to require that students pass a ninth-grade proficiency test in reading, writing, mathematics, and "citizenship skills" before being awarded a high school diploma.

Whoa. What happened to Washington's devotion to "high standards"? Is the ability to read at a ninth-grade level too formidable a standard for high school seniors? What would the Clintonoids consider to be a high standard—third-grade proficiency? Nursery school? (And, oh yes: Whatever happened to "voluntary"?)

Nineteen other states require exit exams. Minimum competency testing has its pros and cons, but it was not the content of Ohio's test that perturbed the grand high educrats at ED-Central. Rather, according to a March 15 letter from ED's Office for Civil Rights to Ohio state superintendent Ted Sanders, the problem was that a "significant and disproportionate number of minority students" failed the first test last fall.

And woe unto Ohio if significant numbers of minority pupils fail a re-test this year. If that happens, says OCR's Chicago regional director Kenneth Mines, "an acute civil rights issue will arise." Mines asserts that OCR will probe "whether minority students will be denied high school diplomas on the basis of race or national origin because they have not had fair opportunities to learn."

That's a clear and ominous tie-in with the "opportunity to learn" standards that states must develop under Goals 2000.

So here we go again. By high standards, Washington actually means lowering standards to the point at which academic outcomes are equalized on a group basis. Individual striving by pupils, including those classified as minorities, to meet standards of excellence are irrelevant. What counts are group results, statistics. There should be proportional A's and B's, proportional diplomas—a bogus, race- normed equality.

Ohio may be out of sync on at least two additional counts:

- One of the eight National Goals codified by Congress states that "the high school graduation rate will increase to at least 90 percent." Putting obstacles like ninth-grade tests in the way is not going to inflate the graduation rate.
- Ohio recently has become the first state to mandate intensive, systematic phonics instruction in the teaching of reading in primary grades. Now, that step could do more than any other to boost pupil achievement and graduation rates legitimately because schools would be giving children the key to all future success: the ability to decode words and read independently.

Unfortunately, however, the Clintonoids (in their plan to "reinvent" the Elementary and Secondary Education Act) have set out to scuttle remaining enclaves of phonetic drill in favor of the "whole language" approach, which encourages children to guess at words and invent their own spellings.

It would not be surprising some day to find teachers busted—fined or even jailed—for bootlegging phonics into their classrooms.

In Virginia, State Superintendent of Public Instruction Bill Bosher is considering dusting off the state's Standards of Learning for English, social studies, math, and other academic subjects, toughening those standards, and making them the basis of a statewide testing program.

Gearing tests to what students actually are being taught has considerable merit. But if the results have disparate impact on any particular group, will Virginia run afoul of the Clintonoids' perverse definition of high standards?

Virginia already has had a bellyful of just how "voluntary" are the nostrums of Clinton's educrats. Acting out of sheer ideology, not legal necessity, ED-Central has reversed an established federal policy and is insisting that local schools not suspend or expel pupils who are identified as disabled, no matter how serious an offense (even selling drugs or carrying a gun to school) they may commit. And the feds are withholding $50 million in special education funds from Virginia because this state insists there should be no special excuse if the misconduct and the disability are unrelated.

Commendably, the Allen administration has gone into federal court to challenge the Clinton administration's perverse interpretation of "full inclusion," which, if carried to a ridiculous extreme, could turn classrooms into utter chaos.

If there really is going to be a return to high intellectual standards in this country, states are going to have to challenge the Ministry of Dumbed-Down Education in Washington.

* * *

July 13, 1994

Reflections Under the Speading Skydome

By Robert Holland

Toronto—Having had my way paid up here to talk to state School Boards Association communicators about Outcome-Based Education, I naturally repaired to the baseball SkyDome to amass a real-life portfolio—complete with a journal of my personal feelings—on OBE's application to baseball.

Dere Dairy: The SkiDumb is like awesum. But how do I feel bout them Word Serious Penknats flying on furrin soil? No problemissimo. One-world base ball is groooovy, like awesum dude, you know? We shud have such a guvment that wud make us all sav the whails and off the develupers and stuf. And stead of singin bout krackerjacks at 7th inn stretuch dig the cheerledurs leding us in 'Shake Yur Bodie!' I luv Kanada! And thanx, Teach, for a nuther 'A' I kno you will giv my hole langage ritin. I feel good. . . .

But, man, like whot wuz that I sawe at bottum of the thurd, havin just klimed to noseblood sektion on a Ten Buck (18 on face) skalpted tickut, the onliest way to get in the SkiDumb? The jays' centurfeilder has just lept his feet and kickked (!) the pill ovur the fence for a homerrun for the othur team, the royuls of kanzus city! Geezo Pitza! Are the jays snakebit or are they tryin to giv games away? Sure looks like it in nintn when guys from bullpin blow a nuther won, 6 to 5.

But like the mind blowingest axshiun wuz in bottum of six, klose game, and the ruuf—dam man, the top of this joint is movin, like groovin! Her come a sektion of the Dummb kreepin over to my side of the nooseblood. And purty soon nurther sektion muves to meet it til 20 minnuts later its klamped titer than a kan of Starkissed Tunna. And all the tim the game is goin on way down bee low! Gotta be purty dizzie if your tryin to snag a hi pop with slidin top. (Ha! A little rhime for you Teach!) But, like, a thundur boommer wuz heded that way and you wanna wait thru a rainlay or whut?

Sure enough, the back-to-back World Champion Toronto Blue Jays are playing exemplary OBE baseball. Consistent with OBE philosophy, they are doing penance for their superior talent—holding back so that players on lesser teams can catch up and have their self-esteem massaged. How else to explain a team with the likes of Roberto Alomar, John Olerud, Paul Molitor, and Joe Carter being 12 games out of second—second!—place at All-Star break?

As for that sliding roof, it reminds me of the top-down restructuring of education going on in this country. How do teachers keep their eye on the ball down at the foundation level, when wooly theorists—abetted by powerful interests—are altering the structure around and above them?

My visit with the school board association folks confirmed for me that OBE-style reform is a scorching hot topic—and getting hotter—across the country. Many of them—particularly from California and Oregon—disagreed vehemently with my views. (Overall, opinion seemed to range from resignation to enthusiastic support for OBE.) But they were seeking to understand the outcry of everyday citizens that is greeting the attempted imposition of OBE in schools from Hawaii to Maine. To use diplomatese, we had a "frank exchange."

The issue entails more than a clash of progressive vs. traditional philosophies. It has to do with whether the real power will reside with Big Government elites or with individual consumers of educational services.

That split is evident even in Governor Allen's strike force on education. Some think the government's control of schools and colleges needs little more than fine-tuning. Others want radical change to put individuals in charge—by letting parents choose their children's schools, for example. And in order to reject the federal government's audacious attempt to seize absolute control of education, they want to turn down the Goals 2000 grants the Clintonoids are dangling in front of the states.

If this males them radicals, consider that the founders of our Republic were radicals also. And here's support for them from a distinguished scholar: Stephen Arons, professor of legal studies at the University of Massachusetts, Amherst. Writes Arons, "The Goals 2000 act adopts a top-down, authoritarian, and systematized model of schooling, and it ought probably to be rejected by teachers, students, families, and subcultures on educational grounds alone."

Even worse, says Arons, by establishing a national curriculum—"official knowledge"—the new law flies in the face of basic principles of our constitutional democracy, such as consent of the governed and First Amendment freedoms of expression. A national curriculum, he says, is just as contrary to the American way as a national religion.

Professor Arons, it gets even worse than that: Goals 2000 is only one part of what Bill Clinton is calling his "human capital" or "lifelong learning" agenda (for a full exposition of which see the June 22 *Education Week*). The Clintonoids regard Goals 2000, the School-to-Work Opportunities Act, the Elementary and Secondary Education Act reauthorization (HR6, S1513), Hillary's health care plan, vast expansion of Head Start for preschoolers, and the bogus welfare reform (consisting mostly of more government make-work) as all of a piece in creating a government-trained and socialized workforce for a global economy.

The agenda took shape during the Reagan-Bush 1980s with several current Clintonoids (Robert Reich, Donna Shalala, Richard Riley, Robert Rubin, Ira Magaziner, and of course Lady Hillary) working closely with big biz- and foundation-supported groups. To be sure, Big Biz and New World Order Republicans found the agenda pleasing—and so we have the current bipartisan atrocity.

Human capital is the technocrats' lingo for our children and grandchildren. These authoritarians should understand that there are many Americans who do not take kindly to their progeny being herded under one SkyDome.

* * *

August 3, 1994

'Systemic' Education Plans Run Roughshod Over Free Individuals

By Robert Holland

The Allen administration has been giving thought to rejecting $14 million in biennial Goals 2000 money being dangled by the feds as an inducement to sign on to a totalitarian form of school reform accurately called systemic by its advocates.

Unfortunately, the decision is more complicated than that. The pending reauthorization of the Elementary and Secondary Education Act (now running to more than 900 dreary pages) could cut Virginia out of another $140 million in aid, largely to high-poverty schools, if it balks at buying into Goals 2000—national school board, national curriculum, and all.

Meanwhile, there is the question of Virginia's participation in the federal School-to-Work Opportunities Act, which Congress quietly passed last spring. Millions more will be at stake. School to Work constitutes the third leg of the triad of national systemic reform; indeed, all three of these measures are cross-referenced and tightly wired together.

An example: Goals 2000 sets up a National Skills Standards Board whereby Robert Reich's Labor functionaries can define the skills necessary for every job in the country. School to Work will specify how the schools are to inculcate and certify those workplace skills (like the notorious SCANS "competencies" of self-esteem and sociability) in children and will begin tracking them early on (through "career majors") toward employment in specific industries. Counseling would begin "at the earliest possible age, but not later than the seventh grade." (Title I, Sec. 101.)

The Allen administration has accepted a $330,000 School-to-Work planning grant, and Cynthia Taylor, a Wilder holdover who heads this initiative, has announced a series of 10 community meetings in September. She plans to hire "professional facilitators" to conduct the sessions, which are to help develop a plan she says will reflect Virginia's own "interests and needs." But the Labor Department already has volumes of specific School to Work guidelines for Virginia and other states. It is possible to tap into those plans via computer by dialing 800-767-0806 with a modem.

Were this simply an effort to keep education abreast of workplace changes in a technological era and to enhance students' career options (as a product of their own free will), then there would be much to commend in School to Work. Unfortunately, however, a strong element of government coercion permeates Labor's files. A 1991 Virginia proposal, for instance, envisioned that persons under 18 who had left school without "establishing their competencies" under the Virginia Assessment of Critical Knowledge and Skills would be required to enter government Youth Work-Learning Centers. They would not be allowed to hold a job until they had mastered the so-called competencies.

Philosophically, School to Work resolves by fiat a long-running debate between the liberal arts and applied education. Workplace knowhow would replace Cardinal Newman's idea of knowledge as a valuable end in itself. No longer would education be about producing well- rounded individuals; instead it would be about well-socialized workers for the global economy.

Governor Allen, who won election as an opponent of state-mandated Outcome-Based Education, has tried to keep faith with concerned citizens who want choice, variety, and strong academics—not one-size-fits-all systemic reform. In a recent letter, he explained to them that while a Governor who believes in local control cannot zap by decree all remnants of OBE-style affective education in certain localities, he stands by their right as parents to have an impact on local policies.

That such everyday parents and taxpayers—the army OBE created—are winning battles not only in Virginia but across the nation greatly offends the powerful establishment that deems its systemic reform the one model for all. Any doubt about that should have been erased by a recent alarum from the Alexandria-based National Association of State Boards of Education.

NASBE director Brenda Welburn lamented that "systemic education reform" is experiencing "setbacks in many states due to the well-organized opposition which has waged a relentless campaign of rallies and sound-bites." She said the Business Roundtable, the organization of big biz CEOs, is organizing a coalition of "national education associations and businesses" to thwart this opposition.

Interestingly enough, one of the touted benefits of joining the coalition will be "tool kits" including "materials on opponents." Totalitarian reform, totalitarian methods.

Among the groups joining so far: the Council of Chief State School Officers, National Alliance of Business, National Association of Secondary School Principals, National Association of State Directors of Special Education, National Middle School Association, National School Public Relations Association, and the New American Schools Development Corporation. These worthies plan to pool their money—ours?—to hire a fancy political campaign consultant to turn public opinion their way.

These elitist pooh-bahs just don't get it. The problem is that their statist scheme stinks, and all the PR in the world won't make it smell sweeter.

In the 1980s, the idea of "outcomes" in education appealed to bottom-line business thinking, as well it should. Solid results should be expected, indeed demanded, from government schools. But as Bruno Manno points out in a trenchant briefing paper on OBE for the Hudson Institute, the outcomes concept was "hijacked" by the education bureaucracy, and the process turned on its head. With outcomes now expressed in the old progressivist mumbo-jumbo about feelings and attitudes, accountability becomes impossible. Jeanne Allen of the pro-choice Center for Education Reform believes that well-meaning business executives have been misled by their staffers and education bureaucrats.

It would be grand if Governor Allen struck a blow for liberty by making Virginia the first state to reject all aid related to the federalization of education. But that's expecting a lot, given the hue and cry sure to arise about "shortchanging" Virginia pupils.

What's more likely is that systemic reform on the current model will be imposed in every district in the land—and as a result we will see a parents' revolt in this country that will make the current uprising seem tame. Maybe then will come true reform—not of the systemic variety, mind you, but rather one that replaces the corrupt, monopolistic system with true diversity and choice.

* * *

August 24, 1994

Parental Choice and OBE: Is Co-Existence Possible?

By Robert Holland

To be or not to OBE.

That is the question for many school districts across the land. But William Spady's High Success Network surely didn't intend to leave the question completely wide open in organizing a "dialogue" this summer with a select few OBE opponents at posh Vail, Colorado.

Spady wants OBE without question. A sociologist, he is the No. 1 guru of Outcome-Based Education, which isn't at all what the name implies if you think of school outcomes as learning Chaucer and Pythagorean Theorems. His Eagle, Colorado, firm markets OBE—complete with warm/fuzzy outcomes such as that students should become Global Stewards and Collaborative Workers—to school systems in more than 30 states. Virginia was wired for state-mandated transformational OBE, Spady-style, until Governor Doug Wilder pulled the plug last September.

Clearly, Spady and other well-heeled OBEists are worried. Citizen uprisings have rendered OBE moribund if not DOA in diverse places—liberal Connecticut, for example, and in Spady's own back yard of Littleton, which had a major experiment going until voters rebelled. All this is bad for business. The Vail conference likely was intended either to soften the opponents or to portray them as know-nothings.

But you know something? It backfired. Spady got cornered on his own turf into publicly endorsing the polar opposite of government-imposed OBE: parental choice. And not just choice among government schools (which is rather like a choice among burger joints) but a choice including private schools, religious schools, even tutoring services for home-schooled children—all aided by vouchers.

For a full transcript of this remarkable exchange I am indebted to the Alexandria-based Foundation Endowment (which I should note—in the interest of full journalistic disclosure—also pays my travel expenses to speak on education issues). The key participants were: Spady; Tom Tancredo, president of the Independence Institute, a think tank in Golden, Colorado; and Professor Arnie Burron, representing Citizens for Excellence in Education, a conservative Christian organization.

Spady set the stage by persistently complaining that critics have misunderstood or misrepresented his objectives. He never intended that states take his outcomes and mandate them (never mind that many have, in almost identical language from state to state). OBE should be "locally driven," he said. Local people should write their own outcomes. Spady said he is an advocate of education deregulation.

Very well. Tancredo pressed the point:

"I don't really care about the extent to which your particular brand of OBE is or is not being accurately reflected in the debate out there. I care a great deal about whether or not parents will be able to select it, whatever it is, from a wide variety of educational options. . . .

"And the only common ground I can think of is [if] you are willing to state at the end of this conference something like this: It is my intent and always has been my intent to have local control over the process and development of outcomes and assessments, understanding that the ultimate in local control is allowing parents to make that choice through the use of a voucher, and to use that voucher at any educational establishment, public or private, or even in the acquisition of materials and tutorial services by home-schooling parents. . . ."

Spady then asked for help in getting his message across to radio talk show audiences, which he said were misunderstanding him, too.

Tancredo: "What I would like to say to that audience—Bill, will you give me permission to say this to that audience?—that Bill Spady supports the idea that parents should be able to choose Outcome-Based Education, Standards-Based Education, back to the basics, or whatever else it is that's presented to them, to give them the opportunity to choose that, and by opportunity I mean the economic ability to make the decision to go to a public school that offers it, a private school that offers it, or . . . even a home-schooling environment. Are you giving me permission to say that about you?"

Spady: "Yes, I am."

Professor Burron called this "the most monumental breakthrough I could possibly imagine. . . ." A little later, however, the back-pedaling began:

Spady: "I want to say that I could support [choice], and I said yes, and I'm not going to withdraw the yes. But for me, the prior issue is that we bring a great deal of informed and civilized dialogue to what these alternatives are before we turn people loose to choose. And I believe that there is an enormous amount of prejudice and stereotyping surrounding whatever alternative is out there."

Okay, get it all out there, all the facts, all the information—and, yes, all the sales pitches. Let Spady put up a model of the ultimate OBE school of the 21st Century. Let advocates of basic education show off their model of a traditional school—a Great Books curriculum, perhaps. Let others set up schools that blend the progressive and structured approaches.

Then let the marketplace decide. Isn't that the way of a free society? But it is extremely doubtful that Spady and other OBE panjandrums want to risk free and fair competition. Their approach anticipates rigging the outcomes.

* * *

October 5, 1994

So This Is the Model for Every Child?

By Robert Holland

A bright young student from the graduate school of education at Virginia Commonwealth University recently visited me before starting her student-teaching. She was enthusiastic about working with children but decidedly less so about the nature of the pedagogical training she had just received.

Actually, she found it to be more like indoctrination. Specifically, she said that her instructors had taught so-called Developmentally Appropriate Practice (DAP) as though it were holy writ and there were no competing philosophy of education. She couldn't give me permission to use her name for fear of being penalized by the education powers-that-be before her teaching career got started. But she did leave behind her voluminous class notes and printed matter, and, sure enough: DAP appears to be The Word.

What's DAP? Particularly in the critical early years of school—

kindergarten, and grades 1–3—it is a linchpin of the Outcome-Based Education philosophy. All learning must be child-directed—with no grades or failure or standardized testing or drills or memorization, and with self-esteem as the paramount objective. Teachers don't assign work or transmit knowledge; they are facilitators. Children of mixed ages circulate from one activity center to another and decide when, if ever, they are ready to learn their ABCs. They learn by play.

Regarding the OBE connection, the student told me a funny story. Last fall, the morning after Governor Doug Wilder had pulled the plug on the state's fuzzy-wuzzy "outcomes," an ed-school professor stormed into class, slammed down a book, and wailed, "OBE is dead. What am I going to teach now?"

The prof needn't have despaired. There's still DAP, which means there's still OBE, and not many parents have caught on yet—although as more and more indoctrinated teachers hit the classrooms and fewer and fewer children learn to read by the third grade, they will.

There is no reason to suppose VCU is any more or less a promoter of this sappy approach than any other teacher factory. Indeed, Rita Kramer spent a year visiting ed-schools from coast to coast and found the mindset to be prevalent. In Ed-School Follies, she wrote:

"Next to the media in general and television in particular, our schools of education are the greatest contributor to the 'dumbing down' of America. They have been transformed into agencies for social change, mandated to achieve equality at all costs, an equality not of opportunity but of outcome. No one can be tested because no one must fail."

Bad ideas never die in education; they just get recycled and given a new name. DAP and OBE are the failed old Progressive Education with 90s' acronyms. But there is something new: The Mandate. DAP is fast becoming official policy.

Under Joe Spagnolo (now Illinois' school chief) DAP became the official methodology for Virginia's elementary schools. Teacher retraining began, model schools were set up, and DAP was inserted into the state's Standards of Quality as something all elementary schools "shall implement." There it remains.

Governor Allen's Champion Schools Commission may recommend scrapping the mandate, but there's no guarantee the State Board of Education and 1995 General Assembly will go along.

Last week the snail mail brought evidence of how deeply the political establishment has bought into ed-school doctrine. A Southern Regional Education Board report hawked—without reservation—the DAP ideology of child-directed learning, calling it the only way—the only way!—to comply with National Education Goal No. 1 of Goals 2000: readiness for school.

It won't be easy, said the SREB. Principals, teachers, and parents must "change their behaviors and their expectations of both children and schools." They must learn that it is "inappropriate" for teachers to direct children in study of subjects such as reading and arithmetic or for them to insist that children be quiet and do their own work.

The Atlanta-based SREB, a 40-year-old consortium of 15 states, once published incisive studies. But this piece of tripe—which simply parrots the dogma of the National Association for the Education of Young Children (NAEYC)—suggests nothing so much as that Virginia ought to withdraw from the SREB and save $276,000 in tax money per two-year budget. (And how did the NAEYC determine "appropriateness" for every child in America? Not from research but from a "working hypothesis," according to the Spring, 1993, issue of *Effective School Practices*. Proponents of DAP "figuratively, if not literally, elbowed" traditional educators out of meeting rooms where the policy was drafted. Well, at least the elbows are sharp.)

Under the doctrine the SREB is peddling, it would be developmentally inappropriate for a grade-school teacher to conduct practice from a phonics chart or to ask her pupils to recite the multiplication tables. Fortunately, there are still teachers who believe in teaching, not facilitating, and in applying discipline (with love) when necessary. There is even an Oregon-based Association for Direct Instruction, which has published copious research on the failures of child-directed learning.

One of the most compelling case histories comes from England, which in 1992 ended a 20-year fling with DAP, known there as progressive education. It had been an abysmal failure. Implemented with the intention of leveling social class differences, it perversely had the opposite effect—locking in poorer children to their existing station. They entered school needing structure and discipline, which they lacked at home, and floundered when left to their own whims.

DAP may have the same deleterious effect on inner-city blacks in this country. Indeed, Lisa Delpit, an African-American educator in Baltimore, has written about moving away from her ed-school progressive training back to traditional methods of drill and direction when she found that her black pupils were failing in droves. What suffices for some kids who come to school already knowing how to construct sentences may be a disaster for inner-city children. What a bitter irony—and tragedy—if the government's effort to equalize outcomes only widens the achievement gap.

* * *

November 23, 1994

Freedom-Based Reform: Now How About Letting Education on That Train?

By Robert Holland

In what may have presaged the recent nationwide vote of no confidence in the Clintons' statist agenda, a citizens' group in Connecticut—normally a bellwether liberal state—not only defeated an OBE scheme for the state's schools last spring but also put forward its own 10-point freedom-based reform plan.

Guess what is Plank No. 1 of Connecticut's Committee to Save Our Schools' (CT:SOS) proposal? Here it is . . .

REJECT FEDERAL INTERFERENCE: Connecticut should follow the example of Governor George Allen of Virginia, who says that rather than cave in to the "dictates of some bureaucrat," he will give up federal education funds. He says, "We'll forgo the money if it's contrary to what we think is best for Virginia's students."

Having taken calls on education reform now from folks in 47 states, I believe I can state with some authority that Virginia is an inspiration for many Americans who want nationalized education no more than they want socialized medicine. Choice is paramount. From California to Connecticut, Americans still want the decisions about how they rear their children, select a family doctor, and generally conduct their personal lives to be in their hands, not Big Mama's in Washington.

Virginia's recent Senate race, which ended in the plurality re-election of Chuck Robb (who has been a dial-a-vote for Bill and Hillary) was an aberration—a result of the flawed candidacy of Oliver North and GOP disunity. Allen's landslide election last year on a populist/conservative platform provides a truer reading of the political barometer. Appropriately, the Governor took to the Republican Governors' Association meeting in Williamsburg this week an action plan for halting the federal over-reach.

Now, even some of the Democratic holdovers on Virginia's Board of Education appear to be getting the message. In the wake of the nation's thunderous repudiation of Big Government, the board backed away last week—on a 5–3 vote—from an expected decision to apply for funds under the Clintons' Goals 2000, the key piece of the scheme to nationalize education.

Michelle Easton of Herndon, one of Allen's two appointees so far, played a key role in convincing a majority that Virginia had nothing to lose—and everything to gain—from steering clear of the Goals shoals. A decision was delayed until March at the earliest.

Indeed, by the time Virginia decides, the substance of the recently enacted federal education laws may have changed. Leaders of the first Republican-controlled Congress in four decades already have said they will "revisit" both Goals 2000 and the reauthorized Elementary and Secondary Education Act early next year. If the government's education directives are found wanting, said Pennsylvania Republican Bill Goodling, who is in line to chair the House Education and Labor Committee, they can be reformed, replaced, or "[thrown] out entirely." Hear, hear!

Since Goodling has voted Badling on most of the Big Education measures (that is to say, for them), he must have had the fear of Speaker Newt thrown into him. So be it if Republicans ever are to live up to their promise of being the party of limited government.

The new federal laws are full of unconstitutional usurpations of power that ought to be stripped out: the National Education Standards and Improvement Council, which would oversee a national curriculum; opportunity to learn standards, which would control what states spend on education; "corrective actions," such as federally mandated firings of local school boards, and dozens of related atrocities.

With the feds at bay, and with newly elected governors, state legislatures, and state superintendents of public instruction carrying the populist torch, a grand opportunity now exists for wholesome education change tailored to diverse community needs. Jeanne Allen, president of the national Center for Education Reform, believes the election has set the stage for expanded parental choice.

Connecticut, Pennsylvania, and Texas are the states most likely to pass comprehensive, freedom-based school reform as a result of the elections, Ms. Allen believes. Charter schools—public schools freed of bureaucratic entanglements and offering varied approaches from which parents may freely choose the best for their children—are going to be a hot item. They are an excellent device when not used as a cover to bring in state-mandated OBE through the back door. And our friends in CT:SOS have some other good ideas, such as:

• A truth-in-reading stipulation that each school report to the local school board its method of reading instruction—phonics or whole language—so the public may know.

• A sunshine law to enable the public to review all state tests and scoring keys after two years' use.

Governor Allen will receive preliminary recommendations of his Champion Schools Commission next week. Charter schools offering alternatives to monopoly control—not least, the freedom to hire teachers who know their stuff but haven't been through the mind-numbing ed-school drill—will be a key plank. There will be more debate as to what kind of academic standards the state should enforce. But this looks like a promising start.

The nation will be looking to Virginia for leadership in education.

* * *

October 19, 1994

Working on the Goals 2000 Systemic-Change Gang

By Robert Holland

Many parents and other citizens across the nation are objecting to school restructuring schemes that have more to do with manipulating children's attitudes than with teaching them to read.

But the systemic-change gang doesn't intend to neglect the adults. Oh, no. It means to adjust their attitudes, too.

In fact, entire communities are in the sights of the Goals 2000 propaganda artillery.

The National Education Goals Panel, an all-politicians' group assembled under the Goals 2000 law, is preparing to distribute a Community Action Tool Kit developed by the U.S. Department of Education and its taxfunded regional laboratories. The five-pound kit is chock full of brightly colored manuals for community-organizing that are printed on spare-no-expense glossy paper. Even sign-up and reminder sheets for local Goals 2000 activists (whom the feds evidently assume to be too inept to draw up their own) are printed on the high-quality slick paper.

Ruth Chacon, the panel's spokesman, claims that by selling 2,500 of these kits to community activists at $37 apiece, the government will recover its costs. Sure. And if you believe that, you probably believe the coming national education standards are going to be "voluntary."

The little 'ol kit-makers leave little to chance. Among the contents:

• Letters to the editor, op-ed pieces, feature stories, radio spots, and even entire speeches endorsing the national education putsch. This is Connect-the-Dots grassroots support: Just sign your name and send in a government-prepared letter.

• A Troubleshooting Guide for dealing with opponents, a.k.a., The Resistance. Identify your opponents, the Kit advises; list their resources. This sounds like something out of one of Chairman Mao's tool kits.

• Case histories of how opponents can be co-opted in order to implement curriculum changes. Educrats in Edmonds, Washington, for example, deliberately put out multiple drafts of the district's OBE plan because "it gives the message that you are open to change."

• Step-by-step plans for manufacturing community support through the use of socalled facilitators and change agents. Those are people who steer public meetings toward a phony consensus. The regional education labs, formed under the 1965 Elementary and Secondary Education Act (recently reauthorized for five years), long ago contracted with behavioral scientists to develop this tool for imposing government-desired innovation. One such manual, for example, was prepared at the University of Michigan's Institute for Social Research.

"Only by changing the attitudes and behavior of community members," the Tool Kit states, "will it be possible to reach the National Education Goals."

That strongly suggests local people are to have little or no choice about the shape education reform will take. Those who believe practice in the basics of literacy more important for first-graders than higher order thinking about globalism and multiculturalism are to be prime candidates for a government re-tooling.

The change being peddled is fraudulent. Real change would break up the education monopoly, enable parents to choose the best schools for their children, and restore intellectual rigor. The systemic-change gang, by contrast, wants to nationalize the monopoly, brainwash parents, and decimate pockets of excellence by assessing for feelings instead of testing for knowledge.

Under Choosing a Facilitator, the kit's Community Organizing Guide makes this remarkable statement: "An organized discussion about education reform will not happen spontaneously." In other words, local rubes cannot be trusted to reach the right conclusions. Their meetings must be facilitated.

That kind of didactic talk—irksome from a nagging aunt but ominous coming from Big Brother's helpers—is common to strategic plans of the systemic-change gang. The National Center on Education and the Economy, a Carnegie offshoot that has become a virtual adjunct of the Clinton Education Department, said this in a 1992 funding proposal:

"If we are to succeed in radically transforming schools, we must alter attitudes outside the schoolhouse door."

The center added that it would be necessary to employ "all the techniques of the modern media strategist as well as the proven methods of community organizing." It said one of its partners, the Public Agenda Foundation, already had "been successful in designing and orchestrating citizen education campaigns" in five communities.

That's where the Tool Kit now comes into play, and sure enough the Public Agenda Foundation's seven-stage journey to correct thinking is contained therein. At Stage One, citizens "may not yet recognize that there is no 'going back to basics' in education; we must go forward to a set of 'new basics' required for success in today's increasingly complex and competitive global economy."

That's Outcome-Based Education jargon right out of the Labor Secretary's Commission on Achieving Necessary Skills (SCANS) reports. The so-called new basics are "competencies" like self-esteem and working in a group.

Indeed, the Colorado-based High Success Network—the lucrative consulting business of OBE guru William Spady—is cited in a section of the Tool Kit on how to sell social change. Interestingly enough, the kit elsewhere advises change agents to avoid using such terms as "outcomes," "outcome-based education," and "self-esteem"—the better to avoid "serious conflict."

Mark this well: The systemic-change gang's preferred new euphemism for OBE is "standards-based education" (SBE). Of course, that's subject to change in Tool Kit II, after The Resistance catches on.

* * *

November 9, 1994

Education That Is Affective—Not Necessarily Effective

By Robert Holland

Worn down by politics? Here are some of the latest potions of Affective Education to pump you up:

• In Chesterfield County, the school system is considering a draft of a new K-10 health curriculum that has "Mental Wellness" as a key section. Starting at the earliest grades, pupils are supposed to brainstorm about their emotions, and engage in assorted stress management and conflict resolution activities.

The curriculum appears to contain some sound knowledge about fitness, nutrition, and other topics. But schools enter dangerous turf when they tinker with emotions and personal feelings.

• In Kentucky, a hotbed of OBE, Ed-Central in Frankfort recently claimed a "dramatic rise" in test scores since systemic restructuring began. Ah, but the gains are on wholly new tests—assessments, really—with open-ended questions in math, reading, science, and social studies. This system features portfolios of student work, evaluated subjectively.

In sum, the secret to miraculous rises in scores is first to dumb-down the tests.

• The U.S. Department of Education is crowing because Wal-Mart has agreed to have Goals 2000 coordinators in every Wal-Mart Store and Sam's Club in America. Why does Big Business so often shill for Big Government, which certainly doesn't have the best interests of business at heart?

• Goals 2000, the linchpin of the systemicchange gang's nationalized education, contains the following requirement for the National Education Standards and Improvement Council, which is to certify the national curr . . . er, standards: "The initial members shall be appointed not later than 120 days after the date of the enactment of this Act." (Title II, Sec. 212).

President Clinton is supposed to appoint the 19 members, some of whom are to be nominated by other lustrous politicians. Well, it's been more than 220 days since the Goals 2000: Educate America Act was passed by Congress, and a White House spokesman told me the NESIC has not been named and she didn't know when it would be.

This should serve as fair warning to expect nationalized education that operates with all the alacrity of the Postal Service and the efficiency of Pentagon procurers of $7,000 coffeepots and $600 toilet seats. Not that we're in any hurry, Mr. President. Let's wait until, say, 1997 to activate this beast.

• Speaking of the 1996 presidential year, the reauthorized Elementary and Secondary Education Act calls for not one, but two, White House Conferences on Education—one for Urban, one for Rural Education. And the ESEA stipulates that both must be held in 1996. I say let The Committee to Re-Elect the President(s) (CREEPS) pick up the tab.

• National panels of subject-matter "experts," working under federal grants doled out by the Bush administration (key operatives of which naively thought national standards would be benign), have begun to check in with national standards for the as-yet-unnamed NESIC to review and certify. The standards for teaching United States history, developed at UCLA, turn out to be the very sort favored at a conclave of America-hating multiculturalists I attended in Los Angeles two years ago. America is to be defined by its worst elements, like the KKK and McCarthyism, and exemplary figures like Robert E. Lee vanish altogether.

But the proposed National Standards for teaching world history are, if anything, even more idiotic. Western civilization becomes a footnote. Skip the Norman Conquest of England, downplay the Magna Charta, but pay great attention to the Olmec civilization in the Oaxaca valley.

Furthermore, the 20th Century's defining struggle between liberal democracy and the totalitarian evils of Fascism and Communism might as well never have happened. The standards setters at UCLA have other causes—minorities, feminists—to glorify.

• True, some of the emerging standards are more reasonable and rigorous. In geography, for example, fourth-graders would have to be able to explain the distribution of the human population on Earth, with the aid of thematic maps. By the end of eighth grade, they would have to be able to explain some of the great human migration streams, and how physical barriers, such as the Berlin Wall, the Appalachian Mountains, and the closed border between North and South Korea have impeded the flow of people.

The National Geographic Society, publishers of National Geographic magazine, had a hand in producing these commendable standards. Unfortunately, however, if students come from dumbed-down history, civics, science, and literature classes, they are going to have a devil of a time handling enhanced geography.

And even if the national standards for all subjects were excellent, there would remain the grave danger of creating "official knowledge," certified by the NESIC, that would be subject to endless political manipulation in Washington.

Which brings me to a final bit of jollity from the systemic-change gang . . .

• The National Association of State Boards of Education, which last summer began mobilizing a coalition to squelch opponents of dictated education restructuring, has blasted an amendment inserted in the ESEA requiring every state that receives ESEA money to expel for at least a year students caught bringing a gun to school. It's better to put the heat-packing young scholars in alternative education than to turn them out on the streets, opines NASBE director Brenda Lilienthal Welburn.

Oh, so national requirements are hunky-dory as long as they are prescribed by liberals or socialists? But when bad old conservatives get in on the game, it's local option time?

If Congress falls under control of the Jesse Helms and Newt Gingrich types, I can hear the sad refrain now: They're breakin' up that ol' systemic-change gang of mine. Sing it, Hank.

* * *

February 1, 1995

Folks Compare Notes on Big Brother's Education Plans

By Robert Holland

St. Louis—It would be more fun to come here in July and see real Cardinals' baseball (post-strike, with Ozzie and the gang) out at

Busch. But the second-best thing is to come here in January and compare notes with education activists from coast to coast.

The spirits soar (as after a successful takeoff from an icy runway) upon meeting hundreds of Americans from every region who are determined to keep education under local control, rather than acquiescing to the nationalized version. Local folks are winning some skirmishes; however, Big Education's tentacles are being detected in new places almost daily. Here are some that were the buzz in Saint Louie:

. Phonics: Wedded to progressive techniques such as invented spelling and look-say (repackaged as whole language), the education establishment demonstrably has failed miserably at its single most important mission—teaching children to read. America has 90 million functional illiterates—and that's disgraceful. Many parents teach their children at home the sounds that letters and letter-combinations make (phonics), so that their kids will not fall victim to this dumbing down.

Big Brother evidently finds home instruction in phonics—the research-proven method—to be threatening. (Is there an agenda to keep the populace semiliterate? Indeed, John Gatto—New York State "Teacher of the Year" in 1991—suggests a deliberate deconstruction of literacy tracing back at least to John Dewey: After all, well-read citizens are independent thinkers, not well-socialized members of a group.)

Whatever the reason, the mighty Federal Trade Commission—using language similar to HR6's blast at phonics last year—is targeting a product, "Hooked on Phonics," that is widely used in American homes, as well as in convention-defying schools.

The FTC is carrying water for the educationists. One of the FTC's preposterous complaints against "Hooked on Phonics" is that it leads people to believe that children can be taught to read in "a home setting" without the services of a certified teacher. The feds are saying implictly, then, that parents can't teach their kids to read—and shouldn't have access to phonetic materials to help them try. But how else will some children learn to read, given that schools of education are indoctrinating new (certified) teachers in "developmentally appropriate practices" that bar systematic instruction of primary-schoolers in phonics (or anything else, for that matter)?

Bob Sweet, Virginia-based director of the National Right to Read Foundation, says that if the FTC's findings are allowed to stand, "Hooked on Phonics" will be just one of many programs for home instruction on the endangered list. Citizens who want to tell the FTC to butt out can send their comments by February 17 to the agency at: 6th Street and Pennsylvania, N.W., Washington, D.C., 20580—referring to FTC File No. 922 3021.

• Accreditation: Hug Therapy is all the rage at the Missouri Scholars Academy, a school for the gifted. "Four hugs per day to survive; eight per day to maintain; 12 per day to grow," advises the school's Personal and Social Dynamics Component. That by-the-numbers approach to feel-good education is maybe worth a chuckle, but some methods other schools have used to probe the Affective Domain are not—i.e., assessment questions about sexual practices, mutilation, callous parents, death and dying, all intended to lay children's emotions raw and provoke their reactions.

Just when parents think they have both the front and back doors closed to Affective (a.k.a. Outcome-Based) Ed, it seeps in through the ventilation shafts. Carol Bond of Stillwater, Oklahoma, has done extensive research documenting the growing role of regional accreditation associations in pushing OBE on schools. A handbook of the North Central Association of Colleges and Schools—Outcomes Accreditation/A Focus on Student Success—proposes to measure education according to how students progress toward emotional well-being, commitment to state-approved values, and self-esteem.

Ms. Bond says that attitudinal OBE is now used in school accreditation in about half the states, and is fast spreading. I don't doubt it. Even if the new Congress should scrap Goals 2000, this brainrot runs deep in the education establishment, and will not be easily expunged.

• The Medicaid Connection: Clearly, physical- and mental-health Outcomes are a big part of New Age ed. But is there a plan to link education restructuring to Medicaid and thereby to bring all, or virtually all, American children under a de facto National Health Care System? Anita Hoge, the Pittsburgh mom who used Freedom of Information laws to expose illegal psychological testing of schoolchildren in Pennsylvania, makes a strong case that this linkage is happening. (And, remember, in last week's State of the Union address, President Clinton did express hope for a national solution to children's health care.)

Wrtiting in a new magazine delightfully named Media Bypass, Ms. Hoge makes the following connections based on recent Pennsylvania experience: Education and welfare departments are collaborating to extend Medicaid funding to schoolchildren under new requirements of the Individuals With Disabilities Education Act (IDEA). This changes Medicaid from a poverty program to one based on a wide assortment of disabilities. Indeed, Ms. Hoge contends that liberal interpretations of IDEA and mental-illness definitions could qualify most children—by dint of the slightest emotional upsets (a bad hair day, breaking up with a boy/girlfriend)—for Medicaid mental-health wraparound services. She sees all of this as plugged in to Big Education's mental health Outcomes, with national data banks tracking intensely personal health and education information in electronic portfolios.

Anita Hoge assembles from many small pieces a big picture not everyone will see. But she's no kook. On December 8, she was called to the Interior Department to testify on the Medicaid connection in the context of security on Al Gore's Information Superhighway. Maybe there is a story here that shouldn't be bypassed by the media.

* * *

January 18, 1995

This Agency Peddles Phony Reform

By Robert Holland

Why should what goes on in the public school system of Johnson City, New York, hold any interest whatsoever for Virginians, or Californians, or even residents of New York City?

Good question. In truth, Johnson City—located north of Valley Forge, Pennsylvania—should be an education irrelevance. It is, after all, a blue-collar school district of fewer than 3,000 pupils, with only one high school. It is hardly America in microcosm.

In the ideological fantasy-land of nationalized education, however, Johnson City is the most exemplary school district in the United States. It is that shining OBE school district on the hill—where failure has been abolished and "high self-esteem" is a graduation requirement. No pupil receives an F, only an Incomplete—and then retest after retest after permissive retest.

When Virginia educrats were pushing mandated Outcome-Based Education in 1993—and they in turn were pushed to say where OBE actually had worked—they responded over and over, parrot-like, with "Johnson City." And from Raleigh to Sacramento, that still is the answer being dished out to concerned parents.

No wonder. The federal Department of Education has pumped hundreds of thousands of dollars into Johnson City through the National Diffusion Network to enable the tiny district to propagandize its supposed successes. According to the Akron (Ohio) Beacon-Journal, Johnson City school administrators collect $500-a-day consulting fees for peddling this line.

Unfortunately for the myth-makers, recent State Regents Exam data from the New York State Department of Education paint a less than idyllic picture. Johnson City is one of 12 school districts in Broome County. Look at how its performance in the February, 1994, report to the governor and New York legislature compared with its peers:

• On high school graduation tests, Johnson City's scores ranked in the lower half of the county in English, history, global studies, math I and II, and Spanish. Overall, the district was in the middle of the pack—a tie for sixth and seventh.

• On the most important subject of all—reading—Johnson City's third-graders ranked dead last and its sixth-graders 11th.

• Its students averaged eighth among the 12 districts in reading, writing, science, and social studies in the lower grades.

• In not a single subject did Johnson City rank higher than fourth within Broome County. And its teacher turnover was the worst in the county.

Far from being a model for the nation, then, Johnson City is not even a beacon in its own backyard. None of the other 11 districts has seen fit to adopt the OBE way in the two decades Johnson City has been implementing the no-failure model.

I am grateful to Aldo Bernardo, a professor at the State University of New York at Binghamton, and Valley Forge parent-activist John Spillane for providing perspective on the print-outs of New York State testing data. Bernardo, a Johnson City resident, was a consultant to the district when it first sought innovation under the name Mastery Learning. But in a letter to a nearby Pennsylvania community being urged to copy Johnson City, Bernardo warned that the "OBE virus" (or ODDM, Outcomes-Driven Developmental Model, as OBE is styled in Johnson City) soon invaded and changed the focus of mastery from academics to "attitudinal and behavioral outcomes."

Spillane warns: In districts implementing OBE, parents may already be noticing some of the same OBE/ODDM practices that caused the failure in Johnson City. Replacement of standardized testing by 'portfolios'. . . . Decreased emphasis on grammar, spelling, multiplication tables, phonics. Cutbacks in advanced and honors classes . . . Weak discipline. Students not grouped in classes according to their abilities. Cutbacks in grading, particularly in the lower grades . . . Use of 'cooperative learning,' 'creative spelling,' 'whole language,' self-esteem courses, group psychology . . . More paperwork for teachers. . . .

That the federal Department of Education would use Americans' tax money to tout Johnson City's warmed-over progressivism shows how the ideological agendas of statists are overwhelming education. Indeed, this Cabinet department was created by President Jimmy Carter as a political payoff to the radical National Education Association for its help in his election. Ronald Reagan was elected on a pledge to dismantle DOE, but his appointee as Secretary of Education, Terrel Bell, played secret good guy to the liberals in preserving this abomination.

How pitiful that the Clintonoid Education Department now is trotting out Bell as an op/ed advocate of its continued existence. (See article on this page.)

As Education Secretary, Bell evidently had a hand in the beginnings of the national OBE movement. On July 27, 1984, Leland Birmingham, state superintendent of public instruction in Bell's home state of Utah, wrote a letter to Secretary Bell stating, I am forwarding this letter to accompany the proposal which you recommended (OBE guru) Bill Spady and I prepare in connection with Outcome-Based Education. This proposal centers around the detailed process by which we will work together to implement Outcome-Based Education using research-verified programs. This will make it possible to put Outcome-Based Education in place not only in Utah but in all schools of the nation.

National OBE is now the agenda that the likes of Hillary Clinton, Ira Magaziner, and Robert Reich ardently push in the guise of education "reform." Contrary to Bell's self-serving arguments equating the department's existence with the well-being of schools, the best favor that the new Congress could do for education would be not just to repeal Goals 2000 but to scuttle the entire politicized U.S. Education Department—leaving decisions about how best to teach children to the people closest to the scene: teachers and parents.

* * *

March 1, 1995

How to Smite the Feds' Education Hydra

By Robert Holland

America Deconstructed: Political Correctness, Multiculturalism, 'Standards,' OBE, and School Reform: A Recipe for Disaster?

What does one say as the leadoff speaker at a Foundation Endowment-sponsored Capitol Hill conference with such an eclectic title? Just this: Yes. Disaster will result from the drive to remake schools and society in one systematized mold, unless Americans reassert local control.

The elements of this compulsory systemic change are very much like the many-headed Hydra of classical mythology—cut off one head, and two grow in its place. Don't they understand over there at the Capitol—not even the vaunted Contractors With America?

The day before, "moderate" Republican members of the House education committee—including Chairman Bill Goodling—had unveiled proudly a plan to merge the Departments of Education and Labor.

Wisconsin Representative Steve Gunderson rhapsodized as to how a reinvented Department of Education and Employment could buttress the federal government's "important role" in training a technologically attuned workforce for the global marketplace.

Federal role? What federal role? Where does education appear in the Constitution as a federal responsibility as opposed to one reserved to the states and the people under the Tenth Amendment?

Perhaps Goodling, Gunderson, et al., were sending a message to House GOP freshmen who had called simply for abolishing the Department of Education: Here is the way we do things in Washington, ye upstarts: We combine, consolidate, and (in that grand Washingtonian euphemism) "streamline for more effective delivery of services"—we don't abolish.

But it is the "moderates" who just don't get it: Over the past two years, Education already has substantially tucked itself under the wing of Labor for purposes of pushing a national model of school restructuring. The *de facto* Labor/Education merger already is well along by way of implementing the School to Work Opportunities Act—which, since its quiet passage last May, is looking more and more like the key to nationally restructured education, perhaps even more so than Goals 2000, to which it is linked.

What Virginians thought they were rid of when the Common Core of Learning (with its intrusive "Outcomes") was scrapped in 1993, they likely will get with School to Work (STW), which is industrial-strength OBE. STW merges academics with work-based learning, steers children into specific industries through career majors and counseling from an early age, and pays inordinate attention to their social utility as quality workers—human capital. So much for the liberal arts and individualism.

No wonder the Clintonoids haven't protested the proposed merger—it's consistent with their grand plan. Harvardite Robert Reich with the twin portfolios of Education and Labor? That makes hearts go pit-a-pat among those who prattle about the "politics of meaning." Herr Reich, the little big man, is just the 'Noid to complete the transformation of education into training for a command economy in the brave new global workplace. As Reich told a like-minded National Education Association confab a few years ago, "Instead of emphasizing individual achievement and competition, the emphasis in the classroom should be on group performance." So there are to be group projects, group grades, group "real-life" projects, group promotions—groupthink all around.

This is the vision that Reich's elitist soulmates—Ira Magaziner and Hillary Clinton, that duplicitous duo from the health reform debacle—sought to advance with their Labor-commissioned reports when George Bush, the wannabe Education President, was still in office. That led to (1) Labor's SCANS system, which asserts that every school in America should teach "workplace competencies" like self-esteem and collaborative skills; (2) Workforce 2000 plans in states like Virginia, which led to the outcomes-based Common Core; and (3) now to School to Work, which only sounds benign.

The late W. Edwards Deming, father of Total Quality Management, is the guru uniting the 'Noids, sadly misguided big-biz CEOs, and educrats. In his declining years, Deming advanced an ever more prescriptive philosophy for society at large (not just TQM for business). It contemplated the demise of merit systems and competition (and grades in school), in favor of a society based entirely on cooperation—with no failure. Utopia.

Deming-downed, double-dumb education requires massive attitude adjustment, and so the push for systematized change has led to such PC garbage as the National History Standards, which would have children learn about Madonna but not Daniel Webster. These so-called standards would teach children about America from the "multiple perspectives" of radical multiculturalists—with just one perspective omitted, that of America as a great and good nation with shared values.

The Family Research Council (which has prepared a competing set of privately financed standards based on sound scholarship) found that the federally funded standards skipped what historian Arthur Schlesinger, Jr., has termed the critical event of the 20th Century—the American astronauts' landing on the moon. Yet those standards cover Soviet accomplishments in space.

It will take far more than one nonbinding "sense of the Senate" resolution to turn things around. The PC mindset permeates Goals 2000 standards advancing down the pike for most other subjects. And attitude-probing is common in pupil assessments coming on line in the states and in the National Assessment of Educational Progress, the nation's so-called report card.

What is needed is a Herculean labor: Don't just remove the national school board from Goals 2000; repeal Goals 2000. Don't stop there: Repeal School to Work, too. By all means, dismantle the three dozen regional laboratories and centers of the Department of Education that are hotbeds of radical, behaviorist experimentation; but don't stop there—abolish DOE, too. And wipe out all of the Labor Department that meddles in education, such as the National Skills Standards Board, yet another new bureaucracy.

Hercules won out over the Hydra when he stopped merely chopping off one head at a time and instead cauterized the whole beast. That is what needs doing if education ever is to be liberated from the federal government's brain-numbing grip.

Appendix G

Resources

Books

• **"Educating for the New World Order,"** by B. K. Eakman, Halcyon House, P. O. Box 8795, Portland, Oregon, 97207-8795, 1-800-827-2499, $21.95 postpaid. (The story of a Pennsylvania woman, Anita Hoge, who, distressed by affective programs given her children without her permission, stood the whole education establishment on its ear when she was declared the winner in a case against the U.S. government.)

• **"Microchipped: How the Education Establishment Took Us Beyond Big Brother,"** by B.K. Eakman, $19.95 postpaid. (A collection of articles and speeches, all on education reform, with thorough documentation provided in the Appendix).

• **"Child Abuse in the Classroom,"** edited by Phyllis Schlafly, (Excerpts from Official Transcript of Proceedings before the U.S. Department of Education), Pere Marquette Press, P.O. Box 495, Alton, Illinois, 62002, $4.95 postpaid.

• **"Research Manual: America 2000/Goals 2000."** (A 700-plus page compendium that contains many useful references and resources. Not all opponents of OBE will agree with the conclusions this book assumes and connections it makes, but it is well worth the cost for the background information it contains). Compiled by James R. Patrick, East Moline Christian School, Building No. 900, 46th Avenue, East Moline, Illinois, 61244. Updated, expanded edition, $20 plus $3.50 for shipping and handling. Those who have the first edition can order the addendum for $7 plus $1 shipping and handling. 1-309-796-1485.

• **"Cradle to College,"** by Brannon Howse (Green Forest, AR: New Leaf Press, 1993). Includes interviews with Jack Kemp, Bill Bennett, Gary Bauer, and Congressman Robert Dornan.

• **"Why Johnny Can't Tell Right From Wrong,"** by William Kirkpatrick (New York: Simon & Schuster, 1992), is available through major bookstores. (This volume makes a case for character education in the schools, as opposed to OBEish approaches that feature "decision-making, higher-order thinking," "values clarification," and other trendy dogmas).

• **"Public Education: An Autopsy,"** by Myron Lieberman (Boston: Harvard University Press, 1993), $27.95, available by special order at most major bookstores. (An analysis of the education crisis and a rallying cry for market-based approaches to school reform).

• **"Inside American Education: The Decline, The Deception, The Dogmas,"** by Thomas Sowell (Free Press, 1993), $24.95, available through major bookstores. (An eye-opening expose of the state of American education today and the need for genuine reform).

• **"Outcome-Based Education: Understanding the Truth About Education Reform,"** by Ron Sunseri (Sisters, Oregon: Questar Publishers, Inc., 1994). (An analysis by an Oregon legislator who is leading the fight to repeal the OBE law in his state.)

Videos

• "Who Controls the Children?," with Peg Luksik, Pennsylvania Parents Commission, Box 73, Johnstown, Pennsylvania, 15907-0073, 1-814-445-6257, $18. (A dynamic dissection of Outcome-Based Education, 58 minutes).

• **"What Did You Learn in School Today?,"** with Jayna Davis, Channel 4 TV, 500 E. Britton Road, P.O. Box 14068, Oklahoma City, Oklahoma, 73113, $14.95. (A TV reporter's in-depth coverage of OBE in her state, 45 minutes.)

• **"Retarding America: The Imprisonment of Potential,"** U.S. Department of Justice, CDR Communications, Inc., 9310-B Old Keene Mill Road, Burke, Virginia, 22015, 1-703-569-3400, $10. (Relationship between illiteracy and methods used to teach reading to wards of the juvenile justice system, 28 minutes).

• **Dr. William Coulson,** speech to Kansas legislators, 1993, Christian Worldview Library, P.O. Box 546, 700 East 37th Street North, Wichita, Kansas, 67201, 832-3319. (Dr. Coulson, along with colleagues Dr. Abraham Maslow and Dr. Carl Rogers, created the psychological methods used in many classrooms today that are commonly referred to as "values clarification." Today, Dr. Coulson travels the nation repudiating that work and apologizing for the damage it has done to many children. 48 minutes).

• **The 1989 Governor's Conference on Education**, Wichita, Kansas, Christian Worldview Library. (This features as key speakers Secretary of Education Lamar Alexander and Dr. Shirley McCune who consulted with the Kansas Department of Education in creating QPA. A long version {about two hours} and an excerpted version (about 30 minutes) are both available.

Booklets

• "To Tell the Truth: Will the Real OBE Please Stand Up?." The Pennsylvania Parents Commission, Box 73, Johnstown, Pennsylvania, 15907-0073, 1-814-445-6257, $10. (A collection of data and articles about OBE from places that have been using it.)

• **OBE Documentation: A Primer,** The Pennsylvania Parents Commission, op. cit., $8. (A collection of documentation from communities where OBE has been in effect).

• **"The SCANS Reports,"** U.S. Government Printing Office, 1-202-783-3238. **"Teaching the SCANS Competencies,"** 029-000-0043802, $11. **"What Work Requires of Schools,"** 029-000-0043301, $3.25. **"Learning a Living, Part 1,"** 029-000-00439-1, $2.50. **"Learning a Living,"** full report, 029-000-00440-4, $6.50. (These are also available by calling 1-800-788-SKILL.)

• **"The Unfinished Agenda,"** Committee for Economic Development, 1700 K Street, N.W., Washington, D. C., 20006, 1-202-296-5860.

• **"The Dawning of the Brave New World: A Primer on OBE, Education Reform, and the Federal Classroom,"** by Donna Hearne, The Constitutional Coalition, P. O. Box 37054, St. Louis, MO 63141, $4 for single copies, bulk rates available.

• **"Beyond Rhetoric: A New American Agenda for Children and Families,"** National Commission on Children, 111 Eighteenth Street, N.W., Suite 810, Washington, D.C.

• **"Outcome-Based Education: The Outcome in Virginia, The Nationwide Controversy."** (A collection of 35 Op/Ed Page columns on OBE and related education issues by Robert Holland, columnist and Op/Ed Page Editor of the Richmond *Times-Dispatch*). Editorial Department, Richmond *Times-Dispatch*, Box 85333, Richmond, Virginia, 23293-0001, 1-804-649-6305, $3.

• **"Outcome-Based Education: Dumbing Down America's Schools,"** by Robert Holland, Family Policy (January 1994 issue), a publication of The Family Research Council, 700 Thirteenth St., N.W., Suite 500, Washington, D.C., 20005, 1-202-393-2100.

Audio Tapes

• Two-tape set: Tape 1 features Robert Holland of the Richmond *Times-Dispatch* discussing OBE in the Commonwealth of Virginia; Tape 2 presents a discussion/debate on OBE with Dr. William Spady of the High Success Network, Dr. Arnold Burrons of Citizens for Excellence in Education, and Chris Helm, a parent and researcher in Ohio. Available from Christian Connection, 715 E. Golf Road, Suite 202, Schamburg, Illinois, 60173, $10/set, 1-708-843-8855.

Printed Materials

- **Goals 2000, Community Update**, the U.S. Department of Education's progress report on national restructuring. Call 1 (800) USA-LEARN to get on the mailing list.
- **Free World Research Report**, P. O. Box 4633, Des Moines, IA 50306. $20 donation for a subscription (monthly).

Honor Roll

(Honoring grassroots organizations that have made a difference for the better in their communities.)

Among the many who are worthy, a salute to these activists is especially warranted. Not only have they made great accomplishments; they have big plans for the future. They are a "beacon" to lead others to "come aboard".

The rationale that "we desire not to know about the education of our children" because we can't do anything about it anyway is "blown-away" by their example.

Salute:

Honor Roll

(Honoring grassroots organizations that have made a difference for the better in their communities.)

The Family Foundation

6001 Forbes Place
Springfield, Virginia 22151-2205

(703) 321-8338; Fax: (703) 321-8406
Walt Barbee, President

The Family Foundation brought a seasoned group of activists together to preview the early "visions" of the educrats OBE planning. From this meeting, a number of assignments were accepted by those present. Also, a communication plan was adopted and the action was "joined."

This is a typical Family Foundation strategy, ie., identify a problem, assess the impact, and alert the appropriate activists. This has proven effective in allowing The Family Foundation to, seemingly, be involved in everything.

They are a great source for information on the Who, What, Where, How, and When of most family values concerns in the State of Virginia.

They would appreciate your call. They are always looking for more seasoned activists to challenge.

Notes

Chapter One

1. Commonwealth of Virginia Department of Education,*The Virginia Common Core of Learning*, (Richmond, Virginia, October 20, 1992).

2. Julia E. Koppich, "The Rocky Road to Reform in Rochester." Paper presented at annual meeting of the American Educational Research Association, (San Francisco, California: April 20–24, 1992), p. 28.

Chapter Two

1. "The ABC's of OBE: Does Your School Have OBE?" (Flushing, Michigan: Michigan Alliance of Families).

2. Kansas State Board of Education, *Kansas Outcomes-Based Health Education Guidelines* . Prepared under cooperative agreement with Division of Adolescent and School Health, Center for Chronic Disease Prevention and Health Promotion, Centers for Disease Control, Atlanta, Ga. (June 1991).

3. Survey, Glasgow (Kentucky) Middle School, (December 14, 1993); reprinted in *Congressional Record*, Proceedings of 103rd Congress, (February 4, 1994) S867.

4. Values Questionnaire, Dayton, Ohio, *Congressional Record* (February 4, 1994) S869.

5. Commonwealth of Virginia Department of Education, *Framework for the Virginia System of Educational Assessment*, Review Draft (Richmond, Virginia: December 9, 1992).

6. Jessica Portner, "At Your Service," feature on Maryland's Community Service Requirement, *Education Week*, (November 23, 1994).

7. Benjamin Bloom, "Taxonomy of Educational Objectives," as cited in *The ABCs of OBE: What's Wrong With Outcome-Based Education* by Dwight Williams and Ed Lederman, (Golden, Colorado: Independence Institute, March 1994), p. 9.

8. Report of the House Committee on Education and Labor on HR6, 268, "Improving America's Schools Act of 1994," (Washington, D.C.: February 16, 1994).

9. Williams and Lederman, p. 9.

10. Dennis Cuddy, "The Grab for Power: A Chronology of the NEA," (The Plymouth Rock Foundation, 1993), pp. 29–30,.

11. *Congressional Record*, S867, (February 4, 1994).

12. Thomas Sowell, "Inside American Education," (New York: The Free Press, 1993), pp. 34–69.

13. "Goals 2000: Educate America Act," Title X, Sec. 439, Conference Report, (March 21, 1994).

Chapter Three

1. Academics First, Box 203, Midlothian, Va., 23113.

2. For reviews of the incipient business-labor-education collaboration, see: the *Monthly Labor Review* (July 1991); *Industry Week* (August 19, 1991); *Employment Relations Today* (Winter, 1992–93); *Educational Leadership* (March 1992); *Public Management* (February, 1993); and *Chemical Week* (March 11, 1992).

3. Brenda Lilenthal Welburn (Executive Director of National Association of State Boards of Education) letter to coalition invitee (June 10, 1994).

4. Attachment to Welburn letter.

5. Marc Tucker, Preface, "A Human Resources Development Plan for the United States," National Center on Education and the Economy (Rochester, New York, 1992), p. 1.

6. "America's Choice: High Skills or Low Wages!," a report to the U.S. Department of Labor by the Commission on the Skills of the American Workforce, National Center on Education and the Economy (June 1990).

7. Hillary Clinton and Ira Magaziner, "Will America Choose High Skills or Low Wages?," *Educational Leadership,* (March 1992), pp. 10–14.

8. "Learning a Living: A Blueprint for High Performance, a SCANS Report for America 2000," (U.S. Department of Labor, April 1992).

9. "Student Data Handbook for Early Childhood, Elementary, and Secondary Education," (National Center for Education Statistics, U.S. Department of Education, Office of Educational Research and Improvement, June 1994).

10. The "New Standards Project, 1992–95, A Proposal," (The Learning Research and Development Center, University of Pittsburgh, and the National Center on Education and the Economy, Rochester).

11. Robert B. Reich, "Education and the Next Economy." Paper presented at National Education Association (April 1988).

Chapter Four

1. See, for example, paper presented by Dr. Janet L. Jones, "Impact of Special Interest Groups on Public Education," to meeting of California Education Research Association, November 17–18, 1994, San Diego, California.

2. Sylvia K. Kraemer, "The Virginia Common Core of Learning: A Bad Idea Whose Time Hasn't Come." (Alexandria, Va., April 1993).

Chapter Five

1. The "New Standards Project, 1992–1995, A Proposal." (Pittsburgh: The Learning Research and Development Center, University of Pittsburgh, and Rochester: The National Center on Education and the Economy).

2. Robert G. Holland, "Big Brother's Test Scores," *National Review,* (September 3, 1990), pp. 35–36.

3. Robert G. Holland, "Testscam," *Reason* (January 1991), pp. 47–48.

4. Robert G. Holland, "Dirty Secrets; Race-Norming Lives On," *Chronicles* (February 1992), pp. 44–46.

5. Senator Steve Symms and Larry Grupp, "The Citizen's Guide to Fighting Government" (Ottawa, Illinois: Jameson Books, Inc., 1994).

Chapter Six

1. B. K. Eakman, "Microchipped: How the Education Establishment Took Us Beyond Big Brother" (Portland, Oregon: Halcyon House, 1994).

Chapter Seven

1. "The Five Fundamental Flaws in Spady's New Paradigm." Paper presented by the Parent-Teacher Communication Network at the San Marcos (Texas) School Board (April 20, 1992).

2. From a Richmond *Times-Dispatch* interview with Cheri Yecke (August 9, 1993).

3. Dr. Robert Slavin, "Mastery Learning Reconsidered." (Baltimore, Maryland: Johns Hopkins University, January 1987).

4. Dwight Williams and Ed Lederman, "The ABC's of OBE: What's Wrong With Outcome-Baseed Education," (Golden, Colorado: Independence Institute, March 1994).

5. "On Outcome-Based Education: A Conversation with Bill Spady," *Educational Leadership* (December 1992/January 1993), pp. 66–70.

6. "Master Teachers Expose Fallacies of OBE 'Mastery Learning'." Richmond *Times-Dispatch* (August 11, 1993).

7. Sylvia Kraemer, "A Bus to Nowhere: Virginia's Education Crisis and the Betrayal of Rosa Parks" (Alexandria, Virginia: June, 1993), p. 23.

8. "Research on Ability-Grouping: Historical and Contemporary Perspective" (Ann Arbor: University of Michigan, 1991), pp. iv-v.

9. "The Well-Rounded Classroom: Applying the Theory of Multiple Intelligence," *Update* , Vol. 36, No. 8 (Association for Supervision and Curriculum Development, October 1994).

10. Denis Doyle, "Issue," *Update* (Alexandria, Virginia: Association for Supervision and Curriculum Development).

11. "Improving America's Schools Act of 1994," Report of the House Committee on Education and Labor on HR6, Title I, Sec. 1001 (c) "What Has Been Learned," (Washington, D.C., February 16, 1994). This language was watered down in the final version after the National Right to Read Foundation and other citizens protested that it was an attack on the use of phonics in teaching reading.

12. J. S. Chall, "Learning to Read: The Great Debate" (New York: Macmillan, 1967.)

13. "Developmentally Appropriate Practice in Early Childhood Programs Serving Children From Birth Through Age 8," (Washington, D.C.: National Association for the Education of Young Children, 1987).

14. "Getting Schools Ready for Children: The Other Side of the Readiness Goal," (Atlanta, Ga.: Southern Regional Education Board, 1994), pp. 6–7.

15. Bonnie Grossen, "Child-Directed Teaching Methods: A Discriminatory Practice of Western Education," *Effective School Practices* (Eugene, Oregon, Spring, 1993), pp. 9–19.

16. Thomas Sowell, "Inside American Education: The Decline, The Deception, The Dogmas," (New York: The Free Press, 1993), p. 90.

17. Joan Herman, Associate Director of the UCLA Center for the Study of Evaluation, paper for Southeastern Regional Vision for Education (SERVE), "What's Happening With Educational Assessment?" (Tallahassee, Florida: June, 1992).

18. Warren Simmons and Lauren Resnick, "Assessment as the Catalyst of School Reform," *Educational Leadership* (February, 1993), pp. 12–13.

19. Ibid. pp. 14–15.

20. Gregory J. Cizek, "On the Disappearance of Standards," *Education Week*, (November 10, 1993), pp. 30 and 24.

21. Daniel J. Singal, "The Other Crisis in American Education," *The Atlantic Monthly* (November, 1991).

Chapter Eight

1. In a December 30, 1993 "Call to Action, " the National School Boards Association's Washington office declared, "The Administration's proposal (HR 3130) for reauthorizing the Chapter 1 program for disadvantaged students contains a new and dangerous State Takeover provision that sanctions the ousting of school boards and superintendents by the state. This provision is heavy-handed, undemocratic, and a direct threat to local supervision of public education. It has no place in federal law."

2. Commonwealth of Virginia Department of Education, "Communications Plan: World Class Education" (Richmond, Va.: June 16, 1993).

3. "Community Action Toolkit: A Do-It-Yourself Kit for Education Renewal," (Washington, D.C.: National Education Goals Panel).

4. See Ms. Eakman's excellent books, "Educating for the New World Order," 1991, and "Microchipped: How the Education Establishment Took Us Beyond Big Brother," (Portland, Oregon: Halcyon House, 1994).

5. Ronald and Mary Havelock,"Training for Change Agents" (Ann Arbor: University of Michigan, 1973).

6. National Center on Education and the Economy, proposal (1992).

7. Janet L. Jones, "Targets of the Right: Public Schools—and School Boards—are under attack from the religious right," (*The American School Board Journal*, April, 1993), pp. 22–29.

8. "Reinventing Outcome-Based Education," a report on the High Success Network Conference in Vail, Colorado, July 6–10, 1994 (The Foundation Endowment, Alexandria, Virginia).

9. Robert Lichter, Stanley Rothman, Linda Lichter, "The Media Elite: America's New Power Brokers " (New York: Hastings House, 1986).

10. "The Decline of American Journalism," *National Review* (June 21, 1993), pp. 34–37.
11. Ibid, p. 55.
12. Davis Merritt, Jr., "Public Journalism: A Movement Toward a Basic Cultural Change," *The Wichita Eagle* (Wichita, Kansas: October 30, 1994).
13. "The Decline of American Journalism," pp. 25–28.
14. Edwin Feulner, "Salute to Talk Radio," Heritage Foundation op-ed distributed by Knight Ridder to 300 daily and 1,000 weekly newspapers (November 2, 1994).

Chapter Nine

1. Leon Wieseltier, "Total Quality Meaning," *The New Republic*, July 19 & 26, 1993, p. 21.
2. Ibid. p. 20.
3. Arnold Packer, "Taking Action on the SCANS Report," *Educational Leadership*, March 1992., p. 30.
4. "Business/Education Insider," No. 35, (The Heritage Foundation, January, 1994).
5. Alan L. Wurtzel, "OBE Is to Public Education as TQM Is to Business and Industry," op-ed article, Richmond *Times-Dispatch* (June 12, 1993), p. A-11.
6. Leila Christenbury, "Factory Breaks Down as a Model for School Reform," op-ed article, Richmond *Times-Dispatch* (June 19, 1993), p. A-11.
7. "The Essential Components of a Successful Education System," (The Business Roundtable, 1989).
8. "Keeping the Promise for New Jersey's Children," The Education Reform Agenda of The Business Roundtable, Education Initiative in New Jersey (1994).
9. Media release on Business Roundtable activities, Center for Education Reform, Washington, D. C., Summer 1994.
10. "The Unfinished Agenda: A New Vision for Child Development and Education," a Statement by the Research and Policy Committee of the Committee for Economic Development (New York, 1991).
11. School to Work Opportunities Act of 1994, Public Law 103–239 (May 4, 1994.
12. See The Secretary of Labor's Commission on Achieving Necessary Skills (SCANS) reports, "Learning a Living: A Blueprint for High Performance" (April 1992), and "What Work Requires of Schools" (June 1991), U.S. Department of Labor.
13. Ibid.
14. Ibid.
15. Ibid.
16. *Research Recommendations*, a weekly newsletter of the National Institute of Business Management (Alexandria, Va.: October 11, 1993).
17. Sticht's comments, originally reported in the August 17, 1987, issue of

The Washington Post, have been cited in several reports, including the Independence Institute's paper, "The ABCs of OBE: What's Wrong With Outcome-Based Education" (March 4, 1994).

18. Excerpted from a videotaped speech of Dr. McCune at the Governor's Summit on Education (Kansas: November, 1989).

19. "Human Capital and America's Future: An Economic Strategy for the '90s," edited by David W. Hornbeck and Lester M. Salamon, (Baltimore, Md.: The Johns Hopkins University Press, 1991).

Chapter 10

1. Reinventing Chapter 1: Annual National Conference of State Chapter 1 Coordinators, September 20–23, 1993, Collected Works; Compensatory Education Programs, Office of Elementary and Secondary Education, U.S. Department of Education, Washington, D.C..

2. Ibid.

3. Ibid.

4. M. Joycelyn Elders and Jennifer Hui, "Comprehensive School Health Services: Does It Matter and Is It Worth the Fight?," Summer Institute papers and recommendations of the Council of Chief State School Officers (1992).

5. Commonwealth of Virginia Department of Education article prepared for suggested use in a 1993 staff or parent newsletter by Office of Public Affairs.

6. Sylvia K. Kraemer, Ph.D., "A Bus to Nowhere: Virginia's Education Crisis and the Betrayal of Rosa Parks," unpublished essay (Alexandria, Va., June 1993), p. 23,

7. Barbara Dafoe Whitehead, "The Failure of Sex Education," *The Atlantic Monthly* (October 1994).

8. "Improving America's School Act," Conference Report to Accompany HR 6 (September 28, 1994), pp. 186–192.

9. "Warning: Feminist Pork Unhealthy Addition to Your Child's School Menu," op-ed release from Independent Women's Forum (Washington, D.C., October 31, 1994).

10. Ibid.

11. HR 6.

12. Chall, op cit.

13. HR 6, "Improving America's Schools Act of 1994," Report of the Committee on Education and Labor, House of Representatives (February, 16, 1994), 268.

14. "Call to Action," National School Boards Association, Office of Federal and National Education Issues Advocacy (December 30, 1993).

15. Bruno V. Manno, "Outcome-Based Education: Miracle Cure or Plague?," Hudson Briefing Paper, Number 165 (Indianapolis, Indiana: Hudson Institute, June 1994).

16. Lynne V. Cheney, "The End of History," *The Wall Street Journal* (October 20, 1994), A22.

Chapter 11

1. "Eagle Forum Recommends Score 100," news release, (Birmingham, Alabama: Eagle Forum of Alabama, November/December 1993).

2. "The Williamsburg Resolves," Republican Governors Conference, (Williamsburg, Virginia, November 1994).

3. Stephen Arons, "The Threat to Freedom in Goals 2000," *Education Week* (April 6, 1994), 52.

Index

About the Author

Robert Holland won the 1992 Mencken Award given by the Free Press Association for best op-ed column or editorial in the nation. He was honored for his work in exposing a racially discriminatory system of job testing contrived by the U.S. Department of Labor.

A native of Savannah, Georgia, Holland is Op/ED Page Editor of the Richmond *Times–Dispatch*. He also has been an editorial writer, education editor, and news bureau reporter. He and his wife, Allyne, have co-authored *The Student Journalist and the Literary Magazine* for Richards Rosen Press of New York.

A 1963 graduate of Washington and Lee University, Holland wrote, as a result of his first full-time reporting assignment, *The Story of the Prince Edward Free Schools*. It told the story of a system of private schools set up for black children when that Southside Virginia county closed its public schools in an attempt to avoid court-ordered desegregation.

Holland's writing has won awards from groups ranging from the Virginia Press Association to the American Academy of Pediatrics. He has lectured on education issues across the United States and in Canada, and has written free-lance articles for many magazines, including *Chronicles*, *National Review*, and *Reason*.

He and Allyne are the parents of two children.

